DYNAMICS OF
PUBLIC BUREAUCRACY

FRED A. KRAMER

University of Massachusetts, Amherst

Winthrop Publishers, Inc.
Cambridge, Massachusetts

DYNAMICS OF PUBLIC BUREAUCRACY

An Introduction to Public Management

SECOND EDITION

Library of Congress Cataloging in Publication Data

Kramer, Fred A
  Dynamics of public bureaucracy.

  Bibliographies
  Includes index.
  1. Public administration.   2. Bureaucracy.
  3. United States—Politics and government.   I. Title.
  JF1351.K69 1981   350   80-26294
  ISBN 0-87626-199-3

Cover and interior design by Janis Capone
Photo research by Carole Frohlich
Illustrations prepared by Mary Reilly

Illustration credits appear on p. xi.

© 1981, 1977 by Winthrop Publishers, Inc.
  17 Dunster Street, Cambridge, Massachusetts 02138

10 9 8 7 6 5 4 3 2 1

*To the memory of my father
and the hopes of my sons*

Contents

CHAPTER SEVEN

Public Sector Labor–Management Relations 196

The Changing Character of Public Unions **197** · The Legal Basis for
Public Sector Collective Bargaining **202** · The Collective Bargaining
Process **209** · What Public Unions Want **218** · Management Rights
and Productivity Bargaining **220** · The Grievance Arbitration Process **225** · Unions on the Defensive **227** · The Political Context Revisited **229**

SUGGESTIONS FOR FURTHER READING **231**

CHAPTER EIGHT

Decision-Making Theory and Policy Analysis 232

Rational-Comprehensive Decision-Making **233** · The Incremental
Method **240** · The Middle Way **245** · Tensions and Ideology **246** · Usefulness of Analysis **249** · A Place for the Analytic Component **252**

SUMMARY **254**
SUGGESTIONS FOR FURTHER READING **255**
APPENDIX TO CHAPTER EIGHT: DECISION ANALYSIS FORECASTING FOR EXECUTIVE MANPOWER PLANNING **256**

CHAPTER NINE

The Budgetary Process: Politics and Policy 276

Public Budgeting Defined **278** · Budget Classification **280** · Cost-
Benefit Analysis Problems **288** · Uncertainty and the Budget
Cycle **293** · Agency Budget Strategies **297** · The Central Budget Office **298** · The Legislative Role **301** · The Effect of Fiscal
Stress **307** · The Audit Stage **309**

SUMMARY **312**
SUGGESTIONS FOR FURTHER READING **313**
APPENDIX TO CHAPTER NINE: THE FEDERAL BUDGET PROCESS **314**

CHAPTER TEN

Administrative Control through the Executive 320

Management Control Is a Problem **321** · PPBS in the Department of
Defense **324** · The Failure of PPBS in the Federal Govern-

ILLUSTRATION CREDITS

Preface

Public administration should be an exciting topic. Almost any measure of economic or political development that one chooses shows the increasing importance of the public sector in American life. Although courses in public administration abound on American campuses, the image of these courses is often that of boring exhortations concerning organization charts and rearranging desks in municipal offices. For too long public administration courses and textbooks have contributed to the view that the study of public administration is a sinkhole where ideas cannot survive, where change is abhorrent, and where substantive problems are not to be confronted but merely processed. This should not be the case.

In this book I deal with the political/administrative responses to policy problems in the American government system. Aside from the value of playing the game, the main reason people express interest in politics is their concern for policy outcomes. These policy outcomes can provide symbolic or tangible benefits for various sectors of the polity. Public bureaucracy is one of the most important governmental institutions involved in public policy formulation and implementation. Public bureaucracy is one of the most direct links determining who gets what, when, and how through the political system.

The aim of this book is to give the student a greater awareness of the workings of public organizations in relation to the policy outputs of government. To achieve this aim, I will stress organization theory and American political practice—notably interest group politics. Along the way, I deal with the traditional areas of public administration like personnel administration, budgeting, administrative law, and administrative responsibility in a democracy.

So that the discussion of organizational and political behavior in American public bureaucracy does not become merely another interesting, although impractical, political science course, specific administrative techniques are treated in appendixes to relevant chapters. The organization development technique, Individual Development Planning, is treated in this manner, as is Decision Analysis Forecasting and Discounting to Present Value. These are fairly simple techniques that beginning students and practitioners could use to improve their on-the-job performance without large-scale organizational support. It is hoped that knowledge of the strengths and weaknesses of these techniques will enable the readers of this book to be more successful government workers.

The idea for this book grew out of my experience as an American Society for Public Administration Fellow in the Department of Housing and Urban Development and the Bureau of the Budget in Washington during 1968–1969. At that time I was exposed to bureaucrats and organizations that ranged from exceptionally skilled and competent to totally incompetent. When I began teaching, I wondered why introductory public administration materials often did not seem to recognize that all was not rosy in American public bureaucracy. In this book, I have tried to describe the American bureaucratic scene as I have experienced it, and to suggest reasons why it is as it is.

The hardest part about writing an introductory textbook in any subject is deciding what to leave out. In this massive revision of *Dynamics,* I have tried to present a more comprehensive view of public administration than was given in the first edition. Still, I have not treated several interesting topics, and I have chosen not to present some data that some may view as relevant. It is not that I think flexitime, for example, is unimportant; or, to use another example, that I do not know where to find the latest figures on women employees in the federal government. Rather, in my judgment, an extended treatment of flexitime should appear in a more specialized book and, in a rapidly changing area such as female employment, even the latest statistics available at press time would soon be out of date. I hope individual instructors and students who are interested in these and other phenomena that are given brief treatment here will use the chapter bibliographies to make the course more comprehensive than the text alone can.

Although any introductory treatment must be selective, I have sought to expand and improve upon the strengths of the first edition. Debbie Cutchin of the University of Georgia gave the first edition solid marks for definitions, explanations, and written illustrations. For this edition, I have expanded each of these areas. In most chapters, case studies, which are new to this edition, are integrated with the text. I have continued to use visual displays and alternative type to highlight key points.

In their study of sexism in public administration books, Ellen Cannon and Valerie Simms of Northeastern Illinois University agreed that the first edition of *Dynamics* was less sexist than most other texts. In this edition, I express my view even more strongly that good management and affirmative action are not antithetical. I believe affirmative action can be an excuse to implement the kind of fair management practices that might develop a public workforce that reflects the flexibility and intelligence that citizens should expect in their civil servants. Better representation of women and minorities at higher levels in the public service will result in more effective government.

Many people have contributed to this volume. Former teachers and colleagues who deserve mention include Guthrie Birkhead, George Frederickson, Lewis Mainzer, Frank Marini, and Victor Thompson. Special thanks are due to Herbert Kagi, who taught me the importance of public administration and enthusiasm. Harry Weiner gave me the opportunity to meet with many practicing administrators in New York City. In this book I try to share some of the things I have learned from them. Marcia Taylor and Deil Wright made helpful comments on the first edition.

Several persons who used the first edition were kind enough to share some of their thoughts with me. I wish to thank James Fairbanks of the University of Houston, Dennis Gilbert of the University of Louisville, David Leonard of the University of California, Norman C. Thomas of the University of Cincinnati, and Charles Williams of the University of Illinois–Chicago Circle. I found their comments useful and have tried to incorporate many of their suggestions in this edition.

Jim Murray and John Covell of Winthrop Publishers did a fine job encouraging me to meet deadlines and then making sure the production of the book went according to schedule.

Although I made those impossible deadlines, my family bore the brunt of my usual end-of-book erratic behavior. I am sure that David, Steven, and Evelynne are glad it is finally finished.

F.A.K.

DYNAMICS OF
PUBLIC BUREAUCRACY

CHAPTER ONE

Public Management and the Dynamics of Public Bureaucracy

"Although the administrative process is politically colorless in that it has no distinctive political character of its own, it does have a particular chameleonic quality of taking on the color of the substantive program to which it is attached, and it is always attached to a substantive program."[1]

Bɪɢ ɢᴏᴠᴇʀɴᴍᴇɴᴛ ʜᴀs ᴊᴏɪɴᴇᴅ Big Business and Big Labor, involving most citizens of the United States in an administered, bureaucratic society. This state of events is not new. Back in the 1940s, a British political scientist succinctly reviewed what was elementary even then:

> The modern state is concerned with a vast sphere of services of a mixed nature. They are repressive, controlling, remedial, and go as far as the actual conduct of industrial, commercial and agricultural operations. The state, which used to be negative—that is to say, which was concerned to abolish its own earlier interventions and reduce such controls as ancient and medieval polity had caused it to undertake—has for some decades now abandoned laissez faire and can be called ministrant. Its work ranges over practically every sector of the modern individual and social interest, from sheer police work, in the sense of apprehending and punishing assaults on person, peace, and property, to the actual ownership and management of utilities.[2]

Clearly, government's role in complex Western democracies has expanded greatly since World War II, and the United States has shared in this expansion of governmental powers into virtually all areas of modern industrial, urbanized life.

We can see the effects of government regulations in the everyday activities in which we engage. When we go to the breakfast table we can see the nutritional information on the side of the Cheerios box, the labeling on the milk carton, the grading standards for meat and eggs. These are the result of regulations developed by various government bureaucracies in response to state or federal laws. We drive to work over roads built to government-approved standards. We drive cars burdened with a variety of pollution control equipment and an assortment of buzzers that government agencies have deemed necessary to implement antipollution, safety, and antitheft laws. Most of us work or will work in institutions that are regulated in some way by government agencies.

---

1. Kenneth Culp Davis, *Administrative Law and Government,* 2nd ed. (St. Paul, Minn.: West Publishing Co., 1975), p. 9.
2. Herman Finer, "Administrative Responsibility in Democratic Government," *Public Administration Review* 1 (Summer 1941): 335–50. This piece has been widely reprinted. This quote appears in Francis E. Rourke, ed., *Bureaucratic Power in National Politics,* 3rd ed. (Boston: Little, Brown, 1978), p. 411.

Not only does government regulate the activities of individuals, corporations, and even other governmental units, but it provides services. These services have a regulatory component because often strings are attached. In order to receive a government service such as public housing, a person will have to meet certain criteria. A public housing authority could ban heroin addicts from living in its projects.

Government provides services either directly or indirectly. For example, fire and police protection are usually directly provided by local governments. The national government directly provides statistical information to businesses, labor unions, ordinary citizens, and professors. Other services may be provided indirectly through other governmental units or through private contractors. The special education programs provided by the local school district are probably funded by the Department of Education in Washington. Perhaps the community mental health facility is a private corporation providing services under a contract with the state mental health office.

Despite an egalitarian ethic that voices the concern that all people are to be treated equally, some groups and individuals benefit from government-sponsored services more than others. At the local level one can see whose streets are plowed first when it snows, who enjoys better schools, and who gets better police and sanitation services. At the national level, although we all share in the benefits of a strong national defense establishment, for example, those working for or owning stock in companies that gain defense contracts enjoy greater benefits than the rest of us.

The complex modern societies of the West are distinguished by a high degree of interaction between government and the private sector. Since the 1930s, government agencies at all levels in the American system have grown in number and power. Increasingly, legislatures have tried to deal with broad policy goals, while the power to decide how and when to implement these goals has become the province of unelected public administrators. Generally it is an unelected public administrator who writes a specific regulation. It is an unelected public administrator who decides which specific business will be checked for compliance with that regulation. It is an unelected public administrator who decides whether Mr. Johnson or Ms. Smith is eligible for some government-provided service. Unelected public administrators have large amounts of discretionary authority.

Regulations and government services are provided through vast networks of public bureaucrats—nurses, policemen, social workers, planners, clerks, and managers—who play important roles in the formation as well as the implementation of public policies. These public administrators do not operate in an antiseptic environment that is free from political forces. Instead, they are key participants in making decisions that affect politics in the most basic way. They are political decision-makers according to Harold Lasswell's classic definition of politics as being the study of "who gets what."[3] They are subject to political pressures, particularly those from groups or individuals who have tangible, often financial, interests in the same area as that in which the bureaucrat is involved.

Administration and Policy

EARLY observers of American public administration assumed there was a distinct separation between administration and politics. According to this view, the legislative process was the policy process. Administrators were supposed to carry out the policies stated in the laws of any jurisdiction or political unit.[4] But if laws are loosely phrased, urging the public administrators to carry out the public interest, there is certainly a great degree of discretion available to the administrators. Administrators, along with judges, have become, in Martin Shapiro's term, "supplementary lawmakers."[5]

An active administrator and educator, the late Paul H. Appleby, observed that although legislatures made policy for the future and the courts interpreted what the law was, neither group had a monopoly over their respective functions.

> Administrators are continually laying down rules for the future, and administrators are continually determining what the law is, what it means in terms of action, what the rights of parties are with respect both to transactions in process and transactions in prospect.[6]

Appleby held that administrators were the key policy-makers by operating within their areas of legitimate discretion in policy execution. In effect, the powers that the legislatures and courts held over administration

---

3. Harold D. Lasswell, *Politics: Who Gets What, When, and How* (New York: Meridian Books, 1958).
4. Luther Gulick, "Notes on the Theory of Organization," in Luther Gulick and Lyndall Urwick, eds., *Papers on the Science of Administration* (New York: Institute of Public Administration, 1937).
5. Martin Shapiro, *The Supreme Court and Administrative Agencies* (New York: Free Press, 1968), pp. 12–29.
6. Paul H. Appleby, *Policy and Administration* (University: University of Alabama Press, 1949), p. 7.

were reserve powers to be invoked only if the administrators violated the implied limits of their discretion.

In addition to their key role in policy-making through control of execution, Appleby noted that administrators played a critical part in policy-making by formulating recommendations for legislation. Because public bureaucrats are specialists in a small area of public policy, they are often the first to see where there may be problems or unexpected consequences of some policy action. Surely, in their efforts to enforce certain policies, they will come in contact with groups and individuals who are affected by that policy. Those groups and individuals will generally express their feelings toward the policy at issue. The bureaucrats will often be on the receiving end of this expression. In many cases those adversely affected by a policy will be able to convince the administrator to make needed changes. Sometimes the affected parties will have to carry the fight to the courts or the legislature. If new legislation is considered, the relevant administrators, as well as the affected groups, will generally have the opportunity to give information to the legislators. Clearly, public administrators have political and policy-making roles in any modern democracy.

These political and policy roles can be troubling to democratic theorists. After all, public bureaucrats are three steps removed from direct participatory democracy. The first step is popularly elected representative government—the legislature. The second step is politically appointed government executives, such as cabinet, subcabinet, and agency appointees. A third step away from direct democracy occurs "with the designation of personnel who are neither elected nor politically appointive and removable.... [These career bureaucrats] are chosen on the bases of stated criteria—social class or caste, family, general competence, specialization in given tasks and skills, etc.—and, once appointed, are protected from removal."[7] Democratic theorists, as well as the citizens who are subject to the interpretations of public bureaucrats, are concerned with keeping public officials *accountable* for their actions to the public. This concern for accountability heavily influences the environment of public administration.

---

7. Frederick C. Mosher, *Democracy and the Public Service* (New York: Oxford University Press, 1968), p. 3.

**The Environment
of Public
Administration**

PUBLIC administration takes place in a complex environment.[8] This is especially true in a highly pluralistic society such as the United States. Environmental frameworks to explain public policies and management have a long history in public administration. During the 1930s and

8. This book will be an effort to define the environment of public administration and to show how that environment presents challenges to and opportunities for public managers. The discussion here will just provide an overview.

FIGURE 1.1
The Environment of an Agency

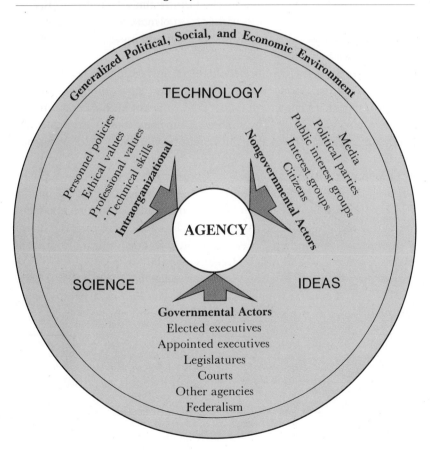

early 1940s, John Gaus called upon political scientists to note ecological factors in studying public administration. Among these factors were "people, place, physical technology, social technology, wishes and ideas, catastrophe, and personality." Knowledge of these aspects might enable one to understand "why particular activities are undertaken through government and the problems of policy, organization and management" resulting from such factors.[9] This may be helpful in understanding why some agencies are effective and others less so.

Governmental Actors

Governmental structure determines many of the actors who become part of an agency's environment. In the American system, the three branches—executive, legislative, and judicial—and federalism have established a structure that affects agency action. Agencies within an executive branch, whether a Department of Public Works in a small city or the Bureau of Public Roads within the Department of Transportation in Washington, have to deal with higher-level elected or appointed executives. Career bureaucrats are not free to act on their own. They must answer to higher-level public managers.

But public bureaucrats are beholden not just to higher-level managers. In most jurisdictions in the United States, legislatures control the funds that agencies need to operate. They also can authorize an agency to perform some task, or they can end an agency's involvement with a particular program. Therefore, public bureaucrats must also respond to legislative masters.

Sometimes the signals that the legislature gives an agency are different from the ones the higher political executives give. During the Nixon years, major battles were fought between the executive branch and Congress over the levels of activity expected from the Economic Development Administration, the Bureau of Public Roads, the Environmental Protection Agency, and others. Usually, legislative-executive conflict is part of the everyday existence of public managers (although not usually on the level of combat seen during the Nixon administration). The necessity to serve two masters—the legislature and the executive—is a complication that is generally lacking in private sector management.

Agency decisions are made within a legal framework. Judges in general courts are the final arbiters of whether agency actions have been taken with regard to the legal rights of individuals and corporations.

9. John M. Gaus, *Reflections on Public Administration* (University: University of Alabama Press, 1947), reprinted in Richard Stillman, II, *Public Administration: Concepts and Cases* (Boston: Houghton Mifflin, 1979), pp. 87–92.

The kinds of agency decisions that may be appealed through the courts are usually spelled out in the legislation that established the agency or in more general administrative procedure acts. Public administrators cannot ignore court action.

Not only must public administrators be open to the wishes of courts, legislators, and higher-ranking political executives, but they often are dependent on other agencies of government to perform the work for which they are responsible. At the national level, some programs in the Department of Housing and Urban Development depend upon information developed by units in the Departments of Commerce and Labor. Often agencies must depend on other agencies at other levels in the federal system to accomplish the purposes of a program. The Department of Education in Washington must depend on state and local school systems to improve the quality of elementary and secondary education. It might provide the money through grants-in-aid, and it might provide some technical assistance, but the effectiveness of programs designed to teach disadvantaged children depends upon those delivering the services to the children.

Nongovernmental Actors

In addition to being aware of structural elements that complicate public management, public administrators must be open to the views of individual citizens and groups who are affected by the agency's action or inaction. Regulatory agencies have to deal with the interests they are regulating. Service agencies must be open to their clients, whether those clients are welfare recipients demanding payments for furniture or business people seeking demographic information before making investments.

Usually, citizens are more able to deal effectively with government agencies when they are organized into interest groups. At the national and state levels especially, powerful interest groups combine with legislative committees or subcommittees and the agencies to form what A. Lee Fritschler calls "policy subsystems."[10] Fritschler describes the tobacco policy subsystem, which consists of the Department of Agriculture, tobacco growing, processing, and marketing interests, and legislators from tobacco-growing states who have risen to powerful positions in congressional committees dealing with the Department of Agriculture.

---

10. A. Lee Fritschler, *Smoking and Politics,* 2nd ed. (Englewood Cliffs, N.J.: Prentice-Hall, 1975). Ripley and Franklin call the same phenomena "sub-governments" in Randall B. Ripley and Grace A. Franklin, *Congress, the Bureaucracy, and Public Policy,* rev. ed. (Homewood, Ill.: Dorsey, 1980).

9

Such policy subsystems can become the dominant feature of an agency's environment.

The tobacco subsystem is not the only one.[11] In virtually every agency, administrators are in a position to help themselves get resources that legislatures have the power to grant. Most agencies are interested in increasing their personnel and budgets. It is possible that administrators might want to maintain favorable relations with the legislature, especially the legislative committees most directly involved with their work. Perhaps agencies would find it to their advantage to do this by working closely with their clientele or the interests that the agency is supposedly regulating.

The regulated interests or clientele of an agency might find that they can get favorable treatment from the agency if they can favorably influence legislators who are in a position to help the agency. Such influence may be in the form of campaign contributions, personal favors, or even construction of a plant in a legislator's district. Often it is in the mutual interest of legislators, agency personnel, and the clientele to resolve problems that may arise at a low level of conflict by keeping political participants who do not have a lasting, tangible interest in the problems of a particular policy out of the policy-making subsystem that develops.

Of course, there is no law that says that only organizations with a significant financial interest can deal with public agencies. Citizens' groups such as Common Cause or a Ralph Nader group might get interested in an issue and affect the agency. Political parties could also take an interest in some agency and seek to influence its behavior. Generally, however, those groups whose principal focus is on work similar to what an agency does will have continuing, effective contact with that agency.

Intraorganizational Aspects

So agencies are subject to governmental and extragovernmental role-players. But important elements of the environment of public agencies are the characteristics of the people who work in those agencies and the personnel policies that govern their actions on the job. Among the most important characteristics of any work force is the level of technical skill. Citizens deserve a capable governmental work force. Government typists should be able to type. Government engineers should be able to read blueprints. Government geologists should know shale from shoe polish. Government planners, architects, doctors, lawyers, and managers should

---

11. See Grant McConnell, *Private Power and American Democracy* (New York: Knopf, 1966; also Vintage, 1970), and Theodore J. Lowi, *The End of Liberalism*, 2nd ed. (New York: W. W. Norton, 1979).

have the ability to do the tasks they are assigned. If new tasks are assigned, government should make sure it gets capable people to fill the new jobs, either by recruiting or by retraining. The level of technical skills in a public bureaucracy influences whether a governmental unit can successfully implement lofty policy goals.

A far larger number of jobs in the public sector than in the private sector are professional or paraprofessional positions. In some agencies, one professional group dominates the others. For example, lawyers run the Department of Justice; physicians virtually own the National Institutes of Health. Similar professional domination occurs in state and local agencies as well. Such domination and professionalism in general bring professional values into government service. All professions socialize their practitioners to certain values through the education and training facilities of that profession. Many of these values are beneficial. Strong professional engineering values might ensure that a street will not cave in. The professional values of an econometrician might produce excellent information regarding the effects of an economic downturn on tax revenues for a city. But sometimes professional values can blind a practitioner to all but his or her narrow specialty. An economist might not see that the destruction of an ethnic enclave in a city to make way for a revenue-producing convention center might have severe social consequences. Or, if the economist recognized these consequences, he or she might downplay them—discount them—since economic values might seem more important than social values to a trained economist.[12]

Not only do public employees act on the basis of professional values, but they should consider other ethical values. What is right or wrong in a democracy hinges on democratic values. Such values, however, may be hard to maintain. People develop commitments to and identifications with particular organizations. Sometimes these may reflect a perversion of the stated goals and values of the organization. As Richard Harris has noted about the Federal Bureau of Investigation (FBI) under J. Edgar Hoover:

> [Even] the most democratically conceived government comes to behave as if its own survival, rather than the people's welfare, is the paramount good. This happens . . . because the government's ordinary day-to-day operations depend on entrenched "public servants"—the bureaucracy—

---

12. For the best discussion of the role of professionals in government, see Mosher, *Democracy and the Public Service,* chapter 4, pp. 99–133. Also see Mosher and Richard Stillman, II, ed., "Symposium on Professions in Government," *Public Administration Review* 37, no. 6 (November–December 1977) and 38, no. 2 (March–April 1978).

who are always most concerned about protecting and expanding their own power. In time, bureaucrats transform government into a kind of private institution that exists for their sake, and this makes them deeply committed to preserving the system—*their* system—as it is. The deeper their commitment, the more alarmed they are likely to be by anything that seems to threaten the system. . . .[13]

Government employees in a democracy should recognize that other actors concerned with the agency's work—especially affected citizens—have legitimate roles to play. Generally, government workers accept this as a condition of employment. For a few, however, official position leads to arrogance and self-promotion.

At a different level of concern, but also important as a force influencing agency action, are the personnel policies of the governmental jurisdiction to which the agency belongs. These policies affect recruitment, selection, promotion, and retention within the agency. They affect pay, benefits, and working conditions. They affect whether the agency employees feel they are being treated fairly. They affect employee morale. All these actions will influence what is done, how much is done, and how well it is done. Overall personnel policies can encourage self-interest or the public's interest, and such policies can sometimes program the agency for failure.

If these environmental factors *determined* the effectiveness of public managers, they would be of interest from an academic viewpoint. But management implies change. Public managers in an agency are not merely products of external forces. Successful ones have resources that enable them to cope with the environment. Through such resources as leadership ability, a sense of mission, and knowledge (among others), a manager tries to mold the environment so it supports agency efforts rather than endlessly challenges them. In some notorious cases, such as Hoover of the FBI and Robert Moses of New York City's Triborough Bridge and Tunnel Authority, public managers have been able to get things done as efficiently as any large private company could.[14] Hoover and Moses violated democratic norms in their single-minded efforts to realize their own visions of a good society. Good public management, however, must seek to change certain aspects of the environment while respecting the basic values of a democratic society.

13. Richard Harris, "Annals of Law: Taking the Fifth-1," *New Yorker* 52, no. 7 (April 5, 1976): 44.

14. For one of the best books on American public management, see Robert Caro, *The Power Broker: Robert Moses and the Fall of New York* (New York: Random House, 1974).

We can see many aspects of the environment of any public agency by looking at some of the problems facing a particular public bureaucrat, John Roland, a ranger in charge of the Cannell Meadow district of the Sequoia National Forest in California. The district is typical of the 187-million-acre National Forest system. Within the virtually uninhabited Cannell Meadow district are timber, rangeland, minerals, trout-filled streams, and unspoiled wilderness. People interested in different aspects of the land in the Cannell Meadow district inspire conflicts—conflicts that have a political character—with which John Roland and the Forest Service must deal.[15]

The Forest Ranger as Public Administrator

The Forest Service is an agency of the United States Department of Agriculture. Its mandate is to manage about 8 percent of U.S. territory for the benefit of many different publics, each of which has differing views of what constitutes good management of these lands. For example, lumbermen believe that good management of the national forests means that they should be allowed to cut much more timber than they currently are permitted. Environmentalists think the Forest Service already allows them to cut too much. Ranchers see proper management as allowing more cattle onto the federal grazing land. Hunters think more cattle will destroy the natural habitat of deer. Skiers and fishermen want more recreational use. Some environmental groups want to see the forests returned to wilderness. Mining interests want the Forest Service to drop restrictions on their activities. Of these conflicting interests, some groups win; some lose. The decisions affecting these interests are made by public bureaucrats within the Forest Service.

Some of the major conflicts among those most interested in the areas within the Forest Service's purview are fought in Washington. Well-organized groups marshal lobbyists to contact influential members of Congress and high-ranking bureaucrats at the Forest Service's national headquarters. But the Forest Service is a highly decentralized agency, which means that many decisions affecting these interests are made in the field by people such as John Roland.

In a decentralized agency, public bureaucrats have considerable power, but they must be aware of the constantly conflicting pressures brought on them by difficulties built into the laws that established their agencies. In the Forest Service, for instance, Roland must balance the interests of people who want him to allow them to cut more trees, or build

---

15. The Forest Service is recognized as one of the more effective federal government agencies. This account is drawn from William M. Bulkeley, "Whatever He Decides, A U.S. Forest Ranger Gets Somebody Upset," *Wall Street Journal,* December 4, 1978, p. 1.

a road to a mining claim, or build paths for bicyclists, or build other trails for hikers, and of people who want none of these things done. At the same time, Roland must keep in mind the wishes of his superiors within the Forest Service and interested legislators who might try to pressure his decisions in individual cases. As a result of these pressures, the administrator often seeks a compromise. As Roland told a reporter for the *Wall Street Journal,* "If one guy is mad at me over a decision we've made and the other is happy, I probably haven't done my job properly. If they're both mad, I've probably done it right."[16]

A person like John Roland does not only deal with conflicting political pressures from those who value the services of his agency, from the superiors within the agency, and from legislators. He or she must also deal with regulations mandated by other governmental agencies. Before Roland can authorize actions that will change almost any aspect of the forest area under his control, he must consider environmental analysis reports which detail the probable effects of any change. Sometimes environmental legislation prevents the Forest Service from doing what it considers to be its job. When a ranger suggested plowing under some sagebrush that grew up in a meadow that had been overgrazed, so that the grass could come back, environmental analysis stopped the action. Government botanists involved in writing the environmental analysis report discovered several rare species of locoweed. Since protection of these endangered species is absolute, the changes that might have restored the meadow to its original condition were set aside. Public managers must learn to live with flexible logic.

Explaining Policy Failures

WE do not have to look far to find areas in which governmental action has not been very successful. Housing, poverty, crime, and racism are just a few issues that have persistently resisted governmental efforts to solve them. Many people would agree with urban planner Robert A. Levine:

> Most public programs in the United States have not worked well; some have not worked at all. Whether one defines "not working well" as failure to solve the problems for which public action is appropriate, failure to substantially improve the situation beyond what it would have been

16. Bulkeley, "Whatever He Decides."

without the programs, or . . . failures of programs to live up to the reasonable expectations of their designers, most public programs have not worked well.[17]

To a degree, these policy failures can be attributed to political accommodation to powerful interests, but such an explanation is too simple. We will try to explain policy failures in a variety of ways throughout this book.

James Q. Wilson has attributed the failure of public programs to what he calls "the bureaucracy problem," which is really a combination of related problems that are tied to conflicting demands from the environment:

> First, there is the problem of *accountability* or control—getting the bureaucracy to serve agreed-on national goals. Second is the problem of *equity*—getting bureaucrats to treat like cases alike and on the basis of clear rules, known in advance. Third is the problem of *efficiency*—maximizing output for a given expenditure, or minimizing expenditures for a given output. Fourth is the problem of *responsiveness*—inducing bureaucrats to meet, with alacrity and compassion, those cases which can never be brought under a single national rule and which, by common human standards of justice or benevolence, seem to require that an exception be made or a rule stretched. Fifth, is the problem of *fiscal integrity*—properly spending and accounting for public money.[18]

Wilson's formulation of the bureaucracy problem suggests that by attempting to solve one aspect of the problem, we probably will aggravate another. For example, if we get bureaucrats to serve agreed-on national goals, perhaps they will not be responsive to a particular situation that might call for compassion. Similarly, controls designed to bring about fiscal integrity might work against the efficient operation of a particular program. Equitable treatment may also violate situations calling for a compassionate response. Wilson gives us a feeling for the complexity of trying to develop a flexible, intelligent public bureaucracy, yet one that is subservient to democratic values.

Although Wilson's criteria suggest contradictory directions for reform, citizens cannot afford to have poorly managed, incompetent public bureaucracies. A measure of competency of bureaucracy must go beyond the routines of what is usually accepted as government work. Pub-

---

17. Robert A. Levine, *Public Planning: Failure and Redirection* (New York: Basic Books, 1973), p. 3.
18. James Q. Wilson, "The Bureaucracy Problem," *The Public Interest* 6 (Winter 1967): 4. Emphasis added.

lic bureaucracies must be prepared to provide advice in areas where government inaction can have great impact on society. Bradford Snell has given a classic example of private sector decisions having great impact—in fact, the ability to mold entire metropolitan regions—in the absence of an intelligent response from public bureaucrats who were in a position to change the course of history.

According to Snell, beginning in the 1920s, General Motors, Standard Oil of California, and Firestone Tires embarked on combined investment programs that eventually enabled them to gain control of and then to dismantle the electric rail systems of forty-five urban areas in sixteen states. Operating through a holding company, National City Line, the three corporations acquired the profitable, efficient electric rail systems, uprooted the tracks, and substituted bus-dominated transit systems. To ensure a monopoly in transportation for gasoline-powered vehicles, "GM extracted from the local transit companies contracts which prohib-

"Your return was neat and accurate and indicated that you understood the forms completely . . . what we want to know is how?"

ited their purchase of any new equipment using any fuel or means of propulsion other than gas."[19]

As in this case, private decisions affecting public policy often bump into government bureaucracy. When the National City Line sought to change from rail to bus mass-transit systems, they petitioned the elected representatives in the cities involved. These elected officials relied on the statements of the National City Line. An uninformed, naive public bureaucracy was not in a position to study the implications of such changes. It had to deal with the more skillful private interests from a weak position. If it is the duty of government agencies to "act in the public interest," as most laws clearly state, surely the public interest can only be protected by an intelligent, well-informed public bureaucracy.

There may be a happy ending to this tale. In San Diego, California, a new generation of public bureaucrats began building a new light rail (trolley) transit system similar to the one that had been abandoned years ago. Their enlightened efforts in the 1970s anticipated the gasoline price crunch of the 1980s.

Is Public Management Different?

CONCERN for grand programs and policies that failed to deliver up to their proponents' expectations became a great intellectual problem among policy scientists in the 1970s. These "implementation studies" renewed a concern for effective public management.[20] Why cannot public managers successfully achieve their policy goals? Are they incompetent? If so, bring in the successful business and industrial managers. Or is public management really different from private management? Obviously, there are some differences. Some observers emphasize these; others note the similarities.

Peter F. Drucker, a highly influential consultant to private industries and the father of "management by objectives" (MBO), has turned much

19. Bradford C. Snell, *American Ground Transport: A Proposal for Restructuring the Automobile, Truck, Bus, and Rail Industries,* report to the Subcommittee on Antitrust and Monopoly of the Committee of the Judiciary, U.S. Senate (Washington, D.C.: U.S. Government Printing Office, 1974), p. 31.
20. Jeffrey L. Pressman and Aaron Wildavsky, *Implementation,* 2nd ed. (Berkeley: University of California Press, 1980).

of his attention toward the public sector in the past decade.[21] He sees many similarities between public service institutions and private businesses and has sought to apply to government management concepts that have proven effective in some businesses. Drucker has suggested there are six "deadly sins" in public administration:

1. *The first thing to do to make sure that a program will not have results is to have a lofty objective—"health care," for instance, or "to aid the disadvantaged."* . . .
2. *The second strategy guaranteed to produce non-performance is to try to do several things at once.* . . .
3. *The third deadly sin . . . is to believe that "fat is beautiful," despite the obvious fact that mass does not do work; brains and muscles do.* . . .
4. *"Don't experiment, be dogmatic" is the next. . . . "Whatever you do, do it on a grand scale at the first try. Otherwise, God forbid, you might learn how to do it differently."* . . .
5. *"Make sure that you cannot learn from experience" is the next prescription for non-performance in public administration.* . . .
6. *The last of the administrator's deadly sins is the most damning and the most common: the inability to abandon.*[22]

Drucker feels that public managers will guarantee failure of their programs if they commit any two of these sins. He suggests that to avoid these pitfalls, public managers should follow the private sector practice of specifically spelling out objectives, focusing on priority items rather than trying to achieve all goals, avoiding overstaffing, trying pilot programs, learning from experience, and getting out of programs that can be better accomplished by other means.

There is much that can be learned from Drucker's criticism, but many of his solutions violate some political realities that an environmental analysis raises. Democratic government is not monolithic. It does not have a single source of power and direction—something a private firm generally has. As Martin Rein and Sheldon H. White have pointed out:

> Governments do not think, nor do individuals joined by an organizational structure think, in unison. In a public bureaucracy, there is a community of actors, whose actions are to some extent interwoven by the system that provides for the division of labor, lines of responsibility, and

---

21. His seminal work was *The Practice of Management* (New York: Harper and Brothers, 1954). He is a prolific and thoughtful observer of management in general. He will deal with MBO as a performance appraisal technique in chapter 6 and as a budgeting technique in chapter 10.
22. Peter F. Drucker, "The Deadly Sins in Public Administration," *Public Administration Review* 40, no. 2 (March–April 1980): 103–106. This piece is reprinted in Fred A. Kramer, ed., *Perspectives on Public Bureaucracy*, 3rd ed. (Cambridge, Mass.: Winthrop Publishers, 1981).

the ultimate integration of their efforts. However, the bureaucratic integration of the actions of individuals is, at best, limited. Cooperative action is only grossly structured, and there is much room for individuals to work at cross-purposes, thus cancelling out one another's actions. Each actor faces his own set of decisions, defined by the position he occupies in the institutional structure. He chooses among courses of action, but his set of possible actions is different from that of others in different positions.[23]

Perhaps there is truth in the late Wallace Sayre's claim that "business and government administration are alike in all unimportant respects."[24]

Public sector managers face constraints not found in the private sector. Political executives tend to have short time horizons because they want results that can benefit them by the next election. Organizational response times, however, are long. To a degree, public sector managers find they lack information to manage effectively because impact measures are hard to develop in many kinds of government work. Generally, public accounting systems tend to be control-oriented rather than geared to provide information needed for management and planning. Even if management had the information it wanted, civil service rules would insulate many workers from management pressures which can be used in the private sector to see that tasks are accomplished.[25] As Gordon Chase, a successful manager in New York City and later a professor of public policy at Harvard and Brandeis, said, "Managing effectively and efficiently in the public sector is not only unlike managing in business. It's harder."[26]

Both the similarities and differences of public and private management are important. This introduction to public management will present both with the hope that the reader will synthesize an effective management style or gain an understanding of the possibilities and limitations of public management. Greater knowledge of what is possible might improve the management of government programs.

---

23. Martin Rein and Sheldon H. White, "Can Policy Research Help Policy?," *The Public Interest* 49 (Fall 1977): 132.
24. Quoted in Joseph L. Bower, "Effective Public Management," *Harvard Business Review* 55, no. 2 (March–April 1977): 132.
25. Ibid., pp. 132–140.
26. Quoted in Mitchell C. Lynch, "Manager's Journal," *Wall Street Journal,* September 10, 1979, p. 30.

The Plan of the Book

WE plan to use the environmental perspective presented here as a rough guide through the thicket of people, politics, policies, and programs that is public management. We make no claims that the environmental perspective is a formal model, and there will be no attempt at pseudoscientific prediction based on vectors, weighting schemes, statistical tests, and canned computer programs. But by the end of the book, the reader should have a better understanding of the political and organizational dynamics of public bureaucracy.

Since the public dimension of public management is a distinguishing feature, chapter 2 will raise the issues dealing with the political nature of public bureaucracy. We will emphasize the formation of the policy subsystems, which was raised earlier, and deal with the reasons that they develop, grow, and are hard to dismantle. The emphasis in this chapter will be on the national government.

In chapter 3 we will look at how state and local governments develop special relations with the national patron and with affected interest groups. Intergovernmental relations is an area of growing importance in American government. The national government mandates aspects of programs that greatly affect policy choices at the state and local level. For instance, Section 504 of the Federal Rehabilitation Act of 1973 requires that all recipients of federal funds provide access for the handicapped. Similar mandates in other policy areas occur at the state level. Despite the innate value of such programs to society as a whole, many jurisdictions wind up paying for policies that they did not support, such as affirmative action, compensatory educational services, and transportation assessments. This can create political problems for the jurisdiction, for its citizens, and for all the other actors in the web of intergovernmental relations.

Organizational dynamics are also important for understanding public bureaucracy. If we believe that public policies have been ineffective in the past in part because of the role bureaucrats have played in helping to formulate and to implement these policies, then we must understand organization theory and human motivation to suggest alternative ways of organizing and leading public employees. We need to explore new ways to open public bureaucracy to the need for change. In chapter 4, we deal with various organizational perspectives on public bureaucracy and some views of human motivation. In chapter 5 we apply these theoretical perspectives to particular techniques that have received some degree of acclaim in the private sector and explore some of the problems involved in applying thee techniques to the public sector.

What Does a Bureaucrat Do?

We worry a lot. People worry about the stock market, the morning's automobile traffic, the government's multiple health insurance policies, and the fortunes of political friends elsewhere in Washington.

Some of the agencies really have to produce. They have a product that people can see, like air traffic controllers landing airplanes, or Social Security checks. But usually you spend at least 50 per cent of the time looking inward—making the agency a better place to work. We've been moving furniture around for more than two years. And you're always satisfying the information requests of other people in the agency, or evaluators. There are all kinds of evaluators—GAO [General Accounting Office] auditors, Budget Bureau people, external contractors evaluating next year's appropriations request, interested staff members from the House Subcommittee . . . and so on.

No social problem has ever been solved this way. . . . It's very frustrating.

SOURCE: George Beckerman, a middle-level manager in the U.S. Department of Commerce, as quoted by Taylor Branch, "We're All Working for the Penn Central," *The Washington Monthly* 4, no. 12 (December 1973): 44.

Organization and motivation theories affect the people who work in the organizations. We must be aware of the range of personnel practices of various governmental jurisdictions within the United States in order to determine how the public sector can attract and retain high-quality individuals capable of serving the public trust. We must know some of the technical aspects of personnel management so we can assess Ralph Nader's low opinion of the government bureaucrat: "The speed of exit of a civil servant is directly proportional to the quality of his service."[27] Chapter 6 is devoted to the general problems of staffing public bureaucracies. This chapter deals with the complex relationships between the merit system, testing, and affirmative action programs. Chapter 7 deals with the most pressing public personnel problem today—labor-management relations. The rise of collective bargaining has resulted in gains by

27. Quoted in Robert G. Vaughn, *The Spoiled System: A Call for Civil Service Reform* (New York: Charter House, 1975), p. 13.

government workers and, in some cases, severe hardships for particular jurisdictions and the citizens within them. The management of "people problems" within government bureaucracies has a strong effect on the policies of that government.

Policy-making, the main interest of this introduction to public administration, is decision-making. Although we are firmly convinced that political factors are the key factors on which decisions hinge, there are several social science techniques that have proven useful in clarifying issues and generally raising the level of policy debate. These decision-making tools have been refined most in those areas of service that have close parallels to private sector marketing. These techniques, it will be argued in chapter 8, often have ideological implications of which practitioners and citizens should be aware. There are serious problems ahead for those who put all their faith in techniques employed by limited or cynical specialists.

The "bottom line" of decision-making in the public sector is the budget for any jurisdiction. Although it is difficult to equate dollar expenditures with the usefulness of any program to a community, there is a rough relationship between money devoted to a program and the perceived importance of that program to the jurisdiction. In chapter 9, we examine the traditional budgeting process, emphasizing administrative strategies for survival and growth in a highly political environment. In chapter 10, we will deal with efforts to change budgetary processes through improved—often centralized—information systems and management techniques.

Modern centralized budgetary systems are really attempts to enforce administrative accountability within the bureaucracy. Concern for administrative accountability extends to the legislatures and the courts, too. In chapter 11, we look at the ways legislative bodies conduct their oversight functions of public bureaucracies. The discussion will emphasize the political realities that often discourage meaningful legislative control. In chapter 12, we will deal with administrative law and the powers of the courts to review administrative decisions. Also in this chapter we will look at the emerging role of courts as policy overseers.

The emphasis on control of possible administrative misbehavior is just one aspect of administrative responsibility. Surely we do not want our public bureaucrats acting arbitrarily or stealing from the public treasury, but we do expect them to be able to react with speed when the situation calls for such action. We expect some independent, professional judgments from them. We do not want to hem our public employees in with strict rules that would add to the red tape and frustration of dealing with our own government. Instead, we want our public bureaucrats to serve the public interest by helping society anticipate and cope with change.

But how is the public interest to be defined? What ethical principles can guide administrators in walking the fine line between getting things done and running roughshod over the rights of individual citizens?

Surely there must be legal and administrative safeguards for the rights of the citizens. But the great amount of paperwork often involved with providing a record to show that proper procedures have been followed might create a situation in which the ordinary citizen loses his or her ability to deal with the bureaucracy at all. In some South American countries, even such relatively routine operations as registering a motor vehicle are so complicated that the services of a *despachante*—an expediter—are necessary to fight through the mass of paperwork. For slightly more complex operations in the United States, hiring an attorney to carry the ball through the bureaucratic maze is a necessity. How can we have a flexible, intelligent bureaucracy, yet provide safeguards for individual liberty? Perhaps in a modern administered democratic state we will have to develop new theoretical notions of individual liberty. Or new notions of the role of the state apparatus. The final chapter deals with these questions.

These are critical questions of political theory. Public administration is more than moving desks from office to office. It is involved at the heart of politics. Indeed, the control of bureaucrats by the citizens or the control of citizens by the bureaucrats is the principal problem facing democratic societies today. Although we cannot promise answers to these questions, this book hopes to provide the background to make it possible for students to deal with them in a more sophisticated manner.

Suggestions for Further Reading

Caro, Robert. *The Power Broker: Robert Moses and the Fall of New York.* New York: Random House, 1974.

Destler, I. M. *Presidents, Bureaucrats, and Foreign Policy.* Princeton: Princeton University Press, 1972.

Fritschler, A. Lee. *Smoking and Politics: Policy Making and the Federal Bureaucracy,* 2d ed. Englewood Cliffs, N.J.: Prentice-Hall, 1975.

Kaufman, Herbert, *Red Tape: Its Origins, Uses, and Abuses.* Washington, D.C.: The Brookings Institution, 1977.

Kaufman, Herbert, with the collaboration of Michael Couzens. *Administrative*

Feedback: Monitoring Subordinates' Behavior. Washington, D.C.: The Brookings Institution, 1973.

Mazmanian, Daniel A., and Jeanne Nienaber. *Can Organizations Change? Environmental Protection, Citizen Participation, and the Corps of Engineers.* Washington, D.C.: The Brookings Institution, 1979.

Mosher, Frederick C. *Democracy and the Public Service.* New York: Oxford University Press, 1968.

Nathan, Richard P. *The Plot that Failed: Nixon and the Administrative Presidency.* New York: John Wiley, 1975.

Ostrom, Vincent. *The Intellectual Crisis in American Public Administration,* rev. ed. University, Ala.: University of Alabama Press, 1974.

Pressman, Jeffrey L., and Aaron Wildavsky. *Implementation,* 2d ed. Berkeley: University of California Press, 1980.

Ripley, Randall B., and Grace A. Franklin. *Congress, the Bureaucracy, and Public Policy,* 2d ed. Homewood, Ill.: Dorsey, 1980.

Seidman, Harold. *Politics, Position and Power: The Dynamics of Federal Organization,* 3rd ed. New York: Oxford University Press, 1980.

Simon, Herbert A., Donald W. Smithburg, and Victor A. Thompson. *Public Administration.* New York: Knopf, 1950.

Waldo, Dwight. *The Administrative State.* New York: Ronald, 1947.

CHAPTER TWO

Politics and Administration

In the years before World War II, most observers of American public administration were preoccupied with the notion that administration could be separated from politics. One of the refrains of the municipal government reform movement, which was active during the first three decades in the twentieth century, claimed there was neither a Republican way nor a Democratic way to pave streets. There was simply the right way to do the job. It was administration's task to accomplish its assigned tasks the right way.

Our view of politics, however, is more inclusive than what Republicans or Democrats want. Our view of politics goes far beyond the stated positions of the parties and electoral politics in general. The term *politics,* as it is used here, is a conflict resolution process that determines "who gets what, when, and how."[1] In this conflict resolution process, power affects the outcome. Power is the ability to make someone do what he or she does not want to do. To this end, potential power resources—wealth, status, position, leadership skills, information, legitimacy, authority— can affect policy outcomes. All the actors affecting an agency's environment, including public managers, have some resources they can mobilize to affect what the agency does. We agree with the definition of politics as "the process by which power is employed to affect whether and how government will act on any given matter."[2]

This chapter presents the theoretical foundation for describing and understanding the dynamics of political bureaucracy. We shall see how an agency's potential power resources, particularly its specialized knowledge, can be used to influence policy from formation through execution, and on to evaluation. We shall see how the power resources of the other actors in the agency's environment force public managers to accommodate political forces and how some accommodations have important consequences to public administration in a democracy.

A View of Conflict

The late E. E. Schattschneider had an insightful view of conflict that partially explains the political role of public administrators. To Schattschneider, conflict was "contagious" in a free society, and as more

---

1. Harold G. Lasswell, *Politics: Who Gets What, When and How* (New York: Meridian Books, 1958).
2. Kenneth M. Dolbeare and Murray J. Edelman, *American Politics: Policies, Power, and Change,* 3rd ed., rev. (Lexington, Mass.: D. C. Heath, 1979), p. 14.

people became involved in the conflict, the scope of the conflict would change and so would its outcome.

> Every fight consists of two parts: (1) the few individuals who are actively engaged at the center and (2) the audience that is irresistibly attracted to the scene. The spectators are as much a part of the overall situation as are the overt combatants. The spectators are an integral part of the situation for ... the *audience* determines the outcome of the fight. The crowd is loaded with portentousness because it is apt to be a hundred times as large as the fighting minority, and the relations of the audience and the combatants are highly unstable. Like all other chain reactions, a fight is difficult to contain. To understand any conflict it is necessary, therefore, to keep constantly in mind the relations between the combatants and the audience because the audience is likely to do the kinds of things that determine the outcome of the fight. This is true because the audience is overwhelming; it is never really neutral; the excitement of the conflict communicates itself to the crowd. *This is the basic pattern of all politics.*[3]

To Schattschneider, political conflicts are resolved in this fashion. The conflict might involve a few individual or group interests, but these original parties would be aware of the potential actions of the audience, the other actors in the polity. To a large degree, the actions of the audience would determine the strategies that the original parties would adopt to seek resolution of the conflict. If additional parties get involved in the actual conflict, the scope of the conflict changes and so may its possible outcome. Schattschneider argued that each level of conflict had a bias in favor of one side of the conflict. People and interests who were losing at a particular level of conflict would seek to involve more people and interests to expand the scope of conflict and raise it to a different level. They would try to use their power resources to raise the level of conflict to an arena where the array of political forces would favor their side. In the ideal case, political conflict would not be resolved until all people and all interests were involved.

In the real world, however, very few political issues get resolved in this idealized fashion. It is in the interest of people and groups who are winning at any particular level of conflict to use their power resources to keep the conflict from changing to a different level. The apparent winners of a conflict want to keep the level low, so they can win. The apparent losers, as we have seen, seek to use their political resources to change the level of conflict to another arena where they might have a better chance of winning. Often the losers of a political conflict at any level lack the resources to carry the conflict to a different one. Not hav-

---

3. E. E. Schattschneider, *The Semi-Sovereign People* (New York: Holt, Rinehart & Winston, 1960), p. 2. *See* his chapter 1 in general.

ing the power to change the arena of conflict, they must accept their fate as losers. Many political conflicts are resolved, therefore, at a low level, involving just a few interests rather than a large portion of the polity. This pattern is typical of the way disputes are handled at the administrative level.

Levels of Conflict in Government

THE low level of conflict, where many of these political issues—political in the sense of who gets what—are resolved, is the administrative level. Figure 2.1 shows, in a rough way, the various levels of conflict in the American governmental structure. If an interest cannot get what it wants at the administrative level, the array of political forces at that level may not be in its favor. It might seek to use what political resources it has to broaden the scope of the conflict, either through litigation in the courts or through lobbying the legislature. Perhaps the interest cannot gain satisfaction either through the courts or the legislature. It might

FIGURE 2.1
Changing Levels of Conflict

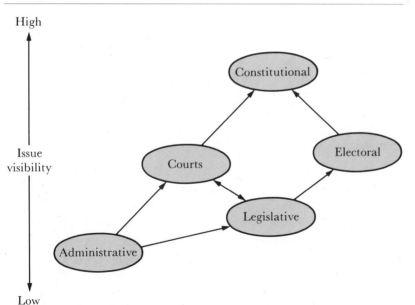

then seek to change the membership of the legislature by raising the issue in the electoral arena. Without success at these levels, an interest might even mobilize its resources for a constitutional amendment.[4]

The antibusing interest is an example of a group that has fought—although unsuccessfully—for its position through the entire range of levels of conflict. Antibusing groups tried to dissuade bureaucrats in the federal Office of Education (now the Department of Education) from using buses as a means to integrate public schools. They failed. They broadened the scope of conflict in order to raise the level to Congress. They failed to get antibusing legislation. They sought to fight in the courts. They lost. They sought to make busing the key electoral issue. They lost. They even advocated a constitutional amendment. Again, they failed.

Although we will generally be dealing with tightly organized corporate interests with financial axes to grind, this example is instructive. It shows that interests must have access to power resources to carry on a fight to expand the level of conflict. In this case, the main resource of the antibusing groups was the sheer number of Americans who disapproved of busing schoolchildren to achieve integration. Antibusing interests were able to stay in the conflict through various levels because many people knew about busing and were affected by it. *A critical aspect of changing the scope of conflict and the level of conflict is publicity concerning that conflict.* Even people who might be affected by some governmental action or inaction are not going to be participants if they do not know that a conflict exists. In the busing example there was reason to believe, based on the polls, that if the conflict could be raised to higher levels, antibusing forces would prevail. It turned out, however, that the busing issue was not the most politically salient issue affecting the potential constituency. Having the power resources to raise an issue through various arenas of conflict resolution does not guarantee that that issue will be resolved in favor of the interest that takes the issue to the higher level. Even though the busing issue got a complete airing, the antibusing forces, who carried the fight, lost.

Policy Subsystems Keep Level of Conflict Low

A more typical example involves the oil interests and the Department of the Treasury. The major American oil companies have extensive foreign operations. Special treatment of expenses involved in these foreign operations has in effect taken money out of the tax coffers and put it at the

---

4. Schattschneider deals primarily with levels of government—local, state, national—rather than with functional levels of the governmental system, as here.

disposal of the oil companies. The special treatment, which was in effect until 1976, was established as a rule by administrative action, not legislation. Furthermore, this special treatment involved interpretations of operating expenses that were contrary to the spirit of the tax laws.

In general, the tax treatment of income earned by firms operating in foreign countries is based upon two principles. The first is that host countries assess the first tax on profits of American corporations operating within their borders. This is a standard international convention. The second principle regarding tax liability of American firms is that the United States seeks to equalize the tax treatment of American firms operating abroad so that neither foreign nor domestic investment is encouraged at the expense of the other. This second principle means that the Internal Revenue Service (IRS) imposes the standard corporate profits tax of 48 percent on all corporate income earned anywhere in the world, but "grants a dollar-for-dollar tax credit for all income taxes already paid to foreign countries on earnings abroad. But it does not allow a dollar-for-dollar tax credit for operating costs such as rents, royalties, and excise taxes."[5]

On the surface, the tax law appears to be quite clear. Foreign income taxes paid by American firms are to be treated as a tax credit against their United States tax liability. Rents and royalties are to be treated as part of operating expenses and deducted before computing taxable income, as shown in part A of Table 2.1. But in the oil-rich countries where the rights to the land are held by the government, it becomes debatable whether a payment to the government is a tax payment or a payment for "rent" or "royalties." If all payments to the government are considered to be taxes, the oil companies save a considerable amount of money in their United States tax liability, as shown in the hypothetical example in part B of Table 2.1.

For years, the Department of the Treasury accepted the oil companies' argument that rent and royalties paid to oil sheiks and foreign governments were really taxes and therefore entitled the companies to the dollar-for-dollar tax credit. In 1973, the oil companies used these tax credits to reduce their United States taxable income by more than $5 billion.[6] That figure did not take into account the great rise of oil prices instituted by the Organization of Petroleum Exporting Countries (OPEC) toward the end of 1973. Even though the bulk of the payments

---

5. Barry M. Blechman, Edward M. Gramlich, and Robert W. Hartman, *Setting National Priorities: The 1975 Budget* (Washington, D.C.: The Brookings Institution 1974), pp. 163–164.
6. "I.R.S. Posts Rule on Oil Tax," *New York Times*, July 15, 1975.

TABLE 2.1
Treatment of Rent and Royalties (R & R) as Expenses Versus Their Treatment as Foreign Income Tax

Part A (R & R as Expenses)		Part B (R & R as Tax)
$2000	Value of oil	$2000
− 1000	Less expenses[a]	− 500
1000	Total income tax liability	1500
× .48	U.S. corporate tax rate	× .48
480	U.S. tax	720
− 0	Tax credit	− 500
$ 480	U.S. tax payment	$ 220

[a] This hypothetical example assumes rent and royalties to be 50 percent of total expenses.

to these governments would have been considered rent or royalties if paid to a private individual or group, the IRS agreed to treat these payments as income taxes. Clearly, the oil companies and the Internal Revenue Service had been able to resolve a conflict at a very low level. The losers in the conflict—the American public—did not even know that oil companies were being granted this special status by the administrative agency's rulings, which had the force of law but which were made in an arena of very low visibility.

In the late 1960s public interest tax reform groups began to study oil taxation policies and began to agitate for meaningful tax reform. Such tax breaks as the oil depletion allowances were cut by legislation from 27 percent of the value of the oil pumped per year to 22 percent. In 1975, the Democratic-controlled Congress eliminated the oil depletion allowance altogether for large oil companies. During the process of "marking up" the 1975 legislation, a provision that would have specified that rent and royalty payments to governments of oil-exporting countries not be considered foreign income taxes was dropped from it. It was not until July 1976 that the IRS, seeing that there was clear support to treat royalties and rent as royalties and rent instead of as tax payments, promulgated a new rule affecting the tax credit position of the oil companies.

Why did this inequitable situation last for so many years? Schattschneider thought that "a powerful and resourceful government is able to respond to conflict situations by providing an arena for them, publicizing them, protecting the contestants against retaliation and taking

FIGURE 2.2
Symbiotic Relationships of Political Bureaucracy

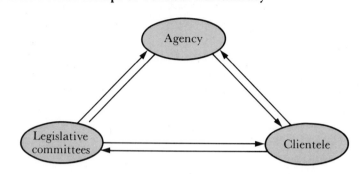

steps to rectify the situations complained of."[7] Clearly, the government of the United States did not act in a powerful and resourceful manner in this case. The oil companies, working closely with the IRS—probably with the knowledge of the tax-writing committees in Congress—were able to keep their favorable treatment hidden from most other actors who might have had an interest in more equitable taxation.

By applying the environmental analysis that was presented in chapter 1, we can see why an agency given the mandate to act in the public interest chose to favor a special interest. To the decision-makers in the agency, the most important environmental relationships—the most salient relationships—were those defining the oil-tax policy subsystem. A policy subsystem consists of those actors who, because they occupy roles in the agency, its clientele, or particular legislative committees, have great concern about a specific policy area. As was pointed out in the first chapter, each of these actors is in a position to help the others. A policy subsystem can be visualized as a triangle of mutually rewarding, or symbiotic, relationships (see Figure 2.2).

In this case, the IRS developed the royalty-as-tax-credit rule for the oil companies at a time when oil companies had relatively minor foreign holdings. To change the rule when the oil companies acquired vast foreign holdings would have meant a dislocation for the agency. It is much easier to continue a friendly relationship with a client than to antagonize it. It especially does not pay to offend a clientele group as powerful as the oil interests. It is no secret that oil money helps many politicians.

7. Schattschneider, *The Semi-Sovereign People*, p. 17.

Among these are powerful members of the House Ways and Means and the Senate Finance committees, who are in a position to affect the jurisdiction of the IRS. Oil money, furthermore, helps people on the appropriations subcommittees, who can most directly affect the agency's budget.

For conflict to be "contagious" it must be publicized. But it was simply not in the interests of any of the participants in the policy subsystem to publicize the potential conflict in equity between the symbolic aspects of the tax structure (all industries are being treated fairly) and the reality (oil companies are getting a big tax break). So all the members of the policy subsystem were content to keep quiet. It was almost as if the actors representing the three points of the triangle of symbiotic relationships had conspired to keep the level of conflict low. Few outside this cozy triangle knew about the preferential treatment until some other industries sought equity with the oil companies and some public interest tax reform groups developed the expertise to research the innermost recesses of tax law and administration.

In this case, it was to the benefit of members of the legislative committees and the agency to allow the clientele to benefit from "tax expenditures." Tax expenditures are special provisions in the tax system that, in effect, allow certain groups and individuals to keep money that ordinarily would have been collected for the government. Some examples of tax expenditures are tax credits given to businesses for new investments, depreciation on real estate and equipment, and deductions for local taxes and interest on mortgages for homeowners. Tax expenditures are indirect subsidies. The effect of tax expenditures, however, is the same as if the government had decided to give direct subsidies to the favored recipients. The beneficiaries of tax expenditures get increased money with which to operate, just as the recipients of direct subsidies, such as growers of certain agricultural commodities and shipping companies, do. Not surprisingly, policy subsystems that protect privileged interests have tended to develop in specific policy areas where government agencies determine who gets tangible benefits.

Implications of Policy Subsystems

Policy subsystems have developed in two ways: (1) by design, and (2) by default. Some agencies were designed to promote or provide services to a particular clientele. At the national level, the Department of Agriculture was the prototype for service-oriented agencies. Other service-oriented agencies in Washington are the Department of Commerce, the Department of Labor, the Veterans Administration, the Department of Transportation, the Department of Housing and Urban Development, and, most recently, the Department of Education, among many others. All these agencies have specific identifiable clients whom they are, by legislative design, supposed to serve.[8]

Policy subsystems develop through default when the legislature authorizes a governmental agency to regulate specific industries or businesses "in the public interest." In most regulatory behavior, however, the public's interest is more fleeting than that of the businesses and industries that are supposed to be regulated. As the fickle public is mobilized to move to a new area of reform, its interest in other specific fields of regulation often fades. This leaves the way open for policy subsystems consisting of highly interested actors to develop.

The result of policy subsystem development whether by design or default is much the same. C. Wright Mills has argued: "The executive bureaucracy becomes not only the center of power but also the arena within which and in terms of which all conflicts of power are resolved or denied resolution. Administration replaces electoral politics; the maneuvering of cliques [interest groups] replaces the clash of [political] parties."[9] This reinforces the decision-making power of some groups at the expense of others that have neither the political power to resolve a conflict favorably at the administrative level nor the power to raise the issue to a higher level where they might be more successful.

The existence of policy subsystems raises problems for democratic control of public policy. Grant McConnell, a political scientist who did much to uncover the many policy subsystems in America, has noted a critical danger:

> A politics of interest groups and small-constituent units is unlikely to develop its own checks. Government offers the best means of limiting both the conflicts between such groups and the agreements by which conflicts are ended or avoided. To give this service, however, government must be formal and distinct. It cannot be either if it is broken into units corresponding to the interests which have developed power.[10]

Theodore Lowi, who was a colleague of McConnell's at the University of Chicago in the 1960s, developed this theme further. Lowi called the

---

8. James Q. Wilson calls this "bureaucratic clientelism" in his "The Rise of the Bureaucratic State," *The Public Interest,* 41 (Fall 1975): 89.
9. C. Wright Mills, *The Power Elite* (New York: Oxford University Press, 1959), p. 267.
10. Grant McConnell, *Private Power and American Democracy* (New York: Knopf, 1966; also Vintage, 1970), p. 363 of the Vintage edition. This book is a goldmine of examples of the interplay of groups and public bureaucracy.

intellectual foundation of modern American government that permits—indeed, encourages—the symbiotic relationships that we have described *interest group liberalism*. To Lowi, the system is liberal because people have a positive view of government as a mechanism for righting wrongs. Liberalism, to Lowi, is the justification for governmental expansion with no blueprint for what government should do after it has expanded into new areas. To Lowi, liberalism has no real concern for formal structure and procedures. Liberalism is afraid of power and seeks to hide behind the smoke screen of pragmatism. Pragmatism, in this case, is when government allows interest groups to define the public interest, with government playing the role of the broker or even another interest among many to be accommodated through bargaining.[11]

Interest group liberalism is weak government. It leads to self-government by groups—agricultural, commercial, industrial, labor—and it keeps the level of conflict low. In interest group liberalism, the government provides the arena for working out problems, but only those with a clear stake in the issue and with strong political organization can effectively participate in the decision. Rarely are decisions presented to the general public in a formal way. Generally, weak government presides over "the private expropriation of public authority."[12]

Lowi credited the pragmatism of interest group liberalism with saving the American society and political system from the Great Depression, but he saw serious long-range effects that we must deal with now. Principally, Lowi saw interest group liberalism contributing to the weakening of the constitutionally created representative bodies like the legislatures. By enhancing executive power, which then, de facto, becomes shared with the clientele of the particular agency, the public itself is cut off from a meaningful role in policy-making. Interest group liberalism creates niches of privilege for those groups that become the clientele of an agency. They are in a position to keep their special privileges at the expense of the public at large. Furthermore, these established groups, through established channels of power, are in a position to resist effectively change that may be desired by the public at large. Interest group liberalism means that policy will effectively be determined at a low level of conflict, with some groups winning and the public probably losing.

11. Theodore J. Lowi, *The End of Liberalism*, 2d ed. (New York: Norton, 1979), chapter 3.
12. Ibid., p. 68.

The Organization
of Effective
Clientele

THAT the level of conflict is so low in American politics and that some interests are able to develop close ties with agencies while other, potentially conflicting interests are relatively ineffective are two of the most interesting phenomena of American politics. Murray Edelman suggested an explanation that relates the types of rewards that groups desire to the way groups are organized. Basically, he saw highly organized, specific-purpose groups gaining tangible benefits from the political process in general and the less organized, less specifically focused groups settling for symbolic rewards.[13]

To Edelman, the apparent lack of conflict in many policy areas could be explained in several ways. It is possible that the lack of conflict reflects a lack of interest—apathy toward the policy area. Or it could be that the lack of conflict means that the groups involved in the policy area, in even a tangential way, are satisfied with existing policy. If they do not agree with the specific policies adopted, they are often satisfied by the symbols of the policy process. For example, citizens might feel that their interests are being protected by an agency. Edelman called this feeling of satisfaction with the symbolic role of the agency *symbolic reassurance.* Edelman argued that people are open to symbolic reassurance— the manipulation of symbols of action—if they lack political organization and have distorted perceptions of how policy is actually made.

Edelman identified two basic patterns of group organization in regulatory policy, patterns A and B, which are summarized in Table 2.2 Groups organized in pattern A have relatively few members and are organized on a rationalist, often bureaucratic, model to deal with the precise information with which the public bureaucracy deals. Pattern A groups want specific, tangible rewards that are in the power of the agency to grant or withhold. It makes sense for the pattern A groups to study the fine print in the *Federal Register,* the weekly publication of new rules and regulations of all federal agencies, and to develop intricate analyses of pending action, because much is at stake for them.

The stakes are not so high for most people associated with pattern B groups. Pattern B groups are more loosely organized and less interested in specific agency action. In both service-oriented and regulatory agen-

---

13. Murray J. Edelman, "Symbols and Political Quiescence," *American Political Science Review* 54, no. 3 (September 1960): 695–704.

TABLE 2.2
Edelman's Two Patterns of Group Organization

Pattern A	Pattern B
High degree of organization	Little organization for purposive action
Rational, cognitive	Protest orientation
Precise information	Distorted, stereotyped, inexact information
Interest in tangible resources	Ineffective in attaining tangible resources through politics
Favored strategic position	Unfavorable strategic position
Relatively small numbers	Relatively large numbers

SOURCE: Murray J. Edelman, "Symbols and Political Quiescence," *American Political Science Review* 54, no. 3 (September 1960): 701.

cies, there is little economic incentive for the membership of pattern B groups to get involved with the policy subsystem. As Herbert Kaufman has pointed out:

> The incentive structure motivates the powerful more effectively than the weak; a regulatory decision meaning millions to a firm often costs individual consumers less than the cost of protesting it, so it would be irrational for individual consumers to fight even though the loss hurts them.[14]

Furthermore, pattern B organizations, of which consumer groups are usually examples, are not organized for purposeful action, often because they are unsure of what that purposeful action would be. Instead, according to Edelman, they are generally satisfied by symbolic rewards. Members of pattern B groups are often satisfied by simply knowing that a government agency has been created ostensibly to look after the interests with which the group is concerned. These groups are often not in a position to follow up to make sure the law is implemented in specific cases. In the regulatory process there is a "divergence between political and legal promises on the one hand and resource allocations and group reactions on the other hand."[15] Generally, pattern B groups are not effective in the resource allocation area, but are content with the promises implied by the mere existence of an agency to regulate freight rates, for example. In truth, those freight rates might be higher than market forces would suggest, but the consumer somehow feels that the rates are equita-

---

14. Herbert Kaufman, *Red Tape: Its Origins, Uses, and Abuses* (Washington, D.C.: The Brookings Institution, 1977), p. 16.

15. Edelman, "Symbols and Political Quiescence," p. 695.

ble because the government is supposedly looking out for his or her interests.

In recent years some good government and consumer groups such as Common Cause and the Ralph Nader affiliates have adopted a pattern A form of organization. These groups have been effective in pressing for tax reform and deregulation. The role of these groups has been institutionalized to a degree through the widespread federal and state practice of having advisory committees for service and regulatory functions. With the many reorganizations of state governments in the past fifteen years, advisory committees have sprung up in those places where the old independent boards have been absorbed into executive departments. But having a self-styled public interest group such as Common Cause on an advisory committee does not mean that the good government and consumer interests will be as effective in influencing policy as the "well-organized, well-heeled, well-informed, well-connected, continuously functioning, experienced" clientele interests that will dominate such groups.[16]

Clientele advisory committees institutionally tie the pattern A, primarily industrial, clientele to the structure of government. There are some real services that advisory committees could provide to the government in a modern democratic state. Government should be able to use the special expertise that only industrial representatives can provide in some cases. Advisory committees can make administrators aware of special problems and conditions in the private sector. Administrators can better judge the impact of programs if they can routinely meet with group representatives through advisory committees. Furthermore, advisory committees enable administrators to get the cooperation of the private sector, which is essential to orderly and efficient administration.[17] This rationale can encourage the kind of flexible and intelligent administration that many desire.

For advisory committees to fulfill the promise of this rationale, however, they must exhibit several attributes. They should be competent and expert. They should be widely representative. They should be independent and critical of the agency in a positive way. But all too often, advisory committees are composed not of experts and technicians but rather of executives seeking to protect their private interests. Often rep-

16. Kaufman, *Red Tape*, p. 16.
17. U.S. Congress, Senate, Committee on Government Operations, Subcommittee on Intergovernmental Relations, *Advisory Committees*, testimony of Henry J. Steck at hearing, 92nd Cong., 1st sess., 17 June, 1971 (Washington, D.C.: U.S. Government Printing Office, 1971), p. 367.

resentatives of the public at large—if they are on the committees at all—lack the staff support to question slickly presented industry claims. Often advisory committees are in a position to obstruct the work of public agencies. They can keep government from finding out about certain corporations. They can sometimes enable some corporations to get inside information about what the government plans to do. In short, advisory committees may be "in a position to define the public interest in private terms."[18]

Advisory committees established or used by federal agencies are governed by the Federal Advisory Committee Act of 1972. The act gives several federal agencies a role in its administration. The General Services Administration (GSA) issues overall administrative guidelines and management controls and reviews the performance of the 1500 or so advisory committees. The Office of Management and Budget (OMB) also provides guidance to the agencies concerning these committees. The law requires each agency to establish more specific management guidance

18. Ibid., p. 358.

An Abuse of the Advisory Committee System

In 1970, Richard Nixon created the National Industrial Pollution Control Council (NIPCC), which was comprised of executives from sixty-three major polluters including airline, utility, coal, oil, chemical, and wood products companies. There were no representatives of conservation associations, consumers, or other public interest groups on the council. The council held its meetings without public announcement or in places such as the Department of State, where access to the meeting could be restricted. The main work of the NIPCC was the preparation of twenty-five "studies" and a "Casebook of Pollution Clean-up Actions"—mainly clippings from trade publications and the companies' own magazines—which showed the remarkable antipollution efforts being made by industry. These reports were widely circulated in booklets bearing the Department of Commerce name and an introductory message from the president of the United States. A small disclaimer indicated that the report did "not necessarily represent the views of the Department of Commerce." As might be expected, this effort was little more than a government-financed propaganda campaign on behalf of the polluters.

SOURCE: *From* Lee Metcalf, "The Vested Oracles: How Industry Regulates Government," *The Washington Monthly* 3, no. 7 (July 1971): 45–57.

and control. Yet despite all these mechanisms, a 1979 study of the Department of Energy's advisory committees suggested there is still much room for potential abuse. The General Accounting Office (GAO), an investigative arm of Congress, found that twelve of the twenty advisory committees in the department did not have specific objectives. These would have helped avoid overlap and duplication and would have contributed to evaluating a committee's usefulness. The GAO found that eighteen of the twenty committees lacked time spans for accomplishing their work. The study further found that guidelines for membership were not specific and the costs of the committees had been improperly allocated.[19] Perhaps having the agencies monitor their own advisory committees does not provide meaningful control.

The Life-Cycle View of Regulation

It is easy to see how service-oriented agencies develop close ties with those they are supposed to serve. The notion of pattern A and pattern B groups can help us see how regulatory agencies often develop close ties with the regulated and how conflicting pattern A groups enable an agency to be a mediating force which can protect the public's interest under certain conditions. Using an implicit notion of symbolic versus tangible rewards, Marver Bernstein has suggested there is a life cycle to the regulatory process. According to Bernstein, many regulatory agencies pass through four stages in their organizational lives: (1) gestation, (2) youth, (3) maturity, and (4) old age.[20] It is important to remember in the following discussion that all agencies are not bound to pass through all of these stages.

During the gestation period, political forces favoring governmental action in a particular area build up. As James Q. Wilson has noted, "Most of the major new social [and regulatory] programs of the United States, whether for the good of the few or the many, were initially adopted by broad coalitions appealing to general standards of justice or to conceptions of the public weal."[21] These broad coalitions get the legis-

19. U.S., General Accounting Office, *Use, Cost, Purpose, and Makeup of Department of Energy Advisory Committees*, Report EMD-79-17 (Washington, D.C.: February 2, 1979), pp. 1–11.
20. Marver Bernstein, *Regulating Business by Independent Commissions* (Princeton: Princeton University Press, 1955), chapter 3.
21. Wilson, "The Rise of the Bureaucratic State," p. 93.

lature to establish certain agencies and programs. At the national level, examples of this kind of legislation are the Commerce Act of 1887, which established the Interstate Commerce Commission (ICC); the Pure Food and Drug Act of 1906, which set up the Food and Drug Administration (FDA); much of the legislation passed during the Great Depression; and consumer and environmental protection legislation of the 1970s. At the state level, occupational licensing laws for everyone from beauticians to plumbers originally had strong majority support. Once legislation is passed, however, many groups in the supporting coalition become symbolically reassured. These pattern B groups receive the rewards they want by seeing a government agency created to protect their interests. They then cease to be a major political force in making policy in the area in which the legislation was passed.

Although the coalition of forces that created the agency begins to break up at its birth, the agency attracts during its youth stage active people who are interested in carrying out the mandate of the legislation. In this stage there is still significant support from broad aspects of the

---

A "Young" Agency's Exercise in
Bureaucratic Trivia and Nonsense

Take what should be a simple matter, the definition of an "exit." The dictionary tells us that "exit" means "a passage or way out." But [to] the [Occupational Safety and Health Administration (OSHA)] enforcers, defining "exit" is a challenge to their bureaucratic instincts, and they are not found wanting. To OSHA, an "exit" is "that portion of a means of egress which is separated from all other spaces of the building or structure by construction or equipment as required in this subpart to provide a protected way of travel to the exit discharge."

"Exit discharge," in turn, is defined merely as "that portion of a means of egress between the termination of an exit and a public way." And "a means of egress" is defined as "a continuous and unobstructed way of exit travel from any point in a building or structure to a public way and consists of three separate and distinct parts: the way of exit access, the exit, and the way of exit discharge. A means of egress comprises the vertical and horizontal ways of travel and shall include intervening room spaces, doorways, hallways, corridors, passageways, balconies, ramps, stairs, enclosures, exits, escalators, horizontal exits, courts, and yards."

SOURCE: Murray L. Weidenbaum, "The Cost of Overregulating Business," *Tax Foundation's Tax Review* 36, no. 8 (August 1975): 34–35.

environment. In regulatory agencies, the youth stage is a period of aggressive regulation. Sometimes, as in the case of the Occupational Safety and Health Administration (OSHA) during the 1970s, exuberant efforts at carrying out the legislative mandate galvanize political forces seeking to reduce the impact of the legislation. These more specialized, pattern A groups set the stage for maturity.

During the mature phase, the attitudes of the personnel of the agency mellow, and the agency tends to look for accommodation rather than confrontation. Agency personnel emphasize being "reasonable" with the regulated. A partnership develops in which the public interest is ostensibly protected by statesmanship on both sides. During this stage, its clientele becomes the most important environmental factor affecting the agency. The regulated groups and the agency develop strong symbiotic relationships during maturity. These relationships are further developed until the teeth fall out of the regulatory agency altogether during old age.

Old age marks the capture of the agency by the groups that it is supposed to regulate. In old age, regulatory agencies become protectors of the regulatees. Although the agency continues to exist and still has its original legislative mandate, during old age it has only symbolic value. It does not perform its stated functions, but it survives. As Kenneth Culp Davis has noted:

> Some of the most important regulatory agencies may be kept, not because of their success, but because the degree of their failure is approved by politically powerful interests that are regulated. An ineffective regulatory agency often goes through the motions of regulating, thereby silencing the sponsors of the legislation that brought the agency into existence, but at the same time the agency is careful for the most part to regulate in the interest of the regulated, thereby silencing them.[22]

Many regulatory agencies provide symbolic reassurance to the public at large while presiding over the division of tangible rewards to their clientele.

---

22. Kenneth Culp Davis, *Administrative Law and Government* (St. Paul, Minn.: West, 1960), p. 39.

The Case of the Interstate Commerce Commission

The ineptitude of the first "independent" regulatory agency, the Interstate Commerce Commission (ICC), is one of the grossest examples of government regulation gone astray.[23] When the ICC was created in 1887, it was supposed to

> represent the diffuse public interest vigorously as a counterforce to highly organized transportation interests. It was Congress' intent that the ICC do more than serve as judge or arbitrator between those transportation forces which might find themselves in conflict. Supreme Court interpretation of the Interstate Commerce Act further indicates that the agency's purpose is to serve as the aggressive and independent representative of the general public interest.[24]

That the Interstate Commerce Commission has failed to carry out this mandate suggests the kinds of pressures on all government agencies charged with regulating aspects of American society.

It is generally acknowledged that the ICC, after a brief period of aggressive regulation, entered a premature old-age stage about the time of World War I. The shoddy performance of the railroads during wartime created a crisis in which the federal government ceased to be a regulator and moved into the position of promoter. Although the stated goals of the ICC did not change, a new goal of helping the railroads make profits at the expense of service was adopted. When the Great Depression of the 1930s devastated American industry, including the railroads, the ICC allowed the railroads to adopt accounting practices that showed that passenger service was too costly to continue. The result was a deterioration in the quality and quantity of intercity passenger train service, from nearly 20,000 trains per day in 1929 to only 250 in 1976.[25] The ICC presided over wholesale mergers of competing lines during the 1960s which cut competition and service even for freight customers.

But by the 1960s the Interstate Commerce Commission was no longer the great protector of the railroads. The ICC, as Leonard Ross has noted, "has modernized in the last few decades by selling out to the truckers. It is now in the business of keeping truck rates high by exclud-

---

23. The independent regulatory commissions are "independent" in the sense that the president cannot dismiss members of the commissions until the end of their terms. Most of the problems of these independent commissions are similar to problems faced by the regulatory agencies in the executive branch. *Also see* chapter 12.
24. Robert Fellmeth, *The Interstate Commerce Omission* (New York: Grossman, 1970), p. xiv.
25. Tracy Kidder, "Trains in Trouble," *The Atlantic Monthly* 238, no. 2 (August 1976): 30.

ing new firms and keeping railroad rates even higher to prevent them from competing. As a sideline, the ICC publishes a tough truck-safety code, which it does not enforce, and a weak household-mover's code, which it also does not enforce."[26] Given the close relationship of the ICC with the truckers, it was not surprising to see the commission and the large truckers in an alliance to fight efforts at deregulating the industry during the mid-1970s.

At that time the Interstate Commerce Commission, allegedly operating under its mandate to provide a transportation policy in the public interest, controlled many aspects of the trucking industry. The ICC assigned routes for interstate carriers. The only way a carrier could get a new route was to prove to the commission that the existing carriers were not properly serving the customers. This was very difficult to prove. The ICC certified carriers to haul specific items under specific conditions. In some cases, trucks had to return empty because they were not certified to carry goods on the back haul. This made little sense at a time of general awareness of energy conservation. Since the industry operated under antitrust immunity, the industry's own rate bureaus set rates, which were routinely sanctified by the ICC. The ICC would even object if some truckers proposed lower rates. No wonder the American Trucking Association, the Washington-based lobbying voice of the large truckers, favored the stability of "regulation" to the uncertainty of freer competition.

Business men and women are constantly seeking to limit the degree of uncertainty with which they must deal. Most administration is also concerned with limiting uncertainty by promulgating rules. It is not surprising that there would be a mutually beneficial relationship between the ICC and its trucker clientele. We will shortly see how this policy subsystem was broken during the late 1970s and early 1980s.

Power and Administration

POLICY subsystems that develop by design and by default have many features in common. The most important one is that the agency must survive if it is to serve or regulate, even in a symbolic way. To survive it

---

26. Leonard Ross, quoted in Robert Sherrill, *Why They Call It Politics,* 2d ed. (New York: Harcourt Brace Jovanovich, 1974), p. 219.

must develop lines of power that can assure it of a budget and personnel. Norton Long has claimed, "The lifeblood of administration is power."[27] To Long,

> It is clear that the American system of politics does not generate enough power at any focal point of leadership to provide the conditions for an even partially successful divorce of politics from administration. Subordinates cannot depend on the formal chain of command to deliver enough political power to permit them to do their jobs. Accordingly they must supplement the resources available through the hierarchy with those they can muster on their own, or accept the consequences in frustration—a course itself not without danger. Administrative rationality demands that objectives be determined and sights set in conformity with a realistic appraisal of power position and potential.[28]

Environmental analysis suggests several sources of power that could be cultivated if an agency is to perform at all. Among these potential power sources are higher political and career executives, including the chief executive, the legislature, other governmental agencies, the clientele, and the general public. These additional sources of power must be developed if an agency is to use its primary potential power resource—its technical expertise.

Of the potential power sources, the ones most easily developed by an agency are those having an intense interest in its work. Not many of the actors in an agency's environment have that intense interest. Higher-level political and career executives are worried about a range of issues in addition to the work of any particular agency. They will not routinely invest their time in an agency that is not giving them problems. An agency that does not make waves often does not make problems for higher executives. Other government agencies may have some peripheral interest in the work of the agency; certainly central budget and personnel offices could either help or hinder the work of any agency. But generally, except when they are protecting their turf from the bureaucratic imperialism of one another, other agencies are not intensely concerned.[29] The general public, whether unorganized or loosely organized in pattern B groups, has such diffuse interests that it would be difficult for most agencies to mobilize the public at large for political support of agency goals.

---

27. Norton E. Long, "Power and Administration," *Public Administration Review* 9 (Autumn 1949): 257.
28. Ibid., p. 258.
29. Matthew Holden, Jr., " 'Imperialism' in Bureaucracy," *American Political Science Review* 60, no. 4 (December 1966): 943–951.

There are, however, two groups of actors in an agency's environment that have a great deal of interest in the agency's work. These are members of legislative committees and subcommittees dealing with the agency, and its clientele. Although the legislature is interested in a wide range of issues, individual legislators in committees or subcommittees specialize in policy areas. Usually legislators get committee assignments because they already have an interest in a particular policy area or agency. Is it so strange that members of Congress from agricultural states like to get on agricultural committees? The choice of committee assignment enables legislators to serve the constituents from their districts better. These people have a strong interest in an agency's work. They are sources of political power that public managers must understand and cultivate.

The clientele of an agency is also extremely interested in the work of the agency. J. Leiper Freeman has pointed out some striking similarities between agencies and their clientele:

> Since a public bureaucracy is concerned with special and limited aspects of public policy, to a degree it resembles the ordinary private pressure group. It is a congregating place for individuals concerned with the same subjects. Some of these interested individuals become members of the administrative agency while others join groups which look to that organization as a rallying point, and the agency takes a leading part in representing their interests. In this representative process perhaps the bureaucracy's most important function is to promote the idea that its special area of concern is important—be it education, air power, or mental health.[30]

Clearly, the political power of the clientele will affect the agency's programs.

A Clientele Typology

So far we have treated the clientele as if they always hold considerable power over the agency—power that can cause the agency to act pragmatically rather than dogmatically and in some cases even to ignore its legislative mandate. An analysis by Eugene Lewis points out that the clientele is not always in a powerful position vis-à-vis the agency. Lewis

---

30. J. Leiper Freeman, "The Bureaucracy in Pressure Politics," *Annals of the American Academy of Political and Social Science* 319 (September 1958): 12.

suggests three modes in which citizens deal with bureaucratic agencies: (1) as constituents, (2) as clients, and (3) as victims.[31]

Bureaucratic constituents are virtually synonymous with the pattern A groups with which we have been dealing. These groups represent the farm, labor, and industrial interests in the administrative arena. Because these groups possess independent sources of power, they are in a position to bargain with an agency in both service and regulatory matters. Because of their power, constituent groups can control the actions of the bureaucracy in the specific policy area in which they both are concerned. Bureaucrats and constituents share policy-making power.

Not all groups are as powerful in dealing with agencies as are those Lewis calls constituents. Clients, in Lewis's terminology, are groups or individuals who are highly dependent on decisions made by an agency, but these people or groups lack the independent sources of power needed to bend the bureaucrats to their will. They lack the power to deal with bureaucrats on a more or less equal basis, as the constituent groups do. The needs and wants of client groups such as welfare mothers are usually articulated by bureaucrats on the basis of agency rules and professional standards. If welfare mothers organize to make demands, the relative political powerlessness of their groups usually enables the bureaucrats to grant or ignore their demands according to rules that were made in the absence of any influence by the welfare mothers. In contrast, the politically powerful constituents bargain with the bureaucrats over rule-making and rule interpretation.

Although clients are highly dependent on the government patron, they are the beneficiaries of services and they can sometimes organize to affect marginally the way the patron deals with them. Victims, according to Lewis, are affected by government policies over which they have no influence at all. There are two types of victims. The first kind is adversely affected by aggregate policy outcomes. For example, if the Federal Reserve Board tightens consumer credit, causing a business to lay off workers, those unfortunate workers are victims of an agency's policy. But rarely are the victims aware of which agency has caused their plight. The government decisions that affect them take place beyond their consciousness. According to Lewis, victims are the unorganized recipients of unintended economic and social effects of government policy. They are powerless to affect key decisions in their own lives, let alone influence particular agencies that indirectly cause them difficulties. The second

---

31. Eugene Lewis, *American Politics in a Bureaucratic Age: Citizens, Constituents, Clients and Victims* (Cambridge, Mass.: Winthrop, 1977), chapter 1.

kind of victims represent those who have come under the jurisdiction of a public agency that has effectively taken away their constitutional rights. Inmates of prisons and mental hospitals often fit this category.

Lewis's typology is interesting because it suggests that government agencies dealing with victims or clients will act in a different manner from those dealing with constituents. When bureaucrats are dealing with victims and clients, professional values seem to be the most important determiner of outcomes. Unless strong groups of "Friends of Prisoners" or "Friends of Mental Patients" spring up, victims have no political voice. Unless client groups can develop their potential power resources into more effective groups, they too will lack a strong enough political voice to challenge the "doctor knows best" attitude of professionals. For instance, the elderly might be a client group that achieves political parity with the government patron as increasing numbers of Americans get older and as they gain better organization. Agencies with politically powerful clientele—the constituents—must make decisions according to political as well as professional criteria. The Lewis typology is summarized in Table 2.3.

TABLE 2.3
Citizen–Bureaucracy Relationships

Dimensions of Interaction	Interaction Modes		
	Constituent	Client	Victim
Character of interest representation	Highly focused; locationally, functionally specific	Highly focused; authoritatively reinterpreted	Disembodied
Efficacy: power to alter policy outcomes	Great	Little	None
Dependence: upon a public agency for viability	Interdependence	Nearly complete	Total

SOURCE: Eugene Lewis, *American Politics in a Bureaucratic Age: Citizens, Constituents, Clients and Victims* (Cambridge, Mass.: Winthrop, 1977), p. 26. Used with permission.

Public Managers
and Power

ALTHOUGH we are now aware that clientele come in at least three varieties, our focus returns to the relationships that define policy subsystems—the triangular symbiotic relationships of Figure 2.2. We have seen that agencies must be attentive to their political environments and that key elements of each agency's environment are the legislative committees that are concerned with its work, and its clientele, who share an intense interest in its work. Both of these elements are the easiest for agencies to deal with because of the shared interests. If the clientele and the legislative committees want basically the same results from the agency, the agency will be under great pressure to give these actors what they want. Conflicts over specific decisions will be resolved at the administrative level. The policy subsystem will effectively cut the public at large off from a policy role.

But the interested legislative committees and clientele do not necessarily speak with one voice. There will sometimes be minority positions within the groups making up the clientele, and there may be minority positions within the legislative committees. Furthermore, these minority positions may be closer to public's interest than the dominant values of the policy subsystem. Public managers, operating under their conceptions of professional and democratic norms, can *choose* to support the claims of the minority positions within the policy subsystems. If they decide to support these claims, however, they will have to mobilize political support from outside the policy subsystem in order to make their decisions effective.

If public managers continually seek accommodation with the powerful interests within the policy subsystem, they will cease to be effective political actors. They will cease to affect their political environment. They will become pawns of strong clientele and legislative committee interests. In the American system, being a tool of such interests has some advantages for the agency. It virtually guarantees a strong budget and support for business as usual. But it also carries the liability of not being able to respond to changing conditions.

Management implies change—the ability to change the organization to meet changing conditions. To manage in the public sector under changing conditions requires the public manager not to get locked into the dominant views of the policy subsystem but to develop alternative sources of power from other actors in the environment. Whether a public manager seeks to develop these alternative sources of power—higher executives, other agencies, different clientele, the media, and so on—is his or her choice.

The manager can choose a strategy of accommodation with the dominant clientele and legislative forces, or he or she can choose a strategy calling for broader political support. The latter course is far more difficult, but it can be done successfully under certain conditions. To return to the example of the Interstate Commerce Commission: for years ICC commissioners and upper-level staff shared a revolving door with first the railroads, then the truckers. The shared values of the policy subsystem dictated inaction in the face of change. The ICC became an object of derision and a symbol of governmental ineffectiveness. A new group of commission members appointed during the Ford and Carter administrations took an active role in leading the ICC toward deregulation of the trucking industry.

These new public managers were able to build political bridges to actors in the executive and legislative branches who favored deregulation but were not vitally concerned with the workings of the ICC. These managers were able to turn minority positions among the clientele (small independent truckers seeking to get certification for routes monopolized by larger firms), press reports of some of the more outlandish examples of regulatory nonsense, and even academic reports into a political resource to use against the politically powerful American Truckers Association (ATA). Within the narrow arena of the ICC, the ATA was apparently overpowering, but in the wider public arena—a higher level of conflict—a combination of other political forces could negate the impact of this powerful lobby.

One aspect that was vital in the rejuvenation of the ICC was the public mood favoring deregulation. Another was presidential support. But the support of a chief executive, although it may be vital in breaking up policy subsystems, is not always forthcoming. As Hugh Heclo has pointed out: "The chief executive has little choice but to act selectively. . . . As he concentrates on what are to him the *crucial* issues, the President and his staff must leave to other executives those issues that are merely *important* to national policy."[32]

32. Hugh Heclo, *A Government of Strangers: Executive Politics in Washington* (Washington, D.C.: The Brookings Institution, 1977), pp. 11–12.

Summary

PUBLIC administration is not apolitical. Although we have not dealt with the kinds of partisan political pressures that are sometimes brought to bear on administrators, administrators are political actors. In the course of deciding how to carry out the law, administrators make decisions that affect "who gets what" in American society. Because administrators do have broad discretionary powers, the administrative arena becomes a political arena—although one less open to the public at large than legislative bodies. It is at this relatively low level, where interests organized to gain tangible rewards through political action are strong, that much public policy is made.

According to many observers, agencies that want to survive, let alone grow, are driven to seek accommodation with clientele and related legislative committees rather than face political battles brought on by conflict that is not contained at a low level. Agencies respond to their immediate political environment and quickly learn to be "reasonable." The symbiotic relationships among agency, clientele, and legislative committee appear to be the natural order of American bureaucratic politics.[33] Yet public managers can adopt strategies to enhance their bargaining position within the policy subsystem by cultivating actors outside the immediate policy area.

In the next chapter we turn our attention to the special case where the government's clientele is another government. We want to explore the managerial implications of intergovernmental relations.

Suggestions for Further Reading

Bernstein, Marver H. *Regulating Business by Independent Commission.* Princeton: Princeton University Press, 1955.

Kaufman, Herbert. *Are Government Organizations Immortal?* Washington, D.C.: The Brookings Institution, 1976.

33. Just some of those who have noted the role of group interaction with bureaucracy in the policy process are Norton Long, *The Polity* (Chicago: Rand McNally, 1962); Francis E. Rourke, *Bureaucracy, Politics and Public Policy,* 2d ed. (Boston: Little, Brown, 1976); Herbert A. Simon, Donald W. Smithburg, and Victor A. Thompson, *Public Administration* (New York: Knopf, 1950); and David B. Truman, *The Governmental Process* (New York: Knopf, 1951, 1971), chapter 14. Grant McConnell, *Private Power and American Democracy,* and Theodore J. Lowi, *The End of Liberalism,* do not subscribe to the notion that such close ties are inevitable and good.

Lewis, Eugene. *American Politics in a Bureaucratic Age: Citizens, Constituents, Clients and Victims.* Cambridge, Mass.: Winthrop, 1977.

Lowi, Theodore J. *The End of Liberalism: The Second Republic of the United States,* 2d ed. New York: Norton, 1979.

McConnell, Grant. *Private Power and American Democracy.* New York: Vintage, 1966.

Mazmanian, Daniel A., and Jeanne Nienaber. *Can Organizations Change? Environmental Protection, Citizen Participation, and the Corps of Engineers.* Washington, D.C.: The Brookings Institution, 1979.

Moynihan, Daniel P. *Maximum Feasible Misunderstanding.* New York: Free Press, 1969.

Schattschneider, E. E. *The Semi-Sovereign People.* New York: Holt, Rinehart & Winston, 1960.

Seidman, Harold. *Politics, Position and Power: The Dynamics of Federal Organization,* 3rd ed. New York: Oxford University Press, 1980.

CHAPTER THREE

Intergovernmental Relations

THE ESSENCE OF MANAGEMENT is to apply resources through an organization to achieve some goals. We have seen that the goals of public bureaucracies are given in legislative mandates, but in practice these goals are subject to some alternation because of political factors arising from the agency's environment. The configuration of political power of the actors surrounding an agency affects the power of the agency to implement its stated goals. An agency's clientele is one of the key factors affecting its effectiveness. In the United States, as one observer has noted, "The growing edge of client-oriented bureaucracy can be found . . . not in government relations with private groups, but in the relations among governmental units."[1]

Not only is one governmental unit able to bring political power to *affect* the actions of another, but agencies at one level of government must *depend on* agencies at another level of government in the American federal system to deliver the services called for by legislative mandates. This complicated web of interdependence is called intergovernmental relations. Today, intergovernmental relations affect the management of virtually all domestic policies in the United States. In this chapter we will define the scope of intergovernmental relations, review the rise of the federal government in the system, explore the mechanisms that coordinate the actions of all the levels of government, and discuss some problems facing the system in the future.

Marble Cakes and Picket Fences

ALTHOUGH intergovernmental relations spring from federalism, they define more inclusive relationships than federalism does. Federalism is the formal sharing of power between the state and national governments. In the Constitution the national government is granted exclusive authority to perform such functions as coining money, conducting foreign relations, and regulating matters of interstate commerce. The states have the power to handle most criminal and civil law, to provide education, and to exercise "police powers"—to protect and nurture the health, safety, welfare and morals of their citizens. The Constitution also spells out some concurrent powers, ones that both state and national governments share, such as the power to tax.

Thus, the constitutionally mandated federal scheme deals with two

---

1. James Q. Wilson, "The Rise of the Bureaucratic State," *The Public Interest* 41 (Fall 1975): 91.

layers, the national and the state. In formal federalism the counties, cities, towns, and numerous special governmental districts designed to provide such services as water and sewer, schools, or recreation, for example, are legal creatures of the state. This view is expressed in Dillon's Rule, which was named after an Iowa judge who asserted in 1868 that there is no common-law right of local self government and that local governmental units can exercise only the powers expressly granted to them by the state legislature.[2]

In addition to enumerating the powers of the national and state governments, the Constitution provides for national supremacy in areas where state and national laws conflict. Article VI states: "This Constitution, and the laws of the United States which shall be made in pursuance thereof; and all treaties made, or which shall be made, under the authority of the United States, shall be the supreme law of the land." This clause was upheld in the landmark case *McCulloch* v. *Maryland* in 1819.[3] Legal federalism, therefore, was often visualized as a two layer cake in which the national layer was on top of the state layer. This metaphor, however, does not deal with the complexities of intergovernmental relations as they are practiced within the United States today.

Deil Wright has noted a critical difference between federalism and intergovernmental relations:

> Whereas federalism emphasizes national-state relationships with occasional attention to interstate relations, the concept of [intergovernmental relations] IGR recognizes not only national-state and interstate relations, but also national-local, state-local, national-state-local, and interlocal relations. In short, IGR encompasses all the permutations and combinations of relations among the units of government in our system.[4]

Instead of a layer cake, Morton Grodzins suggested intergovernmental relations were more like a "marble cake, characterized by an inseparable mingling of differently colored ingredients, the colors appearing in vertical and diagonal strands and unexpected whirls."[5] Not only did

2. *City of Clinton* v. *the Cedar Rapids and Missouri River Railroad*, 24 *Iowa Law Reporter* 455 (1868).
3. 4 Wheaton 316.
4. Deil S. Wright, *Understanding Intergovernmental Relations* (North Scituate, Mass.: Duxbury, 1978), p. 8.
5. Morton Grodzins, "The Federal System," in *Goals for Americans: Report of the President's Commission on National Goals and Chapters Submitted for the Consideration of the Commission* (Englewood Cliffs, N. J.: Spectrum Books, 1960), p. 265. Deil S. Wright attributes the first use of the marble-cake metaphor to Joseph McLean during the 1940s. See Wright's "Intergovernmental Relations: An Analytical Overview," *The Annals of the American Academy of Political and Social Science* 416 (November 1974): 7.

Grodzins describe the seeming overlapping of functions among the levels of government, but he saw such overlapping as a relatively efficient way of serving compatible goals for clientele in the same geographical location. Grodzins argued that it would not make sense to have separate federal, state, and local sanitation inspectors, for example. Instead, one person paid through grants or direct funds from all three levels could enforce the laws of all the levels.

Grodzins and others realized that the marble cake implied that one governmental unit was often dependent on another governmental unit to accomplish certain goals. The federal government, which had the money, depended on state and local governments to deliver services. State and local governments that wanted to provide services were often dependent on the national government for funds. Rather than a diffuse mixing of general governments, however, the pattern of dependency was played out in functional areas.

Terry Sanford, who was governor of North Carolina in the early 1960s, suggested a metaphor that emphasized the functional relationships among the national, state, and local governments. According to Sanford:

> The lines of authority, the concerns and interests, the flow of money, and the direction of programs run straight down like a number of pickets. . . . There is, as in a picket fence, a connecting cross slat, but that does little to support anything. [These cross slats stand] for the governments. [They] hold the pickets in line; [they do] not bring them together. The picket-like programs are not connected at the bottom.[6]

Deil Wright developed this picket fence metaphor in a figure similar to Figure 3.1.[7]

Growth of National Power

THERE has been some federal involvement in the affairs of the states and localities ever since the Northwest Ordinance of 1784 made public land available and the Morrill Act of 1862 provided for land grant colleges, but the scope of that involvement has changed over the years, as new

6. Terry Sanford, *Storm Over the States* (New York: McGraw-Hill, 1967), p. 90.
7. Wright, *Understanding Intergovernmental Relations,* p. 62.

FIGURE 3.1
Wright and Sanford's Picket-Fence Federalism

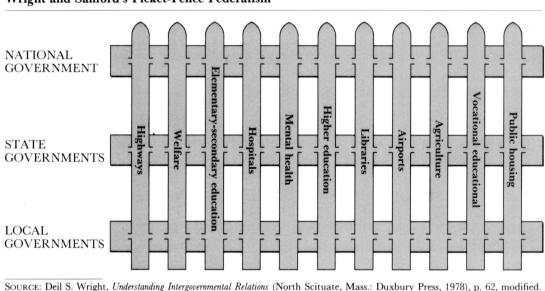

NATIONAL
GOVERNMENT

STATE
GOVERNMENTS

LOCAL
GOVERNMENTS

Highways · Welfare · Elementary-secondary education · Hospitals · Mental health · Higher education · Libraries · Airports · Agriculture · Vocational educational · Public housing

SOURCE: Deil S. Wright, *Understanding Intergovernmental Relations* (North Scituate, Mass.: Duxbury Press, 1978), p. 62, modified.

federal programs have added new "pickets" to the governmental fence. Each new picket was added in response to a promised professional solution to problems of middle-class Americans. To a large degree, the growth of intergovernmental relations is the growth of professional public bureaucracies at all levels.

The inability of the states to cope with the widespread unemployment and misery that afflicted middle-class individuals during the 1930s sparked a growing role for the national government in dealing with the states and local governments. Conflicts could not be resolved at the local level—a low level of conflict, in E. E. Schattschneider's term—so political forces seeking professional solutions to economic and social welfare questions raised the level of conflict to the national arena.[8] Middle-class majorities demanded action. The federal government responded with money and programs. For many, federal money and professional programs became narcotics for whatever ailments were affecting the middle class.

Several observers have commented on the power of the middle class in encouraging federal growth. The Depression showed that working with the states and cities, the federal government was able to mount highly

8. E. E. Schattschneider, *The Semi-Sovereign People* (New York: Holt, Rinehart & Winston, 1960), chapters 1 and 2.

specific programs. These programs were aimed at alleviating welfare and poverty problems, which were middle class concerns during the Depression. After World War II, the middle class sought federal solutions to new problems. As Eugene Lewis argues, "Federal bureaucrats assumed the high ground by identifying problems as national, nonpolitical and capable of professional (and therefore disinterested) solution."[9] Intergovernmental relations, with money flowing from the federal treasury, "fitted middle-class values of professionalism, objectivity, and neutrality. It appeared that objective program needs rather than politics were being served."[10]

A structural component that eased the flow of federal dollars to the state and local governments was the creation of various standing committees in a congressional reorganization of 1946.[11] The reorganization of Congress helped to articulate the middle-class needs for such projects as hospitals and airports, which had been put off during the war. The creation of the standing committees supported the middle class's demands for slum clearance, urban renewal, library construction, and waste treatment facilities as well as other activities that became the fields of professional competence. The committees became the channels through which funds flowed and symbiotic relationships with the agencies and the state and local governmental clientele provided a model for the great increase in grant programs during the 1960s.

The national involvement with the state and local governments has been great. Federal aid has continued to rise as shown in Figure 3.2. As a percent of state and local own source revenue, federal aid rose from 11 percent in 1957 to around 25 percent today, down from a peak of 26.7 percent in 1978.[12] Large cities, however, have seen dramatic increases in federal aid as a percentage of their expenditures in recent years. The Advisory Commission on Intergovernmental Relations (ACIR) estimates that direct federal aid to cities of over 500,000 people amounts to about 50 percent of their expenditure. Direct federal aid does not include federal funds that flow to the state governments and are then passed through to the large cities.[13]

As the political process has brought the federal government more involved in policy concerns that used to be the province of state and local

---

9. Eugene Lewis, *American Politics in a Bureaucratic Age: Citizens, Constituents, Clients and Victims* (Cambridge, Mass.: Winthrop, 1977), pp. 89–90.
10. Wright, *Understanding Intergovernmental Relations*, p. 49.
11. Ibid., p. 49.
12. Advisory Commission on Intergovernmental Relations, *Significant Features of Fiscal Federalism, 1978-79,* Report M-115 (Washington, D.C.: May 1979), p. 2.
13. Advisory Commission on Intergovernmental Relations, *Recent Trends in Federal and State Aid to Local Governments,* Report M-118 (Washington, D.C.: July 1980), pp. 5–9.

FIGURE 3.2
Federal Grants to State and Local Governments

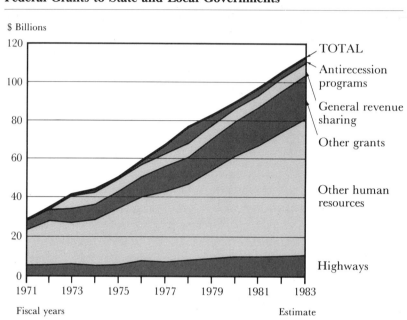

SOURCE: U.S. Office of Management and Budget, *Special Analyses: Budget of the United States Government, Fiscal Year 1981* (Washington, D.C.: U.S. Government Printing Office, 1980), p. 240.

governments, an awareness has grown that the federal government now needs the state and local governments to administer national legislation. Whereas the number of federal civilian employees has not changed significantly in the past twenty years, one only has to look at the great growth at the state and local levels—and through private contracting out for services—to see that the federal government has deputized the state and local governments to carry out national domestic policy. The principal tool by which the federal government achieves this is the grant-in-aid system. Martha Derthick has properly noted: "The essence of the grant system is . . . [the] achievement of federal objectives by proxy."[14]

14. Martha Derthick, *The Influence of Federal Grants: Public Assistance in Massachusetts* (Cambridge, Mass.: Harvard University Press, 1970), p. 197.

The Federal Grant System

THE Advisory Commission on Intergovernmental Relations has developed a taxonomy that classifies federal grants according to three dimensions: by scope, by funds-distribution basis, and by recipient governments.[15] Scope defines the three broad types of grant programs: (1) categorical grants, with narrow scope; (2) block grants, with broader scope; and (3) general revenue sharing, which affords the recipient government the broadest scope in determining how to use the funds. This taxonomy is summarized in Figure 3.3 and discussed below.

Categorical Grants

When people think of the picket fence model of intergovernmental relations, they often think of categorical grants. Categorical grant programs are for specified, often narrow purposes. In recent years, roughly 75 percent of the federal grants-in-aid have been through the almost five hundred categorical grant programs. In 1968, 98 percent of federal aid to

FIGURE 3.3
Taxonomy of Grant Programs

SCOPE	FUNDS DISTRIBUTION			
	Project	Formula-project	Formula-apportioned	Open-ended
Categorical	S, L	S, L	S, L	S, L
Block			S, L	
General revenue sharing			S, L	

Recipient: state = **S**   local = **L**

15. U.S. Advisory Commission on Intergovernmental Relations, *Categorical Grants: Their Role and Design*, Report A-52 (Washington, D.C.: May 6, 1977), pp. 5–9 and 92–93.

state and local governments was through categorical grants. The number of categorical grants has increased drastically since 1960 when there were fewer than 44. The greatest expansion of such grants came during the Lyndon B. Johnson period from 1963 to 1968, but in recent years the number of new categorical grant programs has leveled off.[16]

The number, growth, and specificity of categorical grants have concerned state and local officials. Smaller jurisdictions, especially, find getting through the grant maze to be a formidable task. Until the late 1960s there was not even a central source that indicated which grant programs existed. Now the Office of Management and Budget publishes the *Catalog of Federal Domestic Assistance,* which lists all federal grants, the amount of money appropriated for each program, and the criteria used for selecting the proposals. The growth of categorical-grant programs also led to some duplication. The classic examples of duplication were the four water and sewer programs of four different federal departments, each serving a slightly different, narrowly defined clientele. Categorical grant programs are highly specific because Congress wants to see that its money is used for the things it determines to be important. There are always some strings attached to grant funds, and categorical grants have more strings than block grants or general revenue sharing. Some categorical grants are more closely controlled than other categorical grants, however.

Categorical grants are funded in four different ways, through (1) project, (2) formula-project, (3) formula-apportioned, and (4) open-ended reimbursement. The most common form is the project grant. For the project grant, the potential recipients must submit a specific application for each proposal. The grants are awarded on a competitive basis by the administering federal agencies. Thus, federal grant administrators have power of life or death over project grants, examples of which are those programs designed to improve hospitals or airports.

Formula-project grants allow the federal grant administrator to choose among projects once money has been allocated by a formula to each state. Because of the political realities, even pure project grants often have a rough distribution formula. Politically astute administrators try to spread the money they have among the states, anticipating

16. The number of programs fluctuates from year to year, as some programs are not funded or are absorbed into block grants of consolidated categoricals. Also, the ACIR figures do not match those of the Office of Management and Budget. For the most recent OMB figures, see the annual *Budget of the United States, Special Analyses* (Washington, D.C.: U.S. Government Printing Office).

that influential senators and representatives want to see the benefits spread around as long as they get their share.

Formula-apportioned grants leave little or no discretionary authority to the federal grant manager. In this case, Congress specifically tells the administrators what factors they should consider in giving a grant, or the legislation spells out how much money a state or city is entitled to based on population characteristics, wealth, tax effort, and whatever else Congress wants to include in the grant formula. The reason so many large cities complained about the 1980 census was that alleged undercounts of poor, black, and Hispanic peoples would alter the amounts of money coming into their jurisdictions from formula grants. Many education and housing grants are based on these kinds of formulas.

The fourth group of categorical grants, open-ended grants, effectively takes all discretion away from the federal patron. Examples of such grants are Aid to Families of Dependent Children (AFDC), food stamps and similar entitlement programs that are managed by the states with the federal government picking up a good portion of the bill. Such categorical grants are open-ended because the federal government reimburses a specified proportion of state and local program costs. The participating states and local governments must provide money or services to any individual who meets the qualification standards established by law. If the law says that people earning less than a certain amount of money are entitled to food stamps, the state or local agency responsible for distributing the stamps provides the stamps and files a claim for federal funds.

Block Grants

Since the mid-sixties, groups representing state and local governmental officials have pointed out the need for grant simplification. These groups, which include the National Governors Conference, the Council of State Governments, the National Legislative Conference, the National Association of County Officials, the National League of Cities, the U.S. Conference of Mayors, and the International City Management Association, have sought categorical–grant consolidation and the creation of block grants to cover functional areas. These changes would give greater discretion to local authorities in choosing among various ways to solve problems in housing, health, or social services.

Carl Stenberg of the ACIR has defined a block grant as "a program in which funds are provided chiefly to general purpose governmental units in accordance with a statutory formula for use in a broad functional area largely at the recipient's discretion."[17] Although the term "block grant" has been applied to large formula-based categoricals such as Title I of the Elementary and Secondary Education Act of 1965 and to consolidations of some categorical programs in the maternal and child health and library and learning resources fields among others, Stenberg associates the term with the following five programs: (1) the Partnership for Health Act, (2) the Omnibus Crime Control and Safe Streets Act, (3) the Comprehensive Employment and Training Act of 1973, (4) the 1974 amendments (Title XX) to the Social Security Act of 1935,[18] and (5) the Housing and Community Development Act of 1974.[19]

The proponents of block grants claim that they are a cheaper and more efficient way to accomplish national purposes through state and local governments than categoricals grants are. Block-grant supporters assume that such grants lower administrative costs to both the granting agency and the recipients by eliminating the overlap and duplication of the narrowly defined categorical grants. This has happened with some block grants. For example, federal central and regional offices in the health, community development, and manpower programs needed fewer personnel after grant consolidation to handle the paperwork of the application and review processes.[20] But block grants usually give more responsibility to state and local managers. This greater administrative responsibility for planning, coordinating, monitoring, and evaluating at the state and local level often means that these governments must add employees, thus offsetting the savings accrued when decentralization leads to fewer federal employees.

Block grants attempt to decentralize decision-making in federal programs to the state and local levels. As a result, fewer strings are attached to such grants. The federal government role might be limited to developing certain guidelines for fiscal and personnel management, providing technical assistance, reviewing plans, and evaluating the recipients' performance. Some block grants call for a more intrusive federal role, however. Congressional efforts to keep controls on federal money, even though it is being spent by the cities and states, have led to additional review procedures and, in some cases, to "creeping categorization."

17. Carl W. Stenberg, "Block Grants: The Middlemen of the Federal Aid System," *Intergovernmental Perspective* 3, no. 2 (Spring 1977): 9.
18. Because of loose legislative language and flexible administration in Washington, Title XX programs were treated almost like block grants by some states before the title was amended in 1974. *See* Martha Derthick, *Uncontrollable Spending for Social Service Grants* (Washington, D.C.: The Brookings Institution, 1975).
19. Stenberg, "Block Grants," p. 9.
20. Ibid., p. 10.

Creeping categorization is the tendency for Congress to divide some activities that had formerly come under a block grant into separate categorical grant programs. This was especially true of programs under the Safe Streets Act. Congress split up the block grants by ear-marking funds for corrections, juvenile justice, and neighborhood crime prevention.

Another feature of block grants that concerns us is that such grants are supposed to encourage generalist administrative control at recipient levels. The categorical grants are the raw materials of the picket-fence model. Professionals in highways, welfare, elementary and secondary education, mental health, and the other specialized fields serviced by categorical grants tend to have decision-making power in such grants. Professional educators at the federal level decide on programs with professional educators at the state and local levels, for example. There is little control in this process by elected or appointed "generalist" officials such as governors, mayors, or city managers. But block grants, in part because they are funded according to formulas and in part because they have a broader scope than categoricals, shift some decision-making power away from the professionals. Enhancing the power of the generalists at the expense of the specialists may affect the symbiotic relationships of federal agency professionals and state and local counterparts. With broader scope within grant programs, local and state general administrators may be able to channel federal funds more effectively to meet their needs.

General Revenue Sharing

Even when compared to block grants, general revenue sharing has a much broader scope and gives generalist administrators at the state and local levels almost unlimited discretion. No wonder a strong coalition of state and local officials enthusiastically supported general revenue sharing even before the federal money began to flow in 1972. Although revenue sharing has strong support among the recipients of the funds, Congress has been reluctant to expand the program and has flirted with killing it.

One of the main issues in the congressional controversy is a fiscal one. In a time when talk of balanced budgets has become fashionable, some people have questioned why the federal government, which has been operating with consistently high deficits, should continue to give money away to the states and local governments with virtually no strings attached. Some of these recipients are substantially better off fiscally than the donor government is.

The fiscal argument, however, quickly translates into a philosophical debate concerning accountability and national priorities. National grant programs that have developed since the Northwest Ordinance have always had some national purpose behind them. It is difficult to define the national purpose of letting state and local governments decide how federal tax dollars will be used.

The first general revenue sharing act spelled out some priority areas for expenditure. Among them were expenditures for social services for the aged and poor. Studies of planned and actual expenditures of revenue sharing funds indicated that relatively few funds—2 to 4 percent—were spent in these areas.[21] Since most revenue-sharing funds went for expenditures for health, recreation and education, the argument could be made that these expenditures did help the disadvantaged, although not as directly as specifically targeted expenditures for social services would. Still, the less directly the expenditures of money is to congressional intent, the less control Congress has. The less control Congress has, the less accountable are the state and local officials who are supposed to carry out national priorities.

When budget cutting fever hits Washington, general revenue sharing is particularly vulnerable. Most federal programs have specific aims. These programs, as we have seen, develop their own highly interested clientele. Under normal conditions, many decisions regarding these programs are made at a low level of conflict by the participants of the relevant policy subsystem. It is easier to mobilize political support among the beneficiaries of programs with specific goals. It is harder to mobilize such support for programs with more generalized goals, such as general revenue sharing. As Senator William Proxmire has said: "It is hard to find a place more logical to consider reduction than revenue sharing . . . for many reasons. . . . This is money that does not require accountability. . . . In the revenue sharing area, nobody can say that [these funds] go to the needy. Nobody can say they go to a specific useful purpose, because nobody knows where they go."[22]

Congressional opposition to revenue sharing, while not strong enough to end the program, has been strong enough to keep the program from keeping pace with inflation. Although the number of revenue sharing dollars remained constant, inflation has eroded more than 40 percent of

---

21. Richard P. Nathan and Charles F. Adams, *Revenue Sharing: The Second Round* (Washington, D.C.: The Brookings Institution, 1977), pp. 70–75.
22. Quoted in Will Myers and John Shannon, "Revenue Sharing for States: An Endangered Species," *Intergovernmental Perspective* 5, no. 3 (Summer 1979): 12.

the purchasing power of these funds in recent years.[23] Federal grant revenues as a percentage of state and local expenditures peaked in 1978 because the impact of revenue sharing funds has become less while tax reforms at the state level have enhanced the role of the states in financing intergovernmental programs.[24]

The Golden Rule

ONE cannot dogmatically say that any broad type of grant is better than some other. One has to ask the question, "Which grant is better for whom?" This question gets to the heart of the theory of federalism because it really asks what the powers of the national versus state governments should be. It is natural that state and local general officials would favor grants that give them the most discretion in spending federal funds. But intergovernmental fiscal flows are based on the Golden Rule: "He who supplies the gold makes the rule." National policies, paid for with money raised through the more efficient national tax system, are subject to controls by Congress.

It is natural to expect that the federal government will seek to control the substantive aspects of policies in any particular field where Congress has established a grants program. One would expect to find federal rules and regulations regarding standards for Meals on Wheels programs, recreation for the elderly, or education for the disadvantaged. Such standards are often the subject of negotiation among the professionals from the various levels of government. In addition to these substantive guidelines, grants routinely include provisions affecting such national concerns as environmental protection, citizen participation, prevailing wages, affirmative action, and merit system protection for workers hired under each grant, and many other regulations not directly related to the substance of the program. Even general revenue sharing money is subject to some of these regulations.

These crosscutting regulations are powerful tools for getting the states and localities to carry out national policies. Congress wants federal money to be used consistently with congressionally determined national purposes. It mandates grant recipients must be aware of the environmental impacts of their actions. They must not discriminate on racial or

---

23. Ibid., p. 10.
24. ACIR, *Significant Features,* pp. 1–4, and *Recent Trends,* pp. 1–8.

sexual bases. They must make their facilities available to the handicapped. Private contractors must pay prevailing wage rates if they work on grant-sponsored projects. Congress has mandated these and other general conditions, and if governmental units want federal money, they have to abide by the federal rules.[25]

The effect of these regulations is open to question. If a recipient government is found to have violated the affirmative action component of a grant, for example, all federal aid to that jurisdiction could be withheld. Although some federal bureaucrats might threaten to carry out the letter of the law and turn off the supply of federal money, political realities dictate that the aid will not be cut off entirely for scattered violations of these regulations. Although generalist leaders of the recipient governments would like to see most of these regulations dropped, they seem to have little trouble mobilizing political forces to keep the money flowing despite occasional violations of the crosscutting regulations.

If grant-giving agencies lack the political clout to cut off funds when some regulations are violated by recipient governments, consider the lack of power public managers must have enforcing regulations on other agencies that are not beholden to them for funds. Intergovernmental relations include relationships among governments at the same level as well as at other levels. Sometimes a unit of the national government is supposed to enforce a regulation on another unit of the national government. For example, the Environmental Protection Agency (EPA) is supposed to enforce environmental legislation on public utilities including another arm of the federal government, the Tennessee Valley Authority (TVA). It lacks the political muscle to do so. Similar cases arise at the state level. Interlocal relationships are constantly subject to negotiation rather than one unit of government being able to enforce its rulings on another. Because of political factors, it is difficult for government to regulate itself.[26]

25. There are limits to these rules, however. The Supreme Court has held that state and local governments do not come under the provisions of the Fair Employment Standards Act of 1938, as amended in 1974, when they are performing the traditional functions of government. See *National League of Cities* v. *Usery*, 426 U.S. 833 (1976). For a passionate cry against congressional mandates see Edward I. Koch, "The Mandate Millstone," *Public Interest* 61 (Fall 1980): 42–57.
26. For a discussion of the national government's attempts to regulate itself, see James Q. Wilson and Patricia Rachal, "Can the Government Regulate Itself?" *Public Interest* 46 (Winter 1977): 3–14.

**Rules and Control:
A Case of
Manipulation from
Below**

THE rules and regulations adopted by each grant-giving agency are designed to carry out the congressional mandate in a reasonably fair manner. Formula-based categorical and block grants channel money to recipients on the basis of demographic characteristics. Each recipient gets a predetermined share of the pot. In project grants, however, there is generally not enough money to go to all potential users of the funds, so individual communities, especially those in the same state, are often competing with one another for scarce project grant funds. Sometimes the rules adopted by the agency for control purposes—the criteria by which the grants are awarded—can be manipulated by grant applicants.

Through grant consolidation, Congress ended some elements of competition among larger urban areas for certain housing and development grants with the creation of the Housing and Community Development Act of 1974. This Act does not apply to the smaller urban areas, which still have to apply for specific, project categorical grants. These project grants are awarded on the basis of written applications only, because Housing and Urban Development (HUD) officials have concluded that it is not efficient to make site visits when relatively small amounts of money are concerned. The following case shows how a clever community can use knowledge of the rules to undercut the spirit of congressional intent.[27]

In the late 1970s, Whitehall Township, Pennsylvania, a fairly prosperous town with above average median income went out to get HUD grants for new water lines and housing rehabilitation designed for poorer communities. The town hired a consultant who, knowing that HUD officials would not visit the well-kept town, developed a strong statistical case that the grant would help a poor neighborhood in the town. If the consultant had relied on published census data, his case would not have been strong. Using the relatively large census tract information, the consultant would have shown that only 36 percent of the residents in the area were poor. Using unpublished block data, however,

---

27. This account is drawn from Wayne G. Green, "How a Town Won a Half-Million Pot from HUD Though Poorer Communities Held Strong Hands," *Wall Street Journal,* August 25, 1977, p. 32.

the consultant was able to show that the project would affect an area where 60.6 percent of the occupants of the area were in the lower income category. Whitehall scored well on the HUD criterion that the project should aid lower income people.

Another of HUD's criteria was for recipients to show a willingness to get related financing. The consultant suggested Whitehall get a grant from the Pennsylvania Department of Community Affairs. Knowing that a large grant from the state would take time, the consultant applied for and got a $2000 grant. This was enough to give the Whitehall application the maximum number of points on HUD's related financing criterion, in the agency's highly specific point evaluation system.

Even though the rules were designed to channel money into the poorer communities, wealthier and more clever communities have been able to play the grant game successfully and undermine the broad legislative goals. Cases like the Whitehall example indicate the strength of professionalism among the levels of government involved in one functional area. The Whitehall application was a professional job. The consultant who prepared it knew exactly what the professionals who would pass on the application wanted. The criteria had all been spelled out, and the application was professionally crafted to meet each of them. Perhaps the HUD application evaluators thought that any city or town that could turn in such a professional application would also be able to implement the project in a professional way. Professional implementation would mean fewer problems for HUD. Thus, professionalism can lead to well-designed, well-carried-out programs that do not really conform to the spirit of the legislation. In management, it is always easier to deal with the easiest cases first.

Sometimes grant-giving agencies run into problems not related to professionalism. For example, a few years ago a clerk in the U.S. Department of Transportation represented himself as a subway system and received several hundred thousand dollars earmarked for the Metropolitan Atlanta Rapid Transit Authority. The clerk substituted his name and address on mass transit grant forms that had been approved. These forms were submitted to the Treasury Department for payment. By the time he was arrested while getting off a plane in Las Vegas, the clerk had amassed a suburban house with a swimming pool, twelve luxury cars, a thirty-foot boat, several diamond rings, and a topless bar located near the Justice Department.[28]

---

28. "A Transit Aide Posed as a Subway System, Then Got Derailed," *Wall Street Journal*, November 21, 1977, p. 1.

Fiscal Federalism

THE movement of funds through governmental levels, especially from the national level to the states and local governments, raises some problems for federalism. According to Kenneth Howard, fiscal federalism should allow the state and local governments certain rights or they will become appendages of the national government. Among these are the right to decide how to raise revenues, the right to select the purposes for which the revenues are to be raised, and the right to determine the amount to be raised. Furthermore, Howard notes, governments should have the machinery to administer these decisions.[29]

The rise of federal aid expenditures and the acute financial stress of some jurisdictions have given the illusion that some local governments are wards of the federal government. Some older cities such as Cleveland, Newark, Buffalo, Detroit, and New York depend on the federal government for more than 60 percent of their budgets. The New York City example shows that those governmental levels that supply a good portion of the funds can take some power to make decisions away from elected officials. Since New York's flirtation with bankruptcy in the mid-1970s, some aspects of city administration have been reviewed by the banker-dominated Municipal Assistance Corporation (MAC) and the state appointed Fiscal Control Board. The city's financial problems were precipitated by uncontrollable short-term debts because the city apparently tried to do more than it was capable of financing through standard channels.[30]

One of the channels that local governments use to finance their activities is federal grants. The availability of such grants is sometimes blamed for encouraging recipient governments to get involved in policy areas just to get the federal dollars. As the federal funds are phased out, the recipient governments find they must cut services or make up the difference in money from other sources. Sometimes they do neither.

Whether the availability of federal grants leads unwilling governments down the primrose path is debatable. Federal grants—even highly specific categorical grants—often are an attractive way of financing general government. Many grants call for the recipient government to put up matching funds. The matching formulas are established by

29. S. Kenneth Howard, *Changing State Budgeting* (Lexington, Ky.: Council of State Governments, 1973), p. 81.
30. For an account of the New York City fiscal crisis that emphasizes the role of poor management, see Ken Auletta, *The Streets Were Paved with Gold* (New York: Random House, 1979).

Congress and differ according to the particular program although all matching grants work in the same way. Say a grant program has a 90 percent to 10 percent matching requirement. This means the state or local government must show the federal government its willingness to provide 10 percent of the total cost of the project. Then the federal government will put up the other 90 percent, assuming the project has been approved.

When a grant with a matching formula is approved, federal money then flows directly into the recipient government's general fund. Once in the general fund, the lines between money earmarked for the specific project that qualified for the federal funds and that for other projects of general worth to the community sometimes becomes indistinguishable. Although the accounting system may be able to keep track of the grant funds, in effect they become available to the recipient for other purposes as soon as they enter the recipient's general fund. If a jurisdiction is successful in getting money from several different grant programs and governmental sources, it can keep a little bit ahead of the financial game in much the same way that an individual can "kite" checks without having them bounce. A student may mail the rent payment even though his or her bank balance is less than the payment, hoping that money from home arrives in time to cover the rent check before it clears the bank. Financial managers who deal with grant funds have discovered a property of these funds that enables them to be used more flexibly than a precise legal treatment would allow. They call this property "fungibility."

In addition to mingling grant funds, recipients can achieve fungibility in matching grants in different ways, depending upon what type of match is required by the grant program. Hard match grants, in which the receiving jurisdiction must produce cash, are difficult to manipulate. For example, if the estimate for a building at an airport is $10 million and the federal government will put up 75 percent, the state and local governments wanting the airport building must come up with the remaining 25 percent—in this case, $2.5 million in cash. A soft match, however, allows much greater flexibility. The grant program might call for a 75/25 federal to local split in a program to create a county planning unit, for example. In a soft match, the county's contribution will be not in cash but in services valued at 25 percent of the total project cost. Creative accounting practices can value overhead—office space, desks, personnel services, and so on—in such a way that the recipient government does not have to increase its expenditure to meet the requirements of a soft match. Funds from a soft match are almost free to the recipient.

Conflict and
Coordination

ALTHOUGH it appears that state and local governments have become vassals of Washington, there is considerable opportunity for administrators at the state and local level to take the federal money and channel it toward projects that serve local priorities, too. The intergovernmental system, which relies on one government to carry out the wishes of another government that is paying the bill, has tension built into it. This tension is exacerbated by the competition for grants among neighboring communities. It is further increased when one deals with the conflicting professional values that are built into grant programs, especially categorical grants. For example, transportation improvement programs sometimes underplay the importance of housing patterns in the new system. Housing grants might not consider the educational components of the plan with the same degree of interest as the architectural plans. In short, the conflicts of the federal system and professionalism are played out in the grants system.

Since the late 1960s, the federal government has tried to coordinate grants and grant-giving agencies. It has tried to develop coordinating councils such as the Federal Regional Councils (FRCs) in each of the ten designated regions for domestic agencies. The FRCs and an assortment of federally sponsored joint committees, common planning frameworks, interagency agreements, and various negotiated arrangements were supposed to limit interagency friction. Most of these attempts by the federal government to coordinate federal agencies have not worked. Catherine Lovell suggests some reasons for the failure:

> First, granting agencies have few incentives to coordinate; and second, they failed to recognize that the ultimate purpose of coordination is to harmonize and link programs and projects at the point of impact in the local communities where programs have to be carried out.[31]

Although Lovell found the federal efforts at coordination were not successful, she found significant coordination at the local level. This coordination was achieved by three mechanisms: (1) "orchestration from above," (2) "self-linking among functional professionals," and (3) "meshing the grants from below." Orchestration from above sometimes involved explicit planning coordinated through the chief executives of

---

31. Catherine H. Lovell, "Coordinating Federal Grants from Below," *Public Administration Review* 39, no. 5 (September–October 1979): 432.

"It's either 'Gordian Knot' or 'Government Regulations.'"

the localities, but more often the executives tried to link grants on a project-by-project basis by mixing funds from a variety of sources to achieve their goals. The key to this kind of coordination is the locality's top executive, who "has to want to put things together and has to have the imagination, drive, and ingenuity to do it."[32] In this kind of grant coordination, the fungibility of grant funds is essential.

Lovell found that grants were also coordinated at the local level by functional professionals. At this level, professional values were tempered by community-oriented values. Professionals at the local level tend to work together to ferret out funding sources, which then became the raw material for coordination efforts.

Lovell was especially interested in how community-based organizations like settlement houses tapped into the grant system. She found ex-

32. Ibid., pp. 433–435.

ecutives of neighborhood institutions coordinated grants from a variety of sources in much the same fashion as the local government executives had. Again, the key for successful grant coordination was the fungibility of grant funds. Lovell pointed out that block grants help local and community executives because they provide much more flexibility than the more narrow categorical grants do. The rhetoric of the Reagan Administration supports this position, but other federal interests are still concerned with maintaining federal controls to serve national purposes.

Although local leaders want grant coordination so they can deal with local problems better, the federal government wants better grant coordination so it can control the use of federal funds better. To this end, the Office of Management and Budget, the strongest managerial arm of the Executive Office of the President, has sought to encourage improved accounting practices to limit the fungibility of grants. This effort to ensure that grant money approved for certain projects is spent on those projects runs counter to the recipients' need for flexibility to coordinate grants at the service delivery level.[33]

The Office of Management and Budget has also encouraged grant coordination among various local governments through the A-95 review process. The A-95 process gets its name from the OMB Circular A-95, which describes a procedure for review of all major grants coming into defined areas. The A-95 review procedure established a grants clearinghouse for each standard metropolitan statistical area (SMSA). Grant applications from the jurisdictions in that area are sent to the clearinghouse, which then makes the applications available for comment to other governments in the area. Through the A-95 process, other affected governments are able to delay, discuss, and sometimes even change grant applications to effect some metropolitan coordination of grants (see Figure 3.4).

Summary

INTERGOVERNMENTAL relations are an essential part of the environment of public agencies dealing in domestic policy. Some agencies seek to accomplish their goals by giving money to other agencies at other levels of government. These other agencies have policy priorities that they would

---

33. See the following Office of Management and Budget circulars: Circular A-102, *Uniform Administrative Requirements for Grants in Aid to State and Local Governments,* and Circular A-73, *Audit of Federal Operations and Programs.*

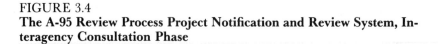

FIGURE 3.4
The A-95 Review Process Project Notification and Review System, Interagency Consultation Phase

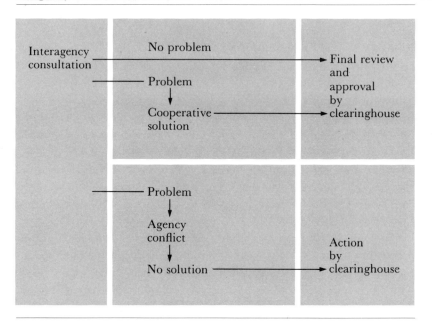

like to pursue, but often they lack the resources. If the priorities of the donor agency match the priorities of the recipient agency, the goals of the donor will be accomplished to the limit of the recipient agency's ability to do so. Often, however, the priorities of both agencies do not quite fit. In such cases, the agency that is supposed to deliver the services that are paid for by another agency may try to channel some of the grant money into projects that are more in tune with its priorities. This can result in the donor agency's not achieving its purpose.

The fiscal and service delivery interdependence among governmental levels reflects conflicts built into the federal system. The perennial debate between advocates of centralization of decision making at the national level and advocates of decentralization of decision making to the state or local levels will continue. The existing grant system provides for an uneasy combination of central control and local flexibility. Generally, categorical grants provide for more central control, while block grants give more flexibility to the recipient governments. In larger jurisdictions especially, many categorical grants have enabled executives to use "multipocket budgeting" to shave a little from several funding sources to enable the recipient government to coordinate grants to deal with local priorities.[34]

There is a political bridge between centralization and decentralization. In the case of federal grants, members of Congress in general want to hold agencies accountable for their expenditures. This is true of agencies that rely on agencies at other levels to deliver services. Members of Congress also want their constituents to benefit from intergovernmental grant programs. When their constituents are seeking grant money, the issue before members of Congress is specific, not general: to help their constituents get the grants. Individual members of Congress work with state and local executives to keep grant funds flowing even if minor violations in the execution of the grant do occur.

The intergovernmental grant system encourages a form of clientele politics. Around each grant-giving agency a policy subsystem develops. Part of this subsystem consists of the professionals within the agency itself. Other parts are the professionals working in counterpart agencies in the recipient governments. Supporting the professionals at the recipient levels are political executives and an assortment of elected officials whose political survival may depend on their ability to mobilize support for grant funds. Additional components of this policy subsystem are the representatives and senators on the relevant committees and subcommittees. Although these actors might want more control and accountability through grants, they are often under pressure from state and local politicians as well as their colleagues to permit flexibility, which can make the grant system work more smoothly.

The political realities of the grant system make compromise necessary. Federal grants must be used to accomplish elements of national purposes, yet they must be flexible enough to fit local needs. Management efforts to wipe out fungibility may hinder local flexibility, thus impeding the local governments' ability to carry out the aim of the grant.

Managing in the atmosphere of clientele politics, which permeates all of public administration, is one factor with which a manager must deal. Another factor relates to organizing, leading, and motivating the people who work in public agencies. The next two chapters will deal with organization theory and its application to governmental organizations.

---

34. "Multipocket budgeting" is a term used by David O. Porter, David Warren, and Teddie Porter, *The Politics of Budgeting Federal Aid: Resource Mobilization by Local School Districts* (Beverly Hills, Calif.: Sage, 1973).

Suggestions for
Further Reading

Break, George F. *Financing Government in a Federal System.* Washington, D.C.: The Brookings Institution, 1980.

Categorical Grants: Their Role and Design. Publication A-52. Washington: Advisory Commission on Intergovernmental Relations, 1978.

Derthick, Martha. *Uncontrollable Spending for Social Service Grants.* Washington, D.C.: The Brookings Institution, 1975.

Haider, Donald. *When Government Comes to Washington: Governors, Mayors and Intergovernmental Lobbying.* New York: Free Press, 1974.

Levine, Charles H. *Managing Fiscal Stress.* Chatham, N.J.: Chatham House, 1980.

Nathan, Richard P., and Mary M. Nathan. *America's Government: A Fact Book of Census Data on the Organizations, Finances, and Employment of Federal, State and Local Governments.* New York: John Wiley, 1979.

Reagan, Michael. *The New Federalism.* New York: Oxford University Press, 1972.

Van Horn, Carl E. *Policy Implementation in the Federal System: National Goals and Local Implementors.* Lexington, Mass.: Lexington Books, 1979.

Wright, Deil S. *Understanding Intergovernmental Relations.* North Scituate, Mass.: Duxbury, Deil 1978.

CHAPTER FOUR

Organization Theories
of Public Bureaucracies

MOST STUDENTS OF GOVERNMENT are interested in the policy decisions of the particular governmental system that they are studying. Given the important role of public bureaucracies in government's public policy-making process, it becomes critical to understand what influences the people who staff these organizations. If people in the organization behave in ways that are bizarre or engage in activities that are in contrast to the values of the general society, observers can reasonably expect the decisions of that organization to be perverse.

There are two main influences on public bureaucrats. One is the impact of large-scale organization on the participants in public agencies, and the other is the overriding political nature of public bureaucracy. Although no firm evidence can be cited to establish with mathematical precision the degree to which each of these variables influences individual bureaucrats and the policies to which they contribute, this author's experience suggests that most of what goes on in American public administration—especially in the larger jurisdictions—can be explained through management and organization theories. The rest of this chapter will deal with several such theories.

The Importance of Theory

OF all the subfields of political science, public administration surely is the most pragmatic. Yet even in so obviously practical a field, knowledge of possible theoretical bases of behavior is helpful to interpret events and activities within public organizations. As the psychologist Mason Haire has suggested, "all managerial policies have a theory behind them," although that theory is generally implicit.[1] Public administrators generally deal with problems—especially organizational problems—in a practical, straightforward manner, without realizing the theories that are implicit in what they do. Often, because they lack awareness of a range of theories, their apparently practical solutions may have overlooked alternative courses that might have proven far superior. If administrators fail to recognize the theoretical bases for their own actions and the actions of others, they may fail to be effective managers.

By dealing with various organization theories here, we hope to open

---

1. Mason Haire, *Psychology in Management* (New York: McGraw-Hill, 1964), p. 19.
PHOTO: Shirley Hufstedler, the nation's first Secretary of Education

our minds to different organizational perspectives. Exposure to several perspectives might enable us to see how people might operate under different conditions. Rather than propose *the* theory of public bureaucratic organization, we will deal with a range of theories. For analytical purposes, we will designate three groups of organization theories: (1) classical, (2) neoclassical, and (3) organizational humanist. As will be shown, each of these organization theories corresponds in a rough way to various political theories. Classical organization theory shares a common intellectual tradition with the more autocratic political theories, such as those espoused by Thomas Hobbes. Neoclassical organization theories bear a rough similarity to liberal political thought and may be traced back to John Locke. Organizational humanist theories have some common features with the theories of Jean-Jacques Rousseau and John Dewey. As will be seen, the basic connection between these organization and political theories involves common assumptions about human nature.[2]

Bureaucracy Defined

ANY discussion of organization theories that influence public bureaucratic behavior must deal with the concept of bureaucracy itself. The term *bureaucracy* carries a negative connotation. Few people have warm feelings when they think of bureaucracy. Generally, people equate bureaucracy—both public and private—with delay, red tape, pettiness, and silly rules that seem only to create barriers that prevent the working of common sense. Victor Thompson saw much of the objectionable bureaucratic activity rooted in what he called "bureaupathetic" behavior. Among the kinds of behavior he saw in large-scale organizations are "excessive aloofness, ritualistic attachment to routines and procedures, and resistance to change; and associated with these behavior patterns is a petty insistence upon rights of authority and status." These features, Thompson noted, are personal behavior patterns. They have little to do with the real work of the organization. They are not necessary to the form of the organization and, indeed, inhibit goal accomplishment.

2. These categories are suggested in part by William G. Scott, "Organization Government: The Prospects for a Truly Participative System," *Public Administration Review* 29, no. 1 (January–February 1969): 43–53. William G. Scott and David K. Hart, "Administrative Crisis: The Neglect of Metaphysical Speculation," *Public Administration Review* 33, no. 5 (September–October 1973): 415–22, suggest the underlying similarities of organization and political theories.

Therefore these behavior patterns are pathological.[3] Informal criticisms of bureaucracy are generally aimed not at the bureaucratic form of social organization but rather at the pathological, often bizarre behavior that occurs in such organizations.

Martin Albrow has traced the term *bureaucracy* back to 1745, when Vincent de Gournay, a French Physiocrat, used it to describe the Prussian government. In the eighteenth and early nineteenth centuries, the term was used to describe the type of government in which power resided with officials. It was used as an addition to Aristotle's typology of governments.[4] Aristotle noted three true forms of government—kingly rule, aristocracy, and constitutional government—and three perversions of the true forms—tyranny, oligarchy, and democracy. *Bureaucracy* was used to represent a fourth type of perversion of government.

Today's formal usage of the term refers less to a neo-Aristotelian typology than to the description of an "ideal type" of social organization developed by the brilliant German sociologist Max Weber. An ideal type is an intellectual construct that attempts to conceptualize or describe a pure or idealized form of a particular phenomenon—for example, bureaucracy. In the real world, one would not find all the elements of the ideal description present in any particular bureaucratic structure. An ideal type corresponds to a pole at one end of a continuum; reality lies along the continuum, but not at the pole position. Whereas ideal types are not subject to proof or disproof by empirical verification, they do provide standards against which specific cases can be compared. The pure bureaucratic organization as described by Weber does not occur in the real world, but it is a set of characteristics that Weber thought contributed to a hypothetically rational and effective organization.

To better understand his view of bureaucracy, one must see some of Weber's larger concerns. Generally, Weber was concerned with the organization of society as a whole and the role of the state in particular. Weber wanted to understand the relationships between power—the ability to make people do what they do not ordinarily do—and authority—legitimate power. Weber developed three ideal types that described authority relationships in society: traditional, charismatic, and legal-rational.[5]

3. Victor A. Thompson, *Modern Organization* (New York: Knopf, 1961), pp. 152–53.
4. Martin Albrow, *Bureaucracy* (New York: Praeger, 1970), p. 3.
5. There are several translations of Weber's most important works. *See* Max Weber, *The Theory of Social and Economic Organization,* trans. Talcott Parsons (New York: Free Press, 1947), pp. 341–342, 358–363. The principal source used here is H. H. Gerth and C. Wright Mills, eds. and trans. *From Max Weber: Essays in Sociology* (New York: Oxford University Press/Galaxy Books, 1958), pp. 196–244.

Traditional authority claims legitimacy on the basis of control patterns that have been handed down from the past and that presumably have always existed. Persons exercising authority in such a system do so according to traditionally transmitted rules. In the ideal traditional authority system postulated by Weber, change is inhibited by precedent. Those exercising authority are afraid to stretch the traditional ways of doing things because the ensuing change might undercut their own sources of legitimacy. One of the attributes of traditional authority, however, is that there is an area of control open to the whims of the persons who occupy places of authority in the system. Capricious behavior by the leaders in traditional societies is to be expected, and this makes ˙ for intensely personal relations between the rulers and the ruled. Reliance on the whims of the rulers in personal dealings within the context of rules that are beyond the power of people to change inhibits traditional authority from dealing with change systematically.

Charismatic authority is intensely personal, too, but the sources of that authority are quite different from those of traditional authority. The charismatic individual has authority by virtue of innate personal qualities through which he or she is able to inspire devotion in his or her followers. The position a charismatic leader occupies in society is not sanctified by traditional criteria. The charismatic person is not bound by traditional rules and is capable of sparking revolutionary changes. Charismatic authority does not accept any system of rules for organizing society. There is no law, no hierarchy, no formalism except the basic demand of devotion to the charismatic figure. His or her followers are duty-bound to follow the leader's commands, which are supposed to lead to accomplishment of his or her mission. The followers obey because of personal devotion, not because rules force them to comply. The leader intervenes whenever and wherever he or she feels like it, unbound by tradition or law. This makes charismatic authority opposed to routines. In recent years the term *charisma* has been overused to such an extent that any politician who looks good on television seems to claim charisma. Weber's complex view of a charismatic leader involves far more than projecting a pleasing media image.

Weber claimed that the traditional and charismatic types of authority were responsible for just about all organized action before the industrial revolution. The early modern period demanded the establishment of social organization on a stable basis, but one that was still open to change. The legal-rational system of authority, to Weber, was such a system. The legal-rational system was based on rules—rules rationally developed by people. Such rules could be intentionally changed to cope with changes

FIGURE 4.1
Key Features of Weber's Ideal-Type Bureaucracy

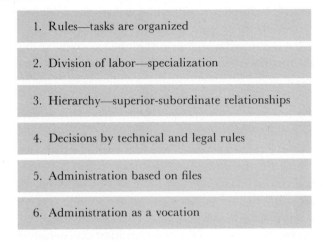

1. Rules—tasks are organized

2. Division of labor—specialization

3. Hierarchy—superior-subordinate relationships

4. Decisions by technical and legal rules

5. Administration based on files

6. Administration as a vocation

Source: H. H. Gerth and C. Wright Mills, eds. and trans., *From Max Weber: Essays in Sociology* (New York: Oxford University Press/Galaxy Books, 1958), pp. 196–204.

in the environment in a systematic, more highly predictable way than could be accounted for by either traditional or charismatic authority. The quintessence of legal-rational authority was the ideal-type bureaucracy. The heart of bureaucracy, to Weber, was the system of authority relations defined by rationally developed rules—rules that could be changed to cope with changes in the organization's environment. See Figure 4.1 for some of the key features of Weber's ideal-type bureaucracy.

Classical Organization Theory

To Max Weber, bureaucracy was superior to other forms of organization because it could coordinate the activities of the more productive functional specialists in society. In the ideal-type bureaucracy, the mission or goal of the organization could rationally be broken down into specific tasks, that would lead to the accomplishment of the goal. The arrangement of work would constitute rules so that the organization could operate on a continuous basis. The members of the organization would know what tasks they were responsible for doing. Once the various tasks that related to the organization goal were identified, functional specialists would be hired to handle these tasks with a high degree of efficiency. The various functional specialists in an organization would be coordinated and directed by bosses within the hierarchy, thus producing the familiar superior-subordinate relationships within the organization and incorporated in the rules of the organization. This view of authority from above defines classical organization theories.

A major advantage that bureaucracy had over other forms of organization, according to Weber, was that decisions would be made on a more equitable, impersonal basis. Decisions would be based on technical and legal rules. Furthermore, these would be based on what had been done in similar situations in the past. The written files were to be the organization's memory, and reliance on the files would, in the ideal type, assure fair administration. Knowledge of the technical and legal rules and the files by the members of the organization who performed specific tasks implied the need for selection of personnel based on merit and the need for training. To assure impersonal treatment, the ideal type of bureaucracy called for full-time activity, and the administrator could not appropriate his or her office; there should be a separation of the person's personal life from his or her work life.

According to Weber, the organization that closely adhered to these key features of his ideal-type bureaucracy would have several benefits over organizations organized along collegial or honorific lines. The bureaucracy would fulfill its goals with "precision, speed, unambiguity, knowledge of the files, continuity, discretion, unity, strict subordination, reduction of friction and of material and personal costs."[6] Weber saw bureaucracy, especially in its monocratic form—with a single head at the apex of the organizational pyramid—as a smoothly running machine that could handle the organizational business "according to calculable rules and 'without regard for persons.' "[7]

Weber seemed to believe in the historical inevitability of the increasing dominance of legal-rational organizations, including bureaucracies, because they were so superior to other forms of organization. He was convinced of bureaucracy's inherent superiority to handle change with stability, based on his own studies in which he strove for a value-free social science. He was, however, a liberal humanist who was concerned

---

6. Gerth and Mills, *From Max Weber,* p. 214.
7. Ibid., p. 215.

that the inevitable growth of bureaucratic administration which he saw would eventually dehumanize the people in the bureaucracy itself. In 1909 he argued:

> ... It is horrible to think that the world could one day be filled with nothing but those little cogs, little men clinging to little jobs and striving toward bigger ones.... This passion for bureaucracy ... is enough to drive one to despair.... That the world should know no men but these: it is in such an evolution that we are already caught up, and the great question is therefore not how we can promote and hasten it, but what can we oppose to this machinery in order to keep a portion of mankind free from this parcelling-out of the soul, from the supreme mastery of the bureaucratic way of life.[8]

Although Weber was aware of the effect of bureaucratization of life on people, he was apparently unaware of, or seriously underplayed, several problems implied by his ideal-type formulation. Weber's ideal-type bureaucracy assumed that superiors in the hierarchy would have the competence as well as the right to give orders to their subordinates. In a highly specialized modern organization, however, competence of the superior cannot be assured. Must the boss be the best budget analyst? Or even a competent one? Furthermore, Weber assumed that the members of the organization would abide by its rationally developed rules. He assumed that people would take orders and carry them out. But in the real world, the rules of an organization or even of society do not have the same meaning to a range of individuals unless they share substantially the same political and social values. These values can change over time and vary from generation to generation.

Obviously, bureaucracies in practice are not paragons of pure efficiency. Weber's belief that rules could be complete guides to action could not be substantiated in practice, especially in periods of rapid change. Rules are generally incomplete in that there rarely is a rule to cover all possible occurrences in a complex social relationship. If there is no rule, the case must be dealt with at higher levels in the hierarchy. Going up through the hierarchy to develop new rules is time-consuming. It produces red tape, but as Herbert Kaufman has pointed out, "One person's 'red tape' may be another's treasured safeguard."[9] Forcing an

---

8. Quoted in Reinhard Bendix, *Max Weber: An Intellectual Portrait* (Garden City, N.Y.: Doubleday/Anchor Books, 1960, 1962), p. 464. Bendix attributes the quote to J. P. Mayer, *Max Weber and German Politics* (London: Faber and Faber, 1943), pp. 127–128.
9. Herbert Kaufman, *Red Tape: Its Origins, Uses, and Abuses* (Washington, D.C.: The Brookings Institution, 1977), p. 4.

accountable official to make decisions can have some positive effects even though the delay of going up the hierarchy is seldom praised.

Weber failed to consider that the hierarchy itself might inhibit truth within the organization. Subordinates may tailor information to please their superiors. Few people wish to be the bearers of bad news, especially to people in a position to control their future progress in their chosen careers. In a hierarchy, one's superiors are in positions to do just that. The hierarchy does not coordinate the subordinate functional specialists merely by rationally convincing them of the best way to accomplish organizational goals. The hierarchy gives people in it the power to reward and punish subordinates. This often encourages false flattery and systematic distortions of the real situation—a distorted organizational view of reality that John Kenneth Galbraith called "bureaucratic truth."[10] A system that depends on the superiors to make decisions based on information given to them by subordinates cannot work well under such conditions.

Scientific Management   Weber certainly was not alone in viewing organizations as social systems in which power and authority flowed from the top downward through the hierarchy. Other administrative practitioners and observers with far fewer global concerns than Weber dealt with organization as such a system. One of the more colorful sidelights of classical administrative theory was the work of Frederick W. Taylor and the scientific management school. The scientific management school developed in the late nineteenth and early twentieth centuries and reflected the world view of the engineers, like Taylor, who sought to refine management techniques by studying how workers might become more complete extensions of machines.[11]

The goal of scientific management, or "Taylorism," was to maximize efficiency. Taylor's principal concern was to discover *the one best way* to get the most out of workers—generally low-level blue-collar workers. He maintained that management did not know how much work each worker could produce, so management could not know what the limits of the productive capacity of each worker were. Taylor advocated re-

---

10. John Kenneth Galbraith, *How to Control the Military* (New York: Signet Books, 1969), p. 17.
11. Frederick Winslow Taylor, *The Principles of Scientific Management* (New York: Harper and Brother, 1911, 1916).

"I don't enjoy *being an unreasonable tyrant, Gregg, but it* works."

search to uncover this capacity. Part of the research identified with the scientific management movement was time and motion study. By observing workers in action, researchers could identify and eliminate useless, wasted motions.

Research led to scientific management's advocacy of standardization of tools for specific tasks. Certain shovels are better for handling certain kinds of material more efficiently. Management should know that such differences exist, then see to it that workers use the right equipment for particular tasks. Standardization is useful in the office, too. If typewriter keyboards were not standardized, typists would have a difficult time maintaining top speed. Research also led to the demand for selection and training of workers. Management would have to pick the person who had the temperament and aptitude to do the required work, then train that person in the manner that observation and analysis indicated was the scientifically proven best way of accomplishing the work.

To keep people doing work according to scientifically established rules, Taylor advocated close supervision of workers by several different functional foremen. Of course, the scientific management people did not expect workers to embrace these new schemes unless there was some payoff in it for them. The incentive to workers to cooperate in a scientific management system was increased pay. Increased pay and the threat of dismissal were the carrot and the stick that allowed scientific management to get results.

Taylor was quite explicit in his view of workers. Workers should be extensions of machines, and scientific management, by providing training and manipulating pay scales, could make individual workers produce more. Taylor emphasized dealing with the individual worker, because he recognized that workers in groups exerted social pressure on individuals to conform to unscientific, more comfortable production norms. Taylor sought to keep such groups from developing by making it in the worker's economic interest to cooperate with the scientific management techniques regardless of social needs or needs to control one's work environment.

The fruits of scientific management are seen today in such activities as cost accounting, industrial engineering, industrial psychology, and the range of activities involved in personnel administration. Barely a year goes by when some observer of the organizational scene fails to produce an article relating some new management technique to Taylor or the scientific management movement. The descendants of the scientific management school are still a force contributing to the behavior of some people in some organizations.

Luther Gulick, the Pragmatic Classical Theorist

Some of the elements of Taylorism still live, but a more significant influence on American public administration today has been the work of Luther Gulick. Gulick sought to explain administrative structures by filling in some of the specifics that were implied in the Weberian ideal-type bureaucracy. From his position as a member of the President's Committee on Governmental Reorganization—called the Brownlow Committee after its chairman, Louis Brownlow—in 1937, Gulick tried to turn "principles" of administrative theory into administrative practice. Despite academic criticism, to a remarkable extent he succeeded. Every major federal governmental reorganization since 1939 has been based to a large degree on ideas that were pulled together in

Gulick's "Notes on the Theory of Organization," which was the lead article in a volume he edited for the Brownlow Committee.[12]

Whereas Weber represented one branch of the classical tradition that dealt with bureaucracy at a cosmic level and Taylor represented a particularistic focus within the classical framework, Gulick's views were midway between the two. His principal concerns were how organizations might be structured and what the roles were of the executives within them. He was not concerned with how the increasing bureaucratization of life affected individuals, nor was he worried about the techniques of specifically dealing with the lower-level cogs in the administrative machine. He was more concerned about the managerial activities that were common to all organizations.

Practically all American public administrators who have had contact with academic public administration through government-sponsored training programs or university study have heard of the acronym POSDCORB, which Gulick used to describe the activities of executives. POSDCORB stands for *p*lanning, *o*rganizing, *s*taffing, *d*irecting, *coo*rdinating, *r*eporting, and *b*udgeting. Gulick explained these functions as follows:

1. Planning, *that is working out in broad outline the things that need to be done and the methods for doing them to accomplish the purpose set for the enterprise*
2. Organizing, *that is the establishment of the formal structure of authority through which work subdivisions are arranged, defined, and coordinated for the defined objective*
3. Staffing, *that is the whole personnel function of bringing in and training the staff and maintaining favorable conditions of work*
4. Directing, *that is the continuous task of making decisions and embodying them in specific and general orders and instructions and serving as the leader of the enterprise*
5. Coordinating, *that is the all-important duty of interrelating the various parts of the work*
6. Reporting, *that is keeping those to whom the executive is responsible informed as to what is going on, which thus includes keeping himself and his subordinates informed through records, research, and inspection*
7. Budgeting, *with all that goes with budgeting in the form of fiscal planning, accounting, and control.*[13]

---

12. Luther H. Gulick, "Notes on the Theory of Organization," in Luther H. Gulick and Lyndell Urwick, eds., *Papers on the Science of Administration* (New York: Institute of Public Administration, 1937), pp. 3–44, reprinted in Fred A. Kramer, ed., *Perspectives on Public Bureaucracy,* 3rd ed. (Cambridge, Mass.: Winthrop, 1981).
13. Ibid., pp. 30–31.

Gulick, who slightly expanded similar categories that had been developed in France by Henri Fayol,[14] thought these seven elements could form the basis of organization for *staff* activities to the executive. Generally, the concept of "staff" refers to supportive activities done by organizational units that are not directly involved in the production of the product or service for which the agency is organized. Staff is usually contrasted with the *line,* those units that are directly engaged in producing the organization's goods or services.

Clearly, not all staff or executive functions are included under the POSDCORB umbrella. Data processing could be considered a staff activity in a governmental organization. Certainly leadership is a key executive role. Criticism of POSDCORB has revolved around this lack of inclusiveness,[15] but the acronym has proven to be a useful summary statement of what executives must do to maintain even a minimal degree of organizational effectiveness. Even into the 1970s, some observers sought to update POSDCORB by pointing to new areas of executive interest. One distinguished academic ended his guest editorial in *Public Administration Review,* the leading journal in the field, with the plea: "Let's give evaluation its due—let's put an E in POSDCORB."[16]

Just as POSDCORB gave easy-to-understand advice to novice administrators, Gulick's presentation of four ways of organizing work has provided useful rules of thumb that many administrators have been able to put into practice. Gulick suggested that each position in an organization could be characterized by the *purpose* served, the *process* used, the *persons or things* dealt with, and the *place* in which the work was done. If people are doing the same work in the same way for the same people at the same place, there would be little difficulty in designing an organizational unit for supervision and control purposes. The unit could be organized on the basis of any of the four categories and the result would be exactly the same from the point of view of the hierarchy. If, however, there is *not* a perfect correlation between the type of work being done, the way that work is being done, the people or things that are benefited by that work, and the place in which the work is being done, then the choice of an organizational unit would not be so simple. The hierarchy would look quite different, depending upon which basis of organization was given precedence in determining how the organizational unit

14. Henri Fayol, "The Administrative Theory of the State," in Gulick and Urwick, *Papers,* pp. 99–114.
15. *See* Herbert Simon, *Administrative Behavior,* 3rd ed. (New York: Macmillan, 1976).
16. Orville F. Poland, "Why Does Public Administration Ignore Evaluation," *Public Administration Review* 31, no. 2 (March–April 1971): 202.

should be established. Figure 4.2 shows alternative ways of organizing a campus police force, for instance.

Gulick tried to guide the executive in deciding upon which basis the organization should be structured at the top levels. Gulick tried to spell out which values would be enhanced and which would be sacrificed by primarily organizing administration along one dimension or another. For example, if one organized by purpose, Gulick saw several advantages accruing: (1) a single-purpose agency would be more certain of attaining its objectives because a whole job would be under a single director; (2) the purpose would be easily understood and recognized by the public; and (3) the central purpose would be useful in motivating the personnel. But these alleged advantages would have to be balanced against several alleged defects of organization by purpose. Among the problems were these: (1) the impossibility of cleanly dividing government work into clear purposes that do not overlap extensively; (2) the strong internal cohesion under the single director, which might lead to serious external conflict and confusion; and (3) several other problems, such as possible failure to make use of modern technology, the danger of overcentralization, and the corresponding lack of democratic control.

Although Gulick's thought has apparently been useful to practitioners—for years he headed the Public Administration Institute, a consulting firm—his work has been savagely attacked by some academics. The sharpest criticism has come from Herbert Simon, who derided the principles as mere proverbs.[17] "Look before you leap" and "He who hesitates is lost" are two proverbs that purport to guide choice under similar circumstances. Which does one follow? Similarly, Simon viewed most of the principles of public administration as offering contradictory advice. To Simon these proverbs were not useful guides to organizational behavior. Surely, Gulick's principles did not constitute the coherent theory implied in the title of his edited volume, *Papers on the Science of Administration*. Simon's logical positivist philosophical stance demanded that organization theory conform to his view of theory in the physical sciences. A meaningful science of organization and management would not present contradictory advice.

Specifically, Simon identified Gulick with the writings of other authors of the *Papers*. Other authors of that volume wrote of such management principles as the unity of command (the view that people in orga-

Herbert Simon's Critique of Classical Theories

---

17. Simon, *Administrative Behavior*, chapter 2.

FIGURE 4.2
Alternative Ways of Organizing a Hypothetical Campus Police Force

BY PLACE

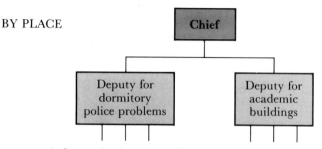

(suborganization probably on some basis other than place)

BY PEOPLE

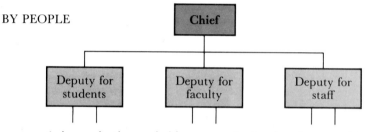

(suborganization probably on some basis other than people)

BY PROCESS

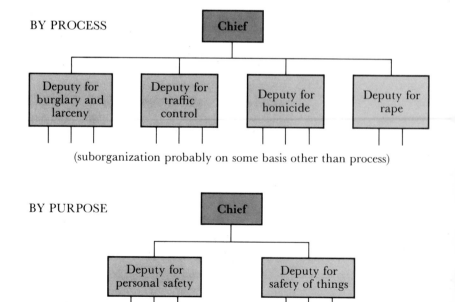

(suborganization probably on some basis other than process)

BY PURPOSE

Chief

Deputy for personal safety   Deputy for safety of things

(suborganization probably on some basis other than purpose)

nizations take orders only from their superiors in the formal hierarchy) and the span of control (the apparent limits on the number of people who could be supervised by one person). The unity of command principle, Simon noted, conflicts with the equally important principle of specialization. People in organizations really take orders from functional specialists as well as from formal superiors. One cannot a priori claim that the formal command structure makes for a more effective organization. Gulick seemed to support the view that the span of control should be limited. In contrast, Simon held that a small span of control might be counterproductive since it would create more vertical levels in the organization. This would produce unwanted delays as conflicts among units were forced to higher levels for resolution.

Gulick had also dealt with the staff and line concepts in the traditional manner, which implied that the line was more important than the staff. The line people could command, whereas the staff only advised. Simon questioned whether that was a true distinction. What is more important in a living organism, the heart or the lungs? Naturally, both are needed. In the organizational organism, staff personnel sometimes command because of their functional expertise. Simon also blasted the notion that the authority to make a decision and the responsibility for it should always be combined in one person. In some cases, authority and responsibility do not match. In Simon's example, the police have the responsibility to fight crime. To do this they use certain equipment—police cars, for example. The police department, however, might not have authority to purchase police cars. The authority to do so resides with the municipal purchasing organization. Therefore, the purchasing organization has formal authority over the police department in this particular area.

Although Simon vehemently fought the principles of administration formulated by the classical school in general because they did not constitute a science of administration, he did admit that Gulick had developed "criteria for describing and diagnosing administrative situations."[18] When Gulick's formulations have been considered as codified common sense rather than rigorous theory, they have been useful, especially to novice administrators. Still, there is very little in Gulick's thought, or that of the entire classical school, that recognizes that large-scale organizations are not monoliths that can be controlled from the top down through the hierarchy.

---

18. Ibid., p. 36.

Neoclassicists

ALTHOUGH it would be a gross oversimplification to claim that Weber, Gulick, and others associated with the classical school of organization theory ignored the role of individuals in organizational effectiveness, surely they underestimated the human factor in administration. Classical organization theory accepted the simplistic view that people in a hierarchical relationship to others would do as they were told. Implicit in classical theories was the idea that specialists could rationally design jobs and divide work. People would automatically accept these decisions based on rational processes and produce more so they could get more from the organization.

If people were simply cogs in a machine, classical theories probably would have produced smoothly run, efficient, and effective organizations. Since people are more complex than fabricated steel or electronic pulsators, the crisp machine models of classical organization proved faulty. Their basic premise was faulty. The human factor had to be considered.

One of the first people to deal systematically with the human factor in organizations was Mary Parker Follett.[19] In the early 1920s, Follett recognized that people constitute the major challenge for modern management. She noted that people deal with people in ever-changing complex relationships, and that in organizations many of the important relationships involve resolution of conflict. Follett saw three basic ways of resolving conflict: (1) domination, (2) balance of power, and (3) integration.

In *domination,* one interest bullies the other. The boss uses the power of the hierarchy to force subordinates to act in accordance with his or her wishes. This, Follett saw, leads to lack of cooperation and repressed behavior. Conflict resolution by domination is generally the way conflict is managed in classical organization theory.

The second means to resolve conflict in organizations, according to Follett, was a *balance of power.* In a balance-of-power relationship, there is no dominant power figure who forces the decision to be made his or her way. In an organizational setting, the boss may have the formal power to make the decision, but the subordinate, who has specialized knowledge of the problem under consideration, has de facto power. Under

---

19. Mary Parker Follett, *Dynamic Administration: The Collected Papers of Mary Parker Follett,* eds. Henry Metcalf and Lyndell Urwick (New York: Harper & Row, 1940).

these conditions a balance of power occurs. A balance-of-power situation becomes a bargaining situation in which compromise is the main way of resolving the conflict. Follett maintained, however, that the bargaining that goes on in a balance-of-power situation allows resentments to remain below the surface. The specialist might not be satisfied with half a loaf and perceives that the boss has really failed to follow his or her advice. The boss may likewise be dissatisfied because he or she feels that the decision has been altered to please the subordinate. Therefore, basic antagonisms remain in the organization, although the immediate decision tends to paper them over.

Follett preferred the third way of resolving conflict—*integration*. Integration, to Follett, meant that decisions regarding conflicts would be resolved through full and free contributions by all participants. There would be real cooperation that would result in mutually beneficial decisions. If people could be honest with each other and not have to worry about taking positions to enhance their bargaining positions, problems could be solved more successfully. The technique for gaining this kind of integration for conflict resolution was to be based not on the relative position of people in organizations or even on their personalities but on the problem situation at hand—the "law of the situation." If people could be led to respond to the objective situation rather than the internal dynamic of the organization's hierarchy, Follett hypothesized, cooperative behavior would ensue.

Whereas Mary Parket Follett was aware of the human problems in organizations and suggested a way to alleviate these problems by encouraging full and free communication aimed at problem-solving, her ideas were not tested experimentally. The key role of people in organizations, which seems second nature to us now, did not achieve standing in the literature of organization theory until the landmark studies conducted by Elton Mayo and Fritz Roethlisberger of the Harvard Business School at the Hawthorne (Chicago) Works of the Western Electric Company in the late 1920s and early 1930s. These Hawthorne experiments brought a new concern for the role of people—especially informal groups—in organizations.[20]

The Hawthorne experiments started out as scientific management experiments. The researchers sought to show that there was a linear rela-

---

20. For an excellent summary of the Hawthorne studies *see* George C. Homans, "The Western Electric Researches," in Schuyler D. Hoslett, ed., *Human Factors in Management,* rev. ed. (New York: Harper and Brothers, 1951). *Also see* Fritz J. Roethlisberger, *Management and Morale* (Cambridge, Mass.: Harvard University Press, 1941).

tionship between the amount of light in the factory and production. In one experiment, the level of light in a test room was increased over a period of weeks. Production went up. This was no surprise to the experimenters, but they were a bit puzzled when production also went up at roughly the same rate in a control group for which the lighting level had remained constant. In another experiment, the test group was subjected to lower lighting levels and a control group continued working under the same lighting conditions as they had in the past. In both the control and the test groups, production went up. In these and other experiments, the researchers came to realize that they were dealing with more complex relationships than the simple physiological effects of illumination on productivity. They embarked on a series of experiments that confirmed that the *workers were responding to the attention that was being paid to them* rather than to the increased illumination.

The recognition that people were not simply responding to changes in the physical environment led the researchers to conclude that people respond favorably when they perceive that others are trying to help them. This "Hawthorne Effect" occurs whether or not the objective criteria of what constitutes help are ever achieved. For example, if a professor had his or her classes videotaped by specialists whose purpose was to help the professor improve his or her teaching, the Hawthorne Effect would suggest that most students would respond favorably toward that professor whether or not his or her teaching improved.

In a series of experiments, the Hawthorne researchers discovered informal organization flourishing within and sometimes creating situations contrary to the needs of the formal organization. In one experiment, the Relay Assembly Test Room, women workers were taken away from the production line and allowed to produce under controlled conditions. Again, the variation of the physical conditions was of secondary importance to the informal group structure that developed and favorably influenced production. In another experiment, the Bank Wiring Observation Room, the fourteen men involved developed an informal group that had a strong effect on production. Even though management had set up an incentive plan that should have encouraged each worker to increase his own production, the experiment showed that the overall group, not management, controlled production. The informal group enforced their norms. If someone was not working hard enough, the group brought pressure to bear on the "chiseler." Similarly, "rate-busters" or "squealers" were brought into line by group sanctions.

Implicit in the findings of the neoclassical school was a new concept of power in organizations. Classical organization theorists saw power and

FIGURE 4.3
Zone of Indifference

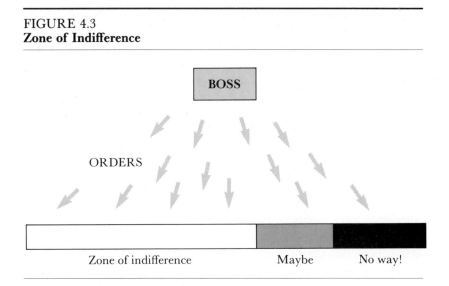

authority as a unidirectional relationship going through the hierarchy from the top down. In the classical organization, the bosses gave the orders and the subordinates obeyed. The neoclassicists, while keeping the hierarchy as the major way for coordinating individual efforts in large-scale organizations, saw power as a relational concept. The bosses might give orders, but the informal organization had real power in determining the extent to which those orders were obeyed.

This new concept of relational power in the hierarchy is best shown by Chester Barnard, a successful manager as president of the New Jersey Bell System and a major influence on administrative thought since the thirties. In *The Functions of the Executive,* Barnard described the power relationship in the hierarchy as involving a zone of indifference (see Figure 4.3).[21] To Barnard, each subordinate was willing to accept certain demands made by the boss. Each employee had a perceptual zone in which he or she would accept the boss's orders as legitimate and carry them out. If an order fell within this perceptual zone, the subordinate would be indifferent to the order; he or she would not give it a second thought. If a secretary were given a letter to type, he or she would not question the demand. A boss, however, could give orders that were clearly outside that secretary's zone of indifference. Perhaps a request to "entertain" an influential legislator might fall outside the zone. The subordinate might

21. Chester I. Barnard, *Functions of the Executive* (Cambridge, Mass.: Harvard University Press, 1938), especially chapters 10 and 11.

not accept such an order as being legitimate and therefore could refuse to carry it out.

An interesting feature about the zone of indifference, or as Herbert Simon called it, the zone of acceptance,[22] is that the zone can be flexible. The zone of acceptance can be broadened by offering incentives. Barnard saw a range of incentives available for management in effect to expand an employee's zone of acceptance. Money could be used to encourage that secretary to treat that influential legislator in ways that he or she might ordinarily not see as part of the job. Barnard, however, was more concerned with other incentives. To Barnard, the attractiveness of the informal social group and the opportunity to show distinction in one's work were more effective incentives to broaden the zone of acceptance than more money or improved working conditions.

To Barnard, one of the key management tasks was to develop a package of incentives that would keep subordinates contributing at a high level to the organization. He developed the concept of a contribution-satisfaction equilibrium (see Figure 4.4). Individuals contributed their talents to an organizaiton in return for a range of satisfactions that they received from the organization. Unless management could continue to provide satisfactions in the form of incentives, employees would not contribute as much as they might.

Barnard was a sophisticated practitioner and observer of organizations. Many of his insights, however, were oversimplified and put into management practice in both private and public organizations under the banner of "human relations." Human relations were a popular offshoot of the neoclassical school during the forties and fifties. Often

---

22. Simon, *Administrative Behavior,* p. 12.

FIGURE 4.4
Contribution–Satisfaction Equilibrium

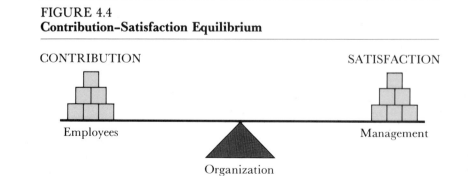

CONTRIBUTION   SATISFACTION

Employees   Management

Organization

human relations were a combination of the glad hand, the backslap, and the big smile. Often they involved replacing the stern, autocratic boss with a more mild-mannered type who would pretend interest in his or her subordinates. At more sophisticated levels, human relations were, in Dwight Waldo's words, "enlightened paternalism."[23]

In all its forms, however, neoclassical organization theory never questioned the hierarchy. It always accepted the goal of efficiency and the belief that workers should be molded to fit the needs of the organization. As such, it rested on the pillars of classical organization theory, but added the recognition that whenever people deal with formal organizations, they must be aware of the informal organization, too.

Maslow and Organizational Humanism

CHESTER Barnard saw that a critical aspect of administration was developing the mix of incentives that would maintain the contribution-satisfaction equilibrium at a level adequate to meet organizational goals. Barnard operated on the basis of an unstated theory of worker motivation that was more complex than the simple view that money was the prime motivator. Such a view had characterized the administrative thought of the classical school. Abraham Maslow, the founder of the psychological humanist school, developed an explicit theory of motivation that went beyond Barnard's implicit views.[24]

Maslow saw humans as having needs and wants. He postulated that people do not randomly need or want things, but that their needs are ordered in a rough hierarchy. Figure 4.5 presents this hierarchy of needs. At a basic level, people have certain physiological needs for food, air, sex, and sleep, among others. To satisfy these needs, Maslow maintained, people are motivated from within themselves to engage in behavior that would be rewarded—i.e., the needs would be satisfied. But when basic physiological needs are more or less satisfied, the motivation mechanism does not grind to a halt. People develop new needs—a higher level of need. According to Maslow's formulation, the next higher level of need is for security and safety. Included in this level are such

---

23. Dwight Waldo, "Development of the Theory of Democratic Administration," *American Political Science Review* 46 (1952): 84.
24. Abraham H. Maslow, *Motivation and Personality*, 2d ed. (New York: Harper & Row, 1970), pp. 35–58.

FIGURE 4.5
Maslow's Hierarchy of Needs

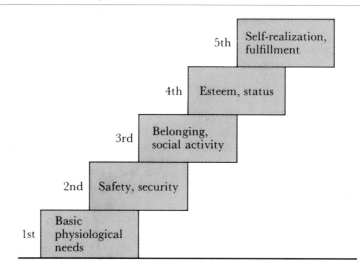

A satisfied need is no longer a motivator of behavior

things as relatively predictable relations with other people and the environment in general. In an organization, job security and fair treatment would be examples of this level of need. Again, as the security and safety needs are satisfied, people develop a still higher order of needs. Belonging and affection needs relate to the desire to be part of a group, to cooperate, and to express and to receive affection. Should this level of need be relatively satisfied, people would seek to behave in such ways as to satisfy an even higher level of need, that for esteem and status—self-respect and the respect of others. If these needs are relatively satisfied, Maslow maintained, people would reach for self-fulfillment or self-actualization—living up to one's full potential.

Maslow's theory of motivation holds that the relationships of the various levels of need are vitally important. One generally will not seek higher levels of need until the lower-level ones are more or less satisfied. Similarly, if the lower-level needs are basically satisfied, the higher order needs—esteem and status and self-actualization—take on increasing importance as a motivating factor for the person. Furthermore, a satisfied need is no longer a motivating factor. If a person's need for safety and security in the job situation is satisfied, no amount of improved lighting or working conditions will motivate that person; but perhaps attempts to enable that person to satisfy some higher level of need will motivate him or her.

Implicit in the hierarchy of needs concept is the notion that people's needs are insatiable. Once they have more or less satisfied their most pressing needs, they will seek to satisfy other needs. As Maslow put it, "Man is a perpetually wanting animal."[25]

Douglas McGregor clearly saw the meaning of this in an organizational context. If the people are perpetually wanting, they will behave in ways that will enable them to satisfy their needs. McGregor saw that the general way in which organizations were structured—along strict hierarchical lines with close supervision—often blocked the efforts of individuals to satisfy their needs, especially the higher levels of need. Blocked efforts led to the kinds of bureaupathetic behavior that concerned Victor Thompson. Such behavior could be explained as defensive reactions developed by individuals to protect their psyches from the frustration of not being able to achieve their personal goals within the organization. If the bureaucratic structure was preventing people from activating the motivation mechanism within themselves, that structure, McGregor felt, should be modified.[26]

McGregor called the classical organization structure "Theory X," the conventional view of organizations. McGregor's propositions regarding Theory X are listed below:

1. *Management is responsible for organizing the elements of productive enterprise—money, materials, equipment, people—in the interest of economic ends.*
2. *With respect to people, this is a process of directing their efforts, motivating them, controlling their actions, modifying their behavior to fit the needs of the organization.*
3. *Without this active intervention by management, people would be passive—even resistant—to organizational needs. They must therefore be persuaded, rewarded, punished, controlled—their activities must be directed. This is management's task—in managing subordinate managers or workers. We often sum it up by saying that management consists of getting them done through other people.*

Behind this conventional theory there are several additional beliefs—less explicit, but widespread:

---

25. Abraham H. Maslow, "A Theory of Human Motivation," *Psychological Review*, 50 (July 1943): 370.
26. Douglas McGregor, in Warren G. Bennis and Edgar H. Schein, with the collaboration of Caroline McGregor, *Leadership and Motivation: Essays of Douglas McGregor* (Cambridge, Mass.: MIT Press, 1960), reprinted in Kramer, *Perspectives on Public Bureaucracy*, 3rd ed., pp. 134–145.

1. *The average man is by nature indolent—he works as little as possible.*
2. *He lacks ambition, dislikes responsibility, prefers to be led.*
3. *He is inherently self-centered, indifferent to organizational needs.*
4. *He is by nature resistant to change.*
5. *He is gullible, not very bright, the ready dupe of the charlatan and the demagogue.*[27]

The most important feature of this view of organization is its view of people. The organizational humanists vehemently reject the view that people are lazy, stupid, and indifferent to the organization's needs.

One leading organizational humanist, Chris Argyris, claimed that if people appear to show their worst sides in most organizations, it is because hierarchically structured organizations encourage such behavior. According to Argyris, healthy personality development takes place along the following seven "developmental dimensions": (1) from passive to active; (2) from dependence to independence; (3) from limited behavior patterns to more complex ones; (4) from casual interests to deep interests; (5) from short time perspectives to long ones; (6) from subordinate roles to peer roles; and (7) from lack of self-awareness to self-awareness. Although Argyris recognized that the world would be a difficult place if everyone progressed toward the more developed end of each continuum at the same rate, he thought that individuals should have the chance to progress as far as their intelligence and inclinations would permit. But bureaucratic organizations generally stifle the development of mature personalities, according to Argyris. In large formal organizations, individuals have minimal control over their work situation, are expected to be passive and have short time perspectives, and are permitted to develop only a few superficial skills. Furthermore, the organizations expect individuals to produce under these conditions, which tend to lead to psychological failure.[28]

McGregor claimed that organizations need not be established along the psychologically repressive lines of Theory X. By assuming that the basic motivating force comes from within an individual and proceeds in the manner suggested by Maslow, McGregor suggested an ideal-type organization that could effectively meet organizational and individual needs. Theory Y, proposed by McGregor, implies that if management can make it possible for people within the organization to satisfy their needs and realize their potential by removing artificial barriers that

---

27. Ibid., pp. 135–136.
28. Chris Argyris, *Personality and Organization* (New York: Harper & Row, 1957), fully develops this argument. *Also see* his "Being Human and Being Organized," *Transaction* 1, no. 5 (July 1964): 1, 3–6.

frustrate need satisfaction, the organization will be more effective. If an organization is to be healthy and capable of creatively responding to and even managing change, an atmosphere conducive to individual growth is essential, according to the organizational humanists. The elements of Theory Y are these:

1. *Management is responsible for organizing the elements of productive enterprise—money, materials, equipment, people—in the interest of economic ends.*
2. *People are* not *by nature passive or resistant to organizational needs. They have become so as a result of experience in organizations.*
3. *The motivation, the potential for development, the capacity for assuming responsibility, the readiness to direct behavior toward organizational goals are all present in people. Management does not put them there. It is a responsibility of management to make it possible for people to recognize and develop these human characteristics for themselves.*
4. *The essential task of management is to arrange organizational conditions and methods of operation so that people can achieve their own goals* best *by directing their own efforts toward organizational objectives.*[29]

It is precisely the need to deal with change effectively that is the raison d'être for a Theory Y type of organization. A Theory Y organization, its advocates claim, would be more democratic and more open to the truth—what is really happening in the organization's environment—than the perverted version of reality tailored to please superiors in the classical hierarchical organization. Warren Bennis, one of the most outspoken advocates of organizational humanism, asserts that *"democracy becomes a functional necessity whenever a social system is competing for survival under conditions of chronic change."*[30] Among the democratic values that he and Philip Slater see being encouraged by organizational humanism are these:

1. *full and free communication, regardless of rank and power*
2. *a reliance on consensus, rather than the more customary forms of coercion or compromise to manage conflict*
3. *the idea that influence is based on technical competence and knowledge rather than on the vagaries of personal whims or prerogatives of power*
4. *an atmosphere that permits and even encourages emotional expression as well as task-oriented acts*
5. *a basically human bias, one that accepts the inevitability of conflict between the organization and the individual, but that is willing to cope with and mediate this conflict on rational grounds.*[31]

---

29. McGregor, in Kramer, *Perspectives,* 3rd ed., p. 142.
30. Warren G. Bennis and Philip E. Slater, *The Temporary Society* (New York: Harper & Row, 1968), p. 4. Emphasis in the original.
31. Ibid. Bennis has stepped back from his advocacy of complete full and free communication. See his "The Cult of Candor," *Atlantic,* 246, no. 3 (September 1980): 89–91.

The True View of
Organizations

DURING the past two decades several organization theorists have developed parallel views of motivation, leadership, and organizational climate. Table 4.1 summarizes and compares some of these organization theories. There is a tendency on the part of many to label those theories associated with McGregor's Theory Y to be "good" and those with Theory X to be "bad," but such judgments are impossible to make in the absence of the main criterion by which these theories must be judged—organization performance.

Since the Theory X–Theory Y formulation was made by McGregor, research has been centered on finding situations in which Theory Y-oriented management works better and the situations in which Theory X seems to hold. The tentative results of this research suggest that success of any particular management theory depends on the appropriateness of the management theory to the task at hand and individuals' motivation patterns. In general, Theory Y assumptions seem to work in science-based organizations that must operate under conditions of environmental turbulence. Theory X seems applicable to many programmatic areas such as certain kinds of manufacturing and processing that are characterized by stable conditions. Yet the situation is not that simple, because some people are motivated under conditions that do not fit either of the theories. The complexity of the situation is outlined below:

1. *Human beings bring varying patterns of needs and motives into the work organization, but one central need is to achieve a sense of competence.*
2. *The sense of competence motive, while it exists in all human beings, may be fulfilled in different ways by different people depending on how this need interacts with the strengths of the individual's other needs—such as those for power, independence, structure, achievement, and affiliation.*
3. *Competence motivation is most likely to be fulfilled when there is a fit between task and organization.*
4. *Sense of competence continues to motivate even when a competence goal is achieved; once one goal is reached, a new higher one is set.*[32]

The major implication of this "contingency theory" is that "we must not only seek a fit between organization and task, but also [we must seek a fit] between task and people and between people and organization."[33]

---

32. John J. Morse and Jay W. Lorsch, "Beyond Theory Y," *Harvard Business Review* 48, no. 3 (May–June 1970): 61–68.
33. Ibid., p. 67. For more on contingency theory see Jay Galbraith, *Designing Complex Organizations* (Reading, Mass.: Addison-Wesley, 1973), chapters 1 and 2.

TABLE 4.1
Parallel Theories about Motivation, Style of Leadership, and Organizational Climate

	Hierarchically Directed				*Participative, Self-Directed, Team Interactive*
Theories about motivation					
Abraham Maslow	Physiological,	safety,	Belonging and security	esteem needs	Self-actualization and growth needs
Frederick Herzberg	Dissatisfiers and hygiene factors			Satisfiers and motivating factors	
Chris Argyris	Dependence, submissiveness, frustration			Aspirations toward psychological success	
Douglas McGregor	Theory X cosmology			Theory Y cosmology	
Theories about style of leadership					
Blake and Mouton	*Style 9.1* Maximal concern for production, minimal concern for people		*Style 5.5* "Middle-of-the-road" concern for both production and people		*Style 9.9* Maximal concern for both production and people
Rensis Likert	*System 1* Exploitive authoritative	*System 2* Benevolent authoritative		*System 3* Consultative	*System 4* Participative group
Theories about organizational climate					
				Principle of supportive relations	
Warren Bennis	Bureaucratic organization				Organic-adaptive organization
Burns and Stalker	Mechanistic systems				Organic systems
Systems Theory	Closed system				Open system

SOURCE: Wendell French, *The Personnel Management Process: Human Resources Administration*, 4th ed. P. 104. Copyright © 1978 by Houghton Mifflin Company. Reprinted by permission of the publisher.

107

Surely we would not want all the people in the Division of Motor Vehicle Registration to be acting innovatively, freed from controls of rules and superiors. To do so would open the door to whimsical treatment of applications and the abandonment of the Weberian goal of a legal-rational system. But we might want to have some employees of that agency freed from strict controls so they could deal innovatively with problems that might affect the agency in the future. The number of people engaged in such functions would be quite small in relation to the number of clerks involved in the routine processing of driver license applications and motor vehicle registrations. Yet an unorthodox organizational form that encouraged the values sought in organizational humanism might be beneficial for this particular unit so that the health of the overall organization could remain sound.

The leading advocates of organizational humanism do not, therefore, claim that it should be universally applied as a panacea for all the ills of public administration, but they would recommend its incorporation in organizational hierarchies. The more sophisticated approaches to organizational humanism recognize that greater organizational effectiveness—a critical goal of the organizational humanism movement—is contingent upon many factors and situations. Organizations involved with rapid change and uncertainty—i.e., planning and research units—which demand a creative organizational response are more likely to respond favorably to the principles of organizational humanism than are more stable units involved with routine application processing.

Organization Theory as Political Theory

As is probably apparent by now, a different view of power and even human nature is at the base of each of the main three divisions of organization theory that we have discussed here. The various views correspond in a rough way to some broad political theories.

The strong leader at the top of an organizational hierarchy, imposing his or her will on the underlings who would otherwise be battling one another, is as at home with classical organization theorists as he or she would be with Thomas Hobbes. Hobbes's governmental system, where power resided at the top, closely parallels organizational systems where control and coordination are accomplished through the hierarchy. In such systems, power emanates from the top of the hierarchy down to the succeeding levels. In the view of Hobbes, as in that of Weber, superiors know better than subordinates, and subordinates realize that they should take orders for their own good.

Employees in a government agency that is run along such lines might limit the amount of extra-agency influence that would be deemed legitimate. In such agencies, most decisions might be made by a select group of people at the top of the hierarchy. Attempts to influence employees at lower levels might be viewed as an infringement of the agency's prerogatives. Thinking back to James Q. Wilson's bureaucracy problem, such a system might emphasize accountability and control as opposed to responsiveness.

Neoclassical organization theory has a view of power and human nature that is quite similar to John Locke's view: power is relational. To Locke, the subordinates might agree to give power to a superior in a hierarchy, but that grant of power would be subject to continual review by the subordinates. In such a political system, as with Chester Barnard's organizational system, the subordinates have a real say in how much power the superiors can wield. The underlings do have power—the power to rebel when they perceive that superiors have overstepped the bounds of the implied contract.

In an agency managed along neoclassical lines, one might expect the employees to be open to attempts to influence their activity from a variety of sources other than the direct hierarchy. In such agencies one might expect significant interest group activity at the lower administrative levels to be perceived as legitimate by the employees of that agency. Such an agency may be open to "reasonable" answers to vexing problems and seek to cut the red tape of strict hierarchical control by being responsive to the pleadings of special interest groups.

Organizational humanist theories have a direct intellectual debt to the political philosophies of Jean-Jacques Rousseau and John Dewey. Even more than in the Lockean view, power in the formulations of Rousseau and Dewey resides in the rank and file. Power is really shared. Participative democracy and participative management are possible because all people have the basic capacity to understand and deal fairly with one another. If people are assumed to have these attributes within the organization, people outside the organization—perhaps consumers of the agency's services—will also have these attributes. Such a view of power as being shared throughout the system by equals might open the agency to far more environmental influences than would be seen as legitimate. In such an organization, not only would lower-level bureaucrats be open to the organized petitions of established interest groups, but perhaps they might equally be open to the needs of individual citizens.

These possible relations between organizational and political theories, and the implications for accepting different environmental influences in agencies characterized by one theory or another, are mere speculation at this time. Much empirical work in public administration must be done to see if the way in which agencies are organized and managed affects their susceptibility to political influences. Although this might be the case, the main importance of organization theories in the public sector today is their effect on how individual public managers attempt to deal with other people in their agencies.

Suggestions for Further Reading

Argyris, Chris. *Integrating the Individual and the Organization.* New York: John Wiley, 1964.

Barnard, Chester I. *The Functions of the Executive.* Cambridge, Mass.: Harvard University Press, 1938.

Beckhard, Richard, and Reuben T. Harris. *Organizational Transitions: Managing Complex Change.* Reading, Mass.: Addison-Wesley, 1977.

Bendix, Reinhard. *Max Weber: An Intellectual Portrait.* Garden City, N.Y.: Doubleday, 1962.

Downs, Anthony. *Inside Bureaucracy.* Boston: Little, Brown, 1967.

Galbraith, Jay. *Designing Complex Organizations.* Reading, Mass.: Addison-Wesley, 1973.

Gulick, Luther, and Lyndall Urwick, eds. *Papers on the Science of Administration.* New York: The Institute of Public Administration, 1937.

Kramer, Fred A., ed. *Perspectives on Public Bureaucracy,* 3rd ed. Cambridge, Mass.: Winthrop, 1981.

McGregor, Douglas. *The Human Side of Enterprise.* New York: McGraw-Hill, 1960.

March, James G., and Herbert A. Simon. *Organizations.* New York: John Wiley, 1958.

Maslow, Abraham H. *Motivation and Personality,* 2d ed. New York: Harper & Row, 1970.

Presthus, Robert. *The Organizational Society,* 2d ed. New York: St. Martin's, 1978.

Simon, Herbert A. *Administrative Behavior,* 3rd ed. New York: Free Press, 1976.

Taylor, Frederick W. *The Principles of Scientific Management.* New York: Harper, 1911.

CHAPTER FIVE

Encouraging Individual Growth and Organization Development for More Effective Performance

CLEARLY, MOST GOVERNMENT AGENCIES in the United States are organized on a hierarchical basis and operate with a gloss of human relations techniques to overcome the drastic human problems that could prevent the agencies from doing anything. But under certain circumstances— uncertainty caused by environmental disturbances such as taxpayer or welfare rights rebellions—it appears that some agencies organized and operated in this fashion are not effective. If, under these circumstances, we want a more innovative governmental response, we might want to encourage a climate of organizational humanism in government agencies. Such a climate would be more theoretically in tune with change. This chapter will deal with some problems involved in attempts to institutionalize organizational humanism in government bureaucracies, some of the techniques used to encourage this kind of behavior in the private sector, and some specific programs that are being used in American governments.

Contingency Theory

SEVERAL studies completed during the 1960s and 1970s have shown that the form of an organization does make a difference in organizational effectiveness.[1] Some forms of organization are more effective under certain conditions; other forms work better under different conditions. Generally, as we have suggested in the previous chapter, hierarchical organization managed through Theory X principles seems to be effective under stable conditions. Under conditions of change, more loosely structured organizations run on Theory Y principles seem to be more effective.

Synthesizing the empirical work, Jay Galbraith suggested a reason that this is so. The key to his explanation is the relationship between uncertainty and information. According to Galbraith:

The greater the uncertainty of the task, the greater the amount of information that has to be processed between decision makers during its exe-

---

1. The classic studies in this area have been done in the private sector. See Tom Burns and G. M. Stalker, *The Management of Innovation* (London: Tavistock Publications, 1961); Joan Woodward, *Industrial Organization: Theory and Practice* (London: Oxford University Press, 1965); Alfred Chandler, *Strategy and Structure* (Garden City, N.Y.: Anchor Books, 1966); and Paul R. Lawrence and Jay W. Lorsch, *Organization and Environment* (Boston: Harvard Business School, 1967.)

PHOTO: The Federal Executive Institute, Charlottesville, Virginia.

cution. If the task is well understood prior to performing it, much of the activity can be preplanned. If it is not understood, then during the actual execution of the task more knowledge is required, which leads to changes in resource allocations, schedules, and priorities. All these changes require information processing *during* task performance. Therefore, *the greater the task uncertainty, the greater the amount of information that must be processed among decision makers during task execution in order to achieve a given level of performance.*[2]

Government work involving new problems or new ways of attacking problems, therefore, requires organizational structures that facilitate rather than hinder this flow of information. Typical government organization, with its emphasis on strict lines of authority (designed to keep the bureaucrats accountable to elected officials), often inhibits the kinds of information processing needed for improved performance.

Galbraith suggests four design strategies that organizations can take to improve performance under conditions of uncertainty. Under these conditions, information must be conveyed to decision-makers while the task is being performed so that they can make changes based on environmental shifts. The four design strategies he mentions are (1) creation of slack resources, (2) creation of self-contained tasks, (3) investment in vertical information systems, and (4) creation of lateral relations.[3]

The *creation of slack resources* amounts to reducing the level of performance. Caseloads can be reduced or schedules for completion of projects can be lengthened through the strategy of creation of slack resources. Fewer things get accomplished in a longer period of time because the organization adjusts to the difficulties of processing information. With taxpayer demands for better service and improved productivity, the creation of slack resources should not be a popular way for government to handle its management problems. Of course, often this strategy is chosen if the program beneficiaries are politically powerless. Middle-class demands to cut welfare fraud may mean that fewer deserving poor people receive services.

Another way to reduce red tape caused by the need to get approval for changes at a higher level is to change the organization permanently to bring all the resources required to accomplish a task under the leadership of one person. By *creating self-contained tasks* congruent with organizational units and providing the resources needed to accomplish the task,

2. Jay Galbraith, *Designing Complex Organizations* (Reading, Mass.: Addison-Wesley, 1973), p. 4. Emphasis in original.
3. Ibid., pp. 14–19.

the organization can bypass some layers of the hierarchy and save time. This time may be saved, however, at the expense of duplication of some functions. For example, if three departments in a local government are sharing a computer programmer, difficulties can arise as to which department is able to employ that programmer on a particular day. If each department had its own computer programmer, high-level decisions regarding the scheduling of the programmer would not have to be made. But if each department could use a computer programmer for only one-third of his or her time, it would be a waste of resources to hire one for each department. That logic would not necessarily stop a local government from hiring three programmers. If the jurisdiction could get a grant to cover the salaries of the new programmers, it might hire them.

The creation of self-contained tasks is behind some of the reorganizations that governments often undergo. This was the case with the creation of the Department of Education in 1980. The Department of Education was broken away from the Department of Health, Education and Welfare (HEW) ostensibly to create a permanent governmental structure that would encompass all educational programs, which formerly had to go through the secretary of HEW. One level of the hierarchy which had stood between the commissioner of education and the president, the secretary of HEW, was dropped. Although it is too early to evaluate the impact of this change, having the chief educational officer of the nation (now the secretary of education) report directly to the president probably will do little to increase the performance of the educational bureaucracy. Instead, the change reflects the power of the politically important National Education Association's ability to collect a political I.O.U. from former President Jimmy Carter.

To keep higher-level executives informed of actions and information required during the performance of a task characterized by uncertainty, the organization could choose to invest in *vertical information systems*. These can take the form of computerized management information systems (MIS), which are proliferating at all levels of government in jurisdictions that have the money to support them. Improved vertical information systems are also reflected in the titles "assistants to"—assistant to the bureau chief for leased rental housing, or assistant to the director for special projects, for example. The aim of improved vertical information systems is to "collect information at the points of origin and direct it, at appropriate times, to the appropriate places in the hierarchy."[4] They

---

4. Ibid., pp. 17–18.

FIGURE 5.1
Improving Lateral Relations Through the "Gangplank"

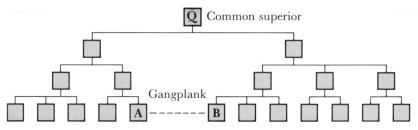

Rather than seeking resolution to problems by going up the hierarchy to Q, A and B negotiate directly with each other and resolve the problem with less red tape.

aim to maintain performance by preventing information overload for top executives.

The fourth organizational design strategy aimed at reducing the effects of uncertainty on organizational performance is the creation of lateral relations. Rather than routinely sending conflicts and problems up the hierarchy for resolution, lateral relations emphasize temporary organizational structures that can resolve such problems at a relatively low level. The results of decisions taken through lateral structures at lower levels are reported to upper-level executives as information rather than as requests for action. (The idea of lateral relations goes back to the theories of Henri Fayol, who advocated the "gangplank" to avoid sending routine conflicts up the hierarchy until they could be handled by a mutual superior. See Figure 5.1.)

Improved lateral relations can range from interoffice or interdepartmental committees that meet on an irregular basis to discuss general problems, to highly specific task forces and project teams that pull together people from several different offices, agencies, or departments for the duration of a specific project. Considering its successs in aerospace, project organization seems to be a promising way to improve governmental performance under certain conditions. Furthermore, it seems compatible with encouraging individual growth and organizational development along with improved performance. Therefore, we want to look more closely at project management.

Project Management and Conflict

EVERY complex organization is faced with two problems: (1) how to divide work to get the advantages of specialization and professionalism, and (2) how to integrate the specialized parts to achieve the organizational objectives. When government is faced with an important problem calling for the participation of many specialized bureaucratic units in an unfamiliar area, it sometimes uses project management to coordinate the problem-solving effort. Project management is "a combination of human and nonhuman resources pulled together in a 'temporary' organization to achieve a specified purpose."[5] It requires people with diversified skills, regardless of their organizational rank. The project organization is not permanent; it is temporary. People chosen to participate in a project know that they will return to their usual bureaucratic units once the project's highly focused goal has been achieved.

Government has become familiar with project management through aerospace and military contracting and through that growing governmental phenomenon, the task force. Often project management is identified with various programming and scheduling techniques such as performance evaluation and review technique (PERT) or the critical path method (CPM).[6] These are important tools, but they might give one an incomplete understanding of what the essence of project management is. By just looking at a PERT chart similar to the one in Figure 5.2, one might surmise that if the chart is correctly drawn—if all the events are correctly identified and all the activities correctly scheduled—the project will run smoothly. PERT charts are used in complex projects, and complexity usually gives rise to problems. Even the most accurate planning under conditions of uncertainty cannot account for materials that arrive late, manpower problems, or equipment failures. When problems do occur in a complex project, the unanticipated changes force changes in the plans. These changes demand continuing management, which is the role of the project manager.

Project management builds conflict into management because each person involved in the project is working for two bosses, his or her usual

5. David I. Cleland and William King, *Systems Analysis and Project Management,* 2d ed. (New York: McGraw-Hill, 1975), p. 113.
6. For explanations of PERT and CPM see Richard I. Levin and Charles A. Kirpatrick, *Quantitative Approaches to Management,* 3rd ed. (New York: McGraw-Hill, 1975).

FIGURE 5.2
Example of a PERT Chart for Project XYZ

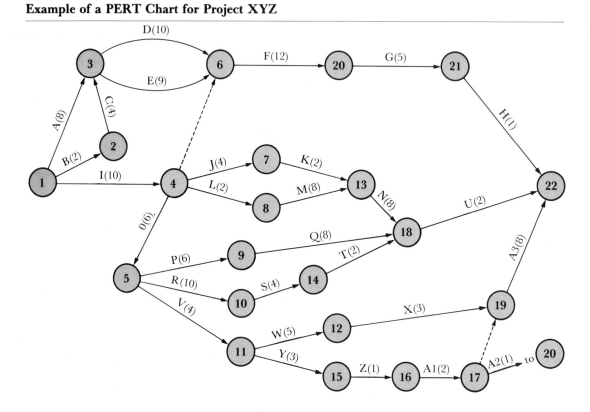

Each numbered circle represents an event; each letter above a line indicates an activity. Numbers in parentheses indicate estimated time to complete activity.

boss in the normal organizational unit and the project manager. As Figure 5.3 indicates, the clear lines of authority are no longer there. Neither are the boundaries separating jobs, agencies, and loyalties. The project manager lacks the power that comes directly through the hierarchy. Instead, he or she must depend on an alternative power source in order to negotiate resources from the various agencies with which he or she must deal. Not surprisingly, power in successful project management comes directly to the project manager from top executives, although not through the standard channels.

This conflict built into project management simply reflects a sharper image of conflicts that exist within an organization. It may strike a stu-

FIGURE 5.3
Hypothetical Metropolitan Transportation Project

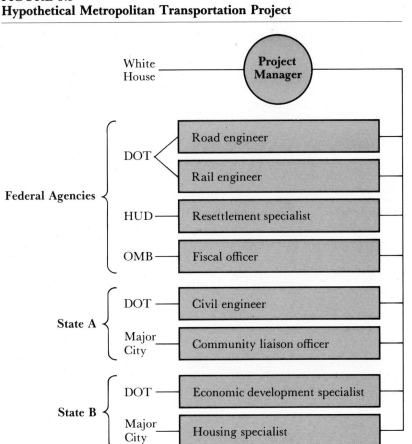

Each individual assigned to this project is in a hierarchical relationship to his or her home agency, but for the duration of the project he or she also has a horizontal relationship with the project manager and others on the project team.

dent as strange that people in the same government or same department or same office are often in conflict over goals, means, and values. Theoretically, since all these people are public servants, to use a quaint term, they should be pursuing the public interest as defined by legislators and elected and appointed political executives. But often one goal appears to be less immediate and relevant than other goals and internal constraints.

119

For example, sometimes professionals in one aspect of an integrated problem-solving effort may feel that special tests must be performed. Perhaps performing such tests might force the project off schedule. Perhaps those tests really are not necessary for successful project completion. If the project is organized in such a way that functional specialists control the schedule, those extra tests will be done and the project will fail to meet its schedule. If a strong project manager is in control, however, he or she might be able to pressure the specialists to stop testing at a negotiated level so the project can meet its schedule. Without project organization, professional goals may seem more important than the management goals of actually completing the project.

Conflict also occurs in organizations according to Miles's Law: "Where you stand depends on where you sit."[7] People in organizations develop loyalties to parts of their organization. A person who works in the Bureau of Public Roads (BPR) is more likely to be loyal to that bureau than to its parent department, the Department of Transportation (DOT). What may be good for the DOT may not appear to be so favorable for the Bureau of Public Roads. Under traditional organization, organizational changes or projects involving BPR and other units of DOT may be treated as institutional loyalty questions. Under those conditions, the BPR and the other bureaus in the department would mobilize their clientele to protect their bailiwicks, possibly at the expense of the overall departmental objectives. The project manager, on the other hand, can often channel political power in support of the overall goal rather than the more parochial bureau interests.

Advantages and Disadvantages of Project Management

PROJECT management has several positive features. It uses the components of existing organizations to achieve organizational goals more efficiently. It does not seek to develop permanent structures because it assumes that plans and structures will change as environmental demands change. It recognizes that there are conflicting goals and multiple sources of authority in organizations. It posits the role of the project

7. Rufus Miles, "The Origin and Meaning of Miles's Law," *Public Administration Review* 38, no. 5 (September–October 1978): 399–403.

manager as a broker or facilitator who brings together elements of the semiautonomous agencies that are needed to solve problems.

The key virtues of project management, however, were recognized implicitly by the classical organization theorist Luther Gulick. In Gulick's terminology, project management is a form of organization by purpose. According to Gulick, organization by purpose had three advantages over organization by process, by persons or things dealt with, or by place.[8] Gulick claimed that organization by purpose would "make more certain the accomplishment" of the objective although he did not appreciate the need for project managers to negotiate with functional specialists or parochial clientele interests. Another advantage was that citizens could readily understand organizations set up by purpose and could evaluate the results. This understanding becomes a power resource for project managers in negotiations with the traditional governmental units. Gulick's third advantage is perhaps the most important. He saw that organization by purpose "apparently serves as the best basis for eliciting the energies and loyalties of the personnel."[9] In short, project management is a way to improve organizational performance and individual motivation.

If project management is the organizational form that can lead to effective performance under conditions of change and uncertainty and that can motivate employees to achieve their personal goals within the context of organizational goals, why is it not used universally when conditions are changing? The simple reason is that project management is a complex organizational scheme, and not all organizations are capable of dealing with the ambiguities it raises. These ambiguities cause problems for project management.

Stanley Davis and Paul Lawrence have listed a number of problems that project management has encountered in the private sector.[10] Many of these problems, such as a tendency toward anarchy and preoccupation with power struggles, come directly from project management's notion of a dual command between the project manager and the functional unit bosses. Other problems arise from the development of project teams. Some project organizations emphasize group decision-making to

---

8. See the discussion in the previous chapter.
9. Both quotes are found in Gulick, "Notes on the Theory of Organization," from Gulick and Urwick, *Papers on the Science of Administration,* in Fred A. Kramer, ed., *Perspectives on Public Bureaucracy,* 3rd ed. (Cambridge, Mass.: Winthrop, 1981), pp. 74–75.
10. Stanley M. Davis and Paul R. Lawrence, "Problems of Matrix Organizations," *Harvard Business Review* 56, no. 3 (May–June 1978): 131–142. Matrix organization is a variant of the project form.

the point of severe "groupitis." Others get confounded by the dual hierarchy and constantly seek to clear all decisions through project managers and the normal hierarchy. Sometimes people in such teams get so wrapped up in the process of maintaining the project organization that they lose track of the goal of the project and just play the negotiation game.

Others have noted different problems with project management. Wendell French has suggested several problems relating to personnel management, among them the following:

1. *What is the impact on employees of the frequent forming and disbanding of project teams?*
2. *What can top management do to facilitate team formation?*
3. *How does the use of a project or matrix form of organization relate to the long-range career development of the employees affected?*
4. *In situations involving two superiors, who reviews performance matters, . . . who makes decisions about salary administration, and what are the consequences?*[11]

Despite the problems that some organizations have encountered with project management, many researchers share the optimism of Davis and Lawrence: "We believe that in the future [project] organizations will become almost commonplace and that managers will speak less of the difficulties and pathologies of the [project form of management] than of its advantages and benefits."[12]

The End of Hierarchy and Accountability

BECAUSE of the expansion of project management, Warren Bennis, one of the leading figures in organizational humanism, has rather recklessly written that the hierarchy is almost dead. He has predicted that within twenty-five or fifty years, hierarchically controlled bureaucracy will no longer be the primary method of organizing complex organizations. Such statements are readily subject to attack, for as Bennis himself noted in paraphrasing Winston Churchill's comments on democracy, "We can say of bureaucracy that it is the worst possible theory of organization, apart from all others that have so far been tried."[13]

---

11. Wendell French, *The Personnel Management Process*, 3rd ed. (Boston: Houghton Mifflin, 1974), pp. 72–73.
12. Davis and Lawrence, "Problems of Matrix Organizations," p. 142.
13. Warren G. Bennis, "Organizational Developments and the Fate of Bureaucracy," in Fred A. Kramer, ed., *Perspectives on Public Bureaucracy*, 3rd ed. (Cambridge, Mass.: Winthrop, 1981), p. 6.

In response to Bennis's penchant for overstatement, Herbert Wilcox was able to make a stirring defense of the principles of classical and neo-classical organization theory:

> We need not be ashamed that the principles of organizations are proverbs, constituting merely diagnostic criteria for the analysis of hierarchical structural problems in organizations. Lacking workable alternatives, we are dependent upon hierarchy and the principles of organization for the attainment of explicit goals by coordinating and controlling the joint action of a multiplicity of persons.[14]

Essentially, Wilcox held that the problems that organizational humanists attributed to the hierarchy may not be quite so serious as members of what he calls the "antihierarchy cult" claim. Wilcox rejected the organizational humanist response to change on ideological and technological grounds. To Wilcox, people do not act as Rousseau and Bennis assumed, and the values of effectiveness, economy, and efficiency, which the public favors, would be lost if classical organization practice were supplanted by organizational humanism.[15]

But Wilcox's defense took Bennis too literally. To Wilcox, the death of bureaucracy meant the absolute demise of bureaucracy and with it the direction, control, and structure that hierarchy gives. Organizational humanism in public administration, however, does not mean the unleashing of 2.8 million federal civil servants. Such a prospect is indeed appalling. But since the mid-1960s, as we have seen, the leading theorists and practitioners of organizational humanism have not made the claim that organizational humanism must be practiced throughout entire organizations and under all circumstances.

If organizational humanism is to be used within parts of agencies where theory indicates that it would improve a unit's effectiveness, the question of accountability becomes easier to handle. Indeed, there are analogous organizational arrangements that have been used in the federal government since the mid-1950s. Elements of organizational humanism are apparent in the project management philosophies of the federal contract research centers (FCRCs)—MITRE, RAND, the Institute for Defense Analysis, among others. These "independent" bodies have relationships with particular government agencies that could provide a model for breaking other parts of government agencies out of the strict hierarchical molds.

---

14. Herbert G. Wilcox, "Hierarchy, Human Nature, and the Participative Panacea," *Public Administration Review* 29, no. 1 (January–February 1969): 54.
15. Ibid., pp. 61–62.

A study of forty FCRCs found that the relationship between government agencies and their FCRCs was not so different from the relationship of line units within the agencies. In most cases the FCRC was financially dependent on a single government agency. There appeared to be a tacit agreement between the agency and the FCRC to provide stable funding from year to year. The sponsoring agencies imposed certain constraints on the performance of work by their FCRCs for other agencies. The agencies also imposed administrative controls and reporting requirements on their FCRCs.[16]

Although there are some similarities between the FCRCs and bureaucratic units in an agency, the FCRCs are more flexible with regard to hierarchical relationships and civil service rules. Advocates of federal contract research centers claim that their performance has been superior to that expected from an organizational unit within the traditional governmental structure. Assuming these claims to be true, it would make sense to incorporate this organizational form in some units within the existing governmental bureaucracy. Certainly by so doing, we would solve one major criticism of contracting out—that contracting out takes most of the interesting, challenging work away from in-house units. If those in-house units were given similar flexibility, they could do the work that they were set up to do. There would be no need to contract with outside organizations on a routine basis.

But the most vocal criticism of contracting out in general and even of contracting out to FCRCs relates to the question of accountability. Just as some people see a need for a strict hierarchy throughout an organization as a prerequisite for accountability, some people feel that contracting out for certain government functions means that government agencies are not to be held accountable for the performance of these tasks. But this should not be the case. The sponsoring agencies are accountable because they make the decisions to let contracts and to whom to give them. The agencies are responsible for monitoring the work. When reports bearing information of a policy-making nature or advice are filed, the agencies are free to reject the recommendations. Government agencies cannot delegate their decision-making role. By keeping the final power of decision, they must take the responsibility for the decision regarding the services of the contractor just as they take responsibility for decisions made by bureaucratic units.

Furthermore, the accountability of work performed by unorthodox

---

16. Dean C. Coddington and J. Gordon Milliken, "Future of Federal Contract Research Centers," *Harvard Business Review* 48, no. 2 (March–April 1970):107.

administrative units such as contractors or temporary, problem-oriented task forces does not remain wholly with the sponsoring agencies. In the case of the FCRCs and other contractors, Congress has the power to control. Congress may order the General Accounting Office to conduct a special investigation of contractor finances. If it chooses, it may enforce budgetary or salary ceilings.

The mechanisms for accountability that Congress has vis-à-vis the FCRCs are really quite similar to the power that Congress has with respect to the rest of the bureaucracy. Legislative bodies in general are reluctant to engage in significant oversight activities of line agencies, let alone contractors or other unorthodox administrative units. Apparently, individual legislators see their role as protector of their constituents' specific interests as more important to them than protection of a more general interest implied in oversight activities.[17] If the legislature has the power to hold administrative agencies—even those that are organized in an unorthodox manner—accountable, but chooses not to use that power, the argument that these organizational units are inherently less accountable to the people and inherently violate democratic theory does not hold up.

Spreading project management through government is not a question of accountability or nonaccountability. Project forms are becoming more common even though they violate traditional organization theory. Organizational practice is conforming to Peter Drucker's view that "sound organization structure requires both (a) hierarchical structure of authority, and (b) a capacity to organize task forces, teams, and individuals for work on both a permanent and temporary basis."[18] If we want more effective project management, we must find ways to encourage its acceptance in government.

Organization Development

A wide variety of techniques have been developed to encourage the organizational humanistic values necessary for effective project management. These techniques generally are called organization development (OD). Organization development is an effort to increase organizational

---

17. Seymour Scher, "Conditions for Legislative Control," *Journal of Politics* 25, no. 3 (August 1963): 531–540. Also see chapter 11.
18. Peter F. Drucker, "New Templates for Today's Organizations," *Harvard Business Review* 52, no. 1 (January–February 1974): 52.

effectiveness through planned intervention in the organization's "processes." Among the processes that concern OD consultants are the following: (1) communication; (2) work group member roles and functions; (3) group problem-solving and decision-making; (4) group norms and group growth; (5) leadership and authority; and (6) intergroup cooperation.[19] Warren Bennis defines organization development as "an *educational strategy* adopted to bring about a *planned organizational change.*"[20] The notion of planned change implies research into the organization's needs and generally means a long-term—two or three year—effort at implementing change deemed necessary by the diagnosis of the organization's problems. Although a wide variety of techniques can be used to educate the members of the organization to deal more effectively with change, Bennis noted, "whatever the strategy, organization development almost always concentrates on the values, attitudes, relations, and organizational climate . . . rather than on the goals, structure, and technologies of the organization."[21]

Although it would be impossible to catalog all the kinds of OD interventions here, a few representative techniques will be discussed briefly. All OD efforts include diagnostic activities. Organization development has a behavioral science basis. Applications of organization development demand data upon which strategies can be formulated for the particular organization under study. The diagnostic activities of organization development relate to fact-finding through a variety of methods, from traditional interviews and questionnaires to sophisticated psychological projective devices. The right to privacy of government workers often rules out the application of some of the more advanced data-gathering techniques.

Once the organization development consultant or "change agent" has built up a data base from which to recommend corrective action, he or she can choose from among a range of implementation techniques and strategies. One of the best known of such techniques is grid® organization development, a technique developed by Robert Blake and Jane Mouton.[22] This technique hypothesizes that organizational health can be plotted on a grid that relates management's concern for people with concern for production. The grid, which is presented in Figure 5.4, indi-

19. Edgar H. Schein, *Process Consultation* (Reading, Mass.: Addison-Wesley, 1969), p. 56.
20. Warren G. Bennis, *Organization Development: Its Nature, Origins, and Prospects* (Reading, Mass.: Addison-Wesley, 1969), p. 10.
21. Ibid., pp. 10–11.
22. Robert Blake and Jane S. Mouton, *Building a Dynamic Corporation Through Organization Development* (Reading, Mass.: Addison-Wesley, 1969).

The Aims of Organization Development

1. to create an open, problem-solving climate throughout the organization
2. to supplement the authority associated with role or status with the authority of knowledge and competence
3. to locate decision-making and problem-solving responsibilities as close to the information sources as possible
4. to build trust among individuals and groups throughout the organization
5. to make competition more relevant to work goals and to maximize collaborative efforts
6. to develop a reward system that recognizes both the achievement of the organization's mission (profits or service) and organization development (growth of people)
7. to increase the sense of "ownership" of organization objectives throughout the work force
8. to help managers to manage according to relevant objectives rather than according to "past practices" or according to objectives that do not make sense for one's area of responsibility
9. to increase self-control and self-direction for people within the organization

SOURCE: National Training Laboratory Institute, "What Is OD?" *News and Reports* 2 (June 1968): 1.

cates that Blake and Mouton see an effective organization as having a balanced concern for these two factors. They encourage the organization's development toward the more favorable positions on the grid through a six-phase change model involving the entire organization. These phases are (1) upgrading the management and leadership skills of individual managers, (2) team improvement, and (3) intergroup relations improvement. Later phases deal with (4) better planning for change and (5) implementation strategies for continued organizational growth. Evaluation of the entire effort is the last phase.

Another technique is third-party peacemaking.[23] In this technique the OD consultant attempts to help members of the organization manage conflict in a manner that is less destructive to the organization's goals

23. Richard E. Walton, *Interpersonal Peacemaking; Confrontation and Third Party Consultation* (Reading, Mass.: Addison-Wesley, 1969).

FIGURE 5.4
The Managerial Grid®

1.9 Management Thoughtful attention to needs of people for satisfying relationships leads to a comfortable friendly organization atmosphere and work tempo.		**9.9 Management** Work accomplishment is from committed people; interdependence through a "common stake" in organization purpose leads to relationships of trust and respect.
	5.5 Management Adequate organization performance is possible through balancing the necessity to get out work with maintaining morale of people at a satisfactory level.	
1.1 Management Exertion of minimum effort to get required work done is appropriate to sustain organization membership.		**9.1 Management** Efficiency in operations results from arranging conditions of work in such a way that human elements interfere to a minimum degree.

Concern for people — vertical axis: High 9, 8, 7, 6, 5, 4, 3, 2, Low 1

Concern for production — horizontal axis: Low ← 1 2 3 4 5 6 7 8 9 → High

SOURCE: R. R. Blake and J. S. Mouton, *The Managerial Grid.* Houston: Gulf Publishing Company, Copyright © 1964, p. 10. Reproduced by permission.

than keeping conflict below the surface. Often confrontation techniques are used to bring the conflict out in the open where it can be dealt with. One of the early governmental efforts at organization development involved such a confrontation between administrative personnel and foreign service officers in the Department of State during 1966.

Process consultation aims to help people in an organization gain insight into the human processes that concern most OD consultants.[24] As was mentioned earlier, these processes include communication, leader

24. Schein, *Process Consultation.*

and member roles in groups, group problem-solving and decision-making, group norms and group growth, leadership and authority, and intergroup cooperation and competition. The objective of process consultation is to enable the client to develop skills at diagnosing process problems and implementing programs to ease these problems.

Another aspect of organization development that relates more directly to the individual's role in the organization is individual development planning. Individual development planning attempts to improve the organization by structuring the growth and development of the individuals who comprise it. It can be a rather simple technique, and as such may be of immediate use in government organizations. A program for individual development planning for prospective government managers in the federal government is presented in an appendix to this chapter.

Although these are just a few of the many OD techniques, they are a representative sample. All OD techniques seek to improve organizational performance by improving the climate for the individuals in the organization. Organization development attempts to implement Douglas McGregor's Theory Y propositions, which were discussed in chapter 4. OD seeks greater congruence between the goals of individuals and the goals of the organization.

The private sector experience with organization development indicates that several factors determine the success of OD interventions. First, there must be a strong desire for improvement from both within the organization and outside it. The top executives must invite the OD consultant and support his or her efforts at diagnosing the organization's problems. This executive support is absolutely essential if meaningful changes are to be made. The extent of this support must be reflected in top management's willingness to get involved in OD implementation activities, including laboratory training and T-groups, in which participants can try out new behavior patterns under supportive, nonhierarchical conditions.

Often the personnel office takes over the major implementation role in organization development as the OD consultant phases out. To facilitate lasting effects of an OD program, the organization may have to alter its reward structure. To this end, it probably is useful for people dealing in such personnel matters as salary administration to be involved in the effort.

Since the goal of organization development is improved performance,

*Successful
Organization
Development*

the organization must continually monitor and evaluate the OD efforts as it unfolds. To most OD consultants, the effort should encompass a period of years.

It is often difficult to achieve the degree of support necessary for a successful OD program in the private sector. Certain features inherent in public sector organizations present some additional challenges to successful OD implementation in government. Robert Golembiewski has raised many of these problems.[25]

In government there is irreconcilable tension between legislative and executive control of the bureaucracy. Even if there is strong executive support for an OD effort in an agency, funds for such activity may not be made available, especially for programs that are supposed to last for a period of years before showing meaningful effects. The legislative bodies that appropriate money might not find such activities justifiable under tight financial conditions. Legislative bodies may question the wisdom of such efforts, thus detracting from whatever support organization development had in the agency hierarchy. Career bureaucrats know that they will have to deal with the same legislators after the current political executives have gone. It often makes long-term strategic sense to cultivate legislative committee members rather than political executives.

Although the private sector experience has indicated a need for a flexible reward structure, civil service rules and regulations (which will be discussed in chapter 6) are quite rigid. These rules and regulations, combined with judicial interpretations, also protect the privacy of government workers more than that of private sector employees. Some diagnostic tests can be seen as an invasion of privacy. Attendance at T-groups can also be viewed as such.

Although these barriers need not be insurmountable, they are serious enough to inhibit government OD efforts on the scale generally assumed by something like grid organization development. The possibility for organizational improvement through organization development in government probably lies more toward the individual development planning end of the OD continuum rather than toward grid organization development. If we value the goals of organizational humanism and see that these values can improve governmental performance, we might want to be aware of OD-oriented techniques that can be employed by individual public managers to improve performance of their immediate organizational units.

---

25. Robert T. Golembiewski, "Organization Development in Public Agencies: Perspectives on Theory and Practice," *Public Administration Review* 29, no. 4 (July–August 1969): 367–77.

Both a full-fledged organization development program and the more decentralized individual development planning concept try to keep the level of an individual's contribution high so he or she can obtain personal goals while working toward organizational goal achievement. Organization development and individual development planning seek to motivate the employee by increasing his or her satisfaction with work. Frederick Herzberg, a leading researcher in motivation in organizations, identifies several factors that contribute to job satisfaction. Moreover, he suggests "that the factors involved in producing job satisfaction (and motivation) are separate and distinct from the factors that lead to job dissatisfaction."[26]

Motivation through Job Satisfaction

Herzberg sees that most organizational efforts to motivate employees are really aimed at affecting the hygiene factors. He derides the efforts to motivate people by cutting the work week. Motivated people do not seek less time on the job; they want more hours of work, according to him. Similarly, spiraling wages and fringe benefits, in Herzberg's eyes, merely motivate the employee to seek another salary increase and join the "fringe-benefit-of-the-month club." Human relations and sensitivity training merely deal with improved supervision and interpersonal relationships, which, according to Herzberg, cannot motivate employees but can merely make them not dissatisfied.

Because Herzberg sees motivational factors related to the work itself, he advocates a strategy of job enrichment. Rather than rationalizing work to increase efficiency, which is the way industrial engineers had approached job development, Herzberg wants to see jobs enriched to use the talents of people more effectively. Job enrichment is different from job enlargement. Job enlargement connotes a restructuring of work that often adds another meaningless task to an already meaningless job. Adding a routine clerical activity to some other routine activity does not make for motivation. Job enrichment, however, would be achieved if jobs could be restructured to involve the motivator factors. Table 5.1 shows the aims of a job enrichment program.

Although organizational humanists would argue that everyone has within him or her the spark of the need to grow and develop personally, some observers have noted "that unless that spark is pretty strong, chances are it will get snuffed out by one's experience in typical organi-

---

26. Frederick Herzberg, "One More Time: How Do You Motivate Employees," *Harvard Business Review* 46, no. 1 (January–February 1968): 53–62.

TABLE 5.1
Aims of a Job Enrichment Program

Principle	*Motivators Involved*
A. Removing some controls while retaining accountability	Responsibility and personal achievement
B. Increasing the accountability of individuals for own work	Responsibility and recognition
C. Giving a person a complete natural unit of work (module, division, area, and so on)	Responsibility, achievement, and recognition
D. Granting additional authority to an employee in his activity; job freedom	Responsibility, achievement, and recognition
E. Making periodic reports directly available to the worker himself rather than to the supervisor	Internal recognition
F. Introducing new and more difficult tasks not previously handled	Growth and learning
G. Assigning individuals specific or specialized tasks, enabling them to become experts	Responsibility, growth, and advancement

SOURCE: Frederick Herzberg, "One More Time: How Do You Motivate Employees," *Harvard Business Review* 46, no. 1 (January–February 1968): 60.

---

zations."[27] Persons who have spent their careers in dull jobs that lack the motivating factors suggested by Herzberg might find it difficult to become internally motivated when given the opportunity. Instead, these persons might have a low psychological need for growth and might lead the fight against making their jobs psychologically rewarding. Such people might see job enrichment as just another way for management to squeeze more work out of them.

Motivation through Understanding

Job enrichment programs can be used as part of an organization development program, but often, especially in the public sector, civil service rules make experiments with job enrichment terribly difficult to effect. Although Herzberg looked down on efforts that were not keyed to the work being done by employees, some managers may be able to get more from their subordinates by improving their interpersonal relationships through transactional analysis (TA). Transactional analysis has been popularized primarily as a psychotherapeutic technique in such books as

27. J. Richard Hackman, Greg Oldham, Robert Janson, and Kenneth Purdy, "A New Strategy for Job Enrichment," *California Management Review* 17, no. 4 (1975): 62.

Games People Play and *I'm OK, You're OK,*[28] but some consultants have applied transactional analysis principles to organizations. Because it involves easy-to-understand terms, transactional analysis is a technique that managers could use successfully without major support activities required for organization development or job enrichment programs.

Examples of Verbal Strokes

Some Positive Strokes:
"You did a good job on that report."
"Thank you for making sure we met the deadline."
"I'm glad you're working in our department."
Some Negative Strokes:
"I wish we'd never hired you."
"Jones, not you again!"
"Of course, you wouldn't be able to handle anything this difficult."
"You did it all wrong again."
Some Mixed Strokes:
"Pretty good job for an old man."
"You really look good for a change."
"You do such a nice job with routine work."

SOURCE: Dru Scott, "Motivation from the TA Viewpont," *Personnel* 51, no. 1 (January–February 1974): 9–10.

Transactional analysis in a management setting recognizes that people want to receive "strokes" from the people with whom they work. A stroke, in transactional analysis, is any unit of recognition. This recognition can be positive, negative, or mixed. According to transactional analysis, people work for strokes; they want recognition. Naturally, a healthy personality would prefer positive strokes, but even negative strokes are better than none at all.

To Dru Scott, a management consultant who has applied transactional analysis to organizations, "stroke satisfaction means motivation."[29] The degree of satisfaction a person gets from various strokes depends on the availability and intensity of the strokes. Since the theory of

---

28. Eric Berne, *Games People Play* (New York: Grove Press, 1964), and Thomas A. Harris, *I'm OK, You're OK* (New York: Harper & Row, 1969).
29. Dru Scott, "Motivation from the TA Viewpoint," *Personnel* 51, no. 1 (January–February 1974): 11.

transactional analysis assumes that people are out to seek stroke satisfaction, management's role is to provide sufficient stroke satisfaction through ways that contribute to the organizational goal rather than inhibit that contribution.

Transactional analysis posits several different ways in which people can spend their time, and the availability and intensity of strokes associated with each. Ways of spending time include withdrawal, rituals, pastimes, psychological games, intimacy, and activity or work. Withdrawal, either physically or mentally, entails avoiding strokes altogether. Rituals like "Good morning, Joe. How's it going?" provide strokes of great availability but of low intensity. Pastimes involve simply talking about everyday topics and also provide many, but low-intensity, strokes. Intimacy involves full and free communication and the development of

"They've taken away my desk, my phone, my secretary, and my 'From the desk of' pads. On the other hand, they haven't fired me, so I guess I'm free to roam the halls."
(Drawing by H. Martin; © 1977 The New Yorker Magazine, Inc.)

authentic relationships. While intimacy provides high-intensity strokes, the risks involved in such relationships tend to cut their availability.

At work, however, the two ways of spending time that most affect the organization are psychological games and work. Game-playing is important in organizations because games waste time and do not solve problems. Scott suggests that people spend from 50 to 90 percent of their waking hours involved in psychological games because games provide high-intensity strokes and are readily available. Also, psychological games usually have predictable outcomes which minimize risks to the players. A typical organizational game is the blemish game, as shown in the accompanying box.

The Game of Blemish

The Blemish player looks over a report, project, or person until he finds something wrong—a too-wide left margin, computations on the wrong-color paper, or a slightly wrinkled collar. The Blemish player's objective is not to solve a problem or improve a situation, but to find something wrong, so there's no stopping him by correcting the fault to which he has called attention. He just moves on. Colleagues and subordinates usually figure out ways to cope with this person, of course. They spend time planning which little mistake to plant or make bets on how many minutes and seconds it will take him to find a mistake.

SOURCE: Dru Scott, "Motivation from the TA Viewpoint," *Personnel* 51, no. 1 (January–February 1974): 12–13.

If people in organizations can be turned away from seeking their stroke satisfaction through game-playing and encouraged to seek it through work, the organization should be more productive. Scott agrees with Herzberg on the centrality of work in providing motivation. She argues that the increase in motivation and productivity is long-lasting when the strokes are derived from the work itself. But if there are constraints on changing the jobs to make the work more interesting, exciting, and challenging, then transactional analysis can indicate directions by which the manager can provide stroke satisfaction while limiting psychological game-playing.

The essence of this effort involves the manager's understanding why certain people engage in nonproductive games. The heart of transactional analysis involves the notion that everyone's personality consists of three "ego states"—the parent, the adult, and the child. The parent, adult, and child are identifiable ways of thinking and feeling and behaving within each person. The parent is the voice of authority in each of us. The adult is the rational problem-solver. The child is the spontaneous, creative, and feeling aspect of us.

Transactional Analysis Ego States: Some Responses to Change

The Parent: "What do you mean, a new system? We've always done it this way."

The Adult: "Here's an announcement of a new system. I'm going to see how it was developed and tested."

The Child: "Wow, I'm curious about this new system we've been hearing about."

SOURCE: Dru Scott, "Motivation from the TA Viewpoint," *Personnel* 51, no. 1 (January–February 1974): 15–16.

In theory, a successful manager can tailor his or her strokes to deal with the ego state that subordinates happen to be expressing at a particular moment. Generally, parent strokes relate to the need to feel that one is doing worthwhile work or helping someone else. Adult strokes might demonstrate respect for a person's analytic or problem-solving ability. Since the child ego state reflects certain ways of coping with the world that persons have developed based on their own patterns of growing up, providing adequate child strokes might be a challenge to a manager. Scott suggested that successful child strokes might be based on trying to give a person something that he or she wanted as a child but never received.[30] Perhaps an individual office, a rug on the floor, an electric pencil sharpener, or a write-up in the agency newsletter would provide a successful child stroke.

In periods of change, when an agency embarks on a new program or installs a new management reporting system, adequate attention to the needs of the parent and the child ego states may be a critical factor in smoothing the transition. The parent can be stroked by paying attention to the older, established rituals while incorporating the desired changes.

---

30. Ibid., p. 13.

Perhaps the child could be stroked by an office party to celebrate the successful implementation of change.

By better understanding what aspect of an individual's personality is driving him or her in a given situation, a manager can better understand what kinds of strokes will be more effective in channeling that person into more productive patterns of behavior. Transactional analysis provides a simple, easy-to-understand way of viewing personality traits in individuals. By applying the concepts of transactional analysis, one might become a more effective worker and a better manager.

Toward a More Effective Public Bureaucracy

PROJECT organization, organization development, job enrichment, and transactional analysis are some of the ways in which an organizational humanist would try to change public bureaucracies to make them more effective. We must keep in mind, however, that organizational humanism does not work under all circumstances. In dealing with organizational and management matters, we should use contingency theory as our guide, although the logic of organizational humanism—an organization can be healthy only if its members are permitted to develop within it and to achieve personal goals while working toward organizational goals—does have powerful appeal.

To a degree, public managers are free to choose among different managerial and organizational strategies. That is what mangerial leadership is. Government organizations need not engage in full-scale, complex OD schemes to encourage individual growth and development in government agencies. Elements of some techniques—individual development planning and transactional analysis, for example—can be applied by individual managers seeking to improve performance in their particular areas of responsibility. By encouraging the values of organizational humanism, managers might encourage more flexible, more intelligent, and more responsive government. Especially in times of rapid change, we probably want governmental organizations capable of responding to the environment.

A healthy organization might be more adept at problem-solving than one characterized by suspicion and fear of reprisal for honest mistakes. A more open organization might consider suggestions from outside the established political channels. Perhaps such an organization would be

137

more responsive to some interests that had been locked out of the policy debates over particular issues in the past. A more open organization might be less susceptible to believing its own press releases and less susceptible to falling prey to its own bureaucratic truths.

The improved, healthier organization envisioned by organizational humanism would not necessarily violate the demands of accountability placed on government organizations. Individual managers could be held accountable for the actions of their organizations, but an open organization would tend to consider more alternatives before acting and would have the ability to develop justifications more in tune with the overall view of public interest, rather than the more typical closed-door, low-level-of-conflict approach that characterizes much public policy making in the United States.

Although moving government bureaucracies more in the direction of organizational humanism might be a worthwhile goal in the abstract, the personnel practices of governmental jurisdictions in the United States often form formidable barriers to this movement. The next two chapters will deal with some of these problems.

Suggestions for Further Reading

Beckhard, Richard, and Reuben T. Harris. *Organizational Transitions: Managing Complex Change.* Reading, Mass.: Addison-Wesley, 1977.

Bennis, Warren. *Organization Development: Its Nature, Origins, and Prospects.* Reading, Mass.: Addison-Wesley, 1969.

Bennis, Warren G., and Philip E. Slater. *The Temporary Society.* New York: Harper & Row, 1968.

Cleland, David I., and William King. *Systems Analysis and Project Management,* 2d ed. New York: McGraw-Hill, 1975.

Galbraith, Jay. *Designing Complex Organizations.* Reading, Mass.: Addison-Wesley, 1973.

Gellerman, Saul W. *The Management of Human Resources.* Hinsdale, Ill.: Dryden, 1976.

Harris, Thomas A. *I'm OK, You're OK.* New York: Harper & Row, 1969.

Herzberg, Frederick, Bernard Mausner, and Barbara Synderman. *The Motivation to Work.* New York: John Wiley, 1959.

Kirkhart, Larry, and Neely Gardner, ed. "Symposium on Organization Development." *Public Administration Review* 34, no. 2 (March–April 1974).

McGregor, Douglas. *The Human Side of Enterprise.* New York: McGraw-Hill, 1960.

Suggestions for Individual Development Planning

Here is a plan for implementing a particular organization development technique. This plan is similar to a consultant's report, which managers in a public organization might receive. Put yourself in the role of such a manager. Would you want to use the plan? What benefits do you see to implementing an individual development plan? What drawbacks might you encounter? Can you think of some easier ways to encourage the humanistic values inherent in an individual development plan?

AN INDIVIDUAL DEVELOPMENT PLAN (IDP) is a periodically prepared schedule of developmental experiences including both work assignments and formal training. IDPs should be designed to meet particular developmental objectives needed to improve current performance and/or to prepare the individual for positions of greater responsibility.

Individual development planning is an integral part of an effective executive manpower management program because it provides a rational and systematic framework for assessing developmental needs in terms of both the individual's career goals and the agency's executive manpower needs. . . .

1. The Individual Development Planning Process

. . . IT is important to remember that employee development at all levels has two facets—development of skills and knowledges needed to im-

SOURCE: Prepared by Executive Manpower Management Technical Assistance Center, Bureau of Executive Manpower, U.S. Civil Service Commission, Washington, D.C., October 1973.

prove performance in present job assignments and/or needed to perform effectively in *future* assignments. There are cases, however, in which special requirements should be taken into account. For example, IDPs for professional specialists who have no desire to be managers could emphasize updating of professional (occupational) skills to improve performance in their present positions. For others, the IDP process might result in a jointly reached conclusion that further development at this time is not needed or is inappropriate.

In any case, the central element of the entire IDP process is the interaction between the supervisor and the individual. There are three steps in this process: (1) preparation for the development planning interview, (2) the interview itself, and (3) implementation of the IDP (*see* figure 5.A).

A. Preparing for the Development Planning Interview

1. THE SUPERVISOR • The supervisor of an incumbent or potential executive should carefully review the organization's goals and objectives. This may require discussions with the supervisor's immediate superior or other top officials in order to clarify both short and long range organizational goals that are relevant to the development of the individual in question. The next step is to assess the individual's performance on the presnt job in terms of professional or technical competence as well as managerial ability. The individual's present capabilities, skills, and areas in which improvement is needed should be carefully examined to determine the types of developmental experiences the individual should receive. This assessment should include consideration of the supervisor's expectations for the individual's potential for advancement, both short and long range. Short-term expectations would include consideration of specific managerial positions for which the individual is a likely candidate.

Preparation for the interview with the subordinate should include an outline of broad development objectives; then information should be collected on the availability of developmental experiences to meet these objectives. It is especially important at this point to identify possible opportunities for developmental work experiences, either through restructuring of the present job or through task force assignments, details, or job transfers. One of the best ways to improve current job performance or to prepare people for higher-level positions is to provide developmental assignments in one or more functional areas which will provide the knowledges and skills deemed necessary for effective performance in a target position. Such experiences are often referred to as "mobility"

FIGURE 5.A
Supervisory and Individual Roles in the Individual Development Planning Process

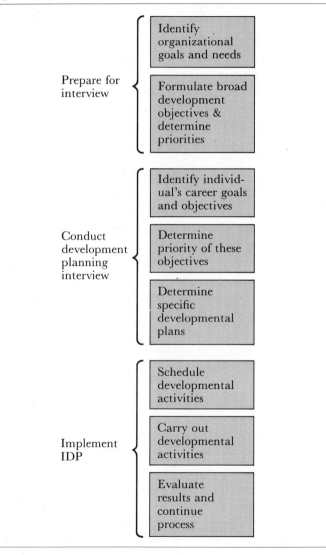

Prepare for interview
- Identify organizational goals and needs
- Formulate broad development objectives & determine priorities

Conduct development planning interview
- Identify individual's career goals and objectives
- Determine priority of these objectives
- Determine specific developmental plans

Implement IDP
- Schedule developmental activities
- Carry out developmental activities
- Evaluate results and continue process

assignments, but they do not necessarily involve geographic relocation. Other types of mobility include role, project, intra- or inter-agency, and occupational.

The supervisor should be prepared to assist and advise employees who desire to undertake self-development activities. Such activities might include taking courses not directly related to present or immediately anticipated work assignments but which may eventually enhance the individual's chances of being selected for broader gauge positions at some point in the future. Another useful and relatively inexpensive self-development practice is selective reading of books, articles, and other publications or issuances. The supervisor could aid in this process by preparing a list of pertinent reading material which would be of benefit to the employee. For certain individuals, participation in "developmental" civic activities or on various types of advisory boards might be beneficial.

Two other factors which should be carefully considered by the supervisor are the background of the individual and the nature of the position occupied. Newly appointed managers would probably need more training in managerial skills and techniques than would individuals who formerly occupied managerial positions. The same holds true for newly appointed executives, especially if they have spent most of their careers in professional or technical positions. Individuals who are relatively new to the organization may need more extensive orientation-type experiences, especially if they were hired from outside the federal government. The main point here is that the supervisor must be prepared to make comparisons between the knowledges and skills the individual brings to the job and those which are required in current or future positions. Then, appropriate developmental experiences to meet these requirements should be identified so that they can be discussed with the subordinate during the development planning interview.

2. THE EXECUTIVE (OR POTENTIAL EXECUTIVE) • The individual should prepare for the IDP planning interview by thinking through and clarifying career goals, plans and developmental needs, both short and long range. It is especially important to consider personal expectations and relate them to those of the organization. Each individual should identify those areas in which knowledge or skills could be acquired to improve present job performance and chances for advancement. Written performance appraisals, previous IDP's and other information sources should facilitate identification of those areas in which improvement is needed. Professional or technical development as well as managerial development needs should be carefully considered.

Individuals should attempt to identify specific positions to which they aspire (especially in the short term) and determine the developmental experiences needed to qualify for those positions. They should be particularly careful to look for ways the present job could be restructured, or what additional tasks could be assigned to provide the needed experiences. It would also be helpful to prepare a list of self-developmental activities which could be undertaken to broaden knowledge and fill in any self-perceived gaps in background, experience, or education.

The above activities should enable the individual to prepare a tentative developmental plan for discussion with the supervisor in the development planning interview.

During this discussion, the supervisor and the individual should jointly review the organization's needs and goals to see how and where the individual fits into their attainment. Once individual and organizational needs have been explored and clarified, broad developmental objectives can be explored. For example, one organizational goal might be to establish new area offices in several cities by the end of the next fiscal year. The organization's *need* in this case would be to have a qualified manager to run each office. As a potential candidate for an area manager position, the individual's short-term *goal* might be to become an area manager by the end of the next fiscal year and an individual *need* might be for additional experience in budgeting. A broad developmental objective for this individual would be "to acquire the budgeting experience necessary to carry out the job of area manager." Possible ways to help achieve this developmental objective would include such things as a developmental assignment to a budget office, participation in training courses on financial management topics, and selective readings of various budget documents.

B. Development Planning Interview

This type of discussion of broad objectives in terms of individual needs will help focus attention on the specific areas of common interest that are likely to be most fruitful for developmental purposes. Priority objectives are usually those that can fulfill an immediate need or goal for *both* the organization and the individual.

Once the high-priority broad objectives have been singled out, specific developmental objectives can be established. If the employee's objectives are reasonable, the supervisor should initiate discussion of specific actions to be taken to reach each developmental objective within a specified period of time. This discussion of specific actions should also include a meeting of the minds between the supervisor and subordinate—prior to the developmental assignment—as to how the planned work experience or formal training will lead to improved job performance. While this certainly cannot be predicted with precision, the discussion should focus on the question of what both the organization and

143

the individual should expect to get out of the developmental experience.

The planned development activities should emphasize on-the-job experiences such as job rotations and task force assignments, supplemented as necessary by formal training. The supervisor and the subordinate should also discuss the possibility of development through job enrichment of the employee's present position. Some methods of achieving this include greater participation in the formulation of organizational goals or policies, service on cross-organizational teams or leadership of such efforts, line experience for staff people and vice versa, and representing the organization in interagency situations. This does not mean indiscriminate increases in workload, although an increase in responsibility may sometimes be involved.

Individuals should be encouraged to supplement developmental assignments with appropriate training such as:

1. *attendance at the Office of Personnel Management's Federal Executive Institute or Executive Seminar Centers;*
2. *taking short-term training courses on specific subjects offered by both government and nongovernment sources;*
3. *participation in professional organization conferences and meetings; and*
4. *study at the university level.*

After the development planning interview, the results (objectives and scheduled activities) should be scheduled and recorded on an official IDP form to be signed by both the employee and the supervisor. At least four copies of the signed IDP will be needed: one each for the employee, the supervisor, the executive manpower management officer and the employee's official personnel folder.

C. Implementing the IDP

At this point the IDP has been signed by both the supervisor and the subordinate and a copy should be sent to the executive manpower management officer for review and eventual consolidation with other agency IDPs to determine aggregate developmental opportunity needs. (This will be covered in detail in section II of this paper.)

The following two steps complete the IDP cycle:

1. *accomplishing the scheduled developmental activities (or revising the schedule as needed); and*
2. *monitoring progress toward meeting the IDP schedule and evaluating results to serve as a basis for developing the next IDP.*

Evaluation of results is the joint responsibility of the individual, the supervisor, and other agency officials. The individual's job performance should be assessed to determine whether, and to what extent, the developmental objectives were achieved. The results of this evaluation can be used to determine the need for further developmental activities and to assess the effectiveness of the developmental experience itself. This evaluation then leads back to whatever step in the cycle is appropriate for both the organization and the individual. The IDP process should be a continuously recurring sequence, with periodic revisions and updating as required (normally, once a year). It may be helpful to time the IDP review cycle to coincide with the performance evaluation and the agency training needs survey.

Figure 5.B illustrates the individual development planning process in terms of the interaction among the three major actors—the supervisor, the individual, and the executive manpower management officer.

II. Role of the Executive Manpower Management Office (EMMO)

THE EMMO is the agency official with primary responsibility for all executive manpower management activities and therefore must develop the policies, procedures, and forms necessary for the effective implementation of the individual development planning process throughout the agency. The EMMO should also play a key role in coordinating the activities of the Executive Manpower Resources Board (EMRB) and ensure that agency top management is kept informed regarding agency-wide executive development needs. Since aggregated IDPs serve as the basis for agency-wide employee development planning, they must be carefully analyzed and summarized by the EMMO to obtain the aggregate data needed to determine agency-wide resource (money and manpower) needs.

Clearly, a successful executive development system will generate high demand for more developmental positions, more formal training programs, and more budget dollars. The EMMO must coordinate the planning and budgeting process throughout the agency and act as liaison between the financial management and manpower management functions to ensure that executive development resource priorities are

FIGURE 5.B
The Individual Development Planning Process

Supervisor and Individual		EMMO
Prepare for interview	Identify organizational goals and needs	Schedule preparation of IDPs for all executives and identified high potentials.
	Formulate broad development objectives & determine priorities	Assist supervisors. Provide or arrange for training of supervisors in coaching and counseling. Counsel individuals as needed.
Conduct development planning interview	Identify individual's career goals and objectives	
	Determine priority of these objectives	
	Determine specific developmental plans	Provide information on developmental opportunities.
Implement IDP	Schedule developmental activities	Review IDPs and extract data for aggregate planning purposes.
	Carry out developmental activities	Monitor and evaluate the process, including: • exercising quality control of IDP documents • ensuring that developmental activities take place as scheduled • evaluating overall process
	Evaluate results and continue process	

established and funds spent where they will do the most good. In those cases where resources are insufficient to achieve the aggregate developmental objectives specified in IDPs, the EMMO must develop recommendations and alternatives to enable top agency management to make proper decisions regarding who gets what and when. In some cases, supervisors will have to be notified that IDPs must be either changed or the schedule for developmental activities delayed.

MOST major agencies have already implemented some sort of IDP system, particularly for their high-potential mid-managers. EMMOs should take steps to ensure that IDPs also cover incumbent executives as well as high-potential mid-managers.

A. Developing the IDP System

Most of the existing IDP systems focus primarily on formal training rather than on development of managerial skills through various types of mobility assignments, job enrichment techniques, and planned rotation to higher managerial positions. This is understandable because management training can identify and order the most important problems found in the day-to-day work situation, assist the participant to recognize how to deal with similar situations, and encapsulate and condense this process into a short time span.

Nevertheless, it must be recognized that one can only *master* the art of management by successfully performing in a variety of progressively more responsible positions which require managerial skills. Therefore, agency guidance to supervisors should stress this face and the forms used for IDPs should by their very design emphasize developmental work assignments as the principal learning experience.

THE EMMO should advise and assist supervisors of incumbent and potential executives in order to:

B. Providing Advice and Assistance

1. *establish broad developmental programs consistent with agency-wide goals;*
2. *determine whether developmental objectives are realisitc and attainable; and*
3. *identify appropriate developmental positions and training sources.*

The EMMO should also consider the training needs of supervisors in employee coaching and counseling. Responses to this need could range from an informal discussion between the EMMO and the supervisor to a formal course in techniques of counseling.

Although the responsibility for counseling individuals rests primarily with the supervisor, the EMMO should inform executives and mid-managers that assistance is available to them at any stage of the IDP process, particularly as regards counseling on career opportunities, plans, and goals.

C. Providing
Developmental
Opportunities

It is important that the EMMO take an active role in providing general information about developmental opportunities such as vacancies, new positions, developmental positions, task force openings, and formal training courses. This information should be provided to supervisors, executives, and mid-managers so that available opportunities can be discussed during the development planning interview. Where necessary, the EMMO should carry the process one step further and actually make arrangements for training courses, developmental assignments, task force placements, and other developmental activities.

D. Monitoring the
System

Completed IDPs are valuable to the EMMO and other top managers for development program planning, manpower planning, and for system monitoring and evaluation. The IDP process supports manpower planning by providing data on the future supply of executive manpower; i.e., information as to when executives with particular skills and knowledges will (or will not) be available. This data, compared to estimates of future requirements, will indicate where shortages or surpluses are likely to occur so that corrective action can be taken.

The EMMO should review all agency IDPs for appropriateness of developmental objectives, specificity, and timing of developmental activities. Assistance and guidance should be given to supervisors who submit inadequate plans. The completed plans provide the framework for monitoring developmental activities to ensure that objectives are being met. From analysis of individual needs as expressed in IDPs, the EMMO can put together a composite picture of individual and organizational needs. Aggregating this data makes it possible to budget for developmental activities, plan for the utilization of both internal and external resources, and determine relative costs, benefits, and trade-offs.

III. Summary

INDIVIDUAL development plans can be of great assistance in keeping an executive development program from becoming a mere collection of activities with little relevance to each other or to the goals and objectives of the organization, the supervisor, and the individual employee. Also, the IDP process forms a sound basis for an executive development program at its most critical point—the day-to-day relationship between the individual employee and the supervisor. Combined with high-level organizational commitment, effective job rotation plans, training resource utilization, and program evaluation, it forms the foundation for ensuring that the government has a sufficient number of top-quality people to meet both its present and future needs for executive leadership. Development of an efficient IDP process will benefit both the organization concerned with maximum resource utilization and the individual aspiring to executive-level positions.

CHAPTER SIX

Public Personnel Administration

Citizens should be concerned about the recruitment, promotion, motivation, and development of their civil servants because the actions of government workers have policy implications and because a substantial element of governmental cost is direct payments to these workers. Around 16 million Americans are nonmilitary public employees working for federal, state, and local governments. The monthly bill for wages and salaries for these workers is over $18 billion. This does not include the costs of pensions, health plans, and other employer-sponsored benefits. Payroll costs run close to 50 percent of the total expenditures for state and local governments, and in 1980 over 13.1 million people worked directly for state and local governments.[1]

Given the great sums being spent and the number of people in government, it is not surprising that public administration in particular should be concerned with developing those people into an effective work force that can improve the delivery of government services and increase the confidence of citizens in our public institutions. Public personnel administration attempts to recruit and develop such a work force.

Until fairly recently, public personnel administration in the United States was mired in a bog of civil service rules and regulations that made effective personnel management almost impossible. Reform efforts at all levels of government have made public personnel administration a dynamic area, yet most reform efforts have only begun to be reflected in changing public personnel management.

Two major federal laws symbolize this reform effort. The first was the Intergovernmental Personnel Act of 1970 (IPA), which tied personnel administration to improved personnel management. The second was the Civil Service Reform Act of 1978, which further recognized personnel management functions in government by separating the United States Civil Service Commission, a product of the previous major civil service reform in 1883, into a Merit Systems Protection Board (MSPB) and the Office of Personnel Management (OPM). The Civil Service Reform Act of 1978 also created a Senior Executive Service (SES), which recognized that public managers could earn substantial bonuses based on performance, and made other changes that will be discussed a bit later. The objectives of these federal laws have been echoed at the state and local levels through reform legislation and attempts to improve the practice of personnel management. (We will deal with one of the principal obstacles

1. U.S. Census of Governments, reported in *Wall Street Journal*, July 3, 1980, p. 5.
Photo: Alan K. Campbell, first Director of OPM, watches as the name change is made at his headquarters.

to personnel management reform in the next chapter when we discuss public sector labor-management relations.)

The objectives of modern public personnel management at any level of government in the United States were spelled out in the preamble to the Intergovernmental Personnel Act. Among these aims are the following:

1. *recruiting, selecting, and advancing employees on the basis of their relative ability, knowledge, and skills*
2. *providing equitable and adequate compensation*
3. *training employees as needed to assure high-quality performance*
4. *retaining employees on the basis of the adequacy of their performance, correcting inadequate performance, and separating employees whose poor performance cannot be corrected*
5. *assuring fair treatment of applicants and employees in all aspects of personnel administration without regard to political affiliation, race, color, national origin, sex, or religious creed, and with proper regard for their privacy and constitutional rights as citizens*
6. *assuring that employees are protected against coercion for partisan political purposes and are prohibited from using their official authority for the purpose of interfering with or affecting the result of an election or a nomination for office.*[2]

Basically, these aims boil down to two main tenets of American public personnel administration: (1) the merit system and (2) equal pay for equal work. The rest of this chapter will examine these fundamental principles of personnel administration and some of the systems designed to attain the lofty aims of the IPA.

Merit versus Spoils

GENERALLY, when people think of government employment—especially in the larger jurisdictions—they see the merit system as the machinery and procedures designed to reward people who can take tests but lack the political clout to get a government job based on "who you know." There seems to be a natural separation between "merit," on the one hand, and the spoils of politics, on the other. The merit system, where appointments and promotions are based on more or less objective measures, is usually contrasted with the spoils system, where personnel decisions are made primarily on political criteria.

2. Intergovernmental Personnel Act of 1970, P.L. 95-454, Title VI, 92 Stat. 1188, 1189.

The spoils system—staffing public bureaucracy on the basis of political connections— is generally identified with President Andrew Jackson, following the 1828 election. Actually, Jackson did not invent the practice, which had been used in various states before he was elected. Nor was he the first president to employ the practice. But Jackson did advertise what he was doing and made a virtue of providing jobs for his backers. Although it would appear to be difficult to defend any system that carries a label such as "spoils," the spoils system must be judged in the context of the times when it was predominant. In the Jacksonian years, the spoils system did broaden representativeness in the bureaucracy. It bound Westerners to what was still a relatively young governmental system. Also, in those less complicated times, almost anyone could do the various clerical jobs that comprised most of the work of nineteenth-century bureaucrats. Furthermore, as Herbert Kaufman has noted, many people who were removed from office when the opposing party came to power were returned to the same positions they had held when their party or faction returned to power. There was a substantial number of employees who held more technical jobs and who were not replaced when different parties held the presidency. These people provided what continuity there was under the spoils system.[3]

Still, one would have difficulty arguing that the spoils system enhanced effective government. Kaufman has mentioned several excesses of the spoils system that stimulated the reformers of the 1870s and 1880s:

> The spoils system put a premium on the creation of extra jobs—both to provide additional political currency and also to lighten the work load so that loyal political partisans would have time for their assigned political tasks.
>
> It resulted in the employment of many individuals who were not qualified to perform the duties for which they were hired.
>
> It tempted government officials to use their official positions for personal gain, for they had generally only four years in which to reap the harvest for which they had labored long and hard in the political vineyards.
>
> It meant that a good deal of energy went into the orientation and basic training of a new work force every four years.
>
> It reduced the President to the level of petty job broker, and diverted his strength and attention from important matters of state. . . .[4]

---

3. Herbert Kaufman, "The Growth of the Federal Personnel System," in Wallace S. Sayre, ed., *The Federal Government Service* (Englewood Cliffs, N.J.: Prentice-Hall, 1965), p. 29.

4. Ibid., p. 31.

During the 1870s reformers sought to establish mechanisms that would mitigate against the worst outrages of the spoils system. Following the assassination of President James A. Garfield at the hands of an alleged disappointed job seeker in 1881, the reform effort finally culminated with the passage of the Pendleton Act of 1883. Implicit in the Pendleton Act were three principles upon which the merit system is based: (1) open competition for available jobs, (2) occupational ability, and (3) political neutrality. Open competition relates to the notion of equal employment opportunity—the idea that no group of people should be arbitrarily closed out of being considered for a government job. The idea of occupational ability means that people who are selected should be competent and qualified for the jobs to which they have been appointed. Political neutrality means that civil servants should not be beholden to partisan politicians. Appointment and retention of employees rest on their abilities to perform in a politically neutral, competent manner rather than to curry the favor of partisan politicos.

Although New York State quickly followed the national government with a civil service law in 1883 and Massachusetts followed with one in 1884, civil service reform at the state level did not gain widespread support until the mid-1900s. Similarly, at the local level civil service reform was slow in developing until the municipal reform movements of the 1900s. Even in the federal service, civil service protection was not granted to all employees with the passage of the Pendleton Act. Successive presidents were able to extend civil service protection to jobs held by their supporters in a gradual process known as "blanketing in." This blanket of civil service protection was gradually extended; about 95 percent of federal civil servants are now covered. Merit system civil service protection is firmly entrenched at all levels of government. All state and county employees paid by federal funds are covered. Most state employees, most of the municipal empoloyees in three quarters of the cities in the United States, and virtually all full-time police and firefighters now enjoy civil service protection.[5]

5. E. S. Savas and Sigmund G. Ginsburg, "The Civil Service: A Meritless System?," *The Public Interest* 32 (Summer 1973): 70–85.

Merit and Testing
for Recruitment
and Promotion

ALTHOUGH the three basic tenets of the merit system—open competition, occupational ability, and political neutrality—need not be dependent on scores on written tests, such standardized tests have practically become synonymous with the system. Standardized group testing was effectively used first by the army during World War I. The Army Alpha test, which proved to be a valid predictor of performance among officer candidates, pioneered the introduction of standardized mental ability testing in industry and government. Today, testing based on "objective" criteria is the principal device used in running the recruitment, and often the promotion, systems in government jurisdictions.

Some of the reliance on this kind of testing stems from a desire on the part of the recruitment authority arbitrarily to exclude large numbers of people. In periods of recession when general government jobs are highly prized, personnel officers often see a need to thin out the ranks of the applicants. Even in good times, some jurisdictions—notably the federal government, which offers relatively high salaries—need some means for weeding out candidates for jobs. The federal government hires only one out of thirty applicants.

Tests that require abilities far beyond the requirements of the job to be filled certainly do serve this function. But this recourse to a method that is administratively convenient for the personnel officer might not be fair to applicants who could perform the job in question. Furthermore, such tests might place someone who is overqualified in a job that would not provide the kinds of job satisfaction that would contribute to a smooth operation. An honors graduate from the state university may not be happy as a clerk-typist and may become a disruptive influence.

In recent years, however, standardized testing as a means of determining recruitment and promotion for government jobs has come under fire from several quarters. Spokesmen from minority groups have been quick to point out that many tests are standardized on a white, middle-class basis which may have no relation to the ability of a minority person to do the job. Tests that are so constituted generally have a discriminatory effect on black and Spanish-speaking applicants. Government jurisdictions that rely on such tests, the minority spokesmen claim, have built institutionalized racism into the recruitment and promotion patterns.[6] In response to such criticism by minority organizations, the federal Office of Personnel Management agreed to drop its main recruiting test for administrative generalists, the Professional and Administrative Career Examination (PACE), in 1981.

Public personnel officers, the people who see themselves as guardians of the merit system, generally are reluctant to abandon competitive examinations. Good tests—tests that validly predict performance in particular jobs—are the principal means with which to implement the values of open competition and occupational ability. Most public personnel officers seem to realize that tests must be realistically tied to job requirements and labor market conditions.

In the early 1970s, the Ford Foundation sponsored research in which the U.S. Civil Service Commission (CSC) and the Educational Testing Service (ETS) studied the problem of relating tests to job requirements. The research involved three types of federal employees: (1) medical technicians, (2) cartographic technicians, and (3) inventory management specialists. The results of the intensive six-year project indicated that "carefully selected written tests predict job performance fairly for minorities and non-minorities." Good test scores reflected good job performance as measured by the supervisor's appraisal, work samples, and job knowledge. The CSC-ETS study indicated that it is possible to develop more or less culture-free, valid tests for specific narrowly defined jobs. The development of these particular tests, however, was extremely time-consuming and costly. Furthermore, more generalized management jobs may not be so amenable to tests that can accurately predict minority performance. The lesson of the research is clear: tests that are accurate predictors of minority and nonminority performance can be developed in some areas if the jurisdiction is willing to spend the money that is needed to develop them.[7]

Court decisions and national legislation, however, have placed the burden of proving the validity of testing on governmental jurisdictions. In *Griggs* v. *Duke Power Company,* the Supreme Court held that a private employer's requirement that a candidate for promotion have a high-school diploma or pass a standardized intelligence test unduly discriminated against black candidates. The court noted that neither require-

---

6. For an excellent critique of testing in general see James M. Fallows, "Tests and the Brightest: How Fair are the College Boards?" *Atlantic* 245 (February 1980): 37–48.
7. An extensive review of this study was presented by William A. Gorham, "Is Testing Fair for All? New Answers on Employment Tests," *Civil Service Journal* 13, no. 2 (October–December 1972): 8–12.

ment was significantly related to the job under consideration and the artificial standard imposed by the requirements worked "to disqualify Negroes at a substantially higher rate than white applicants."[8] The case involved sections of Title VII of the Civil Rights Act of 1964. The Equal Employment Opportunity Act (EEO) of 1972 applied these provisions of the Civil Rights Act to all governmental jurisdictions, as well as to the private sector. The issue is clear: if the racial or gender makeup of a governmental agency differs substantially from the racial and gender composition of its labor market, only a valid job-related test would absolve the agency from discrimination charges.[9]

In a sense, government agencies need not worry about whether their tests for entry or promotion are valid as long as their racial, ethnic, and gender mix falls within Court-recognized guidelines. To a large degree for any jurisdiction, these guidelines follow the federal government's *Uniform Guidelines on Employee Selection Procedures,* which recommends the four-fifths or 80 percent rule. Under the four-fifths rule, if agency personnel selections result in a staff that has less than 80 percent of the proportion of the racial, ethnic, or gender makeup of the relevant labor market, there is a *prima facie* case that the selection criteria of the agency have an "adverse impact" on particular groups that do not get hired in the numbers that one would statistically expect.[10]

Of course, good personnel management consistent with true merit principles calls for tests that are fair and that do measure skills needed for successful job performance. Written tests can be an efficient way to achieve this goal (see Table 6.1). Until equal employment opportunity became legally binding on governments at all levels, validity of tests for many government jobs was not an issue. As a result, testing sometimes brought the best test-takers, not the best workers, into government.

---

8. *Willie S. Griggs et al.* v. *Duke Power Company,* 401 U.S. 424 (1971).
9. *See* Dee Ann S. Horstman, "New Judicial Standards for Adverse Impact: Their Meaning for Personnel Practices," *Public Personnel Management* 7, no. 6 (November–December 1978): 347–353.
10. U.S. Department of Justice and Department of Labor, Equal Employment Opportunity Commission and Civil Service Commission, *Uniform Guidelines on Employee Selection Procedures,* August 1978, Section 4. *Also see* John D. Kraft, "Adverse Impact Determination in Federal Examinations," *Public Personnel Management* 7, no. 6. (November–December 1978): 362–367.

TABLE 6.1
Comparison of Tests with Alternative Ways of Assessing Recruits

Method	Validity	Cost
1. Written tests of knowledge, skill, or ability	Moderate to high	Low to moderate
2. Performance tests/assessment centers	Moderate to high	High
3. Probation period	Moderate to high	High
4. Job element examining	Moderate	Moderate
5. Ratings of experience and education/training	Varies	Moderate
6. Supervisory ratings	Low to moderate	Low
7. Self-ratings	Low	Low
8. Interviews	Low	Varies
9. Reference checks/background investigations	None to low	Varies
10. Physical characteristics	None to low	Low

SOURCE: "Personnel Research Roundup," *Civil Service Journal* 17, no. 4 (April–June 1977): 22.

Rigidities of Testing as a Merit Criterion

TESTING practices in public employment have not just raised the ire of minorities. Public managers who prize flexibility have two main complaints against testing procedures: the time-consuming nature of test administration, and the rigid tying of scores to selection. In state and local bureaucracies, a five- or six-month wait between the time an applicant takes a test for a particular job and the time the position is filled is not uncommon. The long time between examination and getting a job in civil service in many jurisdictions implies that good candidates will be willing to take temporary jobs or collect unemployment insurance while they wait to hear from the personnel office. In a recession, government can operate that way and still find qualified people. For particular jobs that are in demand, however, procedures that delay the appointment of available, qualified candidates almost ensure that they will find employment elsewhere.

There is some evidence that there has been a change in the length of time required for state governments to administer tests to prospective applicants and to prepare the eligibility lists that public managers must use for hiring permanent employees. A nationwide study of state personnel systems, undertaken as part of a major reform effort in New Jersey, reported that the median number of work days between administering an open competitive examination and preparing an eligibility list was twenty days when only one test was involved and thirty-five days when two or more tests were given for a certain job.[11] This length of time—far more reasonable than five months—reflects efforts to offer walk-in exams and continually update lists for such routine positions as typists and stenographers. For these jobs, recognized tests are able to determine a definable level of skill precisely. For less routine jobs—that of a planner, for example—more elaborate tests must be designed. These tests usually take far longer to process.

Rigidly tying test scores to selection of the candidate for the job can create problems for management. Generally, in government jurisdictions in the United States, the testing agent (either the Civil Service Commission or the personnel management agency) administers tests to applicants and draws up the eligibility lists. Depending on the laws covering that particular jurisdiction, the manager in a particular agency that is seeking to fill a position is allowed to choose from among the top few candidates. In some places, the manager must choose the person with the top score. More generally, however, the "rule of three" prevails. Under the rule of three, the manager has the freedom to choose any one of the top three candidates on the eligibility list.

This limited choice can be a problem on two counts. First, in some jurisdictions, test scores are carried out to fractions of a percent. In New York City, some tests are scored to three decimal places. In such a case, a manager might be faced with choosing among three people who had scores of 96.583, 96.582, and 96.581. Perhaps a person who scored 96.579 has certain other skills or aptitudes that would make him or her best for the job. But under the rule of three, *by law,* only the top three can be considered. Many managers feel that the rule artificially constrains their choice and undermines the basic notion of merit as the ability to do the job. Personnel management reform efforts in New Jersey, New York City, Massachusetts, and other places have sought to eliminate the use of fractional percentage scores in developing lists of eligible candidates.

A second problem with the rule of three relates to affirmative action.

11. Robert P. DeNicholas and Carl F. Lutz, "The New Jersey Merit System in Transition," *Public Personnel Management* 8, no. 1 (January–February 1979): 1–6. Data relating to testing are on p. 4.

If women or minority groups are underrepresented at some level in the agency, the agency, by law, is supposed to make an effort in good faith to make sure that equal employment opportunity does exist. But if white males are at the top of the list, the manager cannot violate the rule of three to take a black or a woman who may be number four on the list. The rule of three inhibits managerial discretion and could inhibit agency efforts at affirmative action. Therefore, reform efforts at the state and local levels have tried to change the rule of three to a rule of five or even six.

Yet another reason that managers often feel constrained by the rule of three is the nearly universal practice in American jurisdictions of giving veterans bonus points on tests for government jobs. Generally, following the federal practice, veterans' bonuses amount to five points (or ten for disabled veterans). In some jurisdictions—Massachusetts and New Jersey, for example—veterans have absolute preference. This means that a veteran who passes a test for a state job in those states automatically goes to the top of the list. Even if a woman scored 99.9 on a test and a male veteran got the minimum passing grade, the veteran would have to be hired. Absolute veterans preference has been upheld in the courts. It appears that all veterans preference is immune from court challenge on equal employment opportunity grounds.[12] Furthermore, veterans preference is popular with veterans groups and legislators. President Jimmy Carter's Civil Service Reform Act of 1978 originally included a provision that would have limited veterans preference to a one-time bonus to help the returning veteran. Veterans groups successfully defended the system that allows veterans to claim bonus points for every federal examination they take during their careers and also to have a favored position if they are among the top three on the eligibility list. Personnel professionals generally call for the end of veterans preference, but political realities will ensure that veterans will continue to get additional consideration for government jobs in most jurisdictions.

Although testing procedures tied to the merit system do introduce complications that limit a manager's flexibility in hiring and promotion, there are many ways around such regulations. One way in which many jurisdictions get around the testing lags is through provisional appointments. Sometimes such appointments provide the mechanism for hiring a well-qualified person who might find another job if the red tape of the testing procedures were not cut. At other times, provisional appoint-

---

12. *See* Kraft, "Adverse Impact Determination," pp. 366–367. The key Supreme Court case is *Personnel Administrator of Massachusetts* v. *Feeney,* 440 U.S. 903 (1979).

ments provide an opening for a politician to get a job for a friend. Often provisional appointments are provisional in name only. Such appointments can take on the effective status of regular appointments. In some jurisdictions, some people hold jobs on provisional status for three, five, or even ten years. Since provisional appointments do completely avoid the testing aspects of merit determination, a person who could not meet the stated qualifications for a particular job might nevertheless be sequestered in that job for years on a provisional basis.

If a manager is not able to arrange a provisional or temporary appointment, there are ways to see that a particular person whom the manager wants to hire gets within the top three of the certified eligibles. The longer the time lag between examination and actual job placement, the better the chance that the top scorers will find and accept other jobs. People who have high scores can be discouraged from continuing their interest in a particular job. Bold managers and personnel people may even ask them to decline "voluntarily" the position for which they had expressed interest. Soliciting such a declination is illegal in many jurisdictions, but it is done. These actions could not occur without the knowledge and complicity of personnel officials.[13]

Performance Appraisal

EFFECTIVE personnel management does not stop once a person has been hired. Any good personnel system would reward and promote employees on the basis of merit. In government jurisdictions, a variety of performance appraisal techniques are used to help determine such basic personnel actions as promotion, training and development, disciplinary measures including firing, and (within limits) pay. The Carter reforms at the federal level and similar reforms in some state and local governments have focused increased attention on performance appraisal.

In general, people think the idea of performance appraisal is good. They believe that people should know where they stand in their jobs. Most of the studies of employee motivation have pointed to feedback as an important component of job satisfaction.[14] People at work are often evaluating the performance of others in informal ways. When formal at-

---

13. *See* Jay M. Shafritz, "The Cancer Eroding Public Personnel Professionalism," *Public Personnel Management* 3, no. 6 (November–December 1974): 486–492.
14. *See* chapters 4 and 5.

tempts at performance appraisal are undertaken, however, both supervisors and employees become anxious. Part of this anxiety is caused by lack of confidence in the formal instruments used in much performance appraisal in both government and the private sector. This anxiety is compounded if, as in much of the public sector, supervisors are required to discuss their ratings with the people they rate.[15]

The easy way to alleviate this anxiety is to treat the process as a game that must be played to satisfy the demands of the personnel office. If the performance appraisal process is treated as a game, the potentially valuable management information that an honest appraisal would produce will be lost to the organization. Since performance appraisal can be a useful tool in so much personnel work, we should face up to some of the difficulties and try to improve the process.

Most performance appraisal forms used in government are variants of rating scales for various traits determined to be relevant to job performance. In the rating scale technique, the rater is asked to mark a scale value on a form to describe the degree to which the person being rated displays that particular trait. Any number of traits can be used in the evaluation. Among the traits that are commonly used at lower levels in organizations are quality of work, job knowledge, cooperativeness, dependability, initiative, and attitude toward the job. For higher-level jobs other traits could be used. Among these might be leadership, analytical ability, decisiveness, or emotional stability. Figure 6.1 shows a portion of a typical rating scale form.

Rating scales are widely used because they are so easy to construct and to understand. The results can be treated statistically and can provide a clear comparison among the individuals being rated. Rating scales like the one in Figure 6.1 are subject to several errors that tend to undercut the faith that employees and even supervisors might have in the results, however. There are several kinds of errors that personnel experts have associated with this simple rating scale. The *halo effect* occurs when a person who is exceptionally strong in one trait is incorrectly perceived to be strong in other traits. A negative halo effect, where a person's extreme weakness in one trait is carried over to other traits by the rater, could happen. An *error of central tendency* happens when the evaluator refuses to discriminate among his or her employees. Instead, all employees are rated as virtually the same. The *constant error* occurs in large

15. Herbert H. Meyer, Emanuel Kay, and John R. P. French, Jr., "Split Roles in Performance Appraisal," *Harvard Business Review* 43, no. 1 (January–February 1965): 123–129.

FIGURE 6.1
Example of a Typical Rating Scale

ASSIGN A RATING ACCORDING TO THE FOLLOWING SCALE:

5—EXCELLENT and/or FAR EXCEEDS job requirements
4—ABOVE AVERAGE and/or EXCEEDS job requirements
3—AVERAGE and/or MEETS job requirements
2—BELOW AVERAGE and/or PARTIALLY MEETS job requirements
1—UNSATISFACTORY and/or DOES NOT MEET job requirements
N/A—Not Applicable
N/O—Not Observed

FACTORS	RATINGS	COMMENTS (ATTACH EXTRA SHEETS IF NECESSARY)
JOB KNOWLEDGE: Thoroughness and depth of knowledge of occupational field and its application to specific work duties.		
QUALITY OF WORK: ACCURACY		
SKILL		
THOROUGHNESS		
QUANTITY OF WORK: Output, amount of work performed and organization of work and time.		
COMMUNICATION SKILLS: ORAL		
WRITTEN		

---

organizations when different supervisors apply different standards. Some bosses, like some teachers, are lenient; others are hard. Constant error holds that those employees with the lenient boss will be the recipients of favorable appraisals and those with the tough bosses will lose in the race for whatever benefits a favorable rating bestows on the rated persons. Sometimes bosses consciously reward their employees with good ratings for *organizational reasons.* Bosses can channel some organizational rewards to their subordinates by giving them artificially high ratings.[16]

In addition to these kinds of errors, there are some others. A common problem in performance appraisal is the *recency error.* To clear the desk as soon as possible, some bosses might not consider the whole rating period but only think back to what the employee did last week. Those who were cooperative, dependable, and so on recently might get better ratings than someone who had a series of bad days just last week. In any rating system based on traits, there will be subjective components. If the boss does not like an employee, the rating scale might reflect that feeling. The possibilities of errors in the performance appraisal form because of *personal bias* cannot be ignored.

Because there are problems with trait rating systems is no reason to discard them. Trait rating forms can be improved by assigning statements to describe the degree of the trait qualifying for a certain rating (see Figure 6.2). The raters can be trained. They can be rated on their ratings by their superiors. Raters can be encouraged to keep notes of employee contributions during the full rating period so they will not have to rely on memory when they fill out the forms. Rather than being forced to use the same traits for all jobs, raters might be able to convince the personnel office that some traits are not relevant to the jobs their subordinates are doing. There is a lot of potential flexibility in the way performance appraisal based on traits can be used.

Generally, however, forces combine to make trait rating scales less useful than they could be. Personnel offices usually want to add up all the points on the form and categorize employees by their final scores for all kinds of purposes. Supervisors tend to give their subordinates high scores because those scores will determine the employees' status in the organization. Since a supervisor will be working closely with his or her employee often for years to come, negative evaluations might poison interpersonal relations between supervisor and subordinate. The pressure on the supervisor is to live and let live—to give everyone a better-than-average rating.

Some research supports the contention of those supervisors who do not take performance appraisal seriously. Herbert Meyer, Emanuel Kay, and John French found that criticism has a negative impact on the achievement of goals and that praise has little effect one way or the

---

16. Dale S. Beach, *Personnel: The Management of People at Work,* 3rd ed. (New York: Macmillan, 1975), pp. 326–327.

DIRECTIONS FOR EVALUATORS: Place a check mark in the appropriate box on the numerical scale from 1 to 10, based on the following standards:

- outstanding and far exceeds job standards, check the box numbered 10;
- above average, exceeds job standard, check 7, 8, or 9;
- average, meets job standards, check box 4, 5, or 6;
- below average, does not meet job standards, check box 1, 2, or 3.

SUGGESTIONS: Consider only one factor at a time. Don't let your rating in one influence your rating of another. Base your judgment on the requirements of the job and the subordinate's performance in it as compared with the standards of performance. Carefully read the description of each factor before making each entry, and assign the rating which most nearly describes your objective evaluation.

FACTOR	BELOW AVERAGE 1 2 3	EVALUATION AVERAGE 4 5 6	ABOVE AVERAGE 7 8 9	OUTSTANDING 10
JOB KNOWLEDGE Adequacy of professional/technical skills, experience and knowhow to do the job.	Lacks the understanding, skills and experience to perform the job. Requires constant supervision.	Has sufficient knowledge, skills and experience to perform tasks with a minimum of guidance.	Has a good knowledge of the work to be performed. Above average understanding of procedures.	Has a thorough understanding of the job and all related procedures, laws, regulations and technical tasks. Extensive professional/technical skill and experience.
PRODUCTIVITY: **Quantity of output** Meeting established quantitative standards of work production in terms of projects products, reports or services.	Fails to meet time deadlines. Production does not meet established standards. Requires a high degree of assistance with output.	Production generally meets output standards, with an average amount of assistance and guidance.	Production goals are met on time, and meet output standards. Accepts additional tasks or increased schedule when requested.	Consistently completes complex production goals on time or ahead of schedule. Regularly produces more than agreed-upon output standards.
Quality of work Meeting established quality standards of work for accuracy, reliability and appearance.	Fails to produce output that meets minimum quality standards. High error rate; requires constant checking for correctness.	Work output generally meets quality standards with normal error rate; requires only occasional audit for correctness.	Work output meets quality standards consistently, with minimum errors & corrections. Strives for quality above the standards.	Consistently produces complex work output at or above the quality standards set for the assignment. Regularly analyzes work and establishes new standards that exceed previous norms.
COMMUNICATION: **Oral** Oral facility with language which expedites results while maintaining relationships; interviewing skills.	Frequently fails to achieve understanding from listeners. Speaks in poorly organized fashion. Has difficulty articulating thoughts.	Has adequate ability in making an oral presentation. Occasionally is required to repeat or amend position to achieve desired response.	Presents ideas and material in an effective manner. Has above average ability to obtain agreement and support for desired goals.	Outstanding ability to present ideas and articulate thoughts to diverse audiences and organizations. Expedites results through ability to command positive responses.
Written Presenting and explaining ideas clearly and effectively in writing; developing written work in a logical and comprehensive manner.	Lacks the ability to provide written communications in a logical, timely and understandable manner. Requires constant re-write and editing.	Written communications readable and understandable with only occasional need for editing & re-writing. Usually completes written assignments within prescribed time limits.	Effectively presents thoughts in writing in a very understandable style, with very little need for interpretation or repetition.	Consistently writes complex directives, letters, reports, etc. in a clear, concise, highly understandable style. Writing is convincing and timely, and achieves desired results.

FIGURE 6.2
An Example of a Chart Rating Scale Based on Traits

Performance Appraisal by Results
May Have Some Problems

A Housing and Urban Development performance appraisal sets out to measure the quality of "judgment" in executives. Of the three standards it establishes as a yardstick, two are "decisions rarely, if ever, questioned by client groups" and "decisions consistently praised by affected groups." Now, while it is the function of a bureaucracy to serve the public, it is not its function to yield to every demand by every "client group"—a euphemism for pressure group. But clearly the executive who [clears] the grant, whatever its validity, or lets the contract, however questionable, is less likely to draw static from his [or her] clients. Client groups are the heart of a bureaucracy's lobby, its partner in a mutual back-scratching society. In that light, the judgment of an agency executive who hopes to get a bonus by resisting the pressures of these groups is indeed questionable.

SOURCE: Leonard Reed, "The Joy of SES," *Washington Monthly* 12, no. 7 (September 1980): 47.

other.[17] Instead of trait rating scales, these researchers and others advocate performance appraisal based on the results achieved by the individual employee and the organization. This is a form of management by objectives (MBO), which requires mutual goal-setting between the supervisor and the employee. MBO also calls for specific measures that can indicate whether an employee is achieving an objective. We will deal with these indicators in the next chapter, where we discuss productivity measures, and in chapter 10, where we discuss MBO.

Performance appraisal based on behavior or results will not be applied to most public employees within the next few years. There are some governments, however, that have begun experimenting with results-oriented appraisal systems for managers. The 1978 reforms in the federal government call for a Senior Executive Service (SES) composed of volunteers from the top civil service grades, who will be rewarded for good performance and penalized for inferior work. Not all high-level administrators automatically become part of the SES. SES members become eligible for bonuses based on whether they meet or exceed MBO-like objectives. Unless there is tight control on what these mutually agreed-to objectives are, there can be serious problems with bonuses

17. Meyer, Kay, and French, "Split Roles."

tied to stated objectives. Performance appraisal by results can be rigged by setting objectives that are easily obtained (see box). After the SES program's first year in operation, not one of the 7000 participating career senior executives received an unsatisfactory rating.[18]

Position Classification

THE basic mechanism for achieving the values implicit in the merit system and equal pay for equal work in the public bureaucracy is the job or position classification system. Although there are several different ways of implementing such a system in American public administration, job classification is generally the organizing of all jobs in a governmental jurisdiction into classes based on duties, the actual work that is to be done; responsibilities, the level of responsibility for planning and executing work; and qualification requirements, the educational or skill level deemed necessary for satisfactory performance of the work. The specific objectives of developing and maintaining a job classification plan are presented below:

1. *to determine the qualities, abilities, and skills required to perform successfully in positions, so that personnel capable of accomplishing the governmental jurisdiction's objectives can be employed*
2. *to analyze each position to assure that it is grouped for pay purposes with positions having similar overall values and to arrive at equitable differentials between and among classes of positions on the basis of an objective evaluation*
3. *to provide a method for the determination of fair and adequate salaries for each class of positions through development of procedures for designing a sound compensation structure to eliminate inequalities and to improve morale*
4. *to provide a written record of evaluation data on each class of positions so that the end result—the grading of classes for pay purposes—is supported by records subject to review at any time.*[19]

Perhaps the main objective of job classification plans is to ensure that a secretary in one agency receives roughly the same pay as a secretary doing similar work in another agency. But questions such as what fair pay should be for a computer programmer in one agency versus a social

---

18. Leonard Reed, "The Joy of SES," *Washington Monthly* 12, no. 7 (September 1980): 43–48.
19. *Classification, Evaluation and Relative Grading of Higher Level Professional and Managerial Positions*, vol. 2 (Frankfort, Ky.: Commonwealth of Kentucky, Department of Personnel, July 1973), p. 1.

worker in another agency call for sophisticated personnel classification techniques. This notion of "comparable worth" is especially difficult to develop.

In many jurisdictions, the outlines of job classification plans are determined by statutes. For example, the Classification Act of 1949, which determined the course of the federal government's job classification system for thirty years, includes definitions of each general schedule (GS) grade level. Each grade level is defined by the nature of the work performed, the type of supervision received, the extent of judgment exercised, and the training or experience required to perform the work. In the federal service, all jobs in the general schedule are graded from GS-1 (elevator operators and messengers) to GS-18 (top career executives). The statutory description of the work done by people in GS-11 jobs, for example, is necessarily vague:

> Under general administrative supervision, performs responsible work of considerable difficulty, exercising wide latitude for independent judgment, [and] requiring somewhat extended professional, scientific, or technical training and experience which has demonstrated important attainment and marked capacity for independent work.[20]

One would expect a definition capable of classifying about 150,000 jobs would lack specifics. As in almost all legislation, the executive departments are delegated the authority to develop further standards to make the concepts implied in the hazy definition of GS-11 more applicable to management needs. Until the mid-1970s, the United States Civil Service Commission, now the Office of Personnel Management, developed guidelines for narrative descriptions of various classes of jobs within the various grades. These narrative job descriptions proved to be flexible. Often ambitious people who were willing to take on more responsibility were able to get their jobs upgraded. Managers were often able to add a couple of lines to the narrative description and have a particular job reclassified. Since upgrading meant a raise in pay, this device was used to tie performance to pay if there were no promotional opportunities at a higher grade. This device was especially used when salaries were low. Although such flexibility was good for the manager and often for the individual employee, abuses of the narrative job description threatened the basic goals of job classification—particularly equal pay for equal work and comparable worth.

---

20. Quoted in Milton R. Boss, "Of Job Factors and Benchmarks," *Civil Service Journal* 13, no. 3 (January–March 1973): 12–13.

Study Finds Overgrading Problems in the Federal Government

A Civil Service Commission report has indicated that as many as 150,000 (11 percent) of federal jobs may be overgraded. The report is based on a twenty-one-month study of a random sampling of all federal white-collar jobs. The report also estimated 45,000 jobs (3 percent) may be under-graded, and another 70,000 are likely to have errors in their series or titles. The total cost of all these classification mistakes is estimated at $435 million a year. Agencies are responsible for correcting the misgradings. Reassigning employees and adding duties to misclassified positions are two solutions to the problem, while downgrading employees is generally only a last resort. OPM can authorize agencies to delay demotions associated with correcting classification errors, and the grade and pay retention provisions of the Civil Service Reform Act will give relief to eligible downgraded employees. These two measures are intended to minimize adverse effects on employees while allowing agencies to correct improperly classified positions.

SOURCE: *Civil Service Journal* 19, no. 3 (January–March 1979): 3.

The federal government met the need for a more effective job classification system when it introduced the factor evaluation system (FES) on a pilot basis in 1976. The factor evaluation system, which in other jurisdictions has been called the factor-point evaluation method, attempts to quantify various aspects of each class of jobs in government service. The federal government uses the following nine factors:

1. Knowledge required by the position—*the nature and extent of information and skills needed to perform the work;*
2. Supervisory controls—*the nature and extent of controls over the position, the employee's responsibility, and how the work is reviewed;*
3. Guidelines—*the nature of the guidelines and judgment needed to apply them;*
4. Complexity—*the nature of assignments and difficulty in producing the work products or services;*
5. Scope and effect—*the importance of the job to the work of the agency;*
6. Personal contacts—*the people the employee must deal with to perform the work;*
7. Purpose of contacts—*the reasons that the employee has contact with the people;*
8. Physical demands—*the physical exertion required; and*
9. Work environment—*the employee's physical surroundings.*

Each of these evaluation factors is divided into levels that represent the extent to which each factor is present in the class of jobs being evaluated. Each level in the factor has a certain point value. The point values are assigned on the basis of definitions presented in a key document called the primary standard, which is developed by the Office of Personnel Policies and Standards within OPM. Descriptions that are developed from the factors and levels spelled out in the primary standard are then compared with "benchmark" job descriptions. These are descriptions of real jobs. They are written in the factor format with points assigned.

These benchmark job descriptions are used to determine the classifications of other positions. For example, a personnel specialist or manager can compare the job of a particular operations research analyst with the benchmark for operations research analysts. If the particular analyst whose job is under review does more than the benchmark description, that analyst would get more points—perhaps a large enough number to qualify for a higher GS rating. A higher GS rating means more pay. By using the benchmark, job classifiers supposedly have better guidelines and can establish more equitable grade ratings more easily than they can from traditional narrative job descriptions.[21]

The factor evaluation system does seem to have some advantages over the older narrative technique. The factor format is more systematic and understandable than the rambling narrative descriptions. By relating total points to GS levels and therefore to pay, the classification system supports the equal-pay-for-equal-work and comparable worth concepts more clearly than the more traditional technique does. The system appears to be more consistently applied across very large organizations. Yet the simplicity and quantitative nature of the technique might give one the illusion that job classification is a mechanical process done according to immutable scientific and mathematical principles. The basic definitions in the primary standard could contain flaws that would systematically undervalue some kinds of work and overvalue others. Systems like FES must be periodically reexamined. Perhaps under certain circumstances, the older narrative technique may be more equitable. Although the federal government is committed to FES, most jurisdictions in the United States retain the more traditional format. FES and the traditional narrative technique are compared in Table 6.2.

---

21. For a more detailed account of the FES, *see* Mary Diley, "Personnel Policies and Standards," *Civil Service Journal* 19, no. 2 (October–December 1978): 32–33.

TABLE 6.2
Comparison Between Traditional Classifications System and the Factor Evaluation System in the Federal Government

Traditional Classification System	Factor Evaluation System
Includes eight factors, not all of which apply to all occupations.[a]	Includes nine factors, all of which apply to all occupations covered by FES.
Standards written in long, narrative format.	Standards written in factor format.
Different formats of standards, some with points, some without.	All standards are written in uniform factor format with points.
Position description formats inconsistent.	Position descriptions all written in uniform factor format.
Narrative format makes the classification process quite time-consuming.	Factor format reduces the time needed to classify a position.
Often difficult for employees and supervisors to relate the narrative standard by which their own positions are classified to their own position descriptions.	Easier for employees and supervisors to understand and relate to a standard that is in the same format as their own position descriptions.
Often requires a redescription of the occupation in order to update standards.	Allows flexibility in updating standards by adding benchmarks without need to redescribe occupation.

[a] These are the eight factors formerly used in the traditional classification system: (1) nature and variety of work; (2) nature of supervision received; (3) nature of available guidelines; (4) originality required; (5) personal relationships; (6) recommendations, commitments, decisions made; (7) supervision over others, and (8) qualifications required.

Pay Comparability

THE principle of equal pay for equal work has taken on new meanings in the public sector in the past twenty years. Not only should government workers in roughly the same jobs in different agencies get roughly the same pay, but in some jurisdictions the principle has been established that government workers should be paid roughly the same as people doing the same type of work in the private sector. The idea that public sector salaries should be comparable to those in the private sector is called pay comparability. Because private salaries seem to rise in response to overall economic conditions, governmental jurisdictions that have adopted the pay comparability idea find that their salaries, too, are rising automatically. Therefore, pay comparability plans are often called escalator pay plans.

The federal government has been involved with public-private pay comparability since 1962. A Brookings Institution study of executive manpower in the federal government during the late 1950s uncovered widespread resentment on the part of higher executives. These executives felt they were underpaid for their responsibilities and skills compared to private sector executives. The federal pay scales were such that lower-level employees were marginally better off than their compatriots in the private sector, but higher-level government employees were grossly underpaid if the same comparison were made.[22] Indeed, during the immediate post–World War II era, there seemed to be no guiding pay plan philosophy. Pay increases came through across-the-board cost-of-living adjustments, although recruiting difficulties often influenced pay increases for hard-to-staff positions. Generally, however, as Elmer Staats, the comptroller general, suggested:

> [Pay] legislation was largely a bargaining process in which budgetary costs played a large part and political considerations undoubtedly played even a larger part. Somehow pay bills seemed to come along with surprising regularity in election years, or every two years. Lower paid employees—who were the largest in numbers, the best organized, and hardest hit by price inflation—seemed to fare best in this process.[23]

But as a result of the Federal Salary Reform Act of 1962 and the Federal Pay Comparability Act of 1970, federal salaries are now keyed to those in the private sector. Salaries of the top executives have gone up substantially since 1962. In 1962, top career executives received $18,000. By 1972, because of pay comparability, that figure had doubled. Now, with Senior Executive Service bonus provisions, a top federal executive can earn up to $70,000 once the links of government pay to congressional salaries are severed. Currently career federal employees cannot earn more than congressmen. Those in the middle management grades, GS-11 through GS-15, have seen their salaries go up proportionately, whereas those in the lower grades have not enjoyed such great increases, because salaries in comparable jobs in the private sector have not gone up as sharply as those of the higher-level positions.

The heart of the federal pay comparability process is the annual Na-

22. Franklin P. Kilpatrick, Milton C. Cummings, Jr., and M. Kent Jennings, *The Image of the Federal Service* (Washington, D.C.: The Brookings Institution, 1964).
23. Elmer B. Staats, "Weighing Comparability in Federal Pay," *Tax Review* 34, no. 1 (January 1973): 2.

tional Survey of Professional, Administrative, Technical, and Clerical Pay (PATC survey) conducted by the Bureau of Labor Statistics (BLS). Each year the BLS gathers salary data on roughly eighty jobs in the private sector. These jobs are keyed to similar jobs in the federal job classification scheme. Salaries for these jobs are then adjusted to conform to private sector analogs. A formula is then used to develop a "pay line" that relates the adjusted salaries in the sample jobs to entire GS grades. The Office of Personnel Management and the Office of Management and Budget jointly perform this work, which has resulted in federal workers' receiving an average salary about $2000 higher than the average salary in private industry.[24] Clearly the pay comparability process, designed and managed by federal employees, has been effective in raising federal pay levels without recourse to strikes.

Several questions can be raised about this process. Is the sample of selected jobs broad enough to provide information for determining the entire federal pay scale? Does the sample adequately take into account geographic differences? Does the pay line that is developed adequately reflect differences in responsibilities among grades? Since salaries are only one part of the compensation picture, should fringe benefits also be included in survey?

In 1979, the Carter administration proposed a far-reaching revision of the pay system to bring the salaries and fringe benefits of civilian employees more in line with those of workers doing similar jobs in the private sector. Instead of just *pay* comparability, the proposed revision seeks *total compensation comparability*. For the first time, the value of vacation, health, and other benefits will also be considered in setting federal pay levels. These benefits now make up over 30 percent of the cost of compensating the federal work force.

If the proposed legislation is passed, other problems that the older pay comparability process did not deal with will be addressed. Geographical differences will be a factor. Because prevailing wage rates vary greatly around the country, the federal government has had an advantage in hiring people in areas where the salaries are generally lower, such as the South and Southwest. Similarly, the federal government has had difficulty in holding good people in high-salary areas. It is possible that federal workers in a high-wage area such as New York would receive bigger pay raises if these salary reforms are approved by Congress.

---

24. The 1977 figures were $12,521 for the federal government and $10,522 for the private sector averages. The comparability formulas have probably widened that gap.

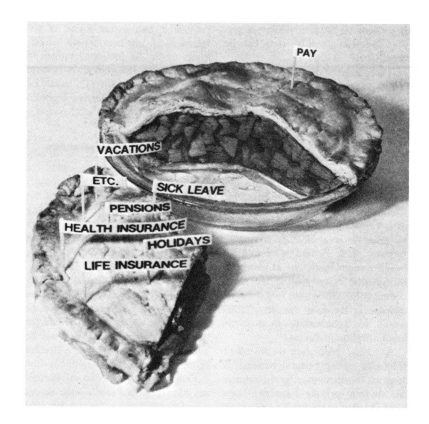

More than a third of the public employee compensation pie goes for benefits. SOURCE: *Civil Service Journal* 19, no. 2 (October–December 1978): 17.

In calculating federal compensation, total compensation comparability also would include the salaries and benefits of state and local government employees as well as those in private industry. Although state and local officials often do work similar to federal government employees, the PATC survey used in the pay comparability process does not look at these jobs. As a result, federal jobs, which have been artificially tied to higher-paying private sector jobs by the pay line, have paid much more than very similar state and local jobs. Therefore, state and local governments have had trouble meeting the competition of the federal government and have had to deal with morale problems caused by the federal-local pay differential.[25]

25. For a concise article on some of the technical and procedural issues in total compensation comparability, *see* Barry E. Shapiro, "What is Total Compensation Comparability?" *Management* 1, no. 4 (Summer 1980): 6–8.

Manpower Planning and Training

ASIDE from trying to develop fair classification and pay plans, public personnel offices are concerned with manpower planning and employee development. Manpower planning is the process by which the personnel needs of the agency are considered in relation to the expected change in mission, growth, and activity of the agency. Manpower planning raises the question of how the organization should be staffed to meet these future needs. As such, manpower planning demands an awareness of future retirements, promotions, and training and development of present employees. It also includes projections for recruiting people with needed skills from outside government.

To this end, government jurisdictions have participated in a wide variety of training activities. Generally this training has emphasized the development of practical, job-oriented skills. There are training programs that cover the specifics of automatic data processing, new techniques in budgeting or personnel classification, and even memorandum

"Not quite—one ankle on top of the other!"

writing. These courses usually last two or three days but might prepare the government worker for further, more specialized work in the particular skills being taught. In the federal government they are conducted by OPM training staffs or consultants, and under the Intergovernmental Personnel Act (IPA), employees of state and local governments have been granted access to those courses run by the Office of Personnel Management.

Often training courses are short-term, one-shot efforts to teach employees a skill that is deemed immediately necessary for a particular agency to have. More recent trends have been to strengthen the training effort by linking a series of these short programs. For example, the Office of Personnel Management runs a series of courses dealing with program evaluation. People who take the basic course could move into related courses and emerge as qualified program evaluators. (Some of these courses are presented in the box.) Similar goals have been met by supporting university study, whether or not it is for degree credit. When the short-lived planning-programming-budgeting system was instituted throughout the federal government in 1965, a limited number of program analysts were trained through a year-in-residence program at selected universities sponsored by the Civil Service Commission, the Bureau of the Budget, and the private National Institute for Public Administration.

Whereas most training in government service at all levels is still oriented to upgrading specific skills of workers on an ad hoc basis, there

---

Office of Personnel Management
U.S. Training Courses in Program
Analysis

Program Evaluation Courses
   Program Evaluation Techniques I
   Program Evaluation Techniques II
   Value Analysis for Management Systems
Systems Approach Courses
   Cost-Benefit Workshop
   Systems Analysis for Government Operations
Technical Courses
   Correlations and Regression Analysis
   Statistical Techniques for Analysis
   Workshop in Decision Logic

are two trends that are now apparent in government training. The first is related to affirmative action programs. Some training programs are designed to upgrade lower-level workers such as clerks and secretaries so that they can qualify for higher-level, professional jobs.[26] The second trend reflects a growing management identity among upper-level public workers. At all levels of government, efforts are being made to create effective public managers through management or executive development programs.[27] Management training is a necessary support for such efforts as the Senior Executive Service in the federal government and the increasingly common managerial pay plans of some larger jurisdictions such as New York City.

Disincentives to Training

ALTHOUGH personnel people tend to see training as a great benefit to the organization, this view is not widely shared outside official public personnel channels. Managers might agree to participate in training programs for a variety of reasons. They may want to reward loyal employees regardless of agency need. This may be especially true if the training involves a three-day retreat to some sylvan grove at a time when there is not too much action at the agency. They may lean on people to participate in training because to do so is in keeping with the standards of that particular agency, where training is seen by top management as a good thing. In these cases, participation in training becomes a sign that the manager follows the forms desired by the personnel office and top management. But he or she need not be concerned with the substance—improvement of skills, performance, or potential—that can help the organization better serve its mission.

Ruth Salinger has noted a disincentive process at work in public sector training. As Figure 6.3 indicates, the benefits of training and development are not clear to many managers, who tend to be more concerned about getting on with the work of the agency or putting out fires in their

---

26. *See* U.S. Civil Service Commission, Bureau of Intergovernmental Personnel Programs, *Improving Opportunities for Employment of the Disadvantaged in State and Local Governments: A Guide for Effective Action* (Washington, D.C.: June 1973).
27. Examples of such programs are the Top Forty Program, run for upper-level New York City managers by the Urban Academy for Management, a private contractor, and the Massachusetts State Agency Management Development Program, which was organized by the University of Massachusetts. Both programs receive money from Intergovernmental Personnel Act funds.

FIGURE 6.3
The Training Disincentives Process

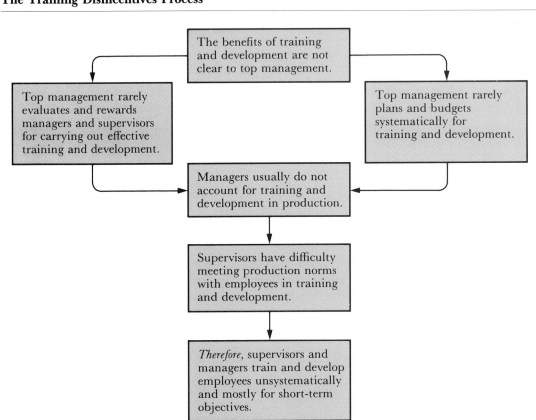

SOURCE: Ruth D. Salinger, *Disincentives to Effective Employee Training and Development* (Washington, D.C.: Bureau of Training, U.S. Civil Service Commission, 1973), p. 13.

bailiwicks. In the absence of meaningful productivity measures, the presumed benefits from training are often the perceived personal happiness and satisfaction of the participants. Top management's belief in the effectiveness of training and development is at best based on faith.[28]

Since reliable productivity measures do not exist for many areas of government work, the only evaluations of the role of training have tended to be a simple numbers game—the number of people participating in training programs during a specified period. Typically, such eval-

---

28. Ruth D. Salinger, *Disincentives to Effective Employee Training and Development* (Washington, D.C.: U.S. Civil Service Commission, Bureau of Training, 1973).

uations, if they may be called that, are simply to see if a manager encourages training, not what effect that training has on the work of the agency. This is not surprising, since a manager's primary responsibility is to see that the work of the agency is done, not to analyze the possible effects of training for his or her employees. But part of effective management is manpower planning. Surely we want human resources available to government when it has to undertake some activity. Training and development with a long-range goal of flexibility of human resources is one way government can be prepared to meet its responsibilities of the future.

Of course, training and development of currently employed workers is not the only way to assure an agency's ability to cope with the challenges of the future. The most obvious alternative to maintaining a vast human resources pool through training and development of current employees would be to contract out to the private sector for services as the need arises. New employees with skills that will be needed in the future also could be recruited when they are needed. The training and development of workers who are already on the job might be more expensive than these alternatives, but training may pay off in better morale if individuals grow through their jobs.

Affirmative Action

IN the United States, governmental jurisdictions have sought to be models of fairness in dealing with women and minority group members. The gross statistics have long shown that employment of minority group workers and women in the federal government has been substantial. In recent years, over 19 percent of the federal civilian work force have been members of minority groups, and roughly 40 percent have been women. A closer look at the data, however, indicates that minority people and women tend to be concentrated in the lower-paying jobs. Although government has thought of itself as a model employer with regard to race and sex—and indeed has outperformed the private sector on this account—the way jobs are distributed in government bureaucracies indicates that there has been institutionalized racism and sexism in government hiring and promotion practices.

The most basic rule of the merit system is that all applicants be considered on job-related qualifications regardless of race, religion, sex, or age. The Civil Rights Act of 1964 sought to outlaw discrimination based on those factors throughout the private sector. Furthermore, that act gave the courts the power to enjoin unlawful conduct and to order relief, including payment of back pay for up to two years prior to filing a charge. The Equal Employment Opportunity Act of 1972 made all government jurisdictions—federal, state, and local—subject to those provisions of the 1964 act.

Merely prohibiting discriminatory practices has not been enough to assure equal employment opportunity. It seems clear that most large-scale employers cannot live up to today's standards of equal employment opportunity unless they consciously develop specific programs of affirmative action to achieve the goals implied in the Equal Employment Opportunity Act. An affirmative action program should not mean that jurisdictions give "preferential treatment" to minority groups or women or that they should "discriminate in reverse." A workable affirmative action program that could gain wide support from all administrative levels must be in keeping with the operational goals of the agency. It should be tied to merit employment concepts of open competition and occupational ability. This can be accomplished by knocking down artificial barriers to equal opportunity, such as inadequate publicity about job openings, unrealistic job requirements, tests that lack adequate validity, and insufficient opportunity for upward mobility.[29]

Interviewing Women Candidates
by Merle Junker

It is difficult to know, sometimes, how to act with someone of another race, another generation, the other sex. What may have been the norm yesterday isn't accepted today and may not be tolerated tomorrow.

Interviewing women as candidates or potential applicants is one situation for which the norms are changing. Here are some rules to go by. They are not intended to establish that any specific behavior is legal or illegal, contrary to federal regulations or not; the perspective is one of common sense, common courtesy, and a professional approach.

As a supervisor filling a vacant position, or as a representative of your agency interviewing potential applicants, you want to do the right thing, to make a favorable impression for your organization, and to avoid embarrassment for yourself and the people you interview. This is an attempt to help.

Use the right words. Try to remember that the women in your office

---

29. For a plan to set up an affirmative action program for state and local governments, see *Improving Opportunities for Employment of the Disadvantaged.*

are not "girls" or "gals." And the woman you're interviewing isn't "swee-tie" or "honey" or "dear"—even if you are a good ol' boy, even if you do call men you've never met before "pal," "chum," or worse.

• Don't inquire into certain areas that are none of your business.

—Her marital status (or nonmarital arrangements) or plans.

—What her husband does, how much he makes, whether he's subject to transfer, how he feels about her working, traveling, or anything else.

—Whether she has any children (or plans to) and how many, what ages or sex they are.

—Arrangements for the care of her children.

—Her views on birth control, abortion, women's lib.

• Don't bring up your prejudices. You're entitled to them, of course, but you aren't entitled to do anything about them on company time.

—Women shouldn't travel alone, shouldn't travel with men, shouldn't stay overnight in another city.

—Women aren't aggressive enough.

—They are too emotional.

—They never stick with a job.

—They won't accept travel assignments.

—That women want to work only until marriage, or that they all want to marry.

—That women are absent from work more than men.

—That they use more sick leave than men.

—Women don't want responsibility.

—Can't supervise men.

—Can't supervise women.

—Aren't interested in certain fields.

—Aren't mobile.

• Don't flirt, don't be patronizing ("you'll find lots of boyfriends"). Don't presume: Interviewers sometimes take advantage of an interviewee's friendliness to act as if there is a degree of friendship.

• Don't joke. Some men find it embarrassing to behave toward women in a completely businesslike way. It can bring on the same kind of feelings you had as a child when you were trying to lie and thought the smirk you were suppressing must be obvious to everyone. The fact is that when women are treated as adult human beings, they don't notice anything strange about it—or you.

• Incidentally, in making a selection or recommendation, it is improper to give consideration to such factors as the following.

—That supervisors or managers might prefer men.

—Customers/clients wouldn't want to deal with women.

—Coworkers might object.

—Women's work lacks credibility.

—The job involves travel, or travel with the opposite sex.

—It involves unusual working conditions.

• It is improper to place undue emphasis on conditions of employment in the hope of discouraging the candidate, i.e., to solicit a declination. It is for the applicant, not the employer, to decide whether or not she wants the job—based, of course, on a clear explanation of what the conditions are.

• Finally, don't indicate your interest in a woman candidate as one whose selection would help improve your EEO picture (it's an insulting suggestion that you'd apply different standards).

The general rule is that one should treat women applicants and men applicants in the same way. But it doesn't make it right if you also go through the motions of asking men, say, about their prospects for parenthood: The point is that in most cases men have no reason to suppose that any improper significance would be attached to the answer, whereas women do.

Discriminatory behavior is as improper when it is not intended as when it is, and the appearance can be as important as the reality. That you ask certain questions not related to the job wouldn't show that you mean to discriminate necessarily, but such questions can be used and have been used in a discriminatory way, and women are increasingly aware of and resentful of this. The fact that certain questions are not relevant to consideration for employment is why they are improper when introduced into an employment interview.

There are a lot of *don'ts.* Where, you may ask, are the *do's?* What *can* you talk about? Simple: There's the job, its duties and responsibilities. The organization, its missions, programs, and achievements. Career possibilities and opportunities for growth, development, advancement and facilities available (especially important with scientists). The individual's qualifications: abilities, experience, education, interests. The wonder is that one can cover all the ground that needs to be covered, let alone have any time left for irrelevancies.

One last rule, though. Don't go the other way: Don't take pains to point out how fair-minded you and your organization are (it will sound phony anyway) or give an instant replay of every female success story. And don't make a big deal about being mature: If you've decided to go along with "Ms." and avoid masculine pronouns when you mean man or woman, at least don't put them in italics.

SOURCE: *Civil Service Journal* 14, no. 2 (October–December 1973): 3–4.

Specific programs for affirmative action in hiring and promoting employees can have both qualitative and quantitative goals. An example of a qualitative goal would be the improvement of attitudes of supervisors and other employees with regard to affirmative action matters. Another

Photo courtesy U.S. Civil Service Commission.

Mary Francis Hoyt, the second appointee under the provisions of the Civil Service Act and the first woman appointee. Miss Hoyt was appointed to a $900-a-year clerkship in the Bank Redemption Agency of the Treasury Department.

example of a qualitative goal might be the improvement of grievance and discrimination appeals processes. Generally, qualitative goals of affirmative action programs are simply extensions of good management practices. Quantitative goals, however, often present management with another problem. Official directives usually take pains to describe quan-

183

titative goals as flexible "targets" rather than mandatory "quotas." There is considerable controversy over the status of such numerical targets or quotas. Yet, as Catherine Lovell has argued:

> Numerical objectives have emerged for the present as the only feasible mechanism for defining with any clarity the targets of action and the criteria for evaluation of progress toward achieving them within a given period of time. Thus, the courts have upheld the validity of goals and quotas in civil rights enforcement efforts and have stated that color-consciousness and sex-consciousness are both aproprirate and necessary remedial postures.[30]

Far from seeing quotas as being bad because they encourage what some feel is discrimination in reverse, Lovell feared that quotas tend to become identified with particular job slots. As such, quotas designed to be targets for progress become maximums rather than minimums and tend to perpetuate race and sex discrimination.

Often the anti-affirmative action forces raise the question of finding "qualified" minority people or women for a particular job. Few people would argue that government bureaucracies should consciously seek to lower the quality of services that they render, even for the sake of some social goal that is external to the immediate agency objectives. The question of quality of service, however, cannot be dealt with on the basis of formal credentials alone. A complex set of factors has excluded women and minority people from pursuing career patterns that follow the standard white middle-class male model. These alternative patterns probably prepare women and minorities to bring additional perspectives to public policy problems. Opting for these different perspectives and different values may enhance the quality of government service rather than lower the level of such service.

One of the ways to use these differing perspectives in government is to upgrade the skills of women and minorities already employed. The Equal Employment Opportunity Act of 1972 maintains that governmental agencies should provide opportunities for their employees to advance so they can perform at their highest potential. The federal government's response to this requirement has been to develop upward mobility programs to upgrade the skills of personnel in the grades below GS-9. The Office of Personnel Management requires that all agencies develop upward mobility plans as part of their general equal employ-

30. Catherine Lovell, "Three Key Issues in Affirmative Action," *Public Administration Review* 34, no. 3 (May–June, 1974): 236. This piece was part of a symposium on affirmative action in public employment, which appeared in the same issue.

ment opportunity planning. To aid in the development of such plans, the OPM has issued the following guidelines:

1. *Establish training and education programs designed to provide maximum opportunities for employees to advance so as to perform at their highest potential.*
2. *Ensure that agency job qualification standards do not constitute unwarranted barriers to upward mobility.*
3. *Create career development plans for lower-level employees who demonstrate potential for advancement.*
4. *Establish personnel procedures and career systems to increase opportunities for advancement, training, and education for lower-grade employees.*
5. *Conduct positive programs of occupational analysis, job redesign, and job restructuring to provide new opportunities for entry employment, advancement, and bridges to higher-grade jobs.*[31]

Such upward mobility plans can only work if they are keyed to projected manpower requirements and specifically to restructured jobs. Furthermore, such plans can work only if management is committed to staffing some projected higher-level jobs through an upward mobility program.

Fair and equal treatment of applicants and employees has been a goal of the federal government since the end of World War II. Now, with the passage of the Equal Employment Opportunity Act, what was an intention has become the law for government jurisdictions at all levels. The development of affirmative action programs, which can eventually enhance government operations without creating undue tensions in the short run, is one of the greatest challenges to the management of public bureaucracies.[32] Already concern to defend agencies from accusations of institutionalized racism or sexism has led public personnel managers to key tests and performance appraisal instruments more to jobs, thus furthering merit principles.

Political Neutrality and the Political Rights of Workers

ATTEMPTS to pursue affirmative action can enhance the open competition and occupational ability features of the merit system. Achieving the third main feature of the merit system, political neutrality, calls for different kinds of personnel action. This action lies at the heart of public-

31. "Equal Opportunity," *Civil Service Journal* 14, no. 4 (April–June, 1974): 21.
32. The exchange between Harry Kranz and O. Glenn Stahl deals with these issues. See *Public Administration Review* 35, no. 1 (January–February 1975): 121–125.

private management differences, because attempts to maintain political neutrality greatly limit management prerogatives. Such attempts also limit the rights of public employees as individuals to express their political preferences.

The ideal of a politically neutral civil servant is almost as old as the republic. President Thomas Jefferson in 1801 thought the best way to achieve an impartial government and protect the rights of all federal workers was to keep government employees out of "the business of electioneering," which he found to be "inconsistent with the spirit of the Constitution and [their] duties to it."[33] Of course, it was much later when the Civil Service Act of 1883 placed some limits on campaign contributions from federal workers. Under the spoils system, federal workers, as a condition of their employment, often were forced to give a percentage of their annual salary to the party in power. In 1907, President Theodore Roosevelt, who had been one of the first U.S. Civil Service commissioners earlier in his career, prohibited career employees from all political activities except voting and stating opinions.

Political activity by federal career employees is proscribed by the Political Activities Act of 1939, which is known as the Hatch Act after its sponsor, Senator Carl Hatch, a Democrat from New Mexico. The Hatch Act prohibits federal employees from using their official authority or influence to interfere with an election and prohibits direct and indirect coercion to force another public employee to contribute to a candidate or party. It also bars employees from taking an active part in partisan political management or political campaigns. The first two prohibitions limit corrupt administrative practices designed to perpetuate an elected official's hold on political office. The political activity prohibition, however, limits political action by public employees as individuals. This provision has been controversial.

Early amendments to the Hatch Act extended the political activity prohibition to District of Columbia employees and to state and local government employees whose principal activities are financed by federal funds. They also permitted federal employees residing in areas where the majority of voters are federal employees to take part in local political activities. Several states passed laws designed to limit the political activities of their employees who were not covered by the expanded Hatch Act. These state acts are called little Hatch acts.

The provisions limiting political activities of individuals have been

---

33. Quoted in Neal R. Peirce and Jerry Hagstrom, "Is it Time to Hatch Federal Workers from their Nonpartisan Shells?" *The National Journal* 9, no. 16 (April 16, 1977): 586.

challenged in the courts, but the Supreme Court has upheld the ability of the Congress and state legislatures to regulate the political activity of public employees to maintain the "efficiency and integrity" of the civil service.[34] The last major court challenge was in *United States Civil Service Commission* v. *National Association of Letter Carriers* in 1973. The court recognizes that the main problem facing the Hatch Act and similar laws is "to arrive at a balance between the interests of the employee, as a citizen, in commenting upon matters of public concern, and the interest of the government, as an employer, in promoting the efficiency of the public service it performs through its employees."[35] By not striking down the Hatch Act, the Court implies that it successfully maintains that balance.

Although the Hatch Act has weathered constitutional challenges in the courts, it continues to face political challenges. The old Civil Service Commission and the successor agency, the Merit Systems Protection Board, have avoided confrontations over the political activity provisions by rarely enforcing them. Only a handful of violations are successfully processed each year, and generally these are glaring violations such as running for office while attempting to hold a career job in the public bureaucracy.

In 1975, the CSC modified the Hatch Act restraints on political activities of state and local officials who come under the federal provision. This was done to conform with the more liberal little Hatch acts of the states. According to these changes, state and local government employees in federally funded grant programs may take active parts in political management and political campaigns and may be candidates for political party office such as a position on the national committee of a political party.[36] These more relaxed standards indicate the direction of change in the Hatch Act and similar laws.

Hatch Act reform measures have been offered in every Congress since 1966. Changes in the restrictions on political activity passed both houses in 1976 but were vetoed by President Gerald Ford. Support for changes comes from government unions and such organizations as the American Civil Liberties Union. These groups contend that the Hatch Act unnecessarily denies First Amendment rights to government employees. They

---

34. *See United Public Workers of America* v. *Mitchell*, 330 U.S. 75 (1947), and *United States Civil Service Commission* v. *National Association of Letter Carriers*, 413 U.S. 548 (1973). For a case supporting a little Hatch act against constitutional challenge, *see Broadrick* v. *Oklahoma*, 413 U.S. 601 (1973).
35. *Letter Carriers*, p. 549.
36. U.S. Civil Service Commission, Bureau of Intergovernmental Personnel Programs, *Summary Statement Regarding Activity of State or Local Officers and Employees* (Washington, D.C.: October 1975), p. 2.

contend that the restrictions on the use of official authority and tough prohibitions against coercion of federal employees are enough to protect the integrity of the civil service. They see competitive selection and promotion as the keys to preventing the return of the spoils system.

Opponents of Hatch Act changes maintain that the need to restrict the political activity of federal bureaucrats continues. The opposition forces often express a strong antiunion bias. It is the inherent political nature of union activity that creates the increasingly strong calls for revisions of the political activity sections of the Hatch Act.

Political Neutrality, Professionalism, and Control

LEGISLATURES and the courts see efforts to maintain political neutrality as necessary for the efficiency and integrity of the governmental work force. Another aspect of this drive toward political neutrality may have far-reaching effects on that efficiency and integrity. The long-term trend toward increased professionalism in public bureaucracies raises some difficult questions about democratic control of the public service. Some recent court cases have made this issue even more important.

Frederick Mosher argues that professionalism is a significant aspect of the public service today.[37] More than one-third of all the people who fit into the census category of "professional, technical, and kindred" workers are employed by government. Even if schoolteachers, who are professionals, are omitted from the figures, governments employ a greater proportion of professional people than the private sector does. The number of professionals within public bureaucracies raises two areas of conflict that concern us: (1) conflict among different professions in agencies, and (2) conflict between professionals and politicians.

Although a large number of people representing different professions is needed to enable government agencies to accomplish their complex missions, some agencies have come to be dominated by one profession. Generally, Mosher notes, in those public agencies that have been in operation for a long time, one occupational group whose skills and knowl-

---

37. This discussion is drawn from Frederick C. Mosher, *Democracy and the Public Service* (New York: Oxford University Press, 1968), pp. 99–133. *Also see* two symposium issues of the *Public Administration Review:* 37, no. 6 (November–December 1977), and 38, no. 2 (March–April 1978).

edge are closely identified with the agency's mission takes on an elite status within that agency. Lawyers rule the roost in the Department of Justice; geologists have the power in the Geological Survey; and physicians are the controlling force in the Public Health Service. This pattern of professional control holds at the state and local levels, too. Civil engineers usually reign in public works agencies and highway departments. Social workers run welfare agencies, and psychiatrists dominate mental health agencies. Professional educators control schools and state and local departments of education. The elite profession within an agency maintains its power vis-à-vis other professions within the agency by controlling access to key decision-making positions. The real power positions within the agency are usually filled by members of that elite profession. Having access to the key jobs enhances the career ladder for members of that profession. It can create tensions, however, with members of other professions, whose skills are also needed for the agency to accomplish its mission but whose career opportunities within the agency are limited.

Elite professions keep their control over their agency by exercising power through personnel matters. The future bureaucratic leaders—as opposed to political appointees—of most professionally dominated agencies must rise through a more or less prescribed career pattern. Generally, this pattern involves a person's entering the agency at a low position after some advanced academic work or other training. That person progresses through a series of jobs, each of which usually demands more responsibility, as he or she progresses up the ladder. As people work their way up the organizational pyramid, competition gets more intense, because there is always less room at the apex than at the base of the pyramid. In some career systems, such as the military or the foreign service, there are specific provisions for "selection out." If one fails to get promoted after a period of time, he or she must leave the organization—be selected out—to make room at the top for people capable of being promoted. In these career systems, there is little "lateral entry" (joining the elite profession within the organization without having started at the bottom).

Such systems tend to be self-perpetuating. People higher up in the professional hierarchy tend to choose people who are acceptable to themselves—often like themselves—for promotion. This puts a premium on conforming behavior. The conformists are promoted; the mavericks are selected out. The personnel in such agencies have not been chosen for their abilities to deal with new problems, but rather for their abilities to handle traditional problems in an acceptable—usually a tradi-

189

tional—manner. The strong control of an agency by its elite profession means that the agency reflects the perspectives and orthodoxies of that profession. Such an agency may not be amenable to new ideas unless the inadequacies of the old ways of handling problems become glaringly apparent. Even then, an elite profession may be hesitant to share its power with another profession whose skills may be needed to fulfill the agency's mission properly.

Of course, not all the elite professions dominate their agencies to the same extent. Mosher suggests five channels through which professional influence can be brought to bear on an agency:

1. *Through the election or appointment of professionals to high political . . . office. . . .*
2. *Through the effective control, often a near monopoly, of the significant managerial and operating positions of administrative agencies by individual professions. . . .*
3. *Through professionals who operate within agencies they do not dominate. . . .*
4. *Through the bringing of ideas, modes of thought and pressures upon political executives and legislative bodies and their appropriate committees by professionals. . . .*
5. *Through the influence of professionals at one level of government on the operations and policies of another level through . . . their counterpart professionals at that other level.*[38]

Table 6.3 presents Mosher's estimates of the relative importance of these five channels of influence for several professions. Only lawyers and military professionals use all five channels.

There is built-in hostility between the professions and politics. As Mosher noted, "Professionalism rests upon specialized knowledge, science and rationality. There are *correct* ways of solving problems and doing things. Politics is seen as constituting negotiation, elections, votes, compromises—all carried on by subject-matter amateurs."[39]

Professionals who are entrenched in particular agencies are able to keep their power and independence by controlling personnel policies within their agencies. That such independence violates the spirit of a democratic society is obvious, but ardent professionals might claim that control by professionals leads to more efficient, more effective, better-run

---

38. Frederick C. Mosher, "Professions in Public Service," *Public Administration Review* 38, no. 2 (March–April 1978): 145–146.
39. Mosher, *Democracy,* p. 109.

TABLE 6.3
Channels of Influence of Different Professions on Governmental Policy and Conduct

	Top Political Office	Professional Agency Control	Professionals Operating in Other Agencies	Professional or Other Interest Group	Inter-Governmental
Military	X	XX	X	XX	X
Foreign Service	X	XX	X	O	O
Education Administration	X	XX	O	XX	XX
City Management	XX	O	O	X	X
City Planning	O	XX	X	X	X
Police	O	XX	O	X	X
Law	XX	XX	XX	XX	X
Accounting-Auditing	O	X	XX	O	X
Engineering	O	XX	X	XX	XX
Economics	X	X	XX	O	O
Mental Health	O	XX	O	XX	XX
Sciences	O	XX	X	X	X

SOURCE: Frederick C. Mosher, "Professions in Public Service," *Public Administration Review* 38, no. 2 (March–April 1978): 146.
Key: XX = strong or frequent channel of influence
    X = moderate or occasional channel of influence
    O = weak or rare channel of influence

government than reliance on amateurs operating through the political process. This claim needs to be examined.

Francis Rourke suggests two criteria by which we can assess the bureaucratic policy-making system:

> The first is the *responsiveness* of the system—the extent to which it promotes a correspondence between the decisions of the bureaucrats and the preferences of the community or the office-holders who presume to speak for the public. The second is the *effectiveness* of the system—the degree to which it leads to decisions which are more likely than alternative choices to bring about the outcomes that are desired.[40]

These criteria, responsiveness and effectiveness—which correspond to political and professional norms, respectively—deal with the difficulties of having administrators act in the public interest.

What combination of responsiveness versus effectiveness seems to produce an acceptable level of quality in what government does? Having

---

40. Francis E. Rourke, *Bureaucracy, Politics, and Public Policy*, 2d ed. (Boston: Little, Brown, 1976), p. 3. Emphasis added.

dealt with the experience of two large cities, Theodore Lowi made some suggestions. The reform movements that brought about a professional bureaucracy have led to a governmental paradox whereby, Lowi maintained, "cities like New York became well-run but ungoverned." The good government reform movements drove out the old-style political machines, which were responsive to public desires. New machines came into the power vacuum that was created. These new machines, according to Lowi, are the "professionally organized, autonomous career agencies," which are not neutral in a policy sense but are certainly independent. Each agency "shapes important public policies, yet the leadership of each is relatively self-perpetuating and not readily subject to controls of any higher authority." Mayors of such modern cities have no way of forcing the new bosses—the bureau chiefs and career commissioners—to be loyal to anything but their agency, its work, and related professional norms.[41] Presidents evidently feel the same way when trying to deal with the federal bureaucracy.[42]

Although Lowi saw most cities as having succumbed to professionalization of their bureaucratic units to an excessive degree, he saw Chicago as a city that was, in fact, governable. He attributed this to the strong political power of the late mayor, Richard Daley, who, more than any mayor in any major American city since 1950, most approached the power of the old-line machine bosses.[43]

Why does Chicago have a different style of power from New York? Why are public bureaucracies highly professional in some areas of the country but more responsive in others? Jay Shafritz has suggested that the political culture of the jurisdiction is one factor that should not be overlooked in assessing merit systems and bureaucratic professionalization. Political culture is important because it significantly contributes to what the citizens within the jurisdiction think constitutes a quality public personnel system. If political culture is considered, there can be no absolute standards by which personnel systems can be judged. As Shafritz pointed out: "While some zealots advocate the tightest possible merit system mechanisms, others with equal vigor and concern for the

---

41. Theodore J. Lowi, "Machine Politics—Old and New," *The Public Interest* no. 9 (Fall 1967): 86–88. For a more explicit statement on Chicago, but one that covers the same ground, *see* Lowi, "Gosnell's Chicago Revisited Via Lindsay's New York: Forward to the Second Edition," in Harold F. Gosnell, *Machine Politics: Chicago Model* (Chicago: University of Chicago Press, 1968), pp. 7–16.

42. Arthur M. Schlesinger, Jr., *A Thousand Days: John F. Kennedy in the White House* (Boston: Houghton-Mifflin, 1965), p. 406.

43. For an excellent discussion of political power and Mayor Daley, *see* Mike Royko, *Boss: Richard J. Daley of Chicago* (New York: E. P. Dutton, 1971).

efficacy of operations cry out for greater discretion on the part of managers and an eventual dissolution of straight jacket civil service procedures. Honest critics may differ on what constitutes quality personnel programs."[44]

The courts, however, have taken a firm stand favoring professional values over political ones. They have steadily narrowed traditional notions of patronage and have effectively elevated a government jobholder's claim to his or her job to a constitutional right to that job. In *Elrod et al., Petitioners* v. *John Burns et al.* in 1976, the Supreme Court held that a public employee cannot be forced to relinquish his or her right to political association as a price for holding a nonpolicy-making government job, even though that job was originally awarded on the basis of patronage.[45] In *Elrod* the Court declared that the patronage firing of sheriff deputies in Cook County (Chicago), Illinois, violated the First and Fourteenth Amendments to the Constitution. In *Branti* v. *Finkel* in 1980, the Court moved its notion of a nonpolicy patronage job higher.[46] In *Branti,* assistant public defenders were ruled not to be policy-makers and not to be confidential employees, two categories of employees that the Court recognizes can be fired solely on the basis of political affiliation. Therefore, the Court held that they could not be fired because of their party affiliation.

The effect of the *Elrod* and *Branti* cases will be to limit the number of upper-level political appointments incoming political executives will be able to make. This will exacerbate the problems of executive control over the permanent bureaucracy and will likely make public employees less responsive to democratic demands.[47]

Summary

FOR years, public personnel administation has hindered effective management in the public sector. As Jacob Ukeles of New York City's Man-

---

44. Jay M. Shafritz, "Political Culture—The Determinant of Merit System Viability," *Public Personnel Management* 3, no. 1 (January–February 1974): 39.
45. 427 U.S. 347 (1976).
46. 99 S. Ct. 3095 (1980). For more background and possible effects of these cases, *see* Robert M. Kaus, "Zbig for Life," *The Washington Monthly* 12, no. 4 (June 1980): 25–32, and Kaus, "How the Supreme Court Sabotaged Civil Service Reform," *The Washington Monthly* 10, no. 9 (December 1978): 38–44.
47. For an excellent discussion of the problems of political control over the permanent government at the national level, *see* Hugh Heclo, *A Government of Strangers: Executive Politics in Washington* (Washington, D.C.: The Brookings Institution, 1977).

agement Advisory Board said: "To manage, you need the ability to hire and fire, to redeploy, to change responsibilities. And [in the public sector] you don't have those things."[48] In the name of the merit system, rigid civil service rules and regulations at all levels chained management to invalid and unreliable testing systems and overly narrow classification systems which prevented the effective use of personnel. In the past ten or fifteen years, however, a greater concern for more effective management has given new meaning to public personnel administration.

Two legislative milestones at the federal level have marked changes in public personnel management at all levels of government in the United States. These laws are the Intergovernmental Personnel Act of 1970 and the Civil Service Reform Act of 1978. In combination, these laws have encouraged several progressive actions in personnel management. Among the more important are these:

1. *Decentralization of personnel decision-making authority;*
2. *Separation of the personnel executive and the merit protection functions;*
3. *Establishment of links between compensation and performance;*
4. *Rationalization of classification systems;*
5. *Creation of a separate managerial identity.*[49]

These changes are occurring at all levels of American government, although not in every jurisdiction.

Changes in personnel practices will not result in vastly improved government in the short run. Customs and laws have governed many personnel actions in the past. These customs and laws will not change overnight. As the *Elrod* case suggests, legal interpretation might further weaken management's hand in attempting to make the personnel functions more responsive to public concerns. In addition to legal barriers to management action, the rise of public sector unions greatly limits managerial control. In the next chapter we will look at this phenomenon, which is the most active force changing public personnel management today.

---

48. Quoted in Ken Auletta, *The Streets Were Paved with Gold* (New York: Vintage Books, 1980), pp. 182–183.
49. Peter Allan and Stephen Rosenberg, "New York City's Approach to Civil Service Reform: Implications for State and Local Governments," *Public Administration Review* 38, no. 6 (November –December 1978): 579–584. The authors do not attribute these actions to federal legislation.

**Suggestions for
Further Reading**

Balk, Walter L., ed. "Symposium on Productivity in Government." *Public Administration Review* 38, no. 1 (January–February 1978).

Beatty, Richard W., and Craig Eric Schneirer. *Personnel Administration: An Experiential Skill-Building Approach.* Reading, Mass.: Addison-Wesley, 1977.

Bolton, John R. *The Hatch Act: A Civil Libertarian Defense.* Washington, D.C.: American Enterprise Institute, 1976.

Cayer, N. Joseph. *Managing Human Resources: An Introduction to Public Personnel Administration.* New York: St. Martin's, 1980.

Gellerman, Saul W. *The Management of Human Resources.* Hinsdale, Ill.: Dryden, 1976.

Hatry, Harry P., Louis H. Blair, Donald M. Fisk, John M. Greiner, John R. Hall, Jr., and Philip S. Schaenman. *How Effective Are Your Community Services? Procedures for Monitoring the Effectiveness of Municipal Services.* Washington, D.C.: Urban Institute, 1977.

Heclo, Hugh. *A Government of Strangers: Executive Politics in Washington.* Washington, D.C.: the Brookings Institution, 1977.

Herbert, Adam W., ed. "Symposium on Minorities in Public Administration." *Public Administration Review* 34, no. 6 (November–December 1974).

Klingner, Donald E. *Public Personnel Management: Contexts and Strategies.* Englewood Cliffs, N.J.: Prentice-Hall, 1980.

Krislov, Samuel. *Representative Bureaucracy.* Englewood Cliffs, N.J.: Prentice-Hall, 1974.

Mosher, Frederick C. *Democracy and the Public Service.* New York: Oxford University Press, 1968.

———, and Richard Stillman, II, eds. "Symposium on the Professions in Government." *Public Administration Review* 37, no. 6 (November–December 1977) and 38, no. 2 (March–April 1978).

Stanley, David T., ed. "Symposium on the Merit Principle Today." *Public Administration Review* 34, no. 5 (September–October 1974).

CHAPTER SEVEN

Public Sector
Labor-Management Relations

THE PHENOMENAL GROWTH OF public sector employee unions since the early 1960s is the single most important change in public personnel management. The policy implications of strong public employee unions are greater than the effects of affirmative action or organization development because of the magnitude of resources involved. Government activity is primarily service activity in which personnel costs are a much greater proportion of the total cost than in manufacturing operations. Organized public employees have sought to improve the salaries and benefits of their members. Insofar as they have been successful, they have contributed to the increased costs of government. Increased costs of government, when combined with taxpayer resistance to pay for these costs, often mean that policy choices will be forced on governmental decision-makers.

In this chapter we will discuss some of the reasons for the rise in public employee unionism, what the unions want, and how they go about getting what they want. We will also deal with ways in which government has sought to develop bilateral labor-management relations which approximate such relations in the private sector in some ways but which differ in other ways because of the public nature of government.

The Changing Character of Public Unions

THERE has been a long history of public employee associations in the United States, but associations designed to negotiate with public sector managers are a relatively recent development. In the federal government, postal employee unions were formed shortly after the passage of the Pendleton Act in 1883. The first permanent postal union, the National Association of Letter Carriers, was influential in convincing Congress to pass an eight-hour work day in 1888. Successor unions and the servicewide National Federation of Federal Employees played a strong role in passing the Lloyd-LaFollette Act of 1912, which protects the rights of federal employees, as well as the Retirement Act of 1920 and the Classification Act of 1923.

Until the 1960s, public employee associations generally were content to seek benefits for their members by lobbying in the legislatures rather than by confronting public managers. Indeed, as Frederick Mosher has pointed out, the aims of the public unions "were fundamentally *simpatico* with civil service; like the career systems, they shared with civil service the common enemy of patronage. Civil service provided a guarantee of tenure and security and an orderly, predictable system for personnel decisions."[1] Furthermore, at the federal level especially, these unions were successful in lobbying for favorable wages, hours, and fringe benefits for the bulk of low- and middle-grade workers. The relationship whereby the public unions accepted the paternalism of civil service commissions and worked to improve pay and conditions of employment through the legislature seemed to work.

What worked at the federal level did not always work so well at the municipal level. During the late 1950s, public employee unions in strong union cities such as Philadelphia, Detroit, New York, Hartford, and others began to negotiate some issues directly with the public managers, not through legislatures or civil service commissions. Generally, however, public sector collective bargaining was considered illegitimate before the 1960s. Whereas collective bargaining had been officially guaranteed and encouraged in the private sector with the passage of the Wagner Act of 1935, arguments had been raised that collective bargaining based on the private sector model would not be possible in the public sector. Most of these arguments centered around the ultimate union weapon in the private sector, the right to strike—an action in which some local public unions had already engaged.

In 1919 Calvin Coolidge, then governor of Massachusetts, ended the Boston police strike with the ringing declaration: "There is no right to strike against the public safety by anybody, anywhere, any time."[2] Coolidge's statement raised two basic arguments that had been used to hinder public sector employee organization and bargaining until the 1960s. These arguments are concern for sovereignty and concern that government continue to supply essential services.

The sovereignty argument was based on the English common law principle that the king, the sovereign, could do no wrong. Sovereignty can be exercised by a king, or, more in keeping with contemporary society, the body politic through its elected representatives. In any case, the sovereign is supposed to have the unilateral power to determine whether an individual or group of individuals can initiate a claim against the state. This sovereignty doctrine assures that public manage-

---

1. Frederick C. Mosher, *Democracy and the Public Service* (New York: Oxford University Press, 1968), pp. 179–180.
2. Quoted in Claude M. Fuess, *Calvin Coolidge: The Man from Vermont* (Hamden, Conn.: Archon Books, 1965), P. 226.

ment and labor cannot be equals at the bargaining table. Since private sector collective bargaining is based on the premise of equality between the parties, many observers held that public sector bargaining could never approach the private sector model.

In its most elemental form, the sovereignty doctrine holds that because the state possesses the power to decide whether a claim can be made against it, the government cannot enter into a contract with a union. This claim, however, is absurd on its face, since governments at all levels in the United States have been making contracts with businesses since the birth of the republic. If a contract negotiated with a corporation does not violate the government's sovereignty, certainly a contract negotiated with a union does not diminish the government's sovereignty.

The view that the sovereignty doctrine only allows the government employer, acting unilaterally, to establish the terms and conditions of employment was accepted civil service dogma as late as 1960.[3] Few people would seriously raise the sovereignty argument today as a means of completely dismissing the rights of government employees to organize for the purpose of collective bargaining. Still, elements of the sovereignty doctrine have been incorporated into the labor-management arrangements that have developed since the early sixties. The sections on "management rights" incorporated in comprehensive public sector labor-management legislation are vestiges of government's attempts to protect its sovereignty. In recent years, however, public employers have been willing to forego "boiler plate" management rights clauses in contracts in favor of reference to past practices. This trend away from formally stated management rights is similar to that in the private sector. As private management developed more experience in bargaining, it felt confident enough to use some management rights as bargaining chips.

Although the sovereignty argument has not kept public employees from organizing and bargaining collectively with public management, the rhetoric of sovereignty still prevails in the widespread American practice of outlawing strikes by public employees.[4] It is not that such laws have much effect, but they are on the books and do force penalties

---

3. U.S. Civil Service Commission, *The Government Personnel System,* Personnel Management Series no. 4 (Washington, D.C.: U.S. Civil Service Commission, November 1960).

4. Several states permit public employee strikes under certain conditions. These states are Alaska, Hawaii, Minnesota, Montana, Oregon, Pennsylvania, Vermont, and Wisconsin. Prince George's County in Maryland also gives public employees a limited right to strike.

*A Typical Managements Rights
Section in Public Sector Labor
Law*

(a) Subject to subsection (b) of this section, nothing in this chapter shall affect the authority of any management official of any agency—

(1) to determine the mission, budget, organization, number of employees, and internal security practices of the agency; and

(2) in accordance with applicable laws—

(A) to hire, assign, direct, layoff, and retain employees in the agency, or to suspend, remove, reduce in grade or pay, or take other disciplinary action against such employees;

(B) to assign work, to make determinations with respect to contracting out, and to determine the personnel by which agency operations shall be conducted;

(C) with respect to filling positions, to make selections for appointments from—

(i) among properly ranked and certified candidates for promotion; or

(ii) any other appropriate source; and

(D) to take whatever actions may be necessary to carry out the agency mission during emergencies.

(b) Nothing in this section shall preclude any agency and any labor organization from negotiating—

(1) at the election of the agency, on the numbers, types, and grades of employees or positions assigned to any organizational subdivision, work project, or tour of duty, or on the technology, methods, and means of performing work;

(2) procedures which management officials of the agency will observe in exercising any authority under this section; or

(3) appropriate arrangements for employees adversely affected by the exercise of any authority under this section by such management officials.

SOURCE: ¶7106, Title VII, Civil Service Reform Act of 1978, P.L. 95–454, 92 Stat. 1111.

on unions and union members who withhold their services.[5] Public employees are not supposed to strike against the public employer because governments are supposed to provide essential services to society. An interruption of the flow of these essential services, it is often held, would

5. Examples of such laws are New York State's Taylor Law and Ohio's Ferguson Law.

repudiate the will of the people who demand that such services be supplied by government. Such an action would violate the canon of representative government whereby the elected representatives of the people provide for the demands of the people.

But what are "essential services" in government? Most people might recognize fire and police services as being essential. But do social workers provide essential services? Ask a welfare recipient whose check did not come. Do teachers? Ask a working couple whose children have to be kept at home. Do transit workers? Try finding another way to get to work. It has been difficult to try to draw the line between nonessential and essential services provided by government, except in the case of police and firefighters.

The question of whether work stoppages by public employees performing essential services can be tolerated becomes more complicated when one considers that government does not have a monopoly on the provision of essential services. As far as the public is concerned, a strike has the same effect whether it occurs in a private hospital or in a public one. With many jurisdictions contracting with private corporations to provide such governmental services as school transportation, garbage collection, and other services, the distinction between private and public employees becomes more blurred. Should government ban all strikes in all essential services provided by either the public or the private sector? The question has profound policy implications, but the political power of labor unions in the private sector makes it moot.

The question of the right to strike boils down to the effect that the right has on collective negotiations. Some observers maintain that there cannot be meaningful negotiations unless the right to strike is available as a sanction for the public union. Although the public union can use political pressure to meet its objectives, such moves are not as dramatic and do not produce results as fast as a strike.[6] Others argue that public sector collective bargaining takes place in a political arena and both parties must develop politically workable agreements. The highly politicized environment serves to encourage bargaining in good faith on both sides.[7]

---

6. Louis V. Imundo, Jr., "Some Comparisons Between Public Sector and Private Sector Collective Bargaining," *Labor Law Journal* 24, no. 12 (December 1973): 810–817.

7. Robert D. Helsby, "A Political System for a Political World—In Public Sector Labor Relations," *Labor Law Journal* 24, no. 8 (August 1973): 504–511.

The Legal Basis
for Public Sector
Collective
Bargaining

ALTHOUGH there is still some controversy over the right of public employees to strike, there is now widespread recognition that public employees have the right to organize. Public employees working for the federal government were granted this right in a historic executive order promulgated by President John F. Kennedy in 1962. This right was reaffirmed in Title VII of the Civil Service Reform Act of 1978, which brought federal labor–management relations under statute law rather than executive orders. State and local government workers, however, depended on the individual states to grant them the kind of bargaining rights that federal law granted to private sector workers in 1935.

Government labor-management relations is one area in which states have been innovators—some states, that is. In the absence of federal law governing public employees' rights to organize and bargain, state practices vary, but several states—notably Wisconsin, Hawaii, and Oregon—have blazed a trail through the thicket of public sector labor relations. In 1959 Wisconsin passed a series of statutes granting public workers the right to organize and bargain with public sector managers rather than the legislature or the civil service commission. Other states followed Wisconsin's lead, some out of predilection backed by strong union political support within the state, and others in order to head off proposed federal attempts to establish national guidelines for structuring governmental labor-management relations at the state and local levels. The effort at federal regulation of state and local public employee relations ended in 1976 when the Supreme Court, by a bare five to four majority, held in *National League of Cities* v. *Usery,* that Congress "may not force directly on the state its choices as to how essential decisions regarding the conduct of integral government functions are to be made."[8] Although *Usery* dealt with an application of the Fair Labor Standards Act to state and local government, the Court's opinion effectively relieved the states of the fear of federal legislation in this area and ended many state legislative efforts to emulate Wisconsin and the other states that had adopted comprehensive legislation regarding governmental labor-management relations. Therefore, state law relating to this area is quite varied, as indicated in Table 7.1.

---

8. 426 U.S. 833 (1976).

TABLE 7.1
State Collective Bargaining Laws

Coverage	States
1. All-inclusive laws	Florida,[a] Hawaii, Iowa, Massachusetts, Minnesota, Montana,[b] New Hampshire, New Jersey, New York,[a] and Oregon
2. "All" employees, separate laws	Alaska, California, Connecticut, Delaware, Kansas, Maine, Nebraska, North Dakota, Pennsylvania, Rhode Island, South Dakota, Vermont, and Wisconsin
3. *Some employees covered:*	
Teachers	Indiana and Maryland
Police and fire	Kentucky, Oklahoma, and Texas
Fire	Alabama,[c] Georgia,[c] and Wyoming
All but state civil service	Michigan and Washington
Local employees and teachers	Nevada
Fire and teachers	Idaho
Local employees and police	Missouri
4. No laws	Arizona, Arkansas, Colorado, Illinois,[d] Louisiana, Mississippi, New Mexico,[d] North Carolina, Ohio, South Carolina, Tennessee, Utah, Virginia, and West Virginia
5. *Employees covered by separate laws (even if other employees covered by other laws):*	
Teachers	Alaska, California, Connecticut, Delaware, Indiana, Idaho, Kansas, Maryland, Nebraska, North Dakota, Oklahoma, Rhode Island, Vermont, and Washington
Police and fire	Kentucky, Oklahoma, Pennsylvania, Rhode Island, South Dakota, and Texas
Fire	Alabama, Georgia, Idaho, Wyoming
State service	California, Connecticut, Maine, Rhode Island, Vermont, and Wisconsin

SOURCE: Hugh D. Jascourt, *Government Labor Relations* (Oak Park, Ill.: Moore, 1979), p. 10. Used with permission.
[a] Allow local governments to have own systems if in conformity with state laws.
[b] Except separate law for nurses.
[c] Law operative only upon enactment of local ordinances.
[d] State service under nonstatutory system.

The Wisconsin statutes and other comprehensive public sector labor-management legislation enacted by the states in the 1960s and early 1970s provided five important elements that structured public sector collective bargaining in those states. First, these laws recognized the rights of government workers to organize for the purpose of collective bargaining. Second, they defined the scope of bargaining. Some laws define certain aspects of working conditions, pay, and benefits as mandatory; that is, if the law so states, grievance procedures (for example) must be discussed at the bargaining table. The comprehensive legislation also defines those areas where bargaining is permitted if both sides agree, and it defines other areas that are deemed beyond the scope of collective bargaining. An area that is generally considered beyond the scope of bargaining is, for example, whether a jurisdiction should have particular programs in elder affairs, youth recreation, or any other area of governmental activity.

The comprehensive public sector labor relations laws provided other essential guidelines. Most of these laws defined *unfair labor practices,* such as failure to bargain in good faith, and prohibited the public employers and the unions from engaging in them. See the box for additional examples of unfair labor practices. A fourth element of comprehensive public labor management laws specified the procedures for dealing with collective bargaining *impasses.* Impasses occur when labor and management cannot reach agreement between themselves. Finally, to administer the law, the states that enacted comprehensive legislation established statewide *public employee relations boards* (PERBs).

Typical List of Unfair Labor Practices in the Public Sector

(a) For the purpose of this chapter, it shall be an unfair labor practice for an agency—

(1) to interfere with, restrain, or coerce any employee in the exercise by the employee of any right under this chapter;

(2) to encourage or discourage membership in any labor organization by discrimination in connection with hiring, tenure, promotion, or other conditions of employment;

(3) to sponsor, control, or otherwise assist any labor organization, other than to furnish, upon request, customary and routine services and facilities if the services and facilities are also furnished on an impartial basis to other labor organizations having equivalent status;

(4) to discipline or otherwise discriminate against an employee because the employee has filed a complaint, affidavit, or petition, or has given any information or testimony under this chapter;

(5) to refuse to consult or negotiate in good faith with a labor organization as required by this chapter;

(6) to fail or refuse to cooperate in impasse procedures and impasse decisions as required by this chapter;

(7) to enforce any rule or regulation (other than a rule or regulation implementing section 2302 of this title) which is in conflict with any applicable collective bargaining agreement if the agreement was in effect before the date the rule or regulation was prescribed; or

(8) to otherwise fail or refuse to comply with any provision of this chapter.

(b) For the purpose of this chapter, it shall be an unfair labor practice for a labor organization—

(1) to interfere with, restrain, or coerce any employee in the exercise by the employee of any right under this chapter;

(2) to cause or attempt to cause an agency to discriminate against any employee in the exercise by the employee of any right under this chapter;

(3) to coerce, discipline, fine, or attempt to coerce a member of the labor organization as punishment, reprisal, or for the purpose of hindering or impeding the member's work performance or productivity as an employee or the discharge of the member's duties as an employee;

(4) to discriminate against an employee with regards to the terms or conditions of membership in the labor organization on the basis of race, color, creed, national origin, sex, age, preferential or nonpreferential civil service status, political affiliation, marital status, or handicapping condition;

(5) to refuse to consult or negotiate in good faith with an agency as required by this chapter;

(6) to fail or refuse to cooperate in impasse procedures and impasse decisions as required by this chapter;

(7) (A) to call, or participate in, a strike, work stoppage, or slowdown, or picketing of an agency in a labor-management dispute if such picketing interferes with an agency's operations, or

(B) to condone any activity described in subparagraph (A) of this paragraph by failing to take action to prevent or stop such activity; or

(8) to otherwise fail or refuse to comply with any provision of this chapter. . . .

Source: ¶7116, Title VII, Civil Service Reform Act of 1978, P.L. 95–454, 92 Stat. 1111.

The success of any of the state laws governing public sector labor relations for state and local employees depends on the quality of the public employee relations board of the state. Because there are no uniform laws covering public employee relations nationwide, each state is free to structure and name its PERB as it sees fit. Some agencies performing the functions of a PERB are called just that. For example, the Hawaii Public Employee Relations Board and the Wisconsin Public Employee Relations Board are easy to identify. The Florida Public Employee Relations Commission serves the same functions for Florida. Similarly, the Massachusetts Labor Relations Commission is a PERB, although not designated as such by name. In the rest of this chapter, the term *PERB* will be used to describe any agency that has the task of carrying out the functions stated in comprehensive public sector labor-management legislation.

Generally, PERBs appear to be growing stronger. Hugh Jascourt of the Public Employment Relations Research Institute reports that courts tend to affirm the rulings of PERBs and that relatively little litigation or legislation challenges their authority. Furthermore, he notes that chairpersons of the PERBs tend to stay in their position even when there are changes in political parties controlling the state.[9] The stability of the PERBs has encouraged the mature development of labor-management relations in many states.

Congress, however, did not pass statutes to define collective rights of federal workers until the Civil Service Reform Act of 1978 and the accompanying Reorganization Plan No. 2 of that year. Instead, labor–management relations in the federal government were controlled by a series of executive orders issued by presidents beginning with John F. Kennedy in 1962. Until Kennedy's *Executive Order 10988,* the federal government did not formally recognize the rights of federal workers to bargain collectively with management on any subject. Kennedy's order upheld the right of federal employees to organize for collective bargaining, but it emphasized management rights and severely limited the bargainable issues to personnel policies and matters affecting working conditions. Negotiation on such items as pay and fringe benefits—the staples of bargaining in the private sector and for public employees in some states—was specifically denied to the federal unions.

Despite the restrictive nature of EO 10988, it did recognize collective bargaining in government as a legitimate activity. As such it spurred tremendous growth of union membership in the federal government.

9. Hugh D. Jascourt, *Government Labor Relations* (Oak Park, Ill.: Moore, 1979), p. 12.

Photo courtesy U.S. Civil Service Commission

President John F. Kennedy signs Executive Order 10988, which first recognized the rights of federal workers to organize.

State and local government employees interpreted the executive order as a mandate for change at their level, too. If collective bargaining were accepted as legitimate by the federal government, the historical denial of such rights at the state and local level could be challenged.

EO 10988 sparked a change in the American labor movement. In 1955, the late George Meany, then AFL–CIO president, had given up the idea of organizing public workers. "It is impossible to bargain collectively with the government," he had said.[10] Before 1962, only two states had laws protecting the rights of government workers to organize. Today, only fourteen do not have such laws, and among some of these, court rulings have effectively given public employees the rights to unionize. Public sector workers, including teachers, fire and police personnel, and general government employees, are more highly unionized than private sector workers. The American Federation of State, County and Municipal Employees (AFSCME) has over a million members. So does

---

10. Quoted in Neal R. Pierce, "Employment Report/Public Employee Unions Show Rise in Membership, Militancy," *National Journal* 7 (August 30, 1975): 1242.

the National Education Association, which is a union in all but name. Virtually all public employees in some states, such as Pennsylvania and Massachusetts, are represented by unions. Even in the South, a traditional anti-organized labor area, union membership and representation is becoming widespread (see box).

Membership Rises in Government Unions

Membership in public employee unions continued to increase in 1976–78, according to latest figures from the U.S. Bureau of Labor Statistics, but at a much slower pace than the dramatic rise for the 1968–78 decade as a whole.

Over 3.6 million government workers belonged to unions in 1978. This membership figure represents an increase of 1.5 million public employees added to union rolls since 1968. Broken down, the 1978 figures show that 38 percent of the 3.6 million total were federal employees, including postal employees, and 62 percent were state and local government employees.

In 1978 over 1.38 million federal employees belonged to unions. This was an increase of 82,000 or about 6 percent over the 1.30 million federal members in 1976.

The largest growth, however, took place in state and local government unions. Over the same two-year period, state-local union membership jumped from 1.71 million to 2.24 million.

Total union membership (combined public and private sectors) inched up from 21.1 million in 1976 to 21.7 million in 1978. Public employees accounted for a significant part of this gain.

BLS notes that while total union membership in the United States has shown a slight increase, union members as a proportion of the total work force dropped somewhat. Organized workers comprised 20.3 percent of the total labor force in 1976, and 19.7 percent in 1978.

The membership figures are based on information provided to BLS by 173 unions and 26 professional and state employee associations.

SOURCE: *Federal Labor Management Consultant* (Washington, D.C.: Office of Personnel Management, October 5, 1979), p. 4.

Despite the positive effect of EO 10988 on the public sector organization movement, the substantive provisions of the order were too weak to permit meaningful bilateral labor-management negotiations. Nixon's EO 11491 in 1969 drastically revised the Kennedy order by expanding the scope of bargaining and by providing administrative mechanisms to perform the functions of PERBs in the states. It established a Federal Labor Relations Council and an Office of the Assistant Secretary of Labor for Labor-Management Relations.

Title VII of the Civil Service Reform Act of 1978 replaced EO 11491 as amended by other executive orders with a congressionally passed law. Federal unions had argued for such a law because it is easier for them to lobby Congress than to depend on executive orders that could be changed on a presidential whim. Title VII did little to change the practice of federal labor relations, but put it on a stronger legal foundation. Reorganization Plan No. 2 of 1978 created the Federal Labor Relations Authority (FLRA), which combined the functions of the old Federal Labor Relations Council and the Assistant Secretary of Labor for Labor-Management Relations. The new Federal Labor Relations Authority, whose three members are appointed by the president with the advice and consent of the Senate, is in effect a PERB for federal agencies and employees.

The Collective Bargaining Process

COLLECTIVE bargaining, especially in the public sector, is not a simple process (see Figure 7.1). Before bargaining can begin, a union must be elected by the workers of a particular bargaining unit. The determination of what constitutes an appropriate bargaining unit is important because it greatly affects which union will be elected to represent the workers in the unit and how powerful that union will be. In the private sector, the National Labor Relations Board (NLRB) has the power to define bargaining units using sketchy guidelines written into the Taft-Hartley Act of 1947. For public employees in states having comprehensive labor-management relations legislation, the public employee relations board usually performs this function, although in some states— Hawaii, for example—the bargaining units are actually defined in the law. For federal workers, the Federal Labor Relations Authority determines the unit.

In those states that rely on the PERB to determine specific bargaining units, the following criteria are generally applied:

1. *a clear and identifiable community of interest among the employees concerned*
2. *the effect of the unit on the efficiency of operations*

209

FIGURE 7.1
The Collective Bargaining Process

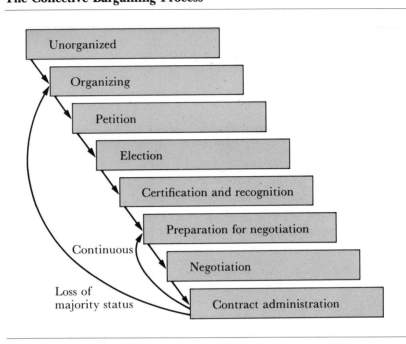

3. *the history, if any, of employee representation*
4. *separation of supervisory and managerial employees from the bargaining unit of nonsupervisory employees*
5. *separation of professional from nonprofessional employees unless a majority of the professional employees vote for inclusion in such a unit.*[11]

In general, public management would like to deal with a few large units representing fairly diverse workers. If there are many smaller bargaining units, a union negotiator can call attention to another contract in a similar jurisdiction: "If you gave X to the teachers, why can't you give Y to us?" In smaller units, union leaders often play a competitive game with other unions to show their membership that they are more militant and better negotiators than some other union's leaders. In smaller bargaining units, there is always the possibility that another union may attempt to gain exclusive recognition as the bargainer for that unit. The

---

11. *1972 Guidebook to Labor Relations: Labor Law Reports* (Chicago: Commerce Clearing House, 1972), pp. 77–88.

possibility of such a challenge to the existing union tends to raise the level of leadership militancy. It is more difficult and expensive for another union to challenge the existing union if the latter represents a very large bargaining unit.

The mechanism for such a challenge is the same as that employed in an effort to seek initial union representation in a bargaining unit. A union petitions the PERB in the relevant state or the FLRA in the federal government for a representation election. Such elections are held in a bargaining unit if a sufficient percentage of employees in that unit sign election petition cards. The percentage required varies according to regulations and laws of the jurisdiction involved. If the PERB or other authorized body recognizes the petition and the appropriateness of the bargaining unit, it conducts a representation election. A majority of the votes cast by the employees in the unit is necessary for the PERB to certify a particular union as the bargaining agent.

Once a union has been certified, the bargaining process can begin. Using the private experience with collective bargaining, Richard Walton and Robert McKersie have developed an analytical framework to explain the labor-management negotiation process. They suggest four types of bargaining: (1) distributive, (2) integrative, (3) attitudinal structuring, and (4) intraorganizational bargaining. Distributive bargaining is the most common form. In distributive bargaining, labor and management are assumed to be in conflict. One side's gain is the other's loss. Integrative bargaining, however, takes place when the parties are not necessarily in direct conflict, but when they recognize that there are common problem areas in which they must cooperate. Attitudinal structuring can be a part of either distributive or integrative bargaining and refers to negotiating activities such as developing trust and respect that serve to change attitudes and relationships. Intraorganizational bargaining concerns those negotiations that take place within the union or governmental jurisdiction to bring about ratification or approval of the agreement reached at the bargaining table.[12]

In the rampant growth years of the public sector union movement, the overwhelming amount of bargaining could be classified as distributive. The expanding public demand for government programs during the 1960s, coupled with generally lagging wages of public employees, created a situation of militant confrontation and general success on the

---

12. Richard E. Walton and Robert B. McKersie, *A Behavioral Theory of Labor Negotiations* (New York: McGraw-Hill, 1965), pp. 4–9.

part of the public unions. In jurisdictions that began to see the very real threat of fiscal collapse during the late 1970s, however, integrative bargaining took hold. Thus in New York, the heretofore powerful unions agreed to "contract regressions"—waiving certain contract provisions that had been previously agreed to—generally realizing that the city's financial plight could be their financial downfall too. As the city's financial position appeared to be less perilous in the early 1980s, however, they did not agree to "give backs"—changes in previously won work rules.

Attitudinal structuring continues to go in the public sector. Originally, unions had to retrain public managers to accept bilateralism as opposed to the old, paternalistic approach that "management knows best." In New York, as well as some other jurisdictions, public managers have been trying to restructure the attitudes of union negotiators to point out that the fiscal wolf is really at the door.

The area of intraorganizational bargaining particularly shows the complexity of public sector labor-management negotiations. On the management side, there is a vast difference in internal ratification activities between public and private employers. In the private sector, once the negotiator gets the backing of the general management group, he or she may sign a binding contract with the union. In the public sector, however, the negotiator must get the backing of the executive branch, then he or she must also get the support of the legislature. In most jurisdictions in the United States, legislative ratification is necessary to implement a negotiated agreement because the legislatures control the purse strings. If a negotiated agreement proves too costly, the legislature can fail to appropriate enough money to cover the costs of the settlement. It might force policy changes that have the effect of abolishing whole programs that may not even have been represented at the bargaining table.

This role of the legislature is a key difference between private and public sector labor negotiations. In the private sector, the principal bargaining issues on either side are economic. In the public sector, as Robert Helsby, a former chairman of the New York State PERB, has claimed, the primary goal of negotiations is political. The parties to the agreement have to balance the needs of the union, the employees, and the public. This must be measured against the level of funding that the executive-employer feels can be committed. Furthermore, the representatives of both labor and management must roughly agree on the political acceptability of any settlement that they work out. Once the union and the executive have arrived at an agreement, Helsby claimed, "both have an obligation to seek legislative approval of their joint product."[13]

Public sector collective bargaining takes place in the political arena. The agreements reached at the bargaining table sometimes affect the level of services provided to the public and the allocation of resources from one area of public concern to another. The outcomes of such bargaining have policy implications of which both parties must be aware. If they fail to understand the policy and political implications of their agreement, the agreement might not survive the political ratification process by the legislature. Failure to achieve political ratification means failure of labor-management negotiation.

A Former Chairman of the United States Civil Service Commission Notes Differences between Private and Federal Labor-Management Relations

The setting for labor-management relations in the Federal service has evolved from the special and unique characteristics of Government as employer—actually, a multiplicity of employers in some 70 departments and agencies employing some 2,000,000 nonpostal civilians. Congressional control over taxation and the budget process, the monopoly character of much of government's activities and the concomitant necessity for uninterrupted service, expression of the public will in Federal personnel affairs—these are some of the conditions that make us a very special and unique kind of employer, and distinguish us from employers in the private economy. They do tend to limit the scope of bargainable matters—in ways deemed to be vitally necessary in the public interest.

Notwithstanding these essential differences, however, some critics of the Federal labor-management program blindly favor a wholesale transplant of private sector law, precedents, and practices into Government—root, trunk, and branch. This might work if Government were just another industry. It is not. The Federal program today is a product of the distinctive conditions that exist in Government, just as the private sector program is a product of the quite different conditions that prevail there. What makes the Federal environment so special?

Labor organizations enjoy long and very important relationships with

---

13. Helsby, "A Political System For a Political World," p. 507.

the Congress. Unions in private industry do not lobby their employers for benefits outside and in addition to those negotiated across the table.

Federal employees benefit immensely from a wide variety of statutory and regulatory policies and protections. These have been achieved through significant union input to the political and administrative processes of Government.

The Executive Order itself has fostered a positive approach toward union organizing and dealings. In contrast to the private sector, the Federal Government has adopted a position of neutrality on union representation of its employees. Government officials do not mount "vote no" campaigns in union elections.

The Congress has outlawed the strike among employees of the Federal Government—in recognition of the paramount need to ensure the uninterrupted delivery of services to the public. In its place, there is viable and effective machinery for determining economic and other major personnel benefits. While this removes concerted job action as a lawful weapon in collective bargaining, the Government—as employer—has no desire to deny Federal employees the general level of rights and benefits secured through negotiations in private industry. On the contrary, the rights and benefits that Federal employees enjoy are fully comparable to—and in some ways better than—those in the private economy.

I think it is eminently clear that labor-management policy in the Federal sector cannot be the same as in the private sector. While we have some things in common with collective bargaining as it is practiced in private industry, there are basic and special differences that demand a special and different program for the Federal service.

SOURCE: Robert E. Hampton, "A Report on Bilateralism in the Federal Service," *Civil Service Journal* 15, no. 1 (July–September 1974): 7–8.

Resolving Impasses   Even when both labor and management representatives understand that their negotiations have political implications, there are times when negotiators for both sides cannot reach an agreement. When such an impasse occurs, the classic economic weapon used in the private sector is the strike. However, even in the private sector, unions have recognized that the strike is a blunt weapon, one that should not be used except as a last resort. Since the legitimate strike is generally denied to public sector unions, strikes are not the main method of resolving impasses. Obviously, public employee strikes do occur. One does not have to think hard to recall press reports of garbage piling up, teachers picketing, and transit riders walking because public employees used a strike as a means of breaking an impasse with management. Whether legal or not, strikes are used, but there are other ways to handle impasses.

In both the public and private sectors three main types of appeals machinery are recognized for ending an impasse in a direct negotiating session rather than by resorting to a strike. These methods are: (1) mediation, (2) fact-finding, and (3) arbitration. They represent an ascending order of appeal. Arnold Zack has succinctly defined these terms:

> In mediation or conciliation, the neutral functions as an extension of the direct negotiation process. By separate and joint meetings with the parties, presumably maintaining the confidence of each side, he seeks to expand the area of agreement until all disputed items are resolved.
>
> In fact-finding, as that term is used in the public sector, the neutral functions in a more judicial role, receiving in joint session evidence from the parties in support of their respective positions, permitting examination and cross-examination of witnesses, until he has collected sufficient evidence to prepare a report of his findings and his recommendations for settlement.
>
> In arbitration, the judicial-type procedure also prevails, but the arbitrators' findings are final and binding on the parties rather than advisory, as in fact-finding.[14]

The appeals machinery has been widely used in the public sector and is generally sanctified by comprehensive public sector labor-management legislation in the states. Generally, the state laws enable PERBs officially to recognize when an impasse in direct negotiations has been reached. Once the impasse has been formally recognized, an impasse resolution timetable automatically takes effect. In Hawaii, for example, the parties have fifteen days from the time the PERB recognizes the impasse to reach an agreement through mediation. If the parties cannot agree after the mediation period has passed, they have three days to agree on the selection of a fact-finder. The fact-finder has ten days to make his or her report. If the parties still disagree, the dispute must go to arbitration. The arbitrator must decide the case within twenty days. The timetable spelled out in the Hawaiian law is quite restrictive in that it does not allow much time for the parties to resume meaningful direct negotiations once the appeals machinery has been activated. Other state laws are not quite so restrictive.

Although labor leaders generally applaud the virtues of free, unbridled direct negotiations, there has been a marked move in the public

---

14. Arnold M. Zack, "Impasses, Strikes and Resolutions," in Sam Zagoria, ed., *Public Workers and Public Unions* (Englewood Cliffs, N.J.: Prentice-Hall, 1972), p. 107.

sector to rely increasingly on the appeals mechanism rather than to settle through the initial direct negotiations. Often a public union feels it must protect itself against charges of "selling out to management" by dissidents within the union or potential organizers from another union. Going through the appeals mechanism often shows the rank-and-file members that the leaders are hard negotiators. By taking a demand all the way to arbitration, the union leadership can gain the symbolic reward of being recognized as tough as well as some tangible rewards should the arbitrator split the difference between the management and union proposals. One observer has noted the "narcotic effect" of conventional arbitration. The parties want to go to arbitration because it is an "easy—and habit forming—release from the obligation of hard responsible bargaining."[15] This has been especially true in fire and police contracts. In effect, the impasse resolution mechanisms provided by comprehensive labor-management legislation tend to discourage meaningful direct collective bargaining.

In an effort to resolve this apparent paradox whereby legislation designed to encourage public sector collective bargaining actually leads to adjudicated settlements dictated by arbitrators, some jurisdictions have experimented with a specialized form of arbitration—*final offer arbitration*. In final offer arbitration, the arbitrator is not allowed to split the difference between labor and management proposals. Instead, each party submits its final offer to the arbitrator. After listening to arguments and studying the facts of the case, the arbitrator must then choose one side's entire package. Since there is no possibility of an arbitrator-declared compromise under final offer arbitration, the parties are faced with an all-or-nothing proposition. The theory behind final offer arbitration is that the possibility of losing completely at the arbitration level will encourage labor and management to seek the safety of compromises hammered out through direct negotiation.

In addition to final offer arbitration, there are other attempts to improve the public sector impasse resolution process. One technique, *med-arb,* combines mediation with arbitration. In med-arb, the neutral third party attempts to get the parties to settle between themselves, but, since he or she also has the final authority as an arbitrator, the neutral party must be concerned about the worth of each party's position. Wisconsin has used this technique with reasonable success since 1978. Massachusetts has experimented with joint labor-management committees to im-

---

15. Willard Wirtz quoted in James L. Stern, "Final Offer Arbitration—Initial Experience in Wisconsin," *Monthy Labor Review* 97, no. 9 (September 1974): 40.

prove communications between the parties even when bargaining sessions for fire and police personnel are not being held. In Massachusetts, the joint committee is composed of six labor members (three representing police officers and three representing firefighters) and six municipal management members plus two neutrals. The guiding force behind this committee, which serves as a mediator with the power to recommend final offer arbitration, is former Secretary of Labor, John T. Dunlop, who has served as the committee chairperson.

The kind of arbitration that attempts to resolve an impasse before the contract is approved is called *interest arbitration* to distinguish it from *grievance arbitration,* which is a process designed to have a third party interpret provisions of the contract to which both labor and management have agreed. Interest arbitration—both regular and final offer—has been attacked as an illegal delegation of authority. Generally, the courts have not gone along with this reasoning. In *City of Warwick* v. *Warwick Firefighters,* the court held that arbitrators became public officers, so there was not an illegal delegation.[16] But in other jurisdictions, courts have found illegal delegation of authority. In a Colorado case, *Greeley Police Union* v. *City Council of Greeley,* the state Supreme Court held that binding arbitration was unconstitutional because it removed government decisions "from the aegis of elected representatives, placing them in the hands of an outside person who has no accountability to the public."[17] Whereas the use of interest arbitration is expanding, taxpayer concern over settlements will probably lead to litigation unless the arbitrators overtly assess the ability of the jurisdiction to pay for any settlement.

Although arbitration is generally the final step in impasse resolution in the public sector, several states provide for legitimate strikes. Again referring to the Hawaiian example, if the union does not accept the ruling of the arbitrator, the union can legitimately strike after a sixty-day cooling-off period and upon giving notice to the PERB. Similar provisions occur in a handful of other states.

Despite established impasse resolution machinery, newspaper headlines attest that crippling strikes do occur in the public sector. Whether legally sanctioned or not, such strikes indicate major differences between management and labor. We will now look at some of the issues that are involved in such disagreements.

---

16. 106 R.I. 109, 256 A.2d 206 (1969).
17. 553 P.2d 790, 93 LRRM 2382 (1976). *Also see* the discussion in Jascourt, *Government Labor Relations,* pp. 26–29.

What Public
Unions Want

CLEARLY, the major demands of public sector unions reflect the desire of the membership for increased compensation. In the state and local jurisdictions that permit bargaining over salary and benefits, these items are always at the top of the agenda. Even in those jurisdictions where the unions are forbidden by law or executive order from bargaining directly over salary and benefits, unions push for better salaries and more benefits through the legislatures. In such activity, the unions resemble any other specialized interest group petitioning the legislature.

In practically all jurisdictions that permit any public collective bargaining at all, there are many subsidiary issues relating to personnel policies and working conditions that are bargainable. Perhaps most important to the employees are union efforts to restrict civil service practices in the areas of promotion and layoffs. Traditionally, public service promotion patterns have emphasized the merit principles of open competition and individual capacity. Union contracts generally seek to make management recognize the role of seniority in promotion. Although unions might want promotion based exclusively on seniority, the general contract language often reflects the idea that, all other things being equal, seniority shall govern promotions. This principle has been upheld even in Hawaii, where the collective bargaining law specifically says that collective bargaining agreements must be consistent with merit principles.[18]

Until several years ago, civil service work meant protection from layoffs. Since the recession of the mid-1970s, some unions found it necessary to spell out provisions for layoffs and recalls in their contracts. As with promotion, unions generally try to deal with layoffs based on seniority. The implications of such policies for equal opportunity employment and affirmative action are obvious. Seniority protects the workers who have been in the agency the longest. This leaves minority group members and women subject to the old employment problem of being the last hired and the first fired. If government employee layoffs become an acute problem, minorities and women within the union itself and probably through the courts will challenge the union's seniority preference efforts. The solution to such a problem might be a guarantee that the propor-

---

18. Jascourt, *Government Labor Relations*, p. 16.

tions of minorities and women in the work force do not fall below some established figure because of layoffs based on reverse seniority.

When considering shift and vacation assignments, unions tend to favor seniority as a determining factor. Seniority in these areas has long been accepted in the private sector. If economic conditions threaten public sector employment, however, unions may accept some flexibility on vacations and shifts to protect seniority rights in the face of layoffs.

Most civil service regulations provide that a person who is temporarily promoted to do work in a job that is classified at a higher level than the job he or she was hired to do should be paid at the higher rate. Sometimes, however, such temporary promotions are not formalized. The person ends up doing the higher-level job, but without any increased compensation. Unions generally seek to formalize arrangements through contracts to enable persons working out of classification to be paid automatically at a higher rate.

Not only are the public sector unions interested in the well-being of their membership, but they are vitally concerned about the survival and well-being of unions themselves. This concern is reflected in attempts to get certain union preservation or security clauses inserted into contracts. Most contracts allow for a union dues check-off whereby the employer automatically deducts union membership fees from the employees' paychecks and gives the money directly to the union. This strengthens the union's financial capacity by guaranteeing funds for union activity and sparing the union the effort of collecting dues from the employees.

Public unions are also interested in collecting fees from all workers within a represented bargaining unit. Ideally, unions have sought to establish *union shop* provisions at the bargaining table. Under a union shop provision, all employees in the bargaining unit must join the union within a specified time period if the union is the exclusive bargaining agent for that unit. This enables the union to increase its membership, increase its treasury, and increase its power. Although such union shop provisions are ruled out in the federal government, a handful of states have legalized union shops in the public sector by making such provisions bargainable items.

The public unions in many jurisdictions have, however, won the right to charge employees in a bargaining unit an agency service fee. *Agency shop* provisions in contracts mean that employees in a bargaining unit who do not choose to join the union must pay the union a fee, since the union represents them in contract negotiations and in grievance cases. Agency shops are becoming increasingly common at the state and local levels. It is likely that they will become even more common as a result of the Supreme Court's decision in *Abood* v. *Detroit Board of Education*, which held that the agency shop does not deprive nonconsenting employees of their First Amendment right to freedom of association.[19] Since the agency service fee generally is equal to union dues, agency shops have the effect of doing what the union shop does for the union—increasing its treasury and power.

The unions' desire to increase their power through agency shop and related provisions is reflected in union positions on recruitment. Generally, the unions favor shorter probationary periods for new workers so employees will be eligible to be dues-paying union members sooner than they would with longer periods of probationary status. Although it rarely comes up in contract talks, unions tend not to favor any lowering of merit standards. Generally, the feeling of rank-and-file members is, "We had to pass the test. Why don't they?" Often this stance, which has strong anti-affirmative action implications, is coupled with the demand to upgrade people who met the earlier requirements. Union leadership, however, sometimes takes the enlightened position favoring minority recruitment. Aside from possible altruistic motives, a dues-paying minority group union member is a dues-paying union member.

Many union desires conflict with elements of the merit system and traditional civil service management. Often unions attempt to deal with legislatures directly to clear the path for favorable conditions at the bargaining table. In some cases, however, union goals run counter to legislatively sanctioned civil service activities. Table 7.2 summarizes some of these areas of difference. Boundaries between the two systems will be defined in the courts.

Management Rights and Productivity Bargaining

UNIONS are not the only parties that seek to increase their power through favorable legislation or executive orders. Public management has sought to base a large measure of its power on statutory or executive provisions, too. Specifically, public management has sought to have certain traditional prerogatives of management sanctified as an immutable

19. 431 U.S. 209 (1977).

TABLE 7.2
Some Areas of Conflict Between Union Desires and the Merit System

Subject	Collective Bargaining	Merit Principles
Employee participation and rights	Union shop, agency shop	Equal treatment to each employee Open shop
Recruitment and selection	Union membership and/or occupational license	Open competitive examination
	Entrance at bottom only	Entrance at any level
Promotion	On basis of seniority	Competitive on bases of merit (often including seniority)
Classification of positions	Negotiable as to classification plan	Intrinsic as to level of responsibilities and duties on basis of objective analysis
Pay	Negotiable and subject to bargaining power of union	On basis of analytically balanced pay plan and subject to prevailing rate
Hours, leaves, conditions of work	Negotiable	On basis of public interest as determined by legislature and management
Grievances	Appealed with union representation to impartial arbitrators	Appealed through management with recourse to civil service agency

SOURCE: Frederick C. Mosher, *Democracy and the Public Service* (New York: Oxford University Press, 1968), pp. 197–198, modified.

foundation on which all public sector labor-management relations must be built, but there is a trend to broaden the scope of bargaining.

Management rights limit the scope of bargaining. Management attempts to interpret its rights to unilateral action broadly. By so doing, management is saying to the unions, "We cannot negotiate on that," not "We will not accept your proposal because . . ." and then listing real reasons for rejecting a proposal, rather than dismissing it out of hand as a violation of management rights (see box on scope of bargaining).

Firm adherence to management rights might deter management's involvement in a promising area of public sector collective bargaining— *productivity bargaining*. Productivity bargaining is the attempt by labor and management to agree on productivity standards and what work

FIGURE 7.2
Scope of Bargaining in the Federal Sector

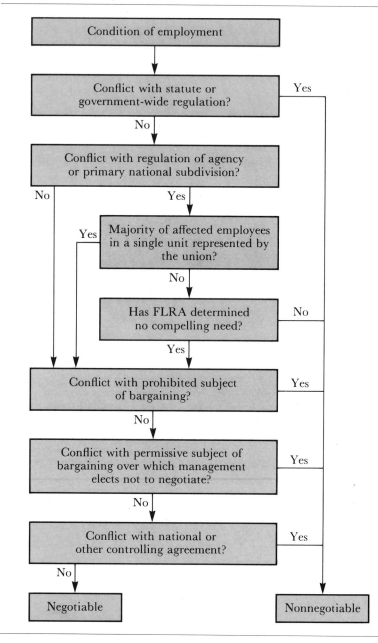

SOURCE: *The Federal Labor-Management Consultant* (Washington, D.C.: U.S. Office of Personnel Management, November 2, 1979), p. 3.

Scope of Bargaining in the Federal Sector

The basic scope of bargaining under the Federal Service Labor-Management Relations Statute is similar to that prescribed in Executive Order 11491. Like the Executive Order, the law contains mandatory, permissive and prohibited subjects of bargaining. The statute imposes a duty to bargain in good faith. That is, the parties must "approach the negotiations with a sincere resolve to reach a collective bargaining agreement."

The chart [Figure 7.2] is a simplified illustration of the key considerations that are involved in deciding whether a proposal is within the legal obligation to bargain.

For example, if a proposal in fact conflicts with a law or a government-wide regulation (Box 2), it is non-negotiable. If there is no conflict, the proposal faces the next criteria of possible "Conflict with Regulation of Agency or Primary National Subdivision" (Box 3). And so on down the line.

rules should be instituted to see that such standards are met. The basis for bargaining over productivity is that both parties generally have an interest in improved productivity. If output increases, which has the effect of decreasing unit labor costs, then the employees have a strong claim on some of the savings. Similarly, if labor costs rise because of wage increases, management should expect some increase in performance for its increase in compensation. Productivity bargaining is Chester Barnard's economy of incentives—the contribution-satisfaction equilibrium—writ large.[20]

On the surface, it is obvious that productivity increases would be in management's interest. If management were willing to share some of the savings from improved productivity, it would also be in the interests of the workers. Yet it is often difficult to agree on how to measure productivity. Are teachers more productive in small classes or in large classes? It depends on what the goals of teachers' efforts in the classroom are. How can we measure the productivity of a police officer? By the number of tickets handed out? By the number of arrests? Or by the number of crimes prevented? And how are we going to measure that? Some sophisticated indicators that purport to measure the unmeasurable can be de-

---

20. *See* chapter 4 for a discussion of Barnard's economy of incentives.

veloped. If productivity is deemed to be bargainable, such measures might even be used.[21] Management, however, is often reluctant to give away what it perceives to be its unilateral right to demand adherence to whatever standards it sets.

Productivity bargaining has been sanctioned in several states—Massachusetts, Michigan, and New York, among others. It has been used successfully in several cases. The Detroit Sanitation Division developed a productivity improvement proposal that was agreed to by the local AFSCME union. In the early 1970s Detroit was faced with a situation in which some sanitation workers, who had completed their routes, were able to go home early while collecting a full day's pay, while others were working overtime to complete their routes. The overtime bill ran to almost $2 million a year. An attempt by management to institute changes in work rules unilaterally to remedy the situation resulted in a strike.

Management realized, although belatedly, that it had to cooperate with the unions. Management sought to redesign routes and improve productivity by increasing the size of the trucks. As an incentive to union cooperation, since the changes would result in loss of overtime for some workers, management agreed to share the savings in overtime with the workers. Management would get 50 percent of the overtime savings, and a bonus fund would get 50 percent. Bonuses for the workers would be distributed from the fund on a quarterly basis. In addition, laborers on larger trucks would receive special wage increases because they would be more productive. All these provisions were on top of the general wage increase won by the union.[22]

Financially hard-pressed New York City entered negotiations with District Council 37 of AFSCME, the largest local unit of the largest public employee union in the country, in 1980. New York was determined to force the union to agree to changes in work rules that the union had successfully bargained for in earlier contracts. Such changes as only having two men on a garbage truck and greater management freedom to reassign individuals would have enhanced productivity, according to the management negotiators. The union negotiator, Victor Gotbaum, moderated his union's salary demands but refused to give management control over disputed work rules. By accepting the "no give-backs"

---

21. For an excellent treatment of a wide range of productivity measures, *see* Harry P. Hatry, Louis H. Blair, Donald M. Fisk, John M. Greiner, John R. Hall, Jr., and Philip S. Schaenman, *How Effective Are Your Community Services?* (Washington, D.C.: The Urban Institute, 1977).

22. National Commission on Productivity, *Improving Municipal Productivity: The Detroit Refuse Collection Incentive Plan* (Washington, D.C.: U.S. Government Printing Office, 1974), pp. 1–22.

package, the New York City negotiators threw productivity bargaining out the window.

After the negotiations were concluded, New York managers attempted to enforce unilaterally some of the work rules they wanted changed. The union's position was clear. Work rules relating to productivity were bargainable items. If the city wanted to change the work rules, the benefits of increased productivity had to be shared with the workers. Although the city seemed to have authority to design work rules unilaterally with an eye toward efficiency, having the authority—that is, the legal right—to make certain decisions does not mean that management has the power to make them. Public sector labor-management relations continually operate in a political environment. The legal principle of management rights might not be in the same power league as citizen reaction to piles of fetid garbage sprouting on the streets.

The Grievance Arbitration Process

THE bargaining that goes into developing a contract is virtually useless unless the agreement can be fairly interpreted. Under the older civil service arrangements, the civil service commission of the jurisdiction was the interpreter of personnel rules and regulations and the arbiter of problems that concerned the application of those rules. With the move toward bilateral determination of personnel policies and working conditions, labor and management representatives have often agreed on grievance procedures different from the paternalistic civil service commission procedures.

Unions have been quite successful in fighting for grievance procedures that provide for arbitration. In fact, most laws covering public sector labor-management relations in the states and the federal governments provide that such mechanisms be established. The main purpose of grievance arbitration is to apply the contract with a degree of justice so that work slowdowns and bad feelings on both sides can be kept to a minimum. The mechanism for doing this is generally a three- or four-step appeals process that enables the aggrieved employee—one with a problem that he or she thinks is a violation of certain contract provisions—to raise the problem with management in an acceptable way. Generally, the first step in the grievance arbitration process happens when the aggrieved employee or a union steward—a low-level union official—files a verbal or written complaint with the employee's immediate supervisor. If the aggrieved employee does not receive satisfaction from the immediate supervisor, the case can be appealed, usually in writing and within a certain number of days, to a higher level as specified in the contract. Depending on contract provisions, the appeals mechanism can culminate in binding arbitration with an independent arbitrator making the final decision, or in an appeal to the PERB. At each step in the appeals process, the employee is represented by union officials.

Aside from resolving the particular issue at hand, the grievance arbitration process has several subsidiary aims. It interprets the language of the contract so that the agreement becomes a dynamic instrument capa-

---

The TM Grievance

A correctional officer, allegedly found asleep at his desk, received a three day suspension. The union filed a grievance, contending that the officer was not asleep but simply practicing transcendental mediation (TM). When the union pursued the matter to arbitration, the arbitrator set aside the suspension and ordered that the grievant be given an official reprimand.

The officer testified that his meditation was a procecss of relaxing with deep rest stages. Awareness was not lost, he explained, and he would be just as alert as a person watching TV.

In reviewing the facts, Arbitrator William S. Rule found no potential danger to the safety of persons as a result of the grievant's meditation. The arbitrator determined that "at best the agency has shown only a brief inattention to duty." The officer was a five year employee with a good record.

But by engaging in TM, concluded Rule, "The grievant created the situation in which it was possible for someone to assume he was asleep. Meditation does interfere with total attention to duty. The grievant had not been given permission to practice meditation. He was inattentive to his duties, at least briefly, and is subject to discipline, but not a three day suspension."

The arbitrator found the suspension was not for just cause and ordered the grievant made whole for loss of three days' pay. The grievant was to be given an official reprimand for his inattention to duty. (Justice, Federal Prison Systems *and* American Federation of Government Employees, Council of Prison Locals—June 18, 1979. LAIRS #1207)

SOURCE: *Federal Labor-Management Consultant* (Washington, D.C.: Office of Personnel Management, October 19, 1979), p. 1.

ble of coping with changes that might not have been considered when the contract was negotiated. The grievance procedure provides a communication link between rank-and-file employees and higher management. Through the grievance appeals process, an employee gets to confront the upper levels of management with problems of concern to the employees in general but of which management might not even be aware. The arbitration procedure often suggests weak areas in the contract. If many grievance cases are spawned by a particular clause, it should serve as a signal to both labor and management that the clause will require modification at the next negotiating period.[23]

The negotiated grievance arbitration procedures have taken a whole body of activity that had formally been the exclusive province of civil service commissions and have shifted it toward PERBs, the unions, and agencies. Except for specified appeals, civil service commissions have no power over determination of employee rights and duties. As the scope of bargaining increases, civil service commission power will be eroded still further. This trend has been reflected in the creation of the Office of Personnel Management (OPM) as the successor to the United States Civil Service Commission, with some appeals functions lodged in a separate Merit Systems Protection Board. Similar arrangements have occurred in some states—Massachusetts and New York, among others. In states having a strong public employee relations board and well-defined bilateral labor-management relations, old-line civil service commissions are superfluous.

Unions on the Defensive

ALTHOUGH it is clear that the role of civil service commissions in public personnel management has been altered, it is not clear whether the dilution of that power means a diminution of managerial power in the public sector.

The general economic slowdown in the 1970s severely cut into the almost universal successes of public unions in their dealings with public management. The economic decline cut into revenues for several large cities and states. Inflation and a revived concern for fiscal conservatism in government, caused by the near-bankruptcy of New York City, gave public executives political backing necessary to force some unions into

---

23. Wendell C. French, *The Personnel Management Process,* 3rd ed. (Boston: Houghton-Mifflin, 1974), pp. 625–626.

defensive positions. After years of riding a crest of favorable public opinion supporting their demands, some unions found themselves having to fight pay freezes, cuts in fringe benefits, and even layoffs.

For nearly two decades, New York City's public unions were among the leaders in public sector unionization. The success of these unions in gaining wage and benefit increases for their members became widely accepted in some quarters as one of the main reasons for New York City's fiscal problems. However, in 1975 and 1976, these unions were forced to accept concessions so that the city could avoid defaulting on its bonds. Wage increases that had been negotiated and affirmed in signed contracts had to be surrendered. Desite strong opposition, the unions had to accept layoffs. Furthermore, the union pension funds were forced to invest $2.5 billion in New York City securities. These initial responses to the city's fiscal plight did not head off strong city efforts to revamp pension systems that had been approved through earlier bargaining efforts.

As a result of the trials brought by governmental fiscal problems and dwindling political support, the public unions in the affected communities have shifted from militancy in support of new demands to militant action to preserve what had been won in the past. For the duration of the hard economic times, survival has become the watchword of the unions. Yet in hard financial times, employees often figure that they need unions more than when times are good. Although some union members might get laid off and thus drop from the union's membership roles, other employees sign up with the unions for protection against being laid off.

The ability of most public unions to maintain and even to increase membership during hard times practically assures a new burst of union gains when the economic picture improves. During the fiscal crunch, unions can sharpen their main arguments that have produced political support in the past—support that has been translated into gains at the bargaining table. Among the strongest of these arguments are fairness and cost-of-living catch-up. Until the fiscal picture improves, however, unions and public managers will probably seek to develop integrative bargaining rather than the more traditional distributive bargaining. When fiscal conditions improve, we can expect a return to distributive bargaining at the state and local levels.

Some conservative groups are trying to outlaw public unions altogether. The American Legislative Exchange Council has developed a draft "public services protection act" for state legislatures. Such an act would prohibit contractual agreements between a state and its subdivisions and public employee unions. Similar laws have been passed in

Virginia and North Carolina and have survived court tests. But given the numerical strength and political power of unions in other parts of the country, it is unlikely that this effort will bear fruit nationally.

The Political Context Revisited

ALTHOUGH there are some similarities between collective bargaining in the public and private sectors, the key factor that differentiates the two processes is the political nature of the public sector. In a study of labor-management relations in New York City, Raymond Horton has noted: "The allocation of public money and the fixing of public and managerial policies, two major functions of the labor relations process, are central political acts in any organized society. . . . [The] labor relations process inevitably is political."[24] The political character of public sector labor-management relations is reflected in several overt ways.

Because of the patterns of demand for government services, even for services that many would not regard as essential, there is more pressure on public officials to settle with unions than there is in the private sector. Most governmental services are provided on a monopolistic basis. If a strike occurs and those services are not provided, the community cannot meet its demands from other sources as easily as it can when there is a strike in the private sector. These unsatisfied demands are reflected in political pressure on the elected leaders to solve the immediate problem.

The frustration created by the unsatisfied demands of the community might be transferred to the political executives of the jurisdiction. Elected officials would probably find a strike detrimental to their re-election bids or their ambitions for higher office. Therefore, they might be more eager to settle with a union, even though the long-range costs to the jurisdiction would be much greater than if the political executives were willing to face the short-run consequences of a strike and the possible negative effect on their subsequent electoral efforts. Voters generally favor political leaders who avoid the inconvenience of strikes as opposed to those who would minimize the costs of settlements at the price of a strike.[25] San Francisco's mayor, Dianne Feinstein, was one of the few to weather a labor storm in a traditionally strong organized-labor area.

24. Raymond D. Horton, *Municipal Labor Relations in New York City: Lessons of the Lindsay-Wagner Years* (New York: Praeger, 1973), p. 123.
25. H. H. Wellington and R. K. Winter, Jr., "Structuring Collective Bargaining in Public Employment," *Yale Law Journal* 79 (April 1970): 847.

It makes more sense for political executives to cozy up to public unions, especially at the local level. As Horton has suggested, public unions "offer two commodities highly valued by the public official in electoral trouble: labor peace and electoral support in the form of endorsements, campaign workers, money, and membership votes."[26] This can be especially effective in local elections where relatively few voters bother to go to the polls. The political executive cannot always purchase an electoral victory by being an easy mark at the bargaining table, but the jurisdiction can and will still have to pay the cost of politically expedient giveaways. In Cleveland in 1979, the incoming mayor, George V. Voinovich, who defeated the incumbent, Dennis Kucinich, was surprised to discover that Kucinich had signed an agreement to give 11 percent raises to members of a municipal foremen's and laborers' union. The agreement was signed five days after the union president endorsed Kucinich for reelection.

Aside from the perceived political pressure from the community and the possibility of union electoral support for political leaders, mutually beneficial or symbiotic relationships can evolve between the career public officials and a particular union. Jay Atwood has described the close relationship that has developed between the Los Angeles Department of Water and Power and the International Brotherhood of Electrical Workers, Local 18:

> Local 18 has been characterized as the "political arm" of the department as a result of its support since the 1930s. Initially, this support was given in a bond election for the embryonic department and more recently in a city charter election which, had it been successful, would have curtailed the administrative independence of the department. Management of the department has generally provided very generous compensation and employee benefits for its employees.[27]

Special treatment at the bargaining table can bring needed political support to both career and elected public officials.

In the political arena of public administration, the political support of one group or another, including the unions that represent the workers in a particular agency, can vitally affect the programs and policies of that agency. Obviously, this fact of political life has major implications for democratic government in America. In the next chapter we will turn our attention to an examination of the decision-making process in public bureaucracies.

---

26. Horton, *Municipal Labor Relations,* p. 134.
27. Jay F. Atwood, "Collective Bargaining's Challenge: Five Imperatives for Public Managers," *Public Personnel Management* 5, no. 1 (January–February 1976): 26.

Suggestions for
Further Reading

Auletta, Ken. *The Streets Were Paved with Gold.* New York: Random House, 1979.

Balk, Walter L., ed. "Symposium on Productivity in Government." *Public Administration Review* 38, no. 1 (January–February 1978).

Cayer, N. Joseph. *Managing Human Resources.* New York: St. Martin's, 1980.

Gershenfeld, Walter J., J. Joseph Loewenberg, and Bernard Ingster, eds. *Scope of Public Sector Bargaining.* Lexington, Mass.: Lexington Books, 1977.

Government Employee Relations Report. Washington, D.C.: Bureau of National Affairs, published weekly.

Hatry, Harry P., Louis H. Blair, Donald M. Fisk, John M. Greiner, John R. Hall, Jr., and Philip S. Schaenman. *How Effective Are Your Community Services? Procedures for Monitoring the Effectiveness of Municipal Services.* Washington, D.C.: Urban Institute, 1977.

Horton, Raymond D. *Municipal Labor Relations in New York City: Lessons of the Lindsay-Wagner Years.* New York: Praeger, 1973.

Jascourt, Hugh D., ed. *Government Labor Relations: Trends and Information for the Future.* Oak Park, Ill.: Moore, 1979.

Public Employee Bargaining. Washington, D.C.: Commerce Clearing House, published biweekly.

CHAPTER EIGHT

Decision-Making Theory
and Policy Analysis

The WAY GOVERNMENT AGENCIES are organized and how the people who staff those agencies are managed merely set the stage for our real interest in public administration—the policy role of the bureaucrats. In the early chapters, we raised the issue that administrators have considerable discretion in carrying out laws. They have meaningful parts to play in the policy process from formulation to implementation. In this chapter, we want to provide a decision-making focus to the policy role of public bureaucrats. We want to explore how administrators actually make decisions.

The decision-making focus has an honorable position in American public administration. Herbert Simon, one of the most influential thinkers in modern public administration, correctly saw the relationship between decision-making and organization in the 1940s. His postulation of the "administrative man," who "satisfices"—seeks to perform at a satisfactory level—rather than the "economic man," who always seeks to maximize utility, is a key to understanding how administrators actually make decisions.[1]

In this chapter, we will look at two broad theories of decision-making. Rational-comprehensive or systems theories emphasize the components of economic rationality in decision-making. The terms *policy analysis* and *systematic program evaluation* are closely tied to these theories. Incremental theories, on the other hand, emphasize political criteria that tend to limit the scope of individual decisions. These two decision-making theories represent poles of a continuum. Rarely are administrative decisions wholly based on systems analysis or wholly based on political criteria. Instead, as Figure 8.1 suggests, there is a broad middle ground where economic criteria and analytic methods can be integrated with political criteria. Decision-making reality for public administrators occupies this middle area of the continuum.

Rational-Comprehensive Decision-Making

THE underlying assumption of this book is that citizens want and deserve capable, intelligent, flexible, creative civil servants. Surely many of us would agree that we should seek to solve society's problems on a "ra-

1. Herbert A. Simon, *Administrative Behavior,* 3rd ed. (New York: Macmillan, 1976), especially chapters 4 and 5.
PHOTO: Former Secretary of Defense Robert S. McNamara.

FIGURE 8.1
Decision Theory Continuum

Systems analysis   Mixed   Incremental

Economic rationality   Political rationality

tional" basis. Maybe many of us would agree with Robert McNamara, the secretary of defense under Presidents Kennedy and Johnson:

> To undermanage reality is not to keep free. It is simply to let some force other than reason shape reality. That force may be unbridled emotion; it may be greed; it may be aggressiveness; it may be hatred; it may be ignorance; it may be inertia; it may be anything other than reason. But whatever it is, if it is not reason that rules man, then man falls short of his potential.[2]

To McNamara, rational decision-making involved having a full range of options from which to choose. Successful management would organize the enterprise so that all the options would be developed. This ideal decision-making organization would encourage what Charles Lindblom has called "rational-comprehensive" analysis.[3]

To Lindblom, the rational-comprehensive analytic method involved several features:

1. *clarification of values*
2. *means-ends analysis*
3. *choice of most appropriate means to desired ends*
4. *analysis that is comprehensive*
5. *analysis that is theory-based*[4]

Basically, the rational-comprehensive method is a variant of scientific investigation and scientific problem-solving. The analysts are supposed to define the problem, develop alternative solutions, place values on the consequences of various alternatives, assess the probability that they will occur, and make the choice based on logical rules—that is, seek to achieve the things that are valued most. Such a method of making deci-

---

2. Robert S. McNamara, *The Essence of Security* (New York: Harper & Row, 1968), pp. 109–110.
3. Charles E. Lindblom, "The Science of 'Muddling Through,'" *Public Administration Review* 19 (spring 1959): 79–88. Lindblom more fully developed his arguments in *The Intelligence of Democracy* (New York: Free Press, 1965). In *Intelligence of Democracy,* he refers to the rational-comprehensive method as the synoptic ideal.
4. Lindblom, "Muddling Through," pp. 80–82.

sions closely approaches the ideal embodied in Max Weber's view of bureaucracy, in which people would make decisions based on impersonal rules and techniques.

But Lindblom argued that such idealized decision-making did not occur in the public policy arena except for small problems where potentially conflicting parties could agree on the values to be sought through alternative programs. On complex issues, Lindblom maintained, there was more likely to be conflict than agreement on values. Lindblom saw that conflicts over values were essentially political questions, which could not be subordinated to economic techniques. He felt that large, complex public policy problems could never be successfully treated in a rational-comprehensive manner because decision-makers would always be operating under constraints—time, money, and, most important, human ability—which would prevent a truly comprehensive analysis of complex social problems. It is impossible to study *all* alternatives. In many cases, agreement on goals might be impossible, and means-ends analysis would be irrelevant under such conditions.

Since means-ends analysis is essential to the kind of analytic enterprise being considered here, we should have a firm understanding of what it means in the public policy area. There are always alternative ways or means to accomplish a goal. There are several possible programs that could be implemented to achieve the same goal. For example, if the goal is to abolish hunger in America, we can give away surplus food. Or we can subsidize food stamps. Or we can give outright cash grants. Or we can establish a corps of nutritionists who will force the poor to forsake junk food for more nutritious fare. We could probably come up with several more alternatives—some reasonable, some absurd—that might, if successfully implemented, enable us to reach our goal of ending hunger in America.

Means-Ends Analysis

Each of the programs or means that we consider will have certain consequences. Some of these consequences may be favorable; some may be unfavorable. Cash grants to solve the hunger problem may have the positive consequence that they are simple to administer, yet there may be the drawback that the recipients of the grants might use this money to buy a more expensive brand of beer and continue to eat dog food. The corps of nutritionists might be able to enforce better eating habits, but that would involve a substantial loss of personal freedom for the individual and in addition great cost to the taxpayer. Good means-ends analysis would spell out the good and bad consequences of each alternative proposal.

Furthermore, good means-ends analysis would attempt to assess the likelihood of any of the various consequences occurring should any particular alternative program be implemented. This can be done mathematically through the use of Bayesian statistical methods.[5] The steps of the Bayesian approach to decision-making, which is fully compatible with the kind of means-ends analysis that is part of the rational-comprehensive method, are listed below:

1. *Identify the objectives toward which the decision-making should be directed.*
2. *Identify the alternative courses of action that should be considered.*
3. *Identify the possible events (environmental conditions or states of nature) that would influence the payoff of each course of action.*
4. *Assign a numerical value to the payoff of each course of action, given each possible event.*
5. *Assign a numerical weight (probability) to the occurrence of each possible event.*
6. *Using the weights (probabilities), compute the weighted average (expected value) of the payoffs assigned to each course of action.*
7. *Assess the exposure to both gain and loss associated with each course of action.*
8. *Choose among the alternative courses of action on the basis of the combination of (a) expected value and (b) exposure to gain and loss that is most consistent with the decision maker's objectives and attitude toward risk.*[6]

Probability and the Problem of Assigning Weights

The heart of the Bayesian approach is the notion of probability—the numerical weight assigned to the occurrence of each possible event. A probability statement is a mathematical representation of the chances of some phenomenon occurring under given conditions. The mathematical expression can run from 0, which would mean absolutely no chance of occurring, to 1, which would mean the event would definitely occur. Since we live in an uncertain world, analysts are reluctant to write off an event's occurring completely. Instead, they would assign it a very low probability, for example, .000001. Similarly, if analysts thought the likelihood of some events occurring was very, very great, they would hesitate to give it a probability of 1, which would indicate absolute certainty, but mighty give it a high probability of, say, .9999.

Once probability statements have been assigned to various consequences of programs, there are standard mathematical techniques for manipulating these probabilities. Through mathematical manipulation of probabilities, analysts are able to recommend various courses of action with varying degrees of certainty. Highly complex problems involving many alternatives and consequences can be handled by computers

---

5. *See* Robert L. Winkler, *An Introduction to Bayesian Inference and Decision* (New York: Holt, Rinehart and Winston, 1972).
6. Joseph W. Newman, *Management Applications of Decision Theory* (New York: Harper & Row, 1971), pp. 6–7.

"We analyzed the trends, plugged in the variables, computed the probabilities, then flipped a coin."

through a technique called *decision analysis* or decision analysis forecasting.[7]

If means-ends analysis through the Bayesian approach depends on probabilities, it is absolutely essential to understand how such probability statements are developed and used. In classical statistics, the probability that a balanced coin will come up heads can be calculated with precision. Since there are two sides to a coin, the chances that the coin will come up heads on any given toss are 50-50, or .5. Similarly, we can calculate the precise probability that a "true" die will come up showing the number 3 to be one in six (a die has six sides; only one side can be up

7. For the best treatment of decision analysis, *see* Howard Raiffa, *Decision Analysis: Introductory Lectures on Choice Under Uncertainty* (Reading, Mass.: Addison-Wesley, 1968).

237

at a time), or .167. Such clear, precise, unquestionable probability statements are called objective probability.

In the social area, we do not have true objective probabilities. Instead, we develop subjective probability statements. Some subjective probability statements may be based on extensive survey data. They may be developed through multiple regression analysis and many other statistical techniques. In such cases, the subjective probabilities may be quite reliable. In other cases, however, probability statements may be generated from personal experience and judgments and may be highly subjective. The degree of validity and reliability of the methods used to develop the probability statements will heavily influence the validity of the results of the means-ends analysis. Probability statements can be no better than the data and the judgments that went into developing them. There is a great danger inherent in decision analysis because even poorly developed probability statements, when manipulated in standard mathematical ways, give the appearance of being scientifically valid.

A simple decision analysis problem is presented in the appendix to this chapter. This problem shows how probabilities can be developed and manipulated.

The Iterative Analytic Cycle

One of the leading analysts in the public sector, E. S. Quade, has refined the rational-comprehensive model of decision-making slightly to present a step-by-step approach for analysts to follow. The heart of Quade's analytic method is the development of a model that is relevant to the decision question. A model is a simplified abstraction of the real situation. As Quade has pointed out:

> Such a model, which may take such varied forms as a computer simulation, an operational game, or even a purely verbal "scenario," introduces a precise structure and terminology that serve primarily as an effective means of communication, enabling the participants in the study to exercise their judgment and intuition in a concrete context and in proper relation to others. Moreover, through feedback from the model (the results of computation, the countermoves in the game, or the critique of the scenario), the experts have a chance to revise early judgments and thus arrive at a clearer understanding of the problem and its context, and perhaps of their subject matter.[8]

8. E. S. Quade, *Systems Analysis Techniques for Planning-Programming-Budgeting*, Report P-3322 (Santa Monica, Calif.: The Rand Corporation, 1966), reprinted in Fred A. Kramer, ed., *Perspectives on Public Bureaucracy*, 3rd ed. (Cambridge, Mass.: Winthrop, 1981), pp. 192–210, quote at p. 195. The rest of this section is drawn from this article. For a fuller explanation of the role of analysis, *see* Quade, *Analysis for Public Decisions* (New York: American Elsevier, 1975).

A critical part of the analytic effort, according to Quade, is the possibility of reexamining objectives and reformulating the decision question.

The key to successful analysis, to Quade, is the repetitive, cyclical process which he called iteration. The various stages in this continuing cyclical process are presented in Figure 8.2. Although most of the stages of the cycle seem self-evident, some items need some explanation. Selecting objectives may seem like a fairly simple task, but often in governmental activities there are multiple objectives to any program. Sometimes these objectives conflict with one another or with objectives of some other program. Alternatives that may work toward obtaining one objective

FIGURE 8.2
Quade's Analytic Process

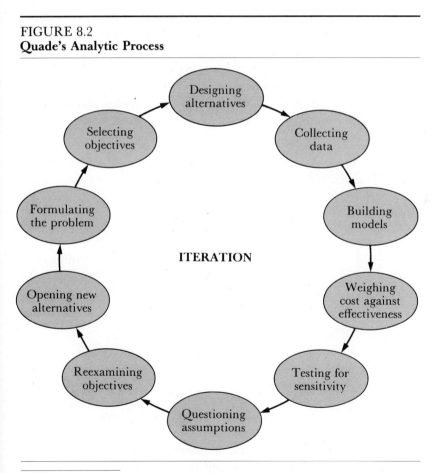

SOURCE: E. S. Quade, *Systems Analysis Techniques for Planning-Programming-Budgeting,* Report P-3322 (Santa Monica, Calif.: The Rand Corporation, 1966), p. 10. Reprinted by permission.

might work against some other objective. Earlier we used the example of a corps of nutritionists to help solve the problem of hunger in America. That alternative would be costly and would work against such overall governmental objectives as personal freedom, but such an alternative might wipe out hunger.

There are similar problems to be encountered in the other stages of iteration. Not all alternatives will be considered. There may be severe data collection problems. Some measures of whether a program is working—effectiveness measures—will not accurately measure the extent to which the objectives of that program are being obtained. Model building is a risky business. It is not easy to develop cause-and-effect models that mirror reality. Neither is it easy to estimate cost and benefits of particular programs. We will return to these problems in the next chapter.

Any model is based on assumptions. Testing for sensitivity means slightly changing one assumption at a time. If a model involves assumptions about inflation rates in ten years, perhaps different decisions will be inferred from the model if one assumes the annual inflation rate to be 10 percent rather than 11 percent. If a change of only 1 percent in the inflation rate assumption alters the recommendation, one would say that the analysis is sensitive to the rate of inflation. If a model is very sensitive to some assumption, one should be wary of the recommendations of that analysis.

To Quade, the analytical iteration process was not revolutionary. He saw it as an attempt to look at problems facing government in a more systematic way, "with emphasis on explicitness, on quantification, and on the recognition of uncertainty."[9] Systematic analysis would improve government decision-making if the iteration cycles could continue until satisfaction were obtained, but Quade was aware that, more likely, the cycle would have to stop at some point short of satisfaction when time and money forced such a cutoff.

The Incremental Method

THE logic of the rational-comprehensive method is appealing to those who seek order and despise chaos. Lindblom, however, argued that the real world presented insurmountable problems to rational-comprehensive analysis on all but the most simple social problems. Whereas Quade

9. Quade in Kramer, ed., *Perspectives,* p. 197.

emphasized the possibilities that analysis could refine the formulation of a problem, open new alternatives, improve the models, and so forth, Lindblom focused on the constraints that impair analysis of complex social problems.[10] These constraints are listed below. According to Lindblom, complex social problems are not adapted:

1. *to man's limited intellectual capacities*
2. *to inadequacy of information*
3. *to costliness of analysis*
4. *to failures to construct a satisfactory set of criteria by which to judge the value of a decision*
5. *to the closeness of fact and value (means and ends) in policy making*
6. *to openness of systems of variables with which they must contend*
7. *to the diverse forms in which policy problems actually arise.*[11]

The principal constraining variable impeding analysis, to Lindblom, is the limit of mankind's ability to conceive all the possibilities inherent in a complex social problem. As Herbert Simon had pointed out, people might intend to be rational, but rationality has its limits. Even the increased use of computers to help deal with masses of data cannot relieve the basic human failing, which is the inability to consider adequately all possibilities that might impinge on a complex problem. Administrators who might want to decide on a rational basis find that they must drastically simplify the problem to deal with it.[12]

This simplification could involve the development of formal models, but these formal models, to Lindblom, would always be deficient. Adequate models of social problems would be extremely costly to develop and keep supplied with information even if people could design them to be flexible enough to cope with changing values. For example, models of transportation planners in the 1950s did not even consider the effect of highway building on breaking up existing communities in urban areas. If an analyst attempts to design a very flexible analytic model, there are no guidelines to suggest when and how the analysis should be limited. There is nothing inherent in the rational-comprehensive method that indicates when the analyst should stop considering aspects of the problem. In some cases—welfare economics, for example—even if one could perform a rational-comprehensive analysis, there is no agreement on what constitutes the proper criteria by which to judge that analysis. Therefore, it would be useless for policy decision-making purposes.

10. Lindblom, "Muddling Through," p. 84.
11. Lindblom, *Intelligence of Democracy,* pp. 138–143.
12. *See* Simon, *Administrative Behavior,* chapter 4, and James March and Herbert Simon, *Organizations* (New York: John Wiley, 1958), chapter 6.

Because of the problems inherent in the rational-comprehensive method, Lindblom rejected reliance on analysis and advocated a method of successive limited comparisons—incremental decision-making—for public policy problems. These limited (as opposed to comprehensive) policy reviews would be defined by the interplay of political forces. To Lindblom, the self-corrective feedback mechanism of the group political system was more reliable than abstract models supported by shaky social science theory. Lindblom saw this political simplification process taking place in a pluralist environment where organized political groups pursued their own interests. He called his arrangement *partisan mutual adjustment*.[13]

Partisan mutual adjustment, based on the ideal of group conflict, forces limited changes from the status quo. Decision-makers—including public administrators—seek to make relatively small policy changes by considering a relatively limited number of alternatives that are raised by political interest groups. Agreement is sought on marginal changes in policy when the political forces at a particular time can be mustered to support a specific change because they agree that change is necessary, not because they agree on the values to be pursued.

The test of good policy in this incremental method is whether the political coalition that supports the change will continue to support it. There is no absolute ethical or social science standard on which the policy can be judged. Instead, there is a relativistic political standard. Floating coalitions of political forces, according to Lindblom, support some changes and create pressure for still more change. These additional changes need not be in the same direction as previous policy changes. If the policy appears to lose political support, new coalitions can take the policy in other directions. In the incremental method of decision-making, political action, especially by organized groups seeking their own interests, provides a feedback mechanism that is alleged to prevent great mistakes in policy choice.

The basic elements of the incremental approach are summarized below:

1. *Rather than attempting a comprehensive survey and evaluation of all alternatives, the decision-maker focuses only on those policies that differ marginally from existing policies.*

---

13. Lindblom, *Intelligence of Democracy*, chapters 1 and 2. In later work Lindblom more favorably presents the role of analysis in defining problems. Even though rational-comprehensive analysis is an ideal, careful analytic work—which he calls strategic analysis—can improve decision-making for public policy. *See* his "Still Muddling, Not Yet Through," *Public Administration Review* 39, no. 6 (November–December 1979): 517–526.

2. *Only a relatively small number of policy alternatives are considered.*
3. *Only a few "important" consequences for each policy alternative are evaluated.*
4. *There is no one decision or "right" solution but a "never-ending series of attacks" on the issues.*
5. *Incremental decision-making is remedial—geared more to the correction of present social imperfections than to the promotion of future social goals.*
6. *Group political interaction plays a leading role in each of the above areas.*[14]

In a pure partisan mutual adjustment environment, the bureaucratic role in policy-making would be to ratify the decisions worked out through the compromise of the relevant group interests. Although the administrator might have the legal authority to make a decision, that decision would be governed by the group political environment. Pure incrementalism would be an extreme case of interest group liberalism.[15]

Problems of Pure Incrementalism

Earlier we argued that the American political system favors resolving disputes at a low level of conflict, often behind closed doors of an administrative office rather than in more open governmental forums. In such situations, groups organized to pursue tangible benefits would have preferential access to public decision-makers at the expense of the public at large. The theory of incrementalism legitimizes mutually beneficial interest group–agency interactions. If agencies were forced to rely on information provided by groups in their efforts at decision-making, and if they based their decisions purely on the political clout of groups most concerned with their sphere of activity, incremental decision theory would sanction action favorable to the affected groups. This seems to be the case in agencies that have become captured by their clientele.

In regulatory areas, there is considerable bargaining between the agency and the affected industries over regulations. Often the regulators hesitate enforcing certain provisions of the law if they think that drastic economic consequences may result. Also the regulators do not want to upset the symbiotic relationships that develop among the agency, its clientele, and relevant legislative committees. There are some dangers inherent in heavily incremental decision-making in those agencies that are content to rely upon the information, arguments, and political clout of their clientele.

By looking at the activity of a young agency that is not a tool for the

---

14. Ibid., pp. 144–148, and Amitai Etzioni, "Mixed-Scanning: 'Third' Approach to Decision Making," *Public Administration Review* 27, no. 5 (December 1967): 385.
15. *See* chapter 2, and Theodore J. Lowi, *The End of Liberalism*, rev ed. (New York: W. W. Norton, 1979), chapter 3.

"private expropriation of public authority,"[16] we can get some idea of the hidden problems of having agencies reach accommodation with their clientele at the low level of conflict sanctioned by incrementalism. In the early 1970s, the Department of Labor's Occupational Safety and Health Administration (OSHA) proposed standards for vinyl chloride gas in the air of chemical plants. The chemical industry fought the implementation of these standards at the agency level and even raised the level of conflict to the courts. The experience under the standards showed that practically all the industry arguments had been false.[17]

Vinyl chloride gas, which is used in manufacturing polyvinyl chloride plastic, is a recognized cancer-producing substance. Aside from causing angiosarcoma, a rare cancer of the liver, vinyl chloride gas has been suspected of causing numerous less serious ailments. In the early days of using vinyl chloride gas for industrial purposes, concentrations of 40,000 or 50,000 parts per million parts of air were not uncommon in some areas of manufacturing plants. Initially, OSHA established a limit of 50 parts vinyl chloride per million. This figure was arrived at in consultation with industry groups and was recognized as reasonable by them. By the time the 50-parts-per-million standard was being considered, most manufactuiring plants had already reduced the vinyl chloride hazard to that level. Given the earlier levels of concentration, many people thought that the risk had been eliminated.

Tests on rats exposed to 50 parts vinyl chloride per million, however, showed that even at the reduced level, vinyl chloride still caused angiosarcoma. These test results prompted OSHA to set the air quality standard at "no detectable" concentration. The no-detectable standard, the chemical industry argued, would close down the billion-dollar industry. They produced a study that purported to prove that the overall economic impact of such a closing would mean 2.2 million people out of work and a cost of $65 to $90 billion.

These arguments convinced OSHA to relax the standards somewhat. The new standards were to be an average exposure of one part per million, with brief exposures to higher levels permitted. Levels of up to 25 parts per million would be acceptable if workers wore respirators. These revised standards were upheld by the courts even though the companies complained that the standards were "simply beyond the compliance capabilities of the industry." They predicted plant closings, job losses, price increases, and massive economic dislocation.

---

16. Lowi, p. 68.
17. This section is drawn from Steven Rattner, "Did Industry Cry Wolf?" *New York Times,* December 28, 1975.

Two years later none of these dire consequences had come to pass. Of course, there was a cost to the industry to comply with the health standards. The main compliance cost was the more rapid implementation of new technology, which was under development anyway. The general costs of compliance, however, were small when compared with doubling of raw material prices during the same period.

The Middle Way

THE vinyl chloride problem was quite simple. Scientific analysis was done by government to determine the level of harmful materials deemed safe. Economic analysis could have been conducted that might have disputed industry claims as to the economic impact of compliance with the stringent regulations. It should be clear from the example that not all regulatory decisions are based on pure politics. There is a role for analysis—scientific, economic, and social analysis—in decision-making by public agencies.

Amitai Etzioni has given the theoretical justification for a middle way between pure economic rationality and pure political rationality. Using a satellite-based weather observation system as an analogy to observing social phenomena, Etzioni suggested how a "mixed-scanning" technique might work:

> The rationalistic approach would seek an exhaustive survey of weather conditions by using cameras capable of detailed observations and by scheduling reviews of the entire sky as often as possible. This would yield an avalanche of details, costly to analyze and likely to overwhelm our action capacities. . . . Incrementalism would focus on those areas in which similar patterns developed in the recent past and, perhaps, on a few nearby regions; it would thus ignore all formations which might deserve attention if they arose in unexpected areas.
>
> A mixed-scanning strategy would include elements of both approaches by employing two cameras: a broad-angle camera that would cover all parts of the sky but not in great detail, and a second one which would zero in on those areas revealed by the first camera to require a more in-depth examination. While mixed-scanning might miss areas in which only a detailed camera could reveal trouble, it is less likely than incrementalism to miss obvious trouble spots in unfamiliar areas.[18]

The common sense of a mixed-scanning approach has indeed been characteristic of many aspects of policy-making since the mid-1960s.

---

18. Etzioni, "Mixed Scanning," p. 388.

The polar positions of decision theory have not changed, but there is an operational accommodation between the two. Very few people would claim that rational-comprehensive decision-making is possible on such major political issues as racism, poverty, the economy, or even national security. Similarly, few people would completely discount the role that systematic planning and analysis can have in clarifying certain aspects of these pressing problems.

Analysis of aspects of public policy problems has contributed to the information available to the various parties at the bargaining table, where the partisan mutual adjustment takes place. Rarely are decisions made wholly on the basis of hard, quantitative analysis, but often hard analysis does contribute something to the level of discussion. Good analysis can help in refining the issues, developing new alternatives, and more fully exploring the probable consequences of such alternatives. If one side in a bargaining relationship makes a strong analytic argument, the other side in the dispute feels it must establish its own analytic operation to counter these analytic arguments. Each of the parties is forced to engage in analytic activity to disprove, or understand, the other side's points.[19] It is clear that there is a significant amount of analysis of public policy problems being done within governments and through contracts with universities and private consulting firms. This analytic work has influenced—although usually in a marginal way—governmental decision-making.

Tensions and Ideology

THE appearance of systematic planning and analysis has created some tension within decision-making circles. Generally, this tension has arisen because of differences in outlook of politicians and generalist administrators, on the one hand, and the analysts, on the other. Analysts tend to see their work as value-free and scientific. Analysts, and people who blindly accept their recommendations, often see people who oppose the

---

19. William M. Capron, "The Impact of Analysis on Bargaining in Government," in Louis C. Gawthrop, ed., *The Administrative Process and Democratic Theory* (Boston: Houghton Mifflin, 1970), pp. 351–371. Also Henry Rowan, "Objectives, Alternatives, Costs and Effectiveness," in H. H. Hinrichs and Graeme M. Taylor, eds., *Program Budgeting and Benefit-Cost Analysis* (Pacific Palisades, Calif.: Goodyear, 1969), pp. 83–93. In Lindblom's later work, he emphasizes that strategic analysis—an attempt to apply rational-comprehensive techniques—is useful in policy-making. *See* his "Still Muddling, Not Yet Through."

conclusions of a piece of analytic work as operating from a political or ideological perspective. To analysts who view themselves as neutral scientists, a political or ideological perspective is inferior to a scientific one.[20] And an ideological perspective may be especially hard for some analysts to take because they are always in an advisory role, not actually making the decisions. Their work can be, and often is, disregarded by political decision-makers, including public administrators.

Many analysts claim to have established a monopoly on the truth in any particular policy area by virtue of their "scientific" model building and quantitative analysis. But, as Quade has cautioned:

> Systems analysis may still look like a purely rational approach to decision-making, a coldly objective, scientific method free from preconceived ideas, partisan bias, judgment and intuition.
> It really is not. Judgment and intuition are used in designing the models; in deciding what alternatives to consider, what factors are relevant, what the interrelations between these factors are, and what criteria to choose; and in interpreting the results of the analysis. This fact—that judgment and intuition permeate all analysis—should be remembered when we examine the apparently precise results that seem to come with such high-precision analysis.[21]

Sometimes analysts become so wrapped up in their views of a particular problem that they fail to see that there may be other legitimate perspectives.

When analysts use the term *politics* as a pejorative to explain why their recommendations have not been followed, they may be avoiding meaningful self-analysis. Perhaps there were problems with the analysis itself. Perhaps the analyst became wedded to some particular assumptions. Perhaps there were flaws in the model that led the analyst to understate the importance of some relationships that were crucial. Perhaps the analyst failed to spell out implicit assumptions. Perhaps the measures being used and the data available had serious weaknesses. Perhaps the analyst lost sight of the cardinal limitation of analysis: *analysis is necessarily incomplete.*

Good analysts are aware of these problems and are willing to confront the issues in a positive manner with administrative and political generalists. But just as there are good practitioners and journeymen in any profession, not all analysts are of the same caliber. Often the analytic work

---

20. For a full discussion of this problem, *see* Fred A. Kramer, "Policy Analysis as Ideology," *Public Administration Review* 35, no. 5 (September–October 1975): 509–517.
21. Quoted in Kramer, ed., *Perspectives,* 3rd ed., p. 204.

that is done—especially for smaller jurisdictions that have to contract out for analysis—is overly simplified. It fails to deal with the weaknesses of the analysis itself. Complex computer simulation models can hide faulty assumptions and data difficulties that would make that analysis worthless.

Generalist administrators and politicians should not be bullied by the results of analysis. What Seymour Martin Lipset said regarding pollsters applies to systems analysts: "Like most businessmen, they do not stress the deficiencies of their product to clients. They do not emphasize the complexities involved in analyzing data, or the frequent need for more expensive research or more detailed and complicated write-ups required for the client to understand the [analysis]."[22] Analysis of public policy—especially contract analysis—is a business. Contract analysis often has severe failings[23] (see box). There is a role for analysis, but generalist policy makers must make sure they and the analysts know the limitations of policy analysis. Table 8.1 summarizes those limitations.

***Controls over Consulting Service
Contracts at Federal Agencies
Need Tightening***

Which of the following best describes consulting service contracts awarded by federal agencies? (Check one)

( )   Perhaps unnecessary.
( )   Extensive sole-source awards.
( )   Lots of modifications.
( )   End products not delivered on time.
(√)   All of the above and more.

These problems will not be resolved until agencies take steps to control the need for the contracting practices related to consulting agencies.

SOURCE: U.S. General Accounting Office, *Monthly List of GAO Reports* 14, no. 3 (April 1, 1980), p. 8.

---

22. Seymour Martin Lipset, "The Wavering Polls," *The Public Interest* no. 43, (Spring 1976): 84.
23. Gregg Easterbrook, "The Art of Further Study: Life in the Consulting Cult," *Washington Monthly* 12, no. 3 (May 1980): 12–26.

TABLE 8.1
Some Limitations of Policy Analysis

1. Analysis is always incomplete.
2. We always operate under constraints.
3. The future is always uncertain.
4. No one has yet found a satisfactory way to predict the future.
5. Many significant aspects of many problems cannot be satisfactorily quantified.
6. There is a danger that analysts and/or customers of analysts will rely too heavily on quantification.
7. Political considerations are sometimes paramount.
8. Not everyone at every time has to ration his resources.
9. One can always use more time to do more analysis.
10. One never has enough facts.

SOURCE: Chester Wright and Michael D. Tate, *Economics and Systems Analysis: Introduction for Public Managers* (Reading, Mass.: Addison-Wesley, 1973), p. 157.

Usefulness of Analysis

DESPITE the tension between social scientists who perform policy analysis and systematic program evaluation and the policy-makers who decide how much weight to give the results of analysis, the view of many remains that "rational intelligence *should* guide policy, at least to some extent."[24] The role of policy analysis in policy-making is further encouraged by bureaucratic politics. All large domestic agencies in the national government and many large state and local agencies have organizational units devoted to policy planning, analysis, or evaluation. Most local jurisdictions now have planning offices. Even within the national government, these units vary widely in size and influence, but they do exist. They are organizational forces that could be used and probably will be by public executives. Since policy analysis and evaluation research is going to be with us in the future, we should assess its usefulness.

Policy analysts who want their work used seem to favor what Martin Rein and Sheldon H. White call a "problem-solving model" to bring social science research and policy-making together. Advocates of the

---

24. Martin Rein and Sheldon H. White, "Can Policy Research Help Policy?" *The Public Interest* no. 49 (Fall 1977): 121. This section draws heavily from the Rein and White discussion on pp. 119–124.

problem-solving model claim that policy research would be more widely used if the following conditions prevailed:

1. *The scientific quality of the research was improved.*
2. *Evaluation research was restricted to those instances suitable for valid social science research.*
3. *Policy-makers were required to define their objectives clearly.*
4. *Centralized decision-makers could implement the results of analysis.*

Rein and White point out that there are difficulties with each of these factors. Although there is much room to improve the quality of analysis, most policy-makers claim they do not use analysis because the studies are not available when the decision must be made. Scientifically valid analysis that hits the decision-maker's desk three weeks after the decision has been made is worthless. Better analysis probably would take longer than the inferior analyses now usually done. The lack of timeliness would insure that it would not be used by decision-makers.

If evaluation research were restricted to those problems in which the proper conditions for a scientifically valid study would have a significant impact on decision-making, Rein and White believe, far fewer studies would be performed than are done today. The conditions necessary for scientifically pure evaluation rarely exist for complex public policy problems. Given the time and money restrictions on analytic efforts, it may not be possible to create suitable control groups. Even with time and money, the state of the art in policy analysis and program evaluation may not permit the development of indices or measures of program performance that would meet scientific criteria.

Many programs lack clearly stated, testable objectives because political factors cause the program goals to be purposely vague. Different political factions can agree on the need for a program but want different things from it. The political process in a democracy seeks to reconcile multiple and sometimes conflicting goals into government programs to alleviate aspects of certain problems that have become political issues. Precise statements of multiple goals, with their weights, might be useful to policy analysts, but might split the coalition of political groups that seeks to implement a vague policy that might marginally make things better. For example, project Head Start, a preschool educational program for disadvantaged children which was one of the key programs in President Lyndon B. Johnson's War on Poverty, was approved for several reasons: "1) to stimulate the development of poor children; 2) to stimulate community action; 3) to coordinate services for poor children and their families; and 4) to provide a basis for experiments in school reform."[25] By not knowing the precise extent to which one of these goals would have been met at the expense of another, diverse groups were able to support the program. Educational groups wanting to stimulate the development of children might have been antagonistic to community action or even the possibility of experimental school reform, yet they could support Head Start. Because of the multiple and sometimes conflicting objectives, the evaluation of Head Start has become a *cause célèbre* for both advocates and opponents of analysis.[26] Policy and programs are not made for the convenience of policy analysts.

The Political Limitations of Analysis

Imagine how the perfectly "rational" Congressman might greet his grieving constituent: "Mrs. Jones, I share your grief about the plight of your husband, but we simply cannot afford to spend $30,000 per year to keep him alive when people are dying elsewhere who could be saved for much less. Moreover, your husband would have to be hooked up to a kidney-dialysis machine for eight hours a couple of times a week, and you must admit that the quality of the lives saved by building safer roads would be much higher. Perhaps it would help if you and Mrs. Smith got together and tried to comfort one another. She lost her husband in the recent air crash, and seemed indignant because the F.A.A. for many years has had a radar system that can prevent such crashes. I tried to explain the high cost of putting those systems in every two-bit airport around the country, and I pointed out that without them if it hadn't been her husband's life it would have been someone else's. I'm not sure that I persuaded her. But just because we *can* save lives doesn't mean we *should* save lives. We've got some pretty complete WTP [willingness-to-pay] surveys now, and it is clear that the public thinks we are spending enough on lifesaving programs."

SOURCE: Steven E. Rhoads, "How Much Should We spend to Save a Life?" *The Public Interest* no. 51 (Spring 1978): 91.

Another aspect of the problem-solving model to encourage the use of policy research in decision-making is the desire for strong leaders and centralized decision-making. We have seen that public management in the United States operates in a highly decentralized milieu. Agencies

---

25. Ibid., p. 123.
26. Joseph S. Wholey, "What Can We Actually Get from Program Evaluation?" *Policy Sciences* 3 (1972): 361–369.

depend on other agencies for resources—both money and expertise—and they can be regulated by other agencies. Intergovernmental relations further decentralize decision-making authority. Policy analysts would like to see strong leaders like former secretary of defense Robert McNamara calling for analysis and using it to make the recommended changes. In government, however, there is generally a rapid turnover of political executives. Often the person who commissions an evaluation is not in office when the study is finally submitted. Since the successor did not call for the particular study, often it is put on the shelf to gather dust while the successor arranges for his or her own evaluation. By the time that study is presented, perhaps there is a new agency head who will ignore it and request yet another evaluation.[27]

Even through Rein and White blast the problem-solving model for postulating a world of public management that is far from the one we know, they believe that social science research can play a role in policy-making. Social scientists can and do report on events with more precision than that available through a limited series of personal encounters. Sampling and statistical manipulation of data can lead to interesting inferences. Data developed by analysts may stimulate particular interest groups to demand specific programs. Policy analysis can clarify the range of choices available on large problems. It can suggest possible tradeoffs between mutually exclusive goals such as preserving work incentives and simultaneously providing income support. Analysis can be useful.

A Place for the Analytic Component

PUBLIC administration, public management, and public policy journals are packed with articles showing the possibilities and (more often) the weaknesses of policy analysis. Generally, these articles point out the difficulties of applying social science techniques to complex public policy problems such as education, race relations, and income distribution. Whereas the analytic techniques have not been as effective as their strongest proponents had hoped in solving problems of this scale, on certain lower-level problems—evaluations of specific programs—policy techniques have been used with some degree of success.

27. Easterbrook, "The Art of Further Study."

Even strong advocates of program evaluation have a feeling for its limitations. Joseph S. Wholey, who defines evaluation as "systematic measures and comparisons to provide specific information on program results for use in policy or management decisions," admits that "evaluation is seldom sufficiently timely, relevant, and conclusive to provide useful feedback to decision makers."[28] Formal, systematic evaluations are supposed to supplement the large amounts of informal feedback on program results that policy-makers and managers already get.

For many programs—especially the bread-and-butter programs of local government, such as public works and sanitation—evaluation techniques that are relatively simple and inexpensive are available. The Urban Institute has developed and tested a variety of such techniques. Among them are telephone surveys of program staffs and program recipients as well as of persons in the target population who do not use the facilities being evaluated. Ingenious scales have been developed to assess whether city streets are cleaner or dirtier than they were at some earlier time. An assortment of measures for library services, crime control, and fire protection as well as for public mass transit have also been developed and tested.[29] The evaluation techniques that have been developed for these areas are groups of measures or indicators, any one of which might not meet stringent social science criteria; but when they are taken together, they provide a package of information that program managers, especially, can use to try to improve program performance.

A major unifying characteristic of all these programs is that a consensus exists on what they are supposed to accomplish. Solid-waste disposal is supposed to clean up the streets. There is very little quarrel about that. Libraries are supposed to serve a variety of clientele. These groups can be identified and contacted regarding the services they seek from libraries. Reasonable people can reasonably agree on what constitutes a decent transit system and whether service is getting better or worse. Not all programs are susceptible to this kind of agreement on goals, but many programs can be evaluated by systematically collecting information that relates to their impact on the community.

Most people who are concerned with better formal evaluation techniques do not want information for the sake of having people fill out

---

28. Joseph S. Wholey, "The Role of the Evaluation and the Evaluator in Improving Public Programs: The Bad News, The Good News, and a Bicentennial Challenge," *Public Administration Review* 36, no. 6 (November–December 1976): 680.

29. Harry P. Hatry et al. *How Effective Are Your Community Services? Procedures for Monitoring the Effectiveness of Municipal Services* (Washington, D.C.: The Urban Institute, 1977). This book is an indispensable guide to program measurement and its use.

more forms. They want the information in order to find out if a program is working or not working. More important, if it is not working, evaluation data will show specifically what aspects are not working so that managers can take corrective action. To this end, evaluators produce reports that "emphasize comparisons of interest . . . such as (a) changes from one year to the next; (b) differences between areas of the community; (c) findings for various clientele groups (different age, sex, income, and racial groupings); and (d) planned performance versus performance achieved."[30] These kinds of information form the data base for all attempts at budget reform, including management by objectives and zero-base budgeting (ZBB), which have become widespread in all levels of American government in the past five years.

Summary

POLITICAL decision-making and policy analysis are both forms of rational behavior, depending on one's perspective. For great issues dealing with societal values, people expect politics to have a role in a democracy. Yet at a lower level of involvement, policy analysis and systematic program evaluation can help define what a political issue is and suggest tradeoffs through means-ends analysis. In the real world of public decision-making, most decisions are not made on purely political grounds. Nor are they made according to strict social science analysis. Real-world public decision-making consciously combines the two in a mixed-scanning mode. Public administrators do use their expert knowledge and do engage in analytic activities aimed at solving problems. They are, however, subject to the political environment.

This interplay of expertise and politics can best be seen in budgetary decision-making. As some of the techniques of program analysis have become more commonplace through information sharing, governments at all levels have been able to include formal evaluation information in their decision processes. Some have chosen not to do so. Others have not used what information they have gathered. Analytic material can be important in budgetary decision-making, but the major decisions in this area still appear to be political. We turn to this vital area of public management in the next chapter.

---

30. Ibid., p. 200.

Suggestions for Further Reading

Beckman, Norman, ed. "Symposium on Policy Analysis in Government; Alternatives to 'Muddling Through.' " *Public Administration Review* 37, no. 3 (May–June 1977).

Hatry, Harry P., Louis H. Blair, Donald M. Fisk, John H. Greiner, John R. Hall, Jr., and Philip S. Schaenman. *How Effective Are Your Community Services? Procedures for Monitoring the Effectiveness of Municipal Services.* Washington, D.C.: The Urban Institute, 1977.

Levin, Richard I., and Charles A. Kirkpatrick. *Quantitative Approaches to Management,* 3rd ed. New York: McGraw-Hill, 1975.

Lindblom, Charles E. *The Intelligence of Democracy.* New York: Free Press, 1965.

Lynn, Laurence E., Jr. *Designing Public Policy: A Casebook on the Role of Policy Analysis.* Santa Monica, Calif.: Goodyear, 1980.

Murphy, Jerome T. *Getting the Facts: A Fieldwork Guide for Evaluators and Policy Analysts.* Santa Monica, Calif.: Goodyear, 1980.

Olson, Mancur, Jr. *The Logic of Collective Action: Public Goods and the Theory of Groups.* Cambridge, Mass.: Harvard University Press, 1965.

Public Administration Review 39, no. 6 (November–December 1979). Several articles dealing with the twentieth annivesary of the publication of "The Science of 'Muddling Through.' "

Rivlin, Alice M. *Systematic Thinking for Social Action.* Washington, D.C.: The Brookings Institution, 1971.

Quade, E. S. *Analysis for Public Decisions.* New York: American Elsevier, 1975.

Simon, Herbert A. *Administrative Behavior,* 3rd ed. New York: Free Press, 1976.

Stokey, Edith, and Richard Zeckhauser. *A Primer for Policy Analysis,* New York: W. W. Norton, 1978.

Schneider, Mark, and David Swinton, eds. "Symposium on Policy Analysis in State and Local Government." *Public Administration Review* 39, no. 1 (January–February 1979).

Wildavsky, Aaron. *Speaking Truth to Power: The Art and Craft of Policy Analysis.* Boston: Little, Brown, 1979.

Decision Analysis Forecasting for Executive Manpower Planning

The simple decision analysis problem that follows is directed toward a manpower-planning problem. The basic methodology and techniques, however, are characteristic of any decision analysis problem. When you assess this piece, consider how much faith you would put in the final recommendations if you were a decision-maker. Is such an exercise helpful? What dangers are involved in dealing with these analytic recommendations?

I. Introduction

THE forecasting technique described in this paper is especially designed to help determine executive manpower needs and resources at the agency level and below. Forecasting changes in executive manpower, program priorities, and organizational structure provide the key component in the overall manpower-planning process and a critical aspect of executive development programs, budget planning, and other phases of agency management. The assumptions and data requirements for most forecasting models and techniques reduce or even preclude their usefulness in executive manpower planning. Decision Analysis Forecasting (DAF) is designed to meet the need for an alternative approach, or, in some instances, a supplementary technique.

SOURCE: U.S. Civil Service Commission, Bureau of Executive Manpower, Executive Manpower Management Technical Assistance Center (EMMTAC), Executive Manpower Management Technical Assistance Paper No. 3, (Washington, D.C.: U.S. Government Printing Office, 1974), p. 30.

II. Brief Description of Decision Analysis Forecasting (DAF)

DAF is a fast, flexible, and extremely responsive method for assisting senior management in forecasting manpower and organizational needs. It is specifically designed for use on problems where the experience and judgments of top-level policy-makers comprise the basic and often the only information.

More technically, DAF is a model for developing executive manpower forecasts by: (1) "decomposing" each manpower planning problem into its relevant factors, (2) quantifying subjective preferences and probability judgments for each problem factor, and (3) combining the available data plus these quantified judgments into a table of predictions. The methodology draws largely on decision analysis theory using "Decision Trees" and some simple mathematics from probability theory.

III. Comparison with Other Methods

A LARGE assortment of elaborate, sophisticated models for manpower forecasting have been developed from the fields of mathematics, econometrics, operations research, and behavioral science. Most of these techniques are either a form of time-series analysis or regression analysis. All such models must rely on the availability of considerable historical data, the appropriateness of large-sample statistics, or the applicability of generalized assumptions about the particular manpower problem. Where historical data are scarce, sampling is impossible, and assumptions are unique to each problem, Decision Analysis Forecasting (DAF) is proposed as a more suitable forecasting model.

The *form* of the resulting outputs, as well as the type of inputs, distinguishes DAF from many other models. Rather than providing only the "best" single forecast, DAF results are in the form of a table or array listing all of the more probable answers, each with a weight or index of its relative likelihood (sometimes interpreted as preference or confidence level depending on the type of problem). The results also include a "branch diagram" breaking the forecast into a complex of alternative

257

branches and intervening factors each with their own prediction indices. This type of output allows the analyst to average, compare, and combine related forecasts.

Another distinction is the durability of the model outputs. Most time-series and regression models are doomed to almost immediate obsolescence or involve great costs in continually updating the data, assumptions, and calculations. DAF uses the most expensive *original* input: namely, the time and judgments of top management; but once this information is obtained, the model makes prudent use of it through the flexibility and prediction adjustment capability provided by probability theory and Bayesian statistics. As new information develops, it can be added to the original analysis with minimal additional inputs from the decision-maker.

IV. Integration with Other Methods

PERHAPS DAF is most valuable in a mixed-mode model with other forecasting methodologies. Frequently, some data are available which provide projection rates for certain variables, while other variables pertaining to the same problem remain strictly a matter of judgment. For example, retirement rates are readily determined from historical data but predicting changes in retirement legislation falls clearly into the realm of Decision Analysis Forecasting. What is needed is a way of quantifying both types of variables (i.e., historical retirement patterns and the likelihood of new retirement legislation) so they can be used together in the same forecasting model. The DAF procedure provides a technique for integrating judgmental data in a mixed-mode forecasting model.

V. Applicable Types of Forecasting Problems

THE DAF Model is particularly suited for forecasting problems which are characterized by:

—agency-level questions and "micro" analysis rather than governmentwide questions and "macro" analysis.
—short-range rather than long-range time horizons.
—considerable change rather than relative stability.

The model can forecast either the timing for a given event or conversely the likelihood that a particular event will occur in a given time range. Examples of forecast events appropriate for DAF are: (1) numbers of executives or other types of personnel, (2) mixes or ratios of personnel such as noncareer/career, (3) location of organizational units, (4) creation or abolition of programs and organizations. For example, you may predict either:

—the number of executives the agency will have in 19XX.
—the future date when the agency will have 12 executives.

The single most important requirement is a *forecasting question,* which can be concisely stated in terms of intervening factors and an array of possible answers. The procedures described in detail in section VII give specific examples and instructions for the meticulous definition of the forecast problems.

VI. The Role of the Analyst

NORMALLY, DAF is carried out by an analyst on the staff of the particular agency. The paramount skills required of the manpower analyst in using the DAF model are in ability to conduct difficult, although highly structured, interviews, and some understanding of decision analysis and probability theory. He does not need to be a specialist in any field of mathematics. In fact, while the calculations involving joint-conditional probabilities may appear at first glance to be very complex, they are actually very mechanical and can be easily interpreted. The analyst also does not need to be an expert in the agency's manpower problems and, in fact, he may be able to be more objective in his analysis if he is not. It is essential, however, that he be able to elicit frank opinions and information from senior managers who serve as a planning panel. In addition to the manpower analyst collecting the judgmental data and calculating forecasts, he serves as the coordinator for the entire DAF procedure.

VII. The DAF
Procedure

THE use of the DAF Model in manpower planning involves a sequence of steps which must be followed for each question in the planning problem. Generally a single planning problem consists of a number of forecast questions. For example, a classic manpower-planning problem involves separate questions concerning the following topics:

—*future staff requirements;*
—*supply within the organization (future promotions, transfers);*
—*supply outside the organization (future recruitment).*

FIGURE A

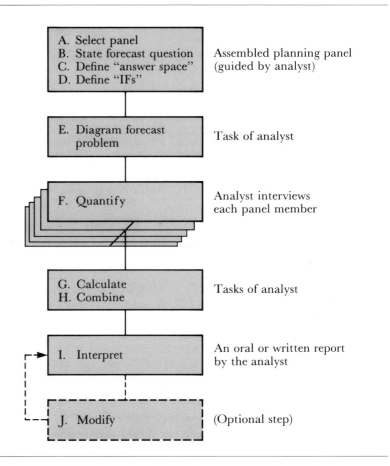

A. Select panel
B. State forecast question · Assembled planning panel
C. Define "answer space" · (guided by analyst)
D. Define "IFs"

E. Diagram forecast problem · Task of analyst

F. Quantify · Analyst interviews each panel member

G. Calculate · Tasks of analyst
H. Combine

I. Interpret · An oral or written report by the analyst

J. Modify · (Optional step)

Figure A illustrates the sequence of meetings and procedures plus the role of panel members and the analyst in each step of the DAF procedure. Following are sections explaining each step in detail.

A. Selecting the Planning Panel

The head of the planning panel should be the executive personally responsible for making the forecasts. The other members of the panel should be those people he would normally consult in making a decision concerning the forecast problem. This first step (panel appointment) cannot usually be separated from the next step, the statement of the forecast question. At least a general notion of the question is needed in order to determine the basic panel membership. Since the forecast question is more explicitly specified in steps B–D, the panel may at that time take on new members or agree to replace some existing member as the more precise definition of the problem indicates. A typical panel should consist of three to five members possibly including top management in the program, personnel training, and legislative areas. If desired, the entire panel can consist of just one person, the policy-maker responsible for the particular planning decision. This choice of a one-man panel would depend on the style of the decision-maker and the characteristics of the particular planning problem.

The assembled group will meet with the analyst for approximately an hour. Following this meeting the analyst will interview the panel members individually for about one hour each. Most of the data required for the analysis can be obtained from these meetings. An optional follow-up meeting is sometimes requested so that the entire panel can discuss the resulting forecasts.

B. Stating the Forecast Question

The panel must first agree on a concise statement of the forecast question. This consists of a statement of the stipulations and the form of "outcome" or answer for the specific question being forecast. The stipulations are fixed conditions such as "headquarters positions only" or "given a budget of X dollars." (Variable conditions, where the question involves consideration of alternatives, such as a range of possible budget levels, are discussed in section D below as intervening factors.) The form of outcome can be in terms of manpower quantity, ratio, timing, or simply a change (e.g., a program change). "Future time" is a part of each of the forecast questions, if not as the answer, then as a stipulation. For example:

261

—When *will the number of executives in the agency be reduced? (Time as the event or answer being predicted).?*

—How many *executives will the agency have in June, 19XX? (Time as a stipulation)?*

C. Defining the "Answer Space"

The panel must agree on a range of possible answers and the analyst will assure that this range or "answer space" meets certain technical as well as practical requirements.

The practical requirements are that the possible answers:

—*are clearly understood by each panel member.*

—*are distinctive (i.e., if the answers are in terms of future dates, years may be distinguishable where days or months are not).*

—*comprise a "short" list (recommend no more than five or ten possible answers rather than a comprehensive catalogue including farfetched possibilities.)*

The technical requirements are that the total range of possible answers be:

—*"mutually exclusive"—meaning only one answer can be "true."*

—*"collectively exhaustive"—meaning the list includes the "true" answer.*

D. Determining Intervening Factors (IF)

When the panel discusses a forecasting question, they typically describe the "related questions," "other considerations," or "intervening factors." For example, if the question is: "How many executives will be needed in 19XX?" the first response from the panel is likely to be: "That all depends on several conditional factors such as the budget, future program emphasis, and reorganization plans." These related considerations, or intervening factors (IF), as they will be called in these DAF procedures, are the very substance of decision analysis.

The panel should construct a basic list of intervening factors although individual members do not need to agree on the importance of each IF or even on the inclusion of a particular IF in their individual analysis. That is, one panel member may consider a particular factor to be relevant even though other members disagree. This step in the procedures is repeated in the individual interviews and at that stage new IFs can be added and others dropped from the panel-developed list. The point is

262

that while the panel must agree completely on the "answer space" or range of alternative answers to the forecasting question, they do not have to agree on intervening factors.

There are two classes of intervening factors:

—Dependent IFs—*These are variable conditions which are logically dependent on some other IF in the same problem. For example, assume the forecast question is: "Will the agency create a new bureau next year?" And some IFs are: "If the new program legislation is introduced," followed by "If Congress passes it," followed by the question itself ("Will a new bureau be created?"). With these dependent IFs, the* order *is important because each is dependent on the one logically preceding it.*

—Independent IFs—*These factors are conditional to the forecast question but are independent of other IFs. Continuing the example about a new bureau: "Could existing bureaus handle the new programs?" This IF is not related in any dependent way to the other two factors concerning congressional action but it is a conditional factor on the forecast question.*

Each IF is really a forecasting question in itself and has its own "answer space" or list of possible outcomes. The IF answer space must meet the same technical and practical requirements as the answer space for the basic forecast question. That is, the list of possible answers must be mutually exclusive and collectively exhaustive (see section C) and should also be concise. A simple two-outcome answer space will be possible for many IFs. For example, "Passage by Congress during this session?" can be answered simply "yes" or "no." It is recommended that wherever possible a very simply two or three answer space be used for IFs. The reason for the strong emphasis on brief, simple IF outcomes will be apparent in the next procedure when the entire problem is diagrammed.

In the Figure B illustration, there are three branching levels. Each level represents an IF with the exception of the top level which is the forecast question itself. The branches are the possible outcomes for each IF. IF-2 is dependent on IF-1 and, therefore, for each IF-1 outcome (1-A, 1-B) IF-2 is repeated, and so forth up the "tree." Figure C shows the same diagram with a specific example.

A branch diagram should be drawn by the analyst describing the entire forecast problem. Its purpose is to lay out each possible combination of outcomes and provide a work sheet for the process of quantifying the

E. Diagramming the Forecast Question

FIGURE B

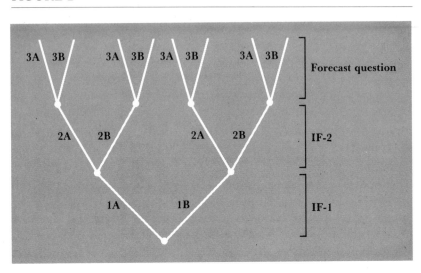

FIGURE C

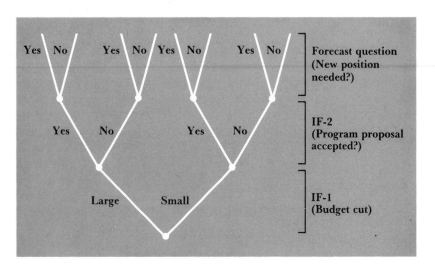

judgments of panel members (section F). Figure B illustrates the basic form of the diagram.

The diagrams for DAF problems grow very complex and "bushy" as the number of IFs and related intermediate outcomes increases. One of the objectives of decision analysis is to reduce this complexity to its essential relationships. Therefore, the diagramming step is more than a simple documentation process. It is also an analytical process to simplify the tree diagram from a "bushy" to a "pruned" version as illustrated in Figure D.

DAF tree diagrams can be pruned in the following ways:

1. Reduce the number of outcomes. *The analyst should particularly seek to streamline the outcome lists of lower level IFs in the diagram. A bushy base will make the diagram extremely difficult to use during step F and the calculations tedious in step G. The number of outcomes per IF can be reduced by:*
    —Grouping outcomes. *The size of the answer intervals represented by an outcome can be increased. For example, if the budget factor is an IF, it might be forecast in intervals of ten-thousands rathers than thousands.*
    —Eliminating insignificant outcome distinctions. *This opportunity to simplify the problem is not always apparent until step F, when the outcomes are given relative values indicating likelihood or preference. At that time whole branches of the diagram can be cut off as being insignificant or redundant to the forecast question.*

FIGURE D

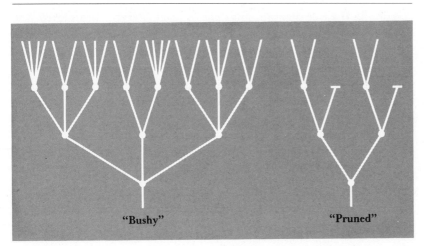

"Bushy"   "Pruned"

2. Terminate illogical branching. *For example, in Figure C, if the program proposal (IF-2) is not accepted there may be no logic to considering the possibility of a new executive position (IF-3). The results of this logical pruning are shown in the "pruned" tree in Figure D.*

3. Diagram independent IFs separately. *These IFs (independent ones as defined in step D) do not need to be a part of the basic diagram because their outcomes are not dependent on other factors. For complex problems, diagramming horizontally, from left to right, is generally preferable over the vertical "tree" format. During pilot tests of the DAF procedures at various government agencies, it was found that horizontal diagrams made the entry of written descriptions and data much easier. Therefore, the examples in the next section will branch from left to right.*

F. Quantifying Judgments

This step requires a particularly high degree of skill on the part of the analyst and cooperation from the members of the planning panel, it is also the most crucial step in the DAF procedure. In individual interviews with each panelist the manpower analyst (1) prunes and tailors the panel's decision diagram to reflect the individual's point of view and special insight, and (2) obtains judgments of the relative likelihood that a decision will go along a particular branch on the diagram.

The process of quantifying judgments consists of giving alternative outcomes relative weights which represent preference or likelihood. The weights (sometimes referred to as probability values or indexes) must lie between .0, 1.0, i.e., be a fraction represented as a decimal such as .5, .33, .07, etc. The sum of these weights representing outcome from a single junction in the tree diagram must *always equal 1.00.* For instance, if it is certain that "yes" is the answer to a given question, "yes" would receive a value of 1.0. On the other hand, if "yes" and "no" were equally likely, each would have a value of .5. In Figure E, these weights are illustrated on an extremely simplified diagram which will be used throughout the rest of this description of DAF procedures. The weights are shown in parentheses.

CONDITIONAL PROBABILITY · With the exception of the IF-1 level of the problem, all of the weights are "conditional probabilities."[1] This means the weight or probability value attached to an outcome in IF-2 is conditional on a "given" outcome in IF-1. In the illustration in Figure E,

---

1. IF-1 weights are not conditional on a prior occurrence since by definition they are the first level of the decision problem.

FIGURE E

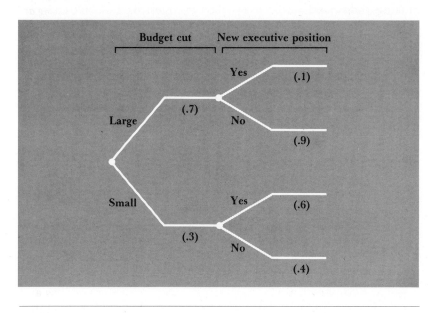

the branch of the forecast question weighted (.1) is the probability of the answer "yes" to the question of the need for a new executive position, given a "large" budget cut.

In the shorthand used in probability mathematics, a vertical bar (|) is the symbol for "given" and p(A) is used to represent the probability or weight of A. The branch of Figure E referred to above would be writtern p(yes | large) = .1.

In discussing each possible outcome with the panelist, the mathematical shorthand should be avoided, but the terms "given" and "conditional" have proven to be very easily understood and useful in eliciting probabilities. The acronym "IF" (intervening factor) is also useful. For example, "What is the likelihood of needing a new executive position IF there is a large budge cut?" Usually all of the decision branches stemming from the same set of conditions can be discussed one after the other with the same premise for each outcome: "Given the conditions as before, how would you judge the likelihood that . . . ?"

ELICITING THE WEIGHTS • During the individual interviews the manpower analyst must be flexible and creative in the approaches he uses to obtain judgments from the panel members. While these *quantified* judg-

267

ments must always take the form described above, they can be converted from many forms of expression used in stating relative weight such as rankings, odds, and verbal terms such as "most likely," "fat chance," and "sure bet." During pilot tests of DAF in a variety of government agencies, experience was obtained in the actual use and conversion of various expressions of relative weight. Based on these pilot tests, the next paragraphs offer advice on interview techniques and instruction on the mechanics for converting each type of statement into standard decimal fractions.

Direct Estimates Some panelists will be able to directly make estimates in the decimal fraction (or percent) form. They may prefer this form if they feel they have very precise preferences or judgments about the relative likelihood of outcomes. The most common way of stating direct estimates is in the form of percentages rather than "point six-five" (e.g., "I'd say there's a 65% chance that we'll have a severe budget cut"). The analyst can simply record these percentages as decimal fractions but must watch that the sum of outcome weights for the same event equal unit (1.0) exactly. That is, a panelist cannot make the above statement and then say, "There's a 50% chance that the cut will be small."

Ranking An approach many panelists will prefer is simple ranking of

TABLE A

		Number of Rank Positions							
		2	3	4	5	6	7	8	9	10
	1	.33	.17	.10	.07	.05	.04	.03	.02	.02
	2	.67	.33	.20	.13	.10	.07	.06	.04	.04
	3		.50	.30	.20	.14	.11	.08	.07	.05
	4			.40	.27	.19	.14	.11	.09	.07
	5				.33	.24	.18	.14	.11	.09
Rank	6					.29	.21	.17	.13	.11
	7						.25	.19	.16	.13
	8							.22	.18	.15
	9								.20	.16
	10									.18

alternative outcomes. Starting by ranking the least likely first will help in converting to fractions. The conversion formula is: rank of outcome divided by sum of ranking positions. For example, if there are five possible outcomes the one ranked fourth is converted to 4/15 or .27. (Note that the denominator is 15, not 5. It is the sum of ranking positions, i.e., 1+2+3+4+5.) Table A is a useful conversion chart for fast calculations during the actual interview. It also helps clarify the relationship between rank and relative weight. The entries in the table have been rounded to two digits. More precision is unnecessary and is usually misleading.

Odds   Some panelists will be most comfortable stating relationships in terms of wagers or odds such as "2 to 1 against a budget decrease" or "4:1 the bill will pass," or "the odds are even." Odds can only be stated between two outcomes at a time. They are converted to fractions by dividing the first number by the sum of both numbers. Thus, X:Y is the same as $\frac{X}{X+Y}$ or in the examples above, 2 to 1 equals ⅔ equals .67; 4:1 equals 4/5 equals .80; and 1:1 equals ½ equals 50.

Verbal Expressions   Perhaps the most common expressions of relative outcome weight are idioms such as "best bet," "fat chance," "no way," "toss up," and so forth. The basic approach here is to:

—*make sure the meaning is clearly understood. ("Fat chance" has an idiomatic meaning the opposite of its literal meaning.)*
—*convert most expressions first to rankings and then to decimals.*
—*some expressions should logically be converted directly such as "no way" (.0) and "toss up" (.50).*

Mixed Modes   Most frequently the manpower analyst will have to deal with a mixed expression such as of the three possible outcomes, A, B, or C, "Outcome A is 80% likely but if not A then I'd lay 4 to 1 against outcome B." The resulting weights are A = .80, B = .04, C = .16. (The 4:1 odds between B and C had only .20 of the total "answer space" and could therefore total only to .20, not to 1.00.) The essential rule, then, in quantifying judgments is to apply each form of estimation to its own portion of the available answer space, which must total 100% overall.

The actual calculations of forecasts for each panelist are surprisingly simple. Two entirely mechanical operations are involved:

G. Calculating Forecasts

—*Multiplying the weights out the entire length of each decision tree branch in order to find the "joint conditional probabilities."*

—Adding the joint conditional probabilities which are common to the same forecast answer.

Completing these two operations results in a *forecast distribution* or array of weighted outcomes covering the answer space of the original forecast question. Figure F demonstrates the two operations and illustrates a completed forecast problem.

H. Combining Forecasts

The final forecast distributions calculated for each panelist in G above can be averaged in order to obtain a panel consensus. The weighted opinions permit the use of either the mean or median summary statistics rather than the simple (and distorting)[2] opinion based on the majority of yes-no votes. The median or "middle weight" is arithmetically possible but generally unsatisfactory because of the small size of most panels. The mean (the sum of weights for a particular outcome divided by the

FIGURE F

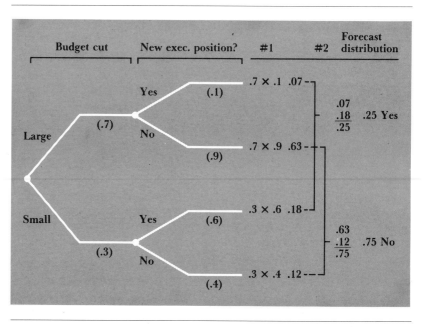

---

2. Simply adding up "yes" and "no" votes overlooks the degree of certainty with which these opinions are registered. For instance, three panel members might all vote "yes" on a question, giving the appearance of great certainty, when actually each of them considered "yes" to be only marginally more likely than "no."

TABLE B

| | Panel Members | | | | | | (*) Panel Vote (unweighted) | Panel's Average Weights |
| | 1 | | 2 | | 3 | | | |
	Ans.	Wt.	Ans.	Wt.	Ans.	Wt.		
YES		.40	*	.85		.45	1	.57
NO	*	.60		.15	*	.55	2	.43

number of panelists making an estimate for that outcome) is perhaps the better measure, but it must also be interpreted carefully because of the small-sized panels and the powerful effect of extreme judgments.

Table B illustrates a very simplified situation where a three-member panel predicts 2 to 1 against an outcome if unweighted judgments were used and the opposite if the weighted judgment averages were used. The obvious case here is that one of the panelists (# 2 with the "yes" judgment) was much surer in his opinion than the other two, who were virtually undecided.

A more realistic situation often requires acknowledgment of unequal status of panel members. The head of the panel may wish to have twice the vote of other members because of his greater familiarity with the particular forecast problem, his personal style of decision-making, or both. In the example in Table B, suppose Panelist 1 is the panel head, and that his response is to be given double weight. Then, the panel average for "yes" would be only .52 [(.40 +.40+.85+.45 ÷ 4)]. Very complex systems can be devised for weighing not only the entire forecast distribution for each panel member but also the specific variables within the problem based on special areas of expertise.

Another use of weighted outcomes in DAF permits combining these forecasts with other manpower planning models. Realistic systems of manpower planning typically must include both objective variables (such as projected retirement based on historical rates) and subjective variables (such as possible congressional action). Using DAF to quantify the subjective variables provides the means for fusing these variables for manpower planning. It overcomes the objection of top management that purely objective systems ignore "real world" variables.

The interpretation of DAF forecasts is very straightforward and this is a major advantage of the technique. The outcome values are in essence prediction weights where the highest weight is the primary forecast and

I. Interpretation Forecasts

TABLE C
Number of Additional Executive Positions Needed Next Year

Possible Answers (answer-space)	Prediction Weights
0	.30
1	.50
2	.20

indicates the certainty of the prediction. For example, in Table C the forecast of one additional executive position is the primary forecast with a prediction weight of .50. There are, however, several precautions in making interpretations of the forecast results:

Significant Intervals within a Single Forecast Distribution   A frequent question is: "How can you tell if the highest weighted answer is 'significantly' more certain than the next answer?" You must obviously interpret the size of the interval between the two outcomes. One suggestion is to compare the interval difference to a "standard interval." Table D gives standard intervals for various numbers of possible outcomes. If the interval between weights is less than the standard interval, the difference can be considered negligible and the two outcomes could be considered equally likely.

For example, looking at Table C, the weight interval between the primary forecast of "1" and the next highest forecast of "0" is .50 − .30 = .20. This is a greater interval than the standard interval of .166 (see Table D) and therefore is significant. Conversely, the weight interval between the "0" answer and the "2" answer is .30 − .20 = .10 and these two answers can be considered equally likely.

Comparing Answers from Different Problems   Remember that the outcome weights are *relative* within their own problem or answer space. To compare a primary forecast of .75 in one problem to a primary forecast of .20 in a different problem and interpret the .75 as a more certain forecast could be entirely wrong. The actual size of the weight depends on

TABLE D

Number of possible outcomes	2	3	4	5	6	7	8	9	10
Standard interval	.355	.166	.100	.066	.048	.036	.027	.022	.018

the number of possible outcomes over which the weights are distributed and the "shape" of that distribution.

If it is necessary to compare weights across problems, standard scores or weights should be used. The formula[3] for standard scores is

$$\frac{x-M}{SD}$$

This is calculated as the difference between the forecast weight (x) and the distribution's mean forecast (M) divided by its standard deviation (SD). For instance, if the forecast weight is .75, the distribution's mean = .50, and the SD = .25; the standard score is

$$\frac{.75-.50}{.25} = \frac{.25}{.25} = 1$$

If the forecast weight is .20, and there are 7 other alternative possibilities with weights of .15, .15, .10, .10, .10, .10, .10, the distribution mean is .125, the SD = .035 and the standard score is 2.1. Actually, then, the prediction of .20 in a field of 8 possibilities is more certain than the prediction of .75 in a field of 2 possibilities.

An important feature of DAF is its durability against obsolescence. The manpower analyst can adjust forecasts to reflect new data and even new IFs without reconstructing the entire problem. Different methods are used depending on whether the new information simply changes the weights of existing IFs or introduces new conditional IFs.

J. Modifying Forecasts with New Information

New Data, Existing IFs   The original process for a particular problem created a detailed diagram and captured the judgments of each panel member. When new information has changed the judgments of some of the panelists on some of the IFs, a recalculation is possible without assembling the entire panel. For example, when estimating the likelihood of passage of a bill by Congress, new data such as press statements by key congressmen on how they plan to vote will change the judgments of some panel members. Revised estimates by these panel members on the particular IFs provide the new weights needed to adjust the entire forecast.

New Data, New IFs   When new information introduces a new IF, a special procedure can be used to adjust the forecasts. Using the example of estimating the likelihood of passage of a bill by Congress, the new information is that the bill has been passed out of House Committee. This is an entirely new IF and the question is how does it affect the total pre-

---

3. J. P. Guilford, *Fundamental Statistics in Psychology and Education* (New York: McGraw-Hill, 1973).

diction. The mathematical calculations developed by Thomas Bayes over two hundred years ago allow us to adjust the estimates of passage by Congress by simply calculating in the conditional probabilities associated with "getting the bill through committee." The formula and proper procedure for this are well presented by Raiffa.[4]

VII. Summary

DAF is a method for assisting senior management in forecasting executive manpower and organizational changes. It is specifically designed for use where the experience and judgments of top-level policy-makers comprise the basic and often the only information. In these cases DAF provides a supplementary technique or alternative approach to the traditional manpower forecasting models.

The technique is practical and responsive, making full use of management's experience and judgment. It is also compatible with other models which must rely solely on historical data. It is durable since its ability to accommodate the constant flow of new information makes its forecasts relatively immune to the immediate obsolescence of most forecast models. Finally, DAF provides forecasts which are easily understood and relevant to top management's paramount task of evaluating alternative plans of action.

---

4. Howard Raiffa, *Decision Analysis* (Reading, Mass.: Addison-Wesley, 1968).

CHAPTER NINE

The Budgetary Process:
Politics and Policy

Policy-making in government covers an extraordinarily wide range of specific activities because government's role in a modern state is so varied. Despite the differences in specific decision areas, each of which requires different skills and knowledge, there is one process that is common to all levels of government and to all agencies. That is the budget-making process by which agencies are able to make claims on society's resources so they may function and, it is hoped, achieve the broad objectives outlined in legislation and in the public's mind.

Expenditures by all levels of government in the United States have gone beyond the $700 billion per year mark (see Figure 9.1). Even in the face of widespread taxpayer concern about government spending, inflationary pressures and demands for services will force government spending still higher. Although we will find that many expenditures are uncontrollable through the annual budget cycle, we must recognize the importance of the budgetary process, which is a legal and administrative process that legitimizes government expenditure. Because of inflation, government expenditures have continued to rise sharply. Federal expenditures for fiscal year 1982 alone were approximately $700 billion.

In this chapter, we will look at the budget-making process, various types of budget documents, and changes that have occurred recently at all levels of government. We will emphasize the key roles that political actors play in the process. Contemporary public budgeting at all levels still operates in a political milieu. Increasingly, however, strong executives have used modern techniques to accomplish two purposes: (1) to develop alternatives to enhance the role of centralized decision-makers, and (2) to demand program results through program analysis and evaluation. These dual purposes of modern budgeting techniques appear at all levels of government, although the more sophisticated techniques are more often employed in larger jurisdictions, which have the resources to support them. Although we will introduce the rationale for techniques such as planning-programming-budgeting systems (PPBS), management by objectives (MBO), and zero-base budgeting (ZBB) here, we will explore them in greater detail in the chapter on executive control, which follows.

PHOTO: Rep. William Brodhead (D-Mich.), left, and Rep. Stephen Solarz (D-N.Y.), right, tape a sign in front of House Budget Committee Chairman Robert Giaimo (D-Conn.) at a 1980 press conference where Giaimo announced more than $15 billion in proposed cuts to the fiscal 1981 federal budget.

FIGURE 9.1
Expenditures by Federal, State, and Local Governments

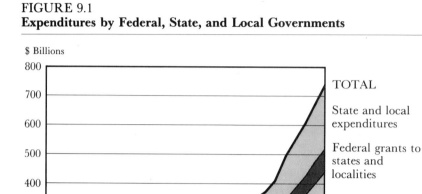

SOURCE: U.S. Office of Management and Budget, *Special Analyses: Budget of the United States Government, Fiscal Year 1981* (Washington D.C.: U.S. Government Printing Office, 1980), p. 256.

Public Budgeting Defined

SIMPLY stated, a budget is a plan. A budget document is a reflection of what we expect to do in the future. Not all plans are budgets, however. We may have a plan to retrain highly specialized aerospace scientists to solve urban problems. We may know what courses and methods of training we would like to use. We may know what organizations we plan to use as consultants on the project, and we may even know what universities or training institutes we want to do the retraining. But even a highly detailed plan is not a budget until we specify how much money we are willing to commit to the project. A budget, therefore, is a special kind of plan in that it is concerned with money. It deals with how much a government plans to spend and how that expenditure is to be financed.

A budget deals with expenditure and revenue questions for a specific future time period, usually a *fiscal year*. A fiscal year is any consecutive twelve-month period a jurisdiction has chosen to define as its budget year. In some jurisdictions the fiscal year is concurrent with the calendar year. For most state governments, the fiscal year runs from July 1 through June 30. The United States government used to operate on that timetable but shifted the fiscal year to October 1 through September 30 as part of congressional reforms of the budget process that were passed in 1974.

When passed by the legislature and signed by the chief executive of a particular jurisdiction, a budget becomes law. The amounts of money specified in the budget document are legally binding during that fiscal year. Agencies cannot spend more than is specified unless they are able to get supplemental or deficiency appropriations through the same legal channels as the original budget. Although a formal budget is legally binding only for the fiscal year for which it was designed, some budget documents show the implications of current budget decisions for spending in future years.

A budget is more than simply a legally binding financial plan. It is also a multipurpose document that reflects and seeks to serve the information needs of the participants in the budgetary process. Allen Schick, one of the foremost authorities on both the politics and techniques of budgeting, has suggested that the budget has three main uses: (1) control, (2) management, and (3) planning.[1] A budget controls administrators by tying them to the stated policies of their superiors and legislative overseers. Control through a budget is obtained through accounting practices and reporting procedures that restrict the transfer of funds from one account to another, limit the number of positions available to an agency, and create mountains of paperwork. Such procedures are thought necessary to keep lower-level bureaucrats accountable to their superiors and to discourage affronts to fiscal integrity—i.e., stealing public funds.

The management function of a budget involves efforts to carry out the approved plans and policies efficiently and effectively. The management function is one of the principal roles of central budgeting offices at all levels of government in the United States. In part, renaming the Bureau of the Budget (BOB) the Office of Management and Budget (OMB) in 1970 was recognition of the potential management role that a budgeting office can play in designing and coordinating organization units. Some budget documents include information on costs and workloads that is

---

1. Allen Schick, "Road to PPB: The Stages of Budget Reform," *Public Administration Review* 26, no. 4 (December 1966): 243–244.

helpful to program managers and higher-level decision-makers in both the executive and legislative branches.

Managerial information needs often influence the planning aspects of a budget. In the budgetary context, as Schick has pointed out, "planning involves the determination of objectives, the evaluation of alternative courses of action and the authorization of selected programs."[2] Planning in this sense is closely linked to broad policy choices, but because of the incremental nature of much policy decision-making, planning in the budgetary process reflects political pressures as much as financial analysis.

Budget Classification

ALTHOUGH Schick maintained that control, management, and planning functions were inherent in every government budget, he was aware that all these functions have rarely been given equal attention in actual budget-making. Generally, these functions compete for attention. To a degree, the relative importance of each is reflected in the type of budget document that jurisdictions use. Using examples from the president's budget, we will be able to see how different formats for presenting data give different information to interested participants.

The federal government and many states present budget documents that contain several different types of budget formats. One of the most common formats is the functional budget. A functional budget for the United States government is presented in Table 9.1. This budget breaks all the activities of the federal government into sixteen functional categories, which correspond to categories approved in the Congressional Budget and Impoundment Act of 1974. As we shall see, Congress uses this functional format to pass resolutions establishing budget targets and ceilings for each functional category.

More generally, however, the functional format is used principally for symbolic purposes. The functional budget shows what the broad priorities of the government are and how they differ from priorities of past years. In the case of the federal government, promilitary observers used to point to the smaller percentage of the budget that was going to national defense, while critics of the defense budget noted how large the absolute amount of money was that went to that function. The limited

2. Ibid., p. 244.

TABLE 9.1
Example of a Functional Budget
(in millions of dollars)

	1979 Actual	1980 Estimate	1981 Estimate
Budget outlays by function:			
National defense	117,681	130,368	146,241
International affairs	6,091	10,401	9,612
General science, space, and technology	5,041	5,889	6,442
Energy	6,856	7,751	8,107
Natural resources and environment	12,091	12,776	12,819
Agriculture	6,238	4,636	2,802
Commerce and housing credit	2,565	5,476	712
Transportation	17,459	19,631	20,159
Community and regional development	9,482	8,467	8,820
Education, training, employment, and social services	29,685	30,654	31,989
Health	49,614	56,563	62,449
Income security	160,198	190,948	219,982
(Social security)	(102,595)	(117,913)	(136,921)
(Other)	(57,604)	(73,037)	(83,063)
Veterans benefits and services	19,928	20,766	21,731
Administration of justice	4,153	4,530	4,699
General government	4,153	4,885	4,931
General purpose fiscal assistance	8,372	8,670	9,617
Interest	52,556	63,330	67,197
Allowances	—	100	2,570
Undistributed offsetting receipts	−18,488	−22,258	−25,119
Total budget outlays	493,673	563,583	615,761

SOURCE: "Budget Receipts, Outlays, and Budget Authority," *The United States Budget, Fiscal Year 1981* (Washington, D.C.: U.S. Government Printing Office, 1980), Table 2, p. 552.

amount of data in the summary form of a functional budget restricts its usefulness for either control, management, or planning. The functional budget's main purpose seems to be to offer the citizen an overview of where his or her taxes are going.

Budget-making takes place in an organizational context, and this is reflected in organizational or agency budgets. Since modern government tends to be organized roughly along program lines, agency budgets tend to reflect the amounts of money being spent for specific program areas. Of course, as Luther Gulick pointed out, there can never be complete agreement between programs and organization because many government organizations serve more than one purpose.[3] For example, labor

---

3. *See* chapter 4.

attachés connected with United States missions overseas perform both a labor function and an international function. Should the labor attaché be paid by the Department of Labor, or should he or she be paid by the Department of State? The labor attaché serves both programs, but his or her salary is reported only in one agency—the Department of Labor. As is the rule for establishing a functional budget, parts of programs that contribute to two or more programs are classified on the basis of the predominant purpose served. In this case, a labor attaché is deemed to serve the labor function more than the international function.

Object Classification versus Activity Budgets

There are several ways of presenting an organizational budget. The traditional way is called an *object classification* budget. In an object classification budget, as is shown in Table 9.2, expenditure levels are presented on the basis of particular accounts. For example, there is the permanent personnel account, the travel and transportation of persons account, and the equipment account. Generally, each jurisdiction's accounts are defined in budget manuals, which give explicit directions as to what types of expenditures should be included under which account. As the example shows, the figures are listed for the past fiscal year, the current fiscal year, and the fiscal year for which the budget is being proposed.

Object classification budgets emphasize program inputs such as the amount of money to be spent on printing and reproduction (code 24.0 in Table 9.2). They do not emphasize program results. From an object classification budget, it is easy to see the increases or decreases in amounts of money budgeted for individual accounts, but it is not possible to see the level of services that is expected if the budgeted amounts for each account are spent. In jurisdictions that use object classification budgets, information on program results are usually provided in auxiliary budget submissions to justify the figures presented in the object classification format.

Despite the difficulty that the object classification budget does not explicitly tie expenditures to program results, this budget format has been useful for legislative control. Legislators and others are able to look at the various account categories and note any major rises over the past expenditure patterns. They can force the administrator who is defending the budget to explain why the travel account, for example, is expected to grow 15 percent. The legislature could, if it chose to, cut the rise in the travel account to 10 percent of the current year's expenditure. Or it could write some special "line items" into the travel account. Such line items might limit the amount of travel by plane, or the amount of inter-

TABLE 9.2
Example of an Object Classification Budget, Federal Agency X

	Previous Fiscal Year	Current Fiscal Year	Future Fiscal Year
Direct obligations:			
Personnel compensation:			
11.1 Permanent positions	188,453	203,377	204,982
11.3 Positions other than permanent	12,188	12,990	13,227
11.5 Other personnel compensation	11,405	12,156	12,426
Total personnel compensation	212,046	228,523	230,635
12.1 Personnel benefits: Civilian	22,959	25,325	26,800
13.0 Benefits for former personnel	1,989	2,403	2,668
21.0 Travel and transportation of persons	7,438	8,103	9,723
22.0 Transportation of things	2,721	3,165	3,257
23.0 Rent, communications, and utilities	36,923	41,678	42,794
24.0 Printing and reproduction	1,841	1,787	2,517
25.0 Other services	81,798	104,970	127,535
26.0 Supplies and materials	21,673	24,301	27,351
31.0 Equipment	29,356	42,579	36,809
32.0 Lands and structures	429	438	615
41.0 Grants, subsidies, and contributions	30,257	32,161	31,891
42.0 Insurance claims and indemnities	16	16	16
Subtotal	449,446	515,449	542,611
95.0 Quarters and subsistence	−703	−703	−703
Total direct obligations	448,743	514,746	541,908
Reimbursable obligations:			
Personnel compensation:			
11.1 Permanent positions	13,696	14,432	14,316
11.3 Positions other than permanent	1,186	1,488	2,515
11.5 Other personnel compensation	827	640	640
Total personnel compensation	15,709	16,560	17,471
12.1 Personnel benefits: Civilian	1,619	1,452	1,499
13.0 Benefits for former personnel	8	8	8
21.0 Travel and transportation of persons	1,465	2,153	2,153
22.0 Transportation of things	297	866	866
23.0 Rent, communications, and utilities	3,419	3,971	3,971
24.0 Printing and reproduction	187	300	300
25.0 Other services	14,861	28,081	27,123
26.0 Supplies and materials	3,996	5,545	5,545
31.0 Equipment	2,401	1,563	1,563
41.0 Grants, subsidies, and contributions	37	320	320
Total reimbursable obligations	43,999	60,819	60,819
99.0 Total obligations	492,742	575,565	602,727

SOURCE: "National Oceanic and Atmospheric Administration," *The Budget of the United States Government, Fiscal Year 1977, Appendix* (Washington, D.C.: U.S. Government Printing Office, 1976), p. 213.

state travel, or any specific item that the legislature wants to control explicitly.

An alternative organizational budget that presents information for agencies in a form that serves the managerial and planning functions more readily is the *activity* budget (see Table 9.3). The activity budget presents expenditure information for each activity or program in which the agency is engaged. Most observers find it more important to know how much an agency is spending to run its ship support services program, for example, than how much it spends for travel. Because activity budgets array data by agency programs, activity budget formats are sometimes called program budgets. A program budget, as we shall see, has a special meaning in academic public administration.

The particular activity budget presented in Table 9.3 also shows the amounts needed for each program for operating expenses and capital improvements. Separate operating and capital expense budgets are quite common on the local level and have recently been incorporated in the data presented in many state and the national budgets. Grouping capital expenditure by activity provides more meaningful information for managerial and planning purposes than simply cramming all capital expenditures into an equipment account for an entire agency does.

A variant of the activity budget is the *performance* budget, which provides additional information for those concerned with program management. Performance budgets attempt to tie expenditures for activities to work-load measures. For example, a local department of public works might have among its activities "maintenance of city vehicles." A work-load measure for this activity might be "cost per tune-up" or "maintenance cost per mile driven." For the snowplowing activity, a work-load measure might be "cost per lane-mile plowed and sanded." Performance budgets, although they do provide detail needed for better management of government activities, do not necessarily deal with accomplishment, impact, or effectiveness measures—measures that indicate how well an agency is meeting its goals or objectives. We will deal more with the difficulties of such measures in the next chapter when we deal with management by objectives and productivity measurements.

Program Budgeting   Since traditional budgetary practice in the United States groups expenditures by accounting categories in the object classification format, which does not permit an observer to tell how cutting or expanding expenditures in one of the account categories will affect the agency's programs, changes to activity budget or performance budget formats have

TABLE 9.3
Example of an Activity Budget, Federal Agency X

Program by Activities	Previous Fiscal Year	Current Fiscal Year	Future Fiscal Year
Direct program:			
Operating costs:			
1. Mapping, charting, and surveying services	32,386	35,082	35,949
2. Ship support services	32,727	39,922	42,596
3. Ocean fisheries and living marine resources	52,794	58,281	62,693
4. Marine ecosystems analysis and ocean dumping	5,929	9,561	7,295
5. Marine technology	3,072	3,981	4,663
6. Sea grant	23,028	23,149	23,214
7. Basic environmental services	104,041	107,779	111,114
8. Environmental satellite services	64,559	66,407	89,669
9. Public forecast and warning services	51,351	60,132	60,333
10. Specialized environmental services	31,704	31,709	32,722
11. Environmental data and information services	12,707	14,710	15,250
12. Global monitoring of climatic change	1,571	1,747	1,826
13. Weather modification	4,468	4,138	4,837
14. International projects	9,672	8,628	8,692
15. Retired pay, commissioned officers	1,781	2,317	2,544
16. Executive direction and administration	21,991	24,190	25,246
17. Construction	—	1,000	970
Total operating costs	453,781	492,733	529,613
Unfunded adjustments to total operating costs: Depreciation included above	−15,705	−16,000	−16,000
Deductions from retired pay	−130	−130	−140
Future cost of retired pay, commissioned officers	−1,160	−1,432	−1,661
Total operating costs, funded	436,786	475,171	511,812
Capital outlay:			
1. Mapping, charting, and surveying services	62	600	600
2. Ship support services	179	198	—
3. Ocean fisheries and living marine resources	165	500	490
7. Basic environmental services	4,096	6,704	6,557
8. Environmental satellite services	2,251	6,724	4,033
9. Public forecast and warning services	791	11,393	14,895
10. Specialized environmental services	13	—	—
12. Global monitoring of climatic change	23	—	—
13. Weather modification	157	5,488	1,528
Total capital outlay, funded	7,737	31,607	28,103
Total direct program	444,523	506,778	539,915

285

TABLE 9.3 (*cont.*)

Reimbursable program:			
1. Mapping, charting, and surveying services	8,749	11,549	11,549
2. Ship support services	311	—	—
3. Ocean fisheries and living marine resources	3,066	7,266	7,266
4. Marine ecosystems analysis and ocean dumping	8,091	17,237	17,237
5. Marine technology	131	131	131
7. Basic environmental services	5,703	6,203	6,203
8. Environmental satellite services	3,314	3,314	3,314
9. Public forecast and warning services	3,337	3,550	3,550
10. Specialized environmental services	5,926	6,172	6,172
11. Environmental data and information services	2,584	2,584	2,584
12. Global monitoring of climatic change	398	398	398
13. Weather modification	74	100	100
16. Executive direction and administration	2,315	2,315	2,315
Total reimbursable program	43,999	60,819	60,819
Total program costs, funded	488,522	567,597	600,734
Change in selected resources (spacecraft and launching inventory and undelivered orders; plus other inventory and undelivered orders)	4,220	7,968	1,993
Total obligations	492,742	575,565	602,727

Source: "National Oceanic and Atmospheric Administration," *The Budget of the United States Government, Fiscal Year 1977, Appendix* (Washington, D.C.: U.S. Government Printing Office, 1976), p. 211.

been hailed as great innovations. As we have mentioned earlier, often these new budget formats are called program budgets. David Novick, the father of program budgeting in government, has pointed out, "Obviously, the word program is available for anyone to use in any manner he sees fit."[4] Most program budgeting today is "program" in little more than name.

Real *program budgeting* is the economists' answer to the principal budgeting question raised by V. O. Key several decades ago: "On what basis shall it be decided to allocate X dollars to Activity A instead of Activity

---

4. David Novick, *Current Practice in Program Budgeting (PPBS): Analysis and Case Studies Covering Government and Business* (New York: Crane, Russak, 1973), p. 15. Accountants generally use the terms *program* and *performance* budgeting as synonyms. *See* Eric L. Kohler, *A Dictionary for Accountants*, 5th ed. (Englewood Cliffs, N.J.: Prentice-Hall), p. 381.

Ten Features of Program Budgeting

1. *definition of the organization's objectives in terms as specific as possible*
2. *determination of programs, including possible alternatives, to achieve the stated objectives*
3. *identification of major issues to be resolved in the formulation of objectives and/or the development of programs*
4. *an annual cycle with appropriate subdivisions for the planning, programming, and budgeting steps to ensure an ordered approach and to make appropriate amounts of time available for analysis and decision-making at all levels of management*
5. *continuous reexamination of program results in relationship to anticipated costs and outcomes to determine need for changes in stated programs and objects. . . .*
6. *recognition of issues and other problems that require more time than is available in the annual cycle so that they can be explicitly identified and set apart from the current period for completion in two or more years. . . .*
7. *analysis of programs and their alternatives in terms of probable outcomes and both direct and indirect costs.*
8. *development of analytical tools necessary for measuring costs and benefits.*
9. *development each year of a multi-year program and financial plan with full recognition . . . that, in many areas, resource allocations . . . require projections of plans and programs and their resource demands for ten or more years into the future*
10. *adaptation of existing accounting and statistical-reporting systems to provide inputs into planning and programming, as well as continuing information on resources used in and actions taken to implement programs*

SOURCE: David Novick, *Current Practice in Program Budgeting* (New York: Crane, Russak, 1973), pp. 5–6.

B?"[5] Advisers to President Lyndon B. Johnson thought they had the answer in the planning-programming-budgeting system (PPBS), which aspired to be a true program budgeting system. Johnson was convinced that program budgeting would enable us to:

1. *identify our national goals with precision and on a continuing basis*
2. *choose among those goals the ones that are most urgent*
3. *search for alternative means of reaching those goals most effectively at the least cost*
4. *inform ourselves not merely on next year's costs, but on the second, and third, and subsequent year's costs of our programs*

5. V. O. Key, Jr., "The Lack of a Budgetary Theory," *American Political Science Review* 34, no. 4 (December 1940): 1137.

5. *measure the performance of our programs to insure a dollar's worth of service for each dollar spent.*[6]

This was a tall order—one that PPBS could not fill. We will discuss some of the reasons for that failure in the next chapter.

Whereas object classification budgeting is control-oriented and activity and performance budgeting is management-oriented, program budgeting is planning-oriented. Program budgeting is principally concerned with developing alternatives for the future and analyzing what the consequences of alternative programs might be and what they will cost. As such the features of program budgeting, as outlined in the box are quite similar to, and certainly compatible with, the rational-comprehensive and Bayesian decision-making methods discussed in chapter 8. As such, program budgeting suffers from the same problems as any future-oriented policy analysis of complex governmental problems does.

Cost-Benefit Analysis Problems

THE heart of program budgeting, as Novick used the term, is analysis—principally economic analysis of future costs and benefits. Since cost-benefit analysis is a key link in the program budget analytical chain, we must examine some of the problems inherent to this form of analysis. We will only deal with some of the data problems involved in attaching dollar values to costs and benefits, to show the enormous difficulties in developing reliable analytic work on government programs.[7]

Most analysts agree with Leonard Merewitz and Stephen Sosnick that the "estimation and prediction of costs are usually on firmer ground than estimation and prediction of benefits."[8] Generally this appears to be so because many examples of cost analysis ignore elements of cost that are not easily quantified. There are serious problems in dealing with cost factors in cost-benefit analysis because there are several kinds

---

6. "Statement by the President to Cabinet Members and Agency Heads on the New Government-Wide Planning and Budgeting System," August 25, 1965, *Public Papers of the Presidents of the United States, Lyndon B. Johnson,* 1965, Book II, pp. 916–917.

7. For general works on cost-benefit analysis, *see* E. J. Mishan, *Cost-Benefit Analysis,* 2d ed. (New York: Praeger, 1976); E. S. Quade, *Analysis for Public Decisions* (New York: American Elsevier, 1975); Edith Stokey and Richard Zeckhauser, *A Primer for Policy Analysis* (New York: W. W. Norton, Inc., 1978). For a critique, *see* Leonard Merewitz and Stephen H. Sosnick, *The Budget's New Clothes* (Chicago: Markham, 1971).

8. Merewitz and Sosnick, *The Budget's New Clothes,* p. 205.

of costs that should be considered if a true picture of the real economic costs of a program or project is to be correctly stated.

Project outlays are relatively easy to calculate. Project outlays may include research and development costs, investment costs, and operation, maintenance, and replacement costs. For a highway through a city, investment costs would include design and planning costs, purchase of the right of way, demolition of existing buildings on that right of way, relocation of occupants, and actual construction costs of the road. Operation, maintenance, and replacement costs would include costs of policing, snowplowing, and repairing the road. Project outlays that must be made soon are easy to spell out with precision. Outlays that must be made in the future are more difficult to estimate.

Project outlays are obvious costs, but a true picture of what the real costs of a particular decision are is much more complicated. An additional type of cost that should be considered in good analysis is *social cost*. Social costs are not paid for directly by any particular organization but must be paid for indirectly by society as a whole. If a private company pollutes the air around its plant, the company does not pay for that pollution, but the people who live there "pay" with shorter lifetimes, less pleasant surroundings, and other problems, all of which are an indirect result of the plant's pollution. Similarly, if a government jurisdiction builds an elevated highway through a neighborhood, there may be social costs as that neighborhood deteriorates, crime rises, pollution from trucks increases, merchants lose business, and so forth. These are all costs that are to be borne by somebody as a result of the government project. As might be imagined, such costs are not easy to identify with precision. Generally, budgetary analysis does not even attempt to do so.

The real economic meaning of cost relates to potential benefits that must be given up when one project or program is chosen over other projects and programs. This is the concept of *opportunity cost*. Opportunity costs are the value of benefits that must be lost since the resources are used for one project rather than for another. As E. S. Quade has pointed out: "Fundamentally, a decision to do one thing implies a decision not to build a hospital, for the resources may no longer be available."[9] To measure the value of all the relevant alternative uses of resources is an incredibly difficult activity that entails knowing what the alternative uses of resources might be, then measuring the benefits from each alternative use.

Any assessment of opportunity costs, therefore, implies estimation of

---

9. Quade, *Analysis*, p. 125.

those benefits of the alternatives that must be foregone when the project or program is chosen. A quantitative estimation of benefits is not always possible. How does one quantify such values as justice or the good feeling of breathing clean air? So, since quantification is a necessary element in cost-benefit analysis, nonquantifiable factors may be played down even though they are critically important. As Bertram Gross has suggested, there may be a kind of Gresham's Law whereby hard data drives out soft data.[10]

Since it is so difficult to measure costs accurately, we need some criteria by which to judge the cost analysis that does go on in government. Quade has suggested some guidelines:

> The responsibility of the cost analyst, however, is not simply to add up any and all costs indiscriminately but to identify and measure that particular collection of costs that is contingent on the specific decision or choice under consideration. To do that he must distinguish the relevant from the irrelevant ones. Any costs that will be incurred no matter what choice is made, any costs that must be borne regardless of the decision at hand, are not costs of that particular choice or decision. Relevant costs are those costs that depend on the choice made, given the choices available.[11]

The Track Record of Cost Analysis

In their attempts to concentrate on the cost information that is most relevant to decisions, cost analysts have tended to stress the more readily available cost figures, such as direct project outlays. These outlays are often compared to outlays for other projects or programs that have similar goals. It is through this type of cost-effectiveness analysis that decisions are made to buy one piece of expensive hardware over another piece that is supposed to do the same thing but that costs more to procure.

Of all jurisdictions in the United States, the Department of Defense (DOD) has had the most experience with cost analysis and cost-effectiveness analysis. In the mid-1970s, the General Accounting Office (GAO) studied forty-five weapons systems' cost histories. The broad results are presented in Figure 9.2. The total cost change from the time

---

10. Thomas Gresham's "law" was that "cheap money drive out good." It was suggested at a time when money meant coin and some coins were inferior to others. People saved the good coins and only used the poorer ones. Gross made the comment at a panel session during the 1968 American Political Science Association annual meeting in Washington, D.C.
11. Quade, *Analysis,* p. 129.

FIGURE 9.2
Analysis of Program Cost Histories on 45 Weapon Systems

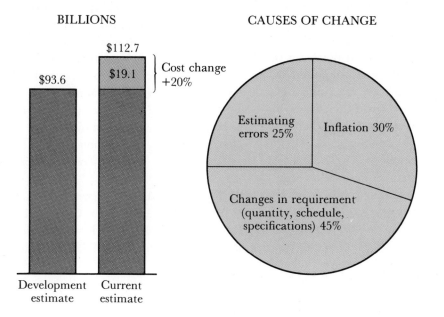

SOURCE: U.S. House of Representatives, *Cost Growth in Major Weapon Systems,* report to the Committee on Armed Services by the Comptroller General of the United States, B-163058 (*Washington, D.C.: General Accounting Office, March 26, 1973*), p. 26.

costs were first estimated and the time of the study was a 20 percent increase. Of this 20 percent increase, less than half was attributable to changes in specifications, quantity, or scheduling—problems over which the cost analysts had no control. But 30 percent of this $19.1 billion cost change was attributable to inflation, something that good analysis attempts to control for. Furthermore, 25 percent of the cost increase was due to estimating errors.[12]

The question not answered by the GAO study is whether the same procurement decisions would have been made if decision-makers had been aware of the inaccuracies of the cost data. In a more limited study of weapons systems' costs, Robert Summers concluded that one of the

12. U.S. House of Representatives, *Cost Growth in Major Weapon Systems,* report to the Committee on Armed Services by the Comptroller General of the United States, B-163058 (Washington, D.C.: General Accounting Office, March 26, 1973).

291

three missile system decisions that he reviewed would have been differ-ent if the uncertainty of the cost factors had been considered.[13]

Some people might snicker and nod knowingly, thinking that this is the way the defense establishment always works—i.e., giving low esti-mates so it can get the weapons systems it wants regardless of cost. But the experience of the Department of Defense with cost analysis serves primarily to point out the severe problems of such analysis. Merewitz and Sosnick reported that cost estimates for civilian projects such as dams and reservoirs are also unrealistically low. Among other projects, they noted, the Verrazano Narrows Bridge in New York City was esti-mated at $78 million in 1948; the bridge cost $300 million by the time it was completed in 1963.[14] Nor is faulty cost projection a monopoly of the public sector. The Playboy Casino in Atlantic City cost 20 percent more than its initial estimates.

One of the more spectacular cost-analysis failures of recent years in-volved the renovation of Yankee Stadium in New York City. Initial studies of renovating the stadium indicated a $17 to $24 million price tag in 1970. By 1973 the cost had grown to "in excess of $80 million," although that year officials reported to the New York City Board of Es-timates, the political body responsible for approving capital expendi-tures in the city, that the cost would be between $40 and $50 million. When the stadium was completed in 1976, the bill came to $97.4 mil-lion. This did not include a $16 million outlay for a nearby highway in-terchange, nor the loss of rent and taxes on the old stadium, nor debt service on borrowed money to complete the project, nor several other items that a meaningful cost analysis would have raised. Perhaps true cost estimates would have killed the entire project.[15]

Cost analysis, it seems, is not too reliable even for the so-called hard-ware projects, such as bridges, stadiums, and weapons systems. Given the complexities of social projects, we can expect even greater discrep-ancies between cost estimates and the final figures. As the Yankee Sta-dium example shows, variable—perhaps falsified—cost estimates ena-bled political forces that favored a particular course of action to have their way.

---

13. Robert Summers, "Cost Estimates as Predictors of Actual Weapon Costs: A Study of Major Hardware Articles," in Thomas Marschak, T. K. Glennan, Jr., and Robert Summers, eds., *Strategy for R & D: Studies in the Microeconomics of Devel-opment* (New York: Springer-Verlag, 1967), mentioned in Merewitz and Sosnick, *The Budget's New Clothes,* pp. 217 and 220.
14. Merewitz and Sosnick, p. 220.
15. John L. Hess, "Stadium's Costs Now Seen as Loss," *New York Times,* April 15, 1976.

If cost estimates are notoriously bad, certainly the budgetary process cannot be left in the hands of the program budgeteers who would plug suspect data into complex models and claim to allocate governmental resources properly. Analysis is advisory. The advisers should remember that cost measurements are approximations that *may* be useful. As Quade pointed out: "To decide between various public policy alternatives, it is usually sufficient to know only that one program costs something like twice as much or three times as much as one program without knowing within hundreds of dollars what either of them will actually cost."[16] There is a place for cost analysis in governmental decision-making. Sometimes it will make the difference in what decision is made. Many times it will not be a factor in the budgetary decision-making process.

Uncertainty and the Budget Cycle

BECAUSE of the deficiencies of cost analysis, budgeting cannot be a mechanical process through which government resources are allocated according to precise economic criteria. Instead it is an administrative-political process. The administrative aspect is reflected in a budget cycle for each fiscal year. This cycle has four identifiable phases: (1) executive preparation and transmittal, (2) legislative authorization and appropriation, (3) budget execution and control, and (4) review and audit. Each of these phases is related to each other. Furthermore, each phase overlaps with other phases in different cycles. For example, while the budget execution phase is going on during a fiscal year, the legislature may be considering appropriations for the next fiscal year that is two years away, and accountants may be reviewing and auditing the fiscal year that has just finished (see Figure 9.3). The overlapping of the budget cycles creates an air of uncertainty that profoundly affects the budget process.

This uncertainty comes about because the information available to the executive branch, which has the main responsibility for the first and third cycles, is incomplete. While the executive branch is trying to prepare a budget for a fiscal year that will begin in fourteen or fifteen months, it may not have had sufficient experience with a particular program to be able to evaluate it. Estimates of program needs and costs fif-

---

16. Quade, *Analysis,* p. 136.

FIGURE 9.3
Budget Cycles Overlap: The Example of the Federal Government

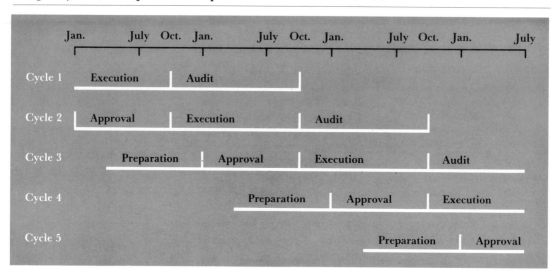

SOURCE: Robert D. Lee, Jr., and Ronald W. Johnson, *Public Budgeting Systems* (Baltimore: University Park Press, 1973), p. 95, modified.

teen months or more into the future cannot be precise. Many times in recent years, legislatures have not completed action on appropriations for the fiscal year already under way at a time when the executive agencies are supposed to present their budgets for the next fiscal year. In cases like these, agency administrators do not know what level of funding they are supposed to be operating under in the current fiscal year, let alone how to make reasonable guesses as to how much they will be able to get for the next fiscal year. Clearly, budget-making under such uncertainty is a complex business.

The budget cycle provides the administrative framework that determines the participants in the budgetary process and the roles that they will perform in various stages of that process. The preparation and appropriations stages involve three institutional actors: (1) the agencies, which must decide how much money to ask for; (2) the central budget office, which must decide how much to recommend; and (3) the legislative appropriations committees, which have the final decision on how much to give.[17]

---

17. Aaron Wildavsky, *The Politics of the Budgetary Process,* 3rd ed. (Boston: Little, Brown, 1979), chapter 2.

To make the complex and uncertain budgetary process manageable, these participants, it appears to many observers, have agreed on ways to simplify the situation. Aaron Wildavsky has suggested two concepts— *base* and *fair share*—that enable the participants to handle budgeting in the real world.

> The base is the general expectation among the participants that programs will be carried on at close to the going level of expenditures but it does not necessarily include all activities. Having a project included in the agency's base thus means more than just getting it in the budget for a particular year. It means establishing the expectation that the expenditure will continue, that it is accepted as part of what will be done, and, therefore, that it will not normally be subjected to intensive scrutiny.[18]

The base, in other words, represents those programs that all participants in the process agree are a legitimate part of an agency's responsibility and should not be seriously questioned.

Fair share differs from the base. According to Wildavsky, "Fair share means not only the base an agency has established but also the expectation that it will receive some proportion of funds, if any, which are to be increased over or decreased below the base of the various governmental agencies."[19] The agencies, the central budget office, and the appropriations committees agree that budgeting should be incremental; that is, changes in agency budgets should be relatively small and in proportion to overall budget changes.

The notions of fair share and base support a picture of the budgetary process that is not grounded in rational-comprehensive analysis. Instead of having to justify all programs every year, as would be the case in a true zero-base budget, the agency (which always has a key role in defining how much money it wants) concentrates on making marginal increases for so-called quality improvements and trying to get new programs accepted as part of the base. Figure 9.4 presents the budgeting activities that go on at the agency level under normal conditions of moderate budget growth.

In recent years, some jurisdictions have felt the sting of fiscal stress and "cutback management."[20] Severe fiscal stress can force changes in budget preparation practices. Even the federal government, which has not been operating under severe stress, puts constraints upon an agency's

18. Ibid., p. 17.
19. Ibid.
20. Charles H. Levine, "Organizational Decline and Cutback Management," in Levine, ed., *Managing Fiscal Stress* (Chatham, N.J.: Chatham House, 1980), pp. 13–30.

actions. Directives from either the president or the director of the Office of Management and Budget (OMB) indicate what the budget request ceilings should be. Under normal conditions these ceilings will be in line with the base and fair-share concepts. In some cases, however, OMB or the White House may force an evaluation of some agency programs. If an agency or bureau is singled out for an in-depth evaluation, it is forced into a defensive posture of trying to justify its program without the luxury of an accepted base.

In the traditional incremental budgeting process, agencies in all jurisdictions must justify their programs. But many of these programs have become accepted parts of the business of government, and other participants do not expect, or want to see, detailed cost-benefit justifications for them. Budget reviewers choose to concentrate on newer programs or areas marked for drastic increases. This means that some programs that have outlived their usefulness will continue to claim their "fair share" for years. Perhaps this is a price that society can afford to pay. Given limited time and expertise, concentrating on new programs or exceptional increases in old ones might be a sensible control strategy for budget reviewers.

FIGURE 9.4
The Real Agency Budget Preparation Process

- Last year's appropriation

- Automatic increases for existing personnel

- Cost of inflation to continue existing level of services

- Cost of additional service by unit

- New program costs—"quality" improvements

Agency Budget Strategies

WILDAVSKY'S seminal work catalogued agency budget strategies that strongly support the triangle of symbiotic relationships among agency, clientele, and legislative committee. Wildavsky found several people active in the budgetary process who firmly felt that success in the budget game for administrators was based not on how good the budget estimates were but how good a politician the administrator was. "Being a good politician . . . requires essentially three things: cultivation of an active clientele, the development of confidence among other government officials, and skill in following strategies that exploit one's opportunities."[21]

Cultivation of clientele involves identifying the groups that benefit from the agency's service, encouraging them to organize so they demand more of the service, and providing them with the service. Depending upon the potential political power of the clientele, agencies can successfully lean on them for support at various places in the budget process. Wildavsky noted that it makes good political sense to encourage advisory groups, to mobilize favorable opinion, and to tie one agency's program to a more popular program (as the Weather Bureau tied itself to the Polaris submarine program during the 1960s). Wildavsky cautioned that agencies should not become the captives of any particular clientele, however.

Since the budgetary process takes place in an uncertain atmosphere, the participants find it beneficial to trust one another. Wildavsky views this as a key element for agencies because they perceive that other participants in the process can hurt them if the agencies prove untrustworthy. Gaining the confidence of others depends on informal contact between agency people and legislative committee members and staff. Such informal contact, especially with members of the legislature, furthers agency success and strengthens the relationships.

Strategies to increase an agency's chances of getting an acceptable budget take many forms. Wildavsky notes that administrators can prepare for hostile questions during legislative appropriation hearings by staging mock hearings in advance. Using informal relationships with legislators, agencies can "plant" favorable questions, or they can comply with requests for information from hostile participants by deluging

---

21. Wildavsky, *Politics of the Budgetary Process*, p. 64. *Also see* his chapter 3.

them with paper. Sympathetic participants can be given information that will help the agency. Although Wildavsky notes that there is no substitute for an administrator's being familiar with his or her budget, an aggressive defense of an agency's request clearly requires much more than accounting expertise.

Agency administrators play the role of advocate for their programs, but this should not surprise us. Agencies are vitally concerned with the programs that they can develop, operate, and expand. As John Wanat points out:

> Agencies prosper—and their personnel prosper—when clients are pleased, and clients are pleased when favorable programs are operational or forthcoming. Since agency personnel do not have any responsibility for collecting money, they do not worry about balanced budgets or fiscal probity but leave such worries to others. Agencies, however, are in constant contact with substantive problems needing solutions and clients desiring service.[22]

Agencies see the budget process from a programmatic perspective that is influenced by the professional needs of their own personnel and the desires of their interest group constituencies.

Thomas Anton, who studied state budgetary behavior, sees a related reason for the agency advocacy role. He suggests that agency administrators seek larger budgets every year to show agency personnel that they are engaged in worthwhile activities that should command a larger share of the public purse each year. Asking for more—even more than the administrators expect to receive—also shows that the administrators are aggressive and competent. By asking for more than they expect to receive, agency administrators allow the central budget officers to play their role of cutting agency requests and deciding how much to recommend.[23]

The Central Budget Office

IN all but the smallest jurisdictions, central budget offices coordinate the executive budget-making process and perform other management func-

22. John Wanat, *Introduction to Budgeting* (North Scituate, Mass.: Duxbury Press, 1978), p. 51. Wanat suggests several additional actors in the budgetary process. *See* his chapter 4.
23. Thomas J. Anton, "Roles and Symbols in the Determination of State Expenditures," *Midwest Journal of Political Science* 11 (1967): 27–43.

tions for the chief executive. In addition to performing the obvious budget estimation, preparation, and execution functions, well-developed central budgeting offices review legislative proposals from the agencies to ensure that they conform to the chief executive's program. They also assess the impact such legislation may have on future budgets. This central clearance of legislation is important since many legislative proposals are developed by the administrative agencies themselves. Central budgeting offices are often involved in standardizing forms, statistical measures, and data processing procedures to aid in governmental management. They also may have responsibilities with personnel, which in many jurisdictions involves a large proportion of governmental expenditures.

The central budgeting office can routinely provide the chief executive with the information it gathers to support budget requests. Information-sharing is a two-way street, however. Not only can the central budget office serve as a channel to let the chief executive know what is happening at the agency levels, but it can also let the agencies know what the chief executive's priorities are. Since the central budget office has frequent contact with the agencies, perhaps this dual educational role is its most important function. Figure 9.5 summarizes these functions, all of which are performed at the national level by the Office of Management and Budget.[24]

Today it is hard to imagine large-scale governments operating without the guidance and coordination of central budgeting offices, but the development of such offices is relatively recent. Even at the national level there was no central budgeting office until 1921. Until then each agency prepared and submitted its budget to the relevant appropriations subcommittees in Congress. The result was chaos and what appeared to be uncontrolled increases in the federal budget. The Budget and Accounting Act of 1921 established a central budgeting office, the Bureau of the Budget, as part of the Treasury Department. The BOB was moved to the Executive Office of the President when that office was established as a result of the Brownlow Committee reforms in 1939. In 1970, acting on recommendations of the Ash Council, President Richard Nixon implemented a reorganization plan that recognized the management role of the BOB by renaming it the Office of Management and Budget.

Although formal organizational arrangements differ, central budget-

---

24. James W. Davis and Randall B. Ripley, "The Bureau of the Budget and Executive Branch Agencies: Notes on Their Interaction," *Journal of Poliltics* 29 (1967): 749–769.

FIGURE 9.5
Central Budget Office Functions

- Budget estimation and preparation

- Budget execution

- Legislative clearance

- Standardization of administrative procedures

- Educational role between chief executive and agencies and vice versa

ing offices at all levels in American government provide needed staff services to the chief executive and usually attract people who consider themselves to be the elite of public bureaucracy. Since one of the principal problems of chief executives is to find out what the bureaucracy is doing, they have a strong tendency to rely on central budget offices to provide that information. These offices have responded by attempting to develop reporting systems that can provide information on agency programs. In the federal government, the Office of Management and Budget and its predecessor agency, the Bureau of the Budget, sought to implement such systems as planning-programming-budgeting (PPBS) and management by objectives (MBO), which were later discarded in favor of zero-base budgeting (ZBB). OMB officials may pay lip service to the needs of individual agencies in implementing budget reforms, but their key role in developing and operating the budget machinery gives them additional power in relation to the other participants in the budgetary process. Even though central budgeting staffers might see themselves as philosopher-kings capable of acting in the public interest, they can become the subject of political controversy.[25]

There is potential for ill feelings between central budget officials and legislators. Legislators jealously protect their prerogatives, especially their powers of the purse. Sometimes they feel that the central budgeting

25. Joel Havemann, "Zero-Base Budgeting," *National Journal* 9, no. 14 (April 2, 1977): 517.

office intends to operate the government as it wishes. Since the central budgeting office is usually identified with the chief executive, legislative criticism of that office is often a way of criticizing the chief executive without appearing to do so. Central budget officials sometimes react arrogantly to legislative efforts to initiate or control programs. This attitude is summed up by the statement of a former OMB official who said, only partly in jest, that he never saw a good idea come out of Congress.[26]

The Legislative Role

ALTHOUGH legislatures at most levels in the United States are laboring under a cloud of public doubt about their competence, they play a key role in the budget process. In most American jurisdictions the executive branch, through the chief executive and the central budgeting office, drafts the budget. The legislators have the power to approve or deny the budget proposals. Historically, control of the public purse by legislatures has been the main control on executive action.

Perhaps, however, the role of legislatures in budgeting is primarily symbolic rather than real.[27] Nevertheless, we can reasonably make several assumptions about legislative intentions concerning budgeting:

First, legislatures review budget proposals with the intent of making decisions about policies, programs, and the allocation of resources. Second, they aim to make these decisions in a more or less rational manner, and rationality, as tempered by the political realities of the time, is deemed a desirable goal. Third, procedures, practices, and organization machinery play an important role in determining the rationality of decision making and the effectiveness of controls over spending.[28]

How close legislatures come to reaching these goals is related to the skill of the legislators and their staff support. Many jurisdictions in the United States lack skilled legislators and staff support of any kind.

At the national level, the appropriations subcommittees of Congress used to view themselves as guardians of the public treasury. In the late

---

26. Joel Havemann, "Executive Report/OMB's New Faces Retain Power, Structure Under Ford," *National Journal Reports* 7, no. 30 (July 26, 1975): 1072.
27. Thomas J. Anton found the state legislature to be practically irrelevant to spending decisions in *The Politics of State Expenditure in Illinois* (Urbana: University of Illinois Press, 1966), p. 246.
28. S. Kenneth Howard, *Changing State Budgeting* (Lexington, Ky.: Council of State Governments, 1973), p. 309.

"This ten billion, of course, includes bullets." (*Drawing by Levin; © 1978 The New Yorker Magazine, Inc.*)

1960s and early 1970s the appropriations committees gave up this role and supported larger budgets for the agencies they were to control. The seemingly uncontrolled rise in the federal budget combined with delays in funding—rarely during the 1960s did Congress complete action on all appropriations bills before the start of the fiscal year—renewed the criticism that the congressional budget review procedure was too fragmented to allow Congress a meaningful role in the budget process.

In an effort to reassert legislative prerogatives in the budgetary process, Congress passed the Congressional Budget Reform and Impoundment Act of 1974. The act set up a Congressional Budget Office (CBO) and changed the fiscal year. Figure 9.6 presents the new budget timetable for congressional action. The president's current services budget spells out the figure needed to keep government programs operating at the same level during the next fiscal year. Presenting the current services budget in November is supposed to give the Congressional Budget Office time to identify ongoing programs that Congress might want to prune. In addition to a current services budget, the Office of Management and Budget must present Congress with a complete list of tax expenditures, which are tax breaks or subsidies to those who qualify. An example of a tax expenditure is the liberal allowance for depreciation of

THE BUDGETARY PROCESS: POLITICS AND POLICY

FIGURE 9.6
Congressional Budget Timetable

ON OR BEFORE	ACTION TO BE COMPLETED
November 10	President submits current services budget.
15th day after Congress convenes	President submits his budget.
March 15	Committees submit reports to budget committees.
April 1	Congressional Budget Office submits report to budget committees.
April 15	Budget committees report first concurrent resolution on the budget to their houses.
May 15	Committees report bills authorizing new budget authority.
May 15	Congress adopts first concurrent resolution on the budget.
7th day after Labor Day	Congress completes action on bills providing budget authority.
September 15	Congress completes actions on second required concurrent resolution on the budget.
September 25	Congress completes action reconciliation process implementing second concurrent resolution.
October 1	Fiscal year begins.

rental property available to real estate owners before they compute their taxes. Tax expenditures used to bypass the entire budget process because they represented revenue that was never collected and so never appeared in agency programs as a subsidy. Still, such tax expenditures constitute federal aid to the beneficiaries in the same way direct payments to airlines or welfare recipients do. The budget reforms of 1974 have enhanced Congress's ability to act in a reasonable fashion in the budget process, although the congressional role is not as strong as the executive role in budgetary matters.

Legislative Budget Politics

Aaron Wildavsky and others who perceive the politics of the budgetary process as primarily an exercise in incrementalism have denigrated the legislature's policy-making role in the budget process. Studies of dollar amounts allocated to agencies and departments have shown that the changes from year to year are slight—that is, incremental.[29] There is, however, a developing body of scholarship that suggests a more positive role for the legislature, at least for Congress. Arnold Kanter has shown that Congress has favored some weapons systems over others and has put up the money to support its preference.[30] Peter Natchez and Irving Bupp have reported similar findings with regard to the Atomic Energy Commission.[31] In these studies, certain agency programs experienced great growth and others survived cutbacks although the overall budget for the agency showed incremental change. The simple incremental model, which assumes that legislatures seek to maintain stability in funding levels, may hold at the agency level but not for specific programs.

Clearly, Congress does have some impact on programs and policies through the budget process. Perhaps as the reforms take hold they will have even greater impact. We can assume, therefore, that most programs are funded with congressional approval if not congressional blessing. Many programs benefit special interests. These remain on the books and are funded because Congress lacks the will to break up the symbiotic relationships among agency, clientele, and the relevant legislative committees. The political pressures that support ongoing programs are real. Policy subsystems based on specialized knowledge and interests do make policy in virtual seclusion unless other political pressures raise the level of conflict to a more visible arena. These policy decisions are reflected in the budget. For legislators to deal effectively with the complexity of budget problems, they must specialize. By specializing, they

29. Wildavsky, *Politics of the Budgetary Process*, and Otto A. Davis, M. A. H. Dempster, and Aaron Wildavsky, "A Theory of the Budgetary Process," *American Political Science Review* 60, no. 3 (September 1966): 529–530.
30. Arnold Kanter, "Congress and the Defense Budget: 1960–70," *American Political Science Review* 66, no. 1 (March 1972): 129–143.
31. Peter B. Natchez and Irving C. Bupp, "Policy and Priority in the Budgetary Process," *American Political Science Review* 67, no. 3 (September 1973): 951–963.

may become part of the symbiotic triangle. This inhibits the legislature from dealing with the budget as a whole although the 1974 reforms have established machinery to do so.

An Effective Bureaucratic Strategy for Dealing with Legislatures

The very first thing Clever Bureaucrat does, when threatened with a budget reduction, is to translate it into specific bad news for congressman powerful enough to restore his budget to its usual plenitude.

Thus Amtrak, threatened with a budget cut, immediately announced . . . that it would be compelled to drop the following routes.

San Francisco–Bakersfield, running through Stockton, the home town of Rep. John J. McFall, chairman of the House Appropriations Transportation Subcommittee.

St. Louis–Laredo, running through Little Rock, Arkansas, the home of Senator John McClellan, chairman of the Senate Appropriations Committee.

Chicago–Seattle, running through the homes of Senator Mike Mansfield, Senate Majority Leader, and Senator Warren Magnuson, chairman of the Senate Commerce Committee.

And in a triumphant stroke that netted four birds with one roadbed, Norfolk–Chicago, running through the home states of Senator Birch Bayh, chairman of the Senate Appropriations Transportation Subcommittee, Senator Vance Hartke, chairman of the Commerce Surface Transportation Subcommittee, Rep. Harley Staggers, chairman of the House Commerce Committee, and Senator Robert Byrd, Senate Majority Whip.

SOURCE: Charles Peters, "Firemen First or How to Beat a Budget Cut," *The Washington Monthly* 8, no. 1 (March 1976): 8–9.

Controlling the overall budget of any government jurisdictions means more than reviewing which special interests get what level of subsidy each year. At the state and national levels, a large proportion of each year's budget consists of expenditures that do not go through the appropriations process at all. These *uncontrollable outlays* are grouped into two categories: (1) open-ended programs and fixed costs, for which outlays are generally mandated by law, and (2) payments from prior-year contracts and obligations, for which outlays are required because of previous action. At the national level such expenditures as general revenue-sharing are fixed-cost programs. The open-ended programs are the *entitlement programs,* such as welfare, unemployment, and veterans' benefits. In these programs people who fall into a specific category are enti-

305

tled by law to certain benefits. If unemployment is widespread because of a sluggish national economy, each unemployed person is entitled to benefits under existing laws. The government must make good on its legal commitment. Congress has no choice but to give money under these conditions. Funds must automatically be allocated to such programs, unless Congress decides to change the law regarding the particular entitlement program. State governments have many similar programs, which make a substantial portion of the budget virtually uncontrollable in any given year.

Legislative control through the budget process depends on many things. Legislatures must have the will to reassess old programs that benefit certain interests. They must understand the implications of entitlement programs before such programs become law. To do so, legislatures need increased budgetary staff. But even with larger staffs, there is only a limited amount of time and energy that a legislator can devote to budgetary problems. Political visibility, therefore, determines which elements in the budget come in for the closest scrutiny.

Uncontrollability in the Federal Budget

Outlays in any one year are considered to be relatively uncontrollable by the President when his decisions can neither increase nor decrease them without changes in existing statutes. Relatively uncontrollable outlays consist of two major categories: open-ended programs and fixed costs, and payments out of prior-year contracts and obligations. The percentage of open-ended programs and fixed costs under current law is projected to reach 62% by 1981. As recently as 1971 open-ended programs and fixed costs amounted to less than 47% of the budget. The substantial growth since then has been due primarily to the rapid increase in benefit payments for individuals.

In addition to open-ended programs and fixed costs, outlays for "prior-year contracts and obligations" amount to an additional 15% to 20% of the budget and should be considered relatively uncontrollable in the short run. Though these outlays cannot be projected beyond the budget year, they suggest that the relatively uncontrollable portion of the budget amounts to 75% to 80% of the total in the short-run.

The degree of uncontrollability in the budget has obvious fiscal policy implications. Without changes in legislation, attempts to control total budget outlays fall on an increasingly smaller proportion of the budget.

SOURCE: *The Budget of the United States Government, Fiscal Year 1977* (Washington, D.C.: U.S. Government Printing Office, 1976), pp. 33–34.

The Effect of
Fiscal Stress

MANY jurisdictions at the state and local levels have experienced fiscal stress in recent years. In many places governments are caught between demands for more services and benefits for clients and public employees at a time when the resources available to governmental units have not been growing. To a large extent the problem is not the fault of the jurisdiction that finds it must somehow cut back programs, ration services, defer maintenance, and even lay off workers. The fault lies to a great degree with the national economic problem of "stagflation"—slow economic growth, high unemployment, and double-digit inflation. Placing the blame for fiscal stress does not make it any easier for affected governments to deal with the condition, however.

Fiscal stress is felt most acutely in those jurisdictions that are required by law to balance their budgets, which includes virtually all state and local governments in the United States. A balanced budget for these governments means that operating expenses, including interest on debts, are covered by revenue raised from taxes, intergovernmental transfers, and fees for each year.

New York City's experience showed that there is a difference between a truly balanced budget and one that appears to be in balance. While New York City was slipping toward the brink of bankruptcy in the mid-1970s, its account books appeared to balance. They appeared to balance because New York officials, probably with the knowledge of the banking community, used various budget gimmicks during the 1960s and 1970s to hide the real financial picture from citizens and potential investors in city bonds. These included waiving the payment of $15 million into a special emergency fund, arbitrarily increasing real estate revenue estimates, inflating the forecast of federal aid, and declaring a 364-day fiscal year for expenditure purposes. Far from being condemned for these ploys, New York's leaders were hailed as fiscal geniuses.[32]

Although the federal budget does not have to be balanced by law, there appears to be a moral commitment to try to put it in balance. Since the 1976 presidential elections, the candidates for both parties have run on platforms advocating a balanced federal budget as an objective. The awareness of gaps between expenditure and revenue levels for the national government has led to the deferral of some programs, such as national health insurance, and the de facto cutback of other ser-

---

32. For many more gimmicks, *see* Ken Auletta, *The Streets Were Paved With Gold* (New York: Random House, 1979), chapter 2.

vices as the rate of inflation outruns the appropriations process. A constitutional amendment requiring a balanced national government budget, which is advocated by some conservative groups, would greatly affect budgets at the state and local levels, too. The prime target for budget-cutting at the federal level would be general revenue-sharing, especially that portion that has gone directly to the states.[33]

Government at all levels is subject to fiscal stress. Diagnosing the problem is not hard; treating it is.[34] Charles Levine has suggested one way of managing fiscal stress.

> In a world without politics, finding the optimal strategy for managing fiscal stress would be a straightforward task. First, one would take a long-range view of the causes of a government's fiscal problems by developing a multiyear forecast of its revenue-raising capacity and the demand for its services and benefits. Second, one would develop a list of priority rankings for all government programs, projects, services, and benefits so that high-priority items could be retained or augmented and low-priority items could be reduced or terminated. Finally, one would design an integrated strategy to generate new resources, improve productivity, and ration services so that both the revenue and expenditure sides of the budget could be neatly balanced. But, instead of an apolitical world that supports a comprehensive approach to the problem of maintaining fiscal solvency, most public management decisions—and especially those that involve cutting back services and benefits—are permeated by politics.[35]

Because the political problems of cutback management are so difficult to deal with, many jurisdictions turn to budget systems that appear to take politics out of budget-making. These systems, such as PPBS, MBO, and ZBB, appear to do just what Levine says should be done if public management were apolitical. Rather than taking decisions out of the political realm, these systems generally provide an analytic gloss that can be used to justify politically motivated decisions. Whether even good analysis can be used to trim a really popular program is questionable, but these budget systems do routinely provide more and better information that managers can use to control programs during the execution phase, as well as improve budget estimates.

In spite of the adoption of these new budget systems in the federal government, budget estimates for expenditure vary substantially from actual expenditures, according to a General Accounting Office study.[36] Of

---

33. *See* chapter 3.
34. The Advisory Committee on Intergovernmental Relations has developed an index to indicate fiscal stress.
35. Charles H. Levine, "The New Crisis in the Public Sector," in Levine, ed., *Managing Fiscal Stress*, p. 5.
36. *Federal Budget Outlay Estimates: A Growing Problem*, Report PAD-79-20 (Washington: D.C.: General Accounting Office, February 9, 1979).

course, agencies have it within their power to make their estimates look realistic if their original estimates were high. Faced with a surplus in their accounts during the execution phase, agencies generally spend that money rather than let it revert to the general fund. When the fiscal year for the federal government ended in June, this annual rush to encumber funds before they reverted to the Treasury Department was called the spring spending spree.[37] With the fiscal year now ending in September, there is a summer spending spree.

The Audit Stage

FISCAL stress has reawakened concern over waste and fraud in government. The budget entrusts agencies with public resources, and the agencies are supposed to use these resources for the benefit of the citizens. This does not always happen. Resources can be mishandled, either by intent or simply by inefficient application. Governmental jusidictions at all levels have shown increased concern for audits to find out how resources actually have been used during the execution phase. In the federal government, the General Accounting Office (GAO), which is an arm of Congress, performs this function. In 1979 President Carter appointed several independent departmental inspectors-general to investigate allegations of waste and fraud further. At the state and local levels, better auditing, including use of independent outside auditors, has been encouraged by the State and Local Financial Assistance Amendments.[38]

Although there are performance as well as financial or compliance audits, we will deal only with the latter kind here. An audit is a process of collecting and evaluating evidence concerning financial information, performed by people who are independent of the agency being audited. External auditors examine the documents, records, systems, and other financial information to see if they comply with generally accepted accounting principles and specific legal requirements. If legal requirements conflict with generally accepted accounting principles, the legal requirements must be met, but the auditor must note that there is a conflict.[39]

---

37. Charles Russell Fisher, "Spring Spending Spree," in Charles Peters and Michael Nelson, eds., *The Culture of Bureaucracy* (New York: Holt, Rinehart and Winston, 1978), pp. 76–78.
38. P.L. 94-488, 90 Stat. 2341.
39. *Statement 1, Governmental Accounting and Financial Reporting Principles* (Chicago, Ill.: Municipal Finance Officers Association, March 1979).

Local Financial
Emergencies Revisited

In the fall of 1979, the Nation's third largest county was confronted with a major fiscal crisis. The situation arose when Wayne County, Michigan—that surrounds Detroit—could not meet its payroll and was denied permission by the state's municipal finance commission to borrow short-term funds. Although that commission had approved such borrowing for the three previous years, it also had warned the county to stop running a budget deficit and to end its reliance on tax anticipation notes. When the county did not comply, the commission blocked further borrowing.

Comparisons inevitably will be made between the Wayne County emergency and the problems encountered by New York and Cleveland. However, a key difference does exist: unlike the two cities, Wayne County has no long-term debt. Rather, its problems have resulted from short-term borrowing necessitated by the growing budget deficit.

Contingency plans were formulated by the county to discharge its work force of about 5,000 employees. Immediately thereafter, essential personnel (about half the total), primarily in the public safety and health areas, were recalled. Those workers who were not recalled were eligible for unemployment compensation.

Further state pressure was applied when Gov. William Milliken line item vetoed money bills which would have helped the county meet its shortfall. His action was based on the contention that the county had not heeded state warnings in the past and had not done enough to find better ways to manage its own affairs. Specifically at issue was a call to reorganize the county's government and provide for a better central management capacity.

As the crisis unfolded, a task force comprised of both state and local officials was appointed to develop a plan to restructure the Wayne County government. . . . .

In the interim, the state funds which were the subject of gubernatorial veto were finally released, and additional state revenue sharing funds for all local governments were approved by the legislature. With these resources at their disposal, Wayne County was able to ride out the remainder of its fiscal year. The basic problems though—i.e., those relating to how the county is organized to conduct its affairs—are still to be resolved. Currently, Wayne County is governed by a 36-member commission and independently elected department heads.

At issue will be what form of government will be acceptable politically in the county as well as by the state, and how quickly the changes will be implemented—in the hope of avoiding the same fiscal problems which were confronted this past year.

SOURCE: *Intergovernmental Perspective* 6, no. 2 (Spring 1980): 25.

The New York City fiscal crisis showed the need for independent auditors at the local level. Local governments depend on estimates of their financial health to float bonds to finance long-term capital improvements. Until the mid-1970s, New York was able to finance capital and even operating expenditures because the city's own financial reporting did not present a true picture of its fiscal condition. When an independent audit was conducted for fiscal year 1978, Peat, Marwick, Mitchell and Company, one of the major national accounting firms, issued a *qualified* opinion on New York's financial dealings. This opinion accurately depicted the city's condition and made would-be investors in the city's securities aware of potential problems.

At the end of the audit process, independent auditors issue a report on the scope of the audit and their findings. An *unqualified* opinion is a clean bill of health. An *adverse* opinion indicates that the auditors found major mistakes in the financial statements of the jurisdiction being audited. The auditors can issue a disclaimer if the audit cannot be performed for some reason. A qualified opinion, such as New York City received, indicates that the financial statements are fair, but there are some problems that could have an impact on the jurisdiction's financial condition.

Improved auditing can be a tool to keep public managers accountable to the legislatures, but sometimes legal requirements for audits add managerial burdens that can, in some cases, force worthwhile programs to close. In 1978 Congress, responding to allegations of fraud in the implementation of the Comprehensive Employment and Training Act, tightened audit requirements on CETA grant recipients. Congress wants each local CETA sponsor to be audited every two years, and Congress and the Department of Labor require that local governments be 100 percent liable for the CETA money they receive. If an audit shows that the sponsoring agency cannot account for some money, whether due to human error or fraud, the local government must repay to the federal government the amount questioned. This means that local governments must run perfect programs or cough up local funds to cover mistakes. Since most CETA programs are run on a contract basis through a combination of public and private nonprofits groups and community organizations with limited accounting experience, the chances of a local sponsoring government's being able to withstand a 100 percent audit are slim. Some local sponsors, such as Berrien County, Michigan, therefore, have dropped CETA programs because they are unwilling to pick up the tab for expenditures that an audit might disallow.[40]

40. Peter W. Barnes, "CETA Audits of Local Funds Spark Protest," *Wall Street Journal,* October 8, 1980, p. 31.

Summary

FISCAL stress is the impetus for management and budgetary reforms. Executives who are pressed by revenue problems caused by economic conditions such as slow growth and inflation and by increased demands for services and benefits sometimes have to recommend unpopular tax increases to balance their budgets. Rather than call for new taxes in a time of taxpayer unrest, executives have concentrated on improving management through the budget process. They have used new budgeting techniques to focus on improved program performance.

But the values implied in this new executive concern for program results may run counter to the values of the traditional budget process. Peter F. Drucker, the father of management by objectives, has argued:

> The importance of a traditional budget-based institution is measured essentially by the size of its budget and the size of its staff. To achieve results with a smaller budget or a smaller staff is, therefore, not "performance." It might actually endanger the institution. Not to spend the budget to the hilt will only convince the budget maker—whether a legislature or a budget committee—that the budget for the next fiscal period can safely be cut.[41]

Under these conditions, Drucker adds, " 'Results' . . . means a larger *budget*. . . . And the budget is, by definition, related not to the achievement of any goals, but to the *intention* of achieving those goals."[42]

Program budgeting, management by objectives, and zero-base budgeting all aim to change these definitions of performance and results in government activities. Each of these techniques seeks to allow or even force government to set priorities and concentrate efforts. Implicit in each of these techniques is the view that executive leadership, backed by information developed through systematic planning and analysis, will be able to break the symbiotic policy subsystems that have been nurtured through the budget-politics-as-usual, traditional budget-making process.

While it is doubtful that these techniques will meet fully the management needs of public executives, they have provided a mechanism by which executive attention can be focused on programs in a systematic way through the budgetary process. These techniques, despite any claims to the contrary, enhance executive control through greater cen-

---

41. Peter F. Drucker, "Managing the Public Service Institution," *Public Interest* no. 33 (Fall 1973): 49–50.
42. Ibid., p. 50.

tralization of the budgetary process. They have the potential to improve budgetary decision-making by systematically evaluating programs. There will continue to be tension between pure politics and pure analysis in the budgetary process. Political considerations will, and should, continue to play a major role in these decisions. But the development of modern budgetary techniques, which have gained limited acceptance in the past, probably will affect future budgetary decisions more and more. Therefore, we will devote the next chapter to a discussion of these techniques.

Suggestions for Further Reading

Berman, Larry. *The Office of Management and Budget and the Presidency.* Princeton: Princeton University Press, 1979.

Fisher, Louis. *Presidential Spending Power.* Princeton: Princeton University Press, 1975.

Havemann, Joel. *Congress and the Budget.* Bloomington, Indiana: Indiana University Press, 1978.

Lee, Robert D., Jr., and Ronald W. Johnson. *Public Budgeting Systems,* 2d ed. Baltimore: University Park, 1977.

Levine, Charles H., ed. *Managing Fiscal Stress.* Chatham, N.J.: Chatham House, 1980.

———, ed. "Symposium on Organizational Decline and Cutback Management." *Public Administration Review* 38, no. 4 (July–August 1978).

McCaffery, Jerry, ed. "Symposium on Budgeting in an Era of Resource Scarcity." *Public Administration Review* 38, no. 6 (November–December 1978).

Merewitz, Leonard, and Stephen H. Sosnick, *The Budget's New Clothes.* Chicago: Markham, 1971.

Nathan, Richard P., and Mary M. Nathan. *America's Government: A Fact Book of Census Data on the Organizations, Finances, and Employment of Federal State and Local Governments.* New York: John Wiley, 1979.

Novick, David, *Current Practice in Program Budgeting (PPBS).* New York: Crane, Russak, 1973.

Schick, Allen, ed. *Perspectives on Public Budgeting.* Washington, D.C.: American Society for Public Administration, 1980.

Wanat, John. *Introduction to Budgeting.* North Scituate, Mass.: Duxbury Press, 1978.

Wildavsky, Aaron. *The Politics of the Budgetary Process,* 3rd ed. Boston: Little Brown, 1979.

The Federal Budget Process

THE BUDGET PROCESS HAS four main phases: (1) executive formulation and transmittal; (2) congressional action; (3) budget execution and control; and (4) review and audit. Each of these phases interrelates with and overlaps the others.

Executive Formulation and Transmittal

THE budget sets forth the President's financial plan of operation and thus indicates his priorities for the Nation for the coming year. The President's transmittal of his budget to the Congress early in each calendar year is the climax of many months of planning and analysis throughout the executive branch. Formulation of the 1982 budget began in the spring of 1980, although tentative goals for some programs were set earlier—when the 1981 budget was transmitted to the Congress in February of 1980.

During the period when a budget is being formulated in the executive branch, there is a continuous exchange of information, proposals, evaluations, and policy determinations among the President, the Office of Management and Budget (OMB), and the various Government agencies.

In the spring, agency programs are evaluated, policy issues are identified, and budgetary projections are made, giving attention both to important modifications and innovations in programs and to alternative long-range program plans. Preliminary plans are then presented to the President for his consideration. At about the same time, the President

SOURCE: "The Budget Process," *The Budget of the United States Government, Fiscal Year 1977* (Washington: U.S. Government Printing Office, 1976), pp. 168–172. Some dates have been changed.

receives projections of the economic outlook that are prepared jointly by the Council of Economic Advisers, the Treasury Department, and OMB and reviewed by the Economic Policy Board. The President also receives projections of estimated receipts prepared by the Treasury Department.

Following a review of both sets of projections, the President establishes general budget and fiscal policy guidelines for the fiscal year that will begin about 15 months later. Tentative policy determinations and planning ceilings are then given to the agencies to govern the preparation of their budgets.

Throughout the fall and early winter the executive branch is involved in two related budgetary processes. One is the preparation of the current services estimates, required by the Congressional Budget Act to be transmitted to the Congress by November 10 of each year. These estimates are projections of budget authority and outlays required to continue ongoing Federal programs and activities in the upcoming fiscal year without policy changes from the fiscal year in progress at the time the estimates are submitted.

The second process is the preparation of the President's budget for transmittal to the Congress. This process involves a detailed review of agency budget requests by OMB. These requests and OMB's recommendations on them are presented to the President for decision. Overall fiscal policy issues—relating to total budget outlays and receipts—are again examined. Moreover, the effects of budget decisions on outlays in the years that follow are also considered and are explicitly taken into account.

The actual budget data from the most recently completed fiscal year and updated estimates for the current fiscal year provide an essential reference base in this review and decision process. Thus, the budget process involves the simultaneous consideration of the resource needs of individual programs and the total outlays and receipts that are appropriate in relation to the outlook for the national economy. The budget reflects the results of both of these considerations.

Congressional Action

THE Congress can act as it wishes on the President's budget proposals. It can change programs, eliminate them, or add programs not requested by the President. It can increase or decrease the amounts recommended by the President to finance existing and proposed new programs. It may

315

also act upon legislation determining taxes and other means of raising receipts.

In making appropriations the Congress does not normally vote on outlays directly, but rather on budget authority. The Congress first enacts legislation that *authorizes* an agency to carry out a particular program and in some cases, sets a limit on the amount that subsequently can be considered for appropriation for the program. Many programs are authorized for a specified number of years, or even indefinitely; other programs, such as nuclear energy, space exploration, defense procurement, foreign affairs, and some construction programs, require annual authorizing legislation.

The granting of *budget authority* is usually a separate, subsequent action. As a normal rule, budget authority becomes available each year only as voted by the Congress. However, in a significant number of cases the Congress has voted permanent budget authority, under which funds become available annually without further congressional action. Most trust fund appropriations [i.e., Social Security] are permanent, as are many Federal fund appropriations, such as the appropriation to pay interest on the public debt.

Congressional review begins when the President transmits his current services estimates to the Congress some 2 months before the President's budget is transmitted. While these current services estimates are neither recommended amounts nor estimates as to what the figures for the budget year will actually turn out to be, the Congress may use these estimates as a base upon which to examine the budget transmitted in January.

Upon receipt of the President's budget, the Congress will follow . . . procedures required by the Congressional Budget Act in addition to its established pattern of considering requests for appropriations and changes in revenue laws.

Under the . . . procedures the Congress will consider budget totals prior to completing action on individual appropriations. The act requires that by March 15, the new House and Senate Budget Committees receive reports on budget estimates from all other congressional committees, as well as a fiscal policy report from the . . . Congressional Budget Office, by April 1. This is followed by the adoption of the first concurrent budget resolution, no later than May 15, containing Government-wide budget targets of receipts, budget authority and outlays to guide Congress in its subsequent consideration of appropriations and revenue measures.

Congressional consideration of requests for appropriations and for changes in revenue laws will continue to follow an established pattern. These requests are considered first in the House of Representatives. The appropriations committee, through its subcommittees, studies the proposals for appropriations and examines in detail each agency's performance. The Ways and Means Committee reviews proposed revenue measures. Each committee then recommends the action to be taken by the House of Representatives.

As appropriations and tax bills are approved by the House, they are forwarded to the Senate, where a similar review process is followed. In case of disagreement between the two Houses of Congress, a conference committee (consisting of Members of both bodies) meets to resolve the issues. The report of the conference committee is returned to both Houses for approval, and when agreed to, the measures are then ready to be transmitted to the President in the form of an enrolled bill, for his approval or veto.

After action has been completed on all money bills, the Congress will, by September 15, adopt a second concurrent resolution. The resolution adopted by the Congress will contain budget *ceilings* classified by function for budget authority and outlays and a *floor* for revenue measures. This resolution may retain or revise the appropriate levels set earlier in the year, and can include directives to the appropriations committees and to other committees with jurisdiction over budget authority or entitlements to recommend changes in new or carryover authority or entitlements. Similarly, the second resolution may direct the appropriate committees to recommend changes in Federal revenues or in the public debt. Changes recommended by various committees pursuant to the second budget resolution are to be reported in a reconciliation bill (or resolution, in some cases) whose enactment is scheduled by September 25, a few days before the new fiscal year commences on October 1.

With enactment of the reconciliation bill, the congressional budget process will be completed. At this point, Congress may not consider any spending or revenue legislation that would breach any of the levels specified in the second resolution. In other words, Congress would not be able to pass a supplemental appropriation if it would cause spending to rise above the levels of the second budget resolution, nor could it cut revenues below the second resolution's totals. However, Congress may adopt a new budget resolution any time during the fiscal year.

If action on appropriations is not completed by the beginning of the fiscal year, the Congress may enact a "continuing resolution" to provide authority for the affected agencies to continue operations until their regular appropriations are enacted.

Budget Execution
and Control

ONCE approved, the budget becomes the financial basis for the operations of each agency during the fiscal year.

Under the law, most budget authority and other budgetary resources are made available to the agencies of the executive branch through an apportionment system. Under authority delegated by the President, the Director of OMB apportions (distributes) appropriations and other budgetary resources to each agency by time periods (usually quarters) or by activities. Obligations may not be incurred in excess of the amount apportioned. The objective of the apportionment system is to ensure the effective and orderly use of available authority and to reduce the need for requesting additional or supplemental authority.

Changes in laws or other factors may indicate the need for more authority during the year, and supplemental requests may have to be transmitted to the Congress. On the other hand, reserves may be established under the Antideficiency Act (31 U.S.C. 665) to provide for contingencies or to effect savings made possible by or through changes in requirements or greater efficiency of operations. Amounts may also be withheld for policy or other reasons, pursuant to the Impoundment Control Act.

Whenever the President determines that all or part of any budget authority provided by the Congress will not be required to carry out the full objectives or scope of a program for which it was provided, or that such budget authority should be rescinded for fiscal policy or other reasons, a special message is transmitted by the President to the Congress requesting a rescission of the budget authority. The budget authority proposed by the President for rescission must be made available for obligation unless both the House and Senate pass a rescission bill within 45 days of continuous session after receiving the President's message.

Whenever all or part of any budget authority provided by the Congress is deferred (i.e., temporarily withheld from obligation) the President transmits a special message to the Congress on such deferrals. Either House may pass a resolution disapproving this deferral of budget authority, thus requiring that the funds be made available for obligation. When no congressional action is taken, deferrals may remain in effect until, but not beyond, the end of the fiscal year.

Review and Audit

THIS is the final step in the budget process. The individual agencies are responsible for assuring—through their own review and control systems—that the obligations they incur and the resulting outlays follow the provisions of the authorizing and appropriating legislation, as well as other laws and regulations relating to the obligation and expenditure of funds. OMB reviews program and financial reports and keeps abreast of agency programs and the effort to attain program objectives.

In addition, the Comptroller General, as agent of the Congress, regularly audits, examines, and evaluates Government programs. His findings and recommendations for corrective action are made to the Congress, to OMB, and to the agencies concerned. The Comptroller General also monitors the executive branch's reporting of special messages on proposed rescissions and deferrals. He reports any items not reported by the executive branch and any differences that he may have with the classification (as a rescission or deferral) of withholdings included in special messages submitted by the President. The Comptroller General may bring civil actions to obtain compliance should the President fail to make budget authority available in accordance with the Impoundment Control Act.

CHAPTER TEN

Administrative Control through the Executive

BUDGETING TECHNIQUES AND THEORIES do have political impact on policy decisions that are made in government. Public administration, however, cannot just be concerned with the kinds of processes that go into deciding policy. Administration must be concerned with actually carrying out policy. In a democratic society where the bulk of administration is left to career bureaucrats, keeping administrative discretion under control is an enormous problem for political executives who are either elected or appointed. Electoral processes mean little unless the results of elections can be felt in the actions of government.

Executives, who have the responsibility for keeping their subordinates accountable for their actions, must have a reporting system that routinely provides them with information on what the bureaucracy is actually doing. In addition to formal reporting systems, alternative means such as press reports, special analytic studies conducted by central budget offices, special task forces, and high-level advisory committees can enable the chief executives to stay on top of what the bureaucrats are doing.

In this chapter we will look at some ways in which American governments have tried to centralize control in the hands of political executives. We will deal with some of the problems that brought about the downfall of planning-programming-budgeting systems (PPBS) in the federal government, and we will discuss management by objectives (MBO), which succeeded PPBS as a centralizing effort in the federal government and is still widely used there and in other jurisdictions. As part of our discussion of MBO, we will emphasize the problems of measurement inherent in much of the productivity data collected by governments. We will also deal with the third major budget innovation of the past twenty years—zero-base budgeting (ZBB), which has been highly touted by various consultants and even presidents. We will see to what extent zero-base budgeting assumes that the base, in Wildavsky's terms, really is zero.[1] We will conclude with some observations about implementing management reforms in the executive branch.

Management Control Is a Problem

INFORMATION concerning what bureaucrats and their programs are actually accomplishing is generally sketchy. Even strong believers in the

---

1. *See* chapter 9 for a discussion of Wildavsky's notion of "base."

efficacy of political mechanisms to bring program information to the attention of legislators and political executives have decried the lack of information with which decisions are made. Aaron Wildavsky has noted:

> Each area one investigates shows how little is known compared to what is necessary in order to devise adequate policies. In some organizations there are no ways at all of determining the effectiveness of existing programs; organizational survival must be the sole criterion of merit. . . . If there is a demand for information, the cry goes out that what the organization does cannot be measured. Should anyone attempt to tie the organization to a measure of productivity, the claim is made that there is no truth in numbers.[2]

That agencies resist collecting and disseminating information concerning their specific accomplishments, or lack thereof, should not surprise us. The success of a policy subsystem of symbiotic relationships among agency, clientele, and legislative committee is dependent upon control of information. Those outside the policy subsystem must have access to information if they are to raise the level of conflict from behind closed doors of administrators' offices to more open political forums. High-ranking centralized executives are in a position to turn disputes, which are usually resolved at a low level of conflict, into open political issues. They are in positions to alter the level of conflict and perhaps the outcome. Without information, however, higher executives are powerless. Under such conditions, participants in the policy subsystem try to amicably resolve their conflicts among one another.

Not only do agencies resist giving information to higher authorities, they sometimes willfully disobey orders from political executives. Graham Allison has related a classic case of bureaucracy's following its own standard operating procedures (SOP) rather than the explicit orders of political superiors trying to coordinate governmental action in a complex policy problem.[3]

During the Cuban missile crisis of 1962, President John F. Kennedy convinced Nikita S. Khrushchev, the Soviet premier, that Soviet missiles in Cuba represented an intolerable threat to the United States. As part of a strategy to get the missiles withdrawn, Kennedy ordered a naval blockade of the island.

---

2. Aaron Wildavsky, "Rescuing Policy Analysis from PPBS," *Public Administration Review* 29, no. 2 (March–April 1969): p 189.
3. Graham T. Allison, *The Essence of Decision: Explaining the Cuban Missile Crisis* (Boston: Little, Brown, 1971). This book has many examples of bureaucratic agencies' propensity to follow their own professional norms and see problems from limited, specialized perspectives.

The object of the operation was not to shoot Russians but to communicate a political message from President Kennedy to Chairman Khrushchev. The President wanted to avoid pushing Khrushchev to extremes. The blockade must be conducted as to avoid humiliating the Russians; otherwise Khrushchev might react in nuclear spasm. By the conventional rules, blockade was an act of war and the first Soviet ship that refused to submit to boarding and search risked being sent to the bottom. Khrushchev must somehow be persuaded to pull back, rather than be goaded into retaliation.[4]

Kennedy wanted a blockade established fairly close to Cuba so Khrushchev would have more time to consider his options before having his ships confronted, which might have set off a nuclear exchange.

The navy, which was given the authority to implement the blockade, had other ideas. Its standard contingency plan for blockading Cuba called for a blockade line to be established 500 miles from the island, so the navy ships would be out of range of Cuban MIGs. Although Allison noted that many observers claimed that President Kennedy and Secretary of Defense McNamara forced the navy to scrap its regular blockade procedures in favor of one closer to the island, he did not believe that the navy actually followed orders. Instead, he charted the course of the first ship to be stopped and convincingly argued that the navy did set up the blockade at the 500-mile mark and only moved it later.[5]

The navy, it appears, was not interested in the logic of the greater problem facing the higher authorities. Instead, its priority was to establish a blockade according to professional military standards. Although the stakes are not nearly so high as the possibility of nuclear war in most executive-bureaucratic agency exchanges, there is often a conflict between professional norms and executive decision. There is the basic tension between standard operating procedures and political flexibility. In this case, it was a conflict between the professional norms of the naval commanders and the political norms of their civilian superiors. In this and other cases, the conflict can be summarized by Miles's Law: "Where you stand depends on where you sit."[6] A person's position influences his or her perspective.

The problem of centralized executive control of administration is real. It can affect future policy decisions as well as execution of stated policies. If the executive branch is to be held accountable for more efficient and

---

4. Elie Able, *The Missile Crisis* (Philadelphia: J. B. Lippincott, 1966), p. 155, quoted in Allison, *Essence of Decision,* p. 131.
5. Allison, pp. 129–130.
6. Rufus E. Miles, Jr., "The Origin and Meaning of Miles' Law," *Public Administration Review* 38, no. 5 (September–October 1978): 399–403.

more effective government, we must expect it to have the capacity to develop some meaningful control devices.

PPBS in the Department of Defense

THE budgetary process is one of the key control mechanisms available to both the higher reaches of the executive branch and to the legislature. Modern budgeting techniques—specifically, the program budgeting ideas of David Novick—are ideally suited to improving the executive's ability to make better policy choices and to see that existing policies are implemented. Unfortunately, serious problems have been encountered when program budgeting systems have been attempted. In chapter 9, we dealt with some of the theoretical and practical difficulties of doing high-quality cost-benefit or cost-effectiveness analysis. Now we want to look at the federal government's experience with the planning-programming-budgeting system.

The planning-programming-budgeting system was originally developed for the air force by the Rand Corporation and implemented by Charles Hitch and Robert S. McNamara in the Department of Defense (DOD) in 1961.[7] In 1965, as we have seen, President Lyndon B. Johnson announced that the system, which had achieved apparent success in the DOD, would be spread to all agencies of the federal government. The "success" in DOD included a role in the selection of such weapons systems as the TFX fighter plane, a highly sophisticated plane that was to be used by the air force and the navy with great cost savings to the DOD. There was a bit of a problem when this plane, later called the F-111, was flown in Vietnam. The highly sophisticated aircraft had difficulty staying in the air, even when enemy missiles and antiaircraft artillery were silent.

But in 1965 it looked as if PPBS had worked, and worked well, in the Pentagon. It did not work nearly as well in the other agencies of the federal government. Frederick C. Mosher and John E. Harr, in a study of the failure to implement a programming system in foreign affairs, compared the DOD with other agencies. They noted that the Rand Cor-

---

7. For a brief history of program budgeting, *see* David Novick, "Introduction: The Origin and History of Program Budgeting," in Novick, ed., *Program Budgeting: Program Analysis and the Federal Budget,* 2nd ed. (New York: Holt, Rinehart and Winston, 1969), pp. xix–xxviii.

poration had been at work on defense programming questions for years and had developed a "bag of rather sophisticated tools and a trained body of carpenters skilled in the use of these tools."[8] They noted that there were relatively few overlaps with other organizations and that DOD's mission was clearly defined.

They attributed a great deal of importance to the person of the secretary of defense, Robert S. McNamara, whom they characterized as "a strong executive and an able administrative politician possessing amazing capabilities of intellectual grasp, analytical ability, and memory."[9] This emphasis on the unique characteristics of McNamara was reflected in the Rouse report, a Bureau of the Budget study that sounded the death knell for the PPBS in 1969. The Rouse report found that PPBS-like analysis was useful in domestic agencies when agency heads demanded systematic planning and analysis. The BOB found few domestic agency heads who wanted analysis, let alone understood it as well as McNamara did.[10]

Mosher and Harr suggested that the Department of Defense had additional advantages. It had a relatively simple organizational structure and reported only to one appropriations subcommittee and one substantive committee in each house of Congress. Few other agencies have this luxury of organizational and legislative simplicity. The DOD had a unified accounting system that was especially useful in assessing the costs of hardware items, the principal expenditure focus of the department. Although we have seen that DOD cost estimates for weapons procurement programs were significantly under the real costs, estimating the costs of hardware programs is much easier than assessing the costs and benefits of social programs.

Another factor that favored the implementation of the PPBS in the Department of Defense was that the amount of money available to the department greatly increased during the McNamara years. This was true even before the Vietnam buildup in 1965. Defense expenditures went from $45.8 billion in fiscal 1961 to over $54 billion in fiscal 1965, which was before the real push for Vietnam was reflected in the budget. The domestic agencies were forced to try to use the program budgeting

---

8. Frederick C. Mosher and John E. Harr, *Programming Systems and Foreign Affairs Leadership: An Attempted Innovation* (New York: Oxford University Press, 1970), pp. 9–11; quote on p. 9.
9. Ibid., p. 10
10. For a shortened version of the Rouse report, *see* Edwin L. Harper, Fred A. Kramer, and Andrew M. Rouse, "Implementation and Use of PPBS in Sixteen Federal Agencies," *Public Administration Review* 29, no. 6 (November–December, 1969): 623–632.

TABLE 10.1
Factors Favoring PPBS in the Defense Department During the Early 1960s

1. trained, experienced analysts from Rand
2. clear-cut, definable mission within organization
3. strong agency head with intellectual grasp and analytical ability
4. simple organizational structure and appropriations procedures
5. large share of the budget devoted to hardware
6. expansion of the budgetary pie

---

system at a time when program growth was being curtailed to support the war in Southeast Asia. The advantages of the PPBS effort in the Department of Defense are summarized in Table 10.1.

The Failure of PPBS in the Federal Government

THE planning-programming-budgeting system as it was adopted in the federal government was based on a rationalized, integrated program structure. In theory, all programs in the federal government were to be broken down into distinct elements and put together so those elements contributed to larger programs. The program structure that was adopted consisted of each agency's mission being divided into several *program categories*. These were divided into submissions called *program subcategories,* which were made up of *program elements*. At each level the mission of each program was to be specifically defined. Figure 10.1 presents a partial program structure for a PPBS-like system that was used in the State of Washington. The Washington state program structure was based on the same logic as that used in the federal government.

PPBS in the federal government called for three new documents to accompany the budget presentation. These documents were the program memorandum (PM), the program and financial plan (PFP), and special analytic studies (SAS). The program memorandums were supposed to be analytic justifications that would set out the alternatives and recommendations for each program element. The program and financial plan was to show future implications of programs advocated in the

FIGURE 10.1
Sample Program Structure Logic, Washington State Government Protection of Persons and Property Program

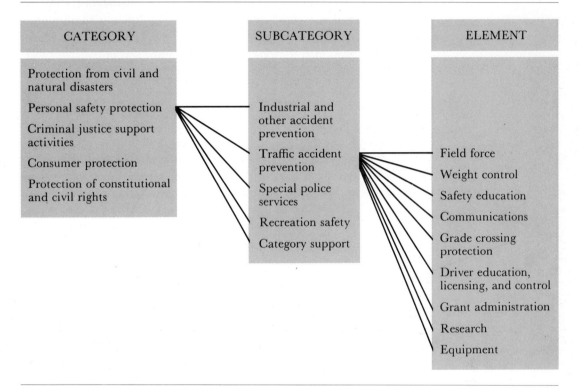

PM by projecting budget figures five years into the future. Special analytic studies were to be full-scale analytic efforts on issues identified by the central budgeting office and agency heads.

In practice, the federal PPBS operation specialized in creating paper, much of it demanded but never used by the Bureau of the Budget in its policy-making deliberations. The program memorandums emphasized the justification of existing practices over poorly constructed alternative proposals. The program and financial plans contained suspect data for which the agencies were not held accountable since the real decisions involved only the budget year under consideration.

In some cases, however, particularly when the agency head wanted to use analytic work, the PPBS exercise was moderately successful. When agency personnel saw that the PPBS materials were being used in

327

agency decision-making rather than for the BOB, they developed better materials, which did prove to be marginally useful.[11]

But generally, PPBS in the federal government failed to live up to the expectations of its advocates. Several reasons were offered for the failure. William Niskanen, formerly a high official in the Office of Management and Budget, declared that the multiple objectives of many government programs meant that a clean program structure was impossible to develop. Niskanen was amused by the planning orientation of PPBS, since the pressure of the budget process forces participants in the process to look only one year ahead. Most of the participants did not have the time or the inclination to deal with five-year projections. The phony figures developed for the PFP undercut the credibility of the whole effort. The heart of PPBS—analysis—also came in for severe criticism from Niskanen. Most of the analytic efforts were based on a national income economic model and failed to identify all the beneficiaries of the various programs.[12]

Perhaps the most important factor that Niskanen brought out, however, related to the political implications of PPBS. Although PPBS was sold as if it had no political impact, Niskanen pointed out, any system designed to help administrators keep track of how subordinate agencies are performing their work will have a centralizing effect.[13] There is a strong tendency in any large organization for incomplete information to flow from top to bottom and vice versa. In government agencies much of the information that flows upward is forced through a filter that permits only self-serving information to pass up. Through this control of information, policy subsystems can continue to make symbiotic accommodations at a low level of visibility.

This action, however, leads to overall inefficiency and ineffectiveness, which is exactly why the higher levels of government administration are trying to develop reliable reporting systems. But as the case with PPBS shows, it is threatening to call for information other than what the agencies want to let out. Most agencies did little to alleviate this threat. As Allen Schick has pointed out: "PPBS died in part because new men of power were arrogantly insensitive to budgetary traditions, institutional loyalties, and personal relationships. PPBS died because of inadequate support and leadership."[14]

11. Ibid., pp. 630–631.
12. William A. Niskanen, "Improving U.S. Budget Choices," *Tax Foundation's Tax Review* 32, no. 11 (November 1971): 41–44.
13. Ibid.
14. Allen Schick, "A Death in the Bureaucracy: The Demise of Federal PPBS," *Public Administration Review* 33, no. 2 (March–April, 1973): 148.

TABLE 10.2
Factors Contributing to Failure of PPBS in the Federal Government

1. PPBS advocates insensitive to institutional loyalties
2. inadequate support and leadership
3. lack of skilled analysts and useful data
4. planning orientation at expense of budgeting needs
5. faulty analytic models
6. inadequate program structure

Indeed, sensitivity and leadership are probably two key items needed to implement any change in public bureaucracy successfully. Creating mountains of meaningless paperwork does not alter the political relationships of the policy subsystems. It might momentarily reassure top-echelon executives that they are enforcing accountability on subordinates in various agencies, but that reassurance might be merely symbolic. With strong leadership that can excite lower-level personnel to live up to the ideals and stated objectives of an agency, meaningful change may be possible. As suggested by the Rouse report, strong leadership was not forthcoming in most agencies. Even though PPBS was not as successful as its advocates had hoped, it did contribute to the greater acceptance of systematic planning and analysis in government budgeting. Table 10.2 summarizes the factors that contributed to the failure of PPBS in the federal government.

Management by Objectives

PPBS quietly faded from the federal budget process in the spring of 1971. No apologies were made and probably few tears were shed when the Office of Management and Budget announced the end of PPBS as part of an effort to simplify budget submission requirements. In less than two years another management technique was being pushed by OMB as the successor to PPBS. Management by objectives was groomed to provide the centralized information and control that PPBS had failed to furnish.

Few persons disagree with the logic of management by objectives. On the surface, it seems like codified common sense. It seems to be what good managers have intuitively done for years. The general aims of management by objectives are quite similar to those of rational decision-making and the PPBS. Management by objectives is a professional approach to management that determines:

1. *what must be done (after careful analysis of why it must be done), including establishment of priorities*
2. *how it must be done (the program steps or plan of action required to accomplish it)*
3. *when it must be done*
4. *how much it will cost*
5. *what constitutes satisfactory performance*
6. *how much progress is being achieved*
7. *when and how to take corrective action.*[15]

Objectives should be precisely defined. Programming—that is, scheduling how tasks must be done to accomplish the goal—should take place. Costs should be considered. Indicators should be developed to show what progress is being made toward those goals. Furthermore, MBO represents a continuous process in which problems are called to management's attention for corrective action. The main difference between MBO and PPBS is that management by objectives does not claim to be a way of allocating resources through the budget. The PPBS did claim to have a powerful role in resource allocation. MBO emphasizes management control of operations.

Management by objectives attempts to incorporate strong controls into program planning. According to George Morrisey, "A plan is only as good as the controls it has to ensure its achievement."[16] Since we have assumed that American citizens want an intelligent, flexible governmental administration that is able to plan, yet one that is controlled by elected officials, MBO appears to fill the bill.

Not only is MBO touted as a management planning and control device, but many management-by-objectives enthusiasts claim that it is rooted in the organizational humanism implied in Douglas McGregor's Theory Y.[17] Henry Tosi and Stephen Carroll, for example, have identified three activities involved in management by objectives: (1) goal-setting, (2) participation, and (3) feedback.[18] The development of clear goals—particularly goals that can be achieved—can be a strong motivator. This is especially true if subordinates are involved in setting the

---

15. George L. Morrisey, *Management by Objectives and Results* (Reading, Mass.: Addison-Wesley, 1970), p. 3.
16. Ibid.
17. *See* the discussion in chapters 4 and 5.
18. Henry L. Tosi and Stephen Carroll, "Management by Objectives," in Jay M. Shafritz, ed., *A New World: Readings on Modern Public Personnel Management* (Chicago: International Personnel Management Association, 1975), pp. 179–183.

goals and developing plans to achieve them. MBO assumes that partici-pation leads to greater commitment to organizational goals and encour-ages people within an organization to work harder to achieve those goals. Feedback is necessary to permit the organization to adapt to new circumstances that can affect a plan's effectiveness.

Many advocates of MBO have stressed the role of participation. The editor of a symposium issue of the *Public Administration Review* devoted to public sector MBO viewed participation as the key aspect of the tech-nique:

> For our purposes, we define management by objectives as a process whereby organizational goals and objectives are set through the partici-pation of organizational members in terms of results expected. . . . Al-though participation in the goal-setting process is not a panacea for ef-fective management, the existing literature supports the idea that participative management can increase individual motivation toward or-ganizational objectives, promote interdependence between managers and subordinates, and create more flexibility, increased efficiency, and greater job satisfaction.[19]

We would expect, therefore, that an environment open to decentraliza-tion of authority would produce the most benefits through MBO. In-stead, the federal government's experience with MBO has suggested that management by objectives is a way of centralizing control rather than a way of decentralizing it to make government more productive.

The basic MBO cycle as used in the federal government during the early 1970s appears in Figure 10.2. This diagram suggests that the mis-sion and goals of an agency are supplied by superiors in the hierarchy or by statute. Analysis of agency problems indicates areas of management concern. Specific objectives are developed and tied to agency goals; suit-able indicators to determine whether the objectives are being achieved must be developed. Agency activities are related to goals and resources through planning. Reporting systems provide the feedback necessary to change plans and programs. Program success is evaluated by the degree to which the activities achieve the stated objectives.

The objective-setting phase is supposed to tie the subordinates to the organization's objectives through participation. But just as private sec-tor objectives in MBO are often dictated by the hierarchy with minimal reference to participation, so too are those in the federal government.[20]

---

19. Jong S. Jun, "Management by Objectives in the Public Sector," *Public Adminis-tration Review* 36, no. 1 (January–February, 1976): 3.
20. Wendell French, *The Personnel Management Process: Human Resources Administration,* 3rd ed. (Boston: Houghton Mifflin, 1974), p. 385.

FIGURE 10.2
MBO in Federal Government

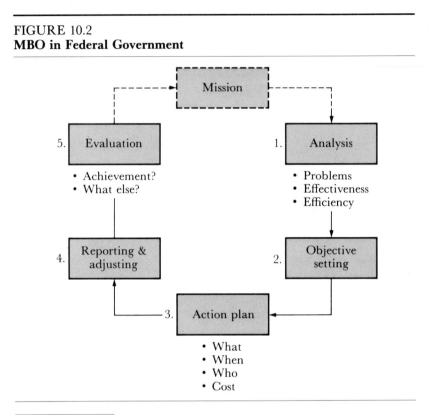

SOURCE: William L. Ginnodo, "A View of MBO . . . From the Middle," *Civil Service Journal* 16, no. 1 (July–September 1975): 14, modified.

At the top levels, the Office of Management and Budget does the dictating. This filters down until operating officials responsible for meeting the objectives are given the orders. As one bureaucrat said: "They force-feed their objectives on us, and we don't swallow."[21]

If it is generally the case that MBO in government operates in a unilateral, authoritarian fashion with the central budgeting agency enforcing objectives that it has determined, then the participative promise of management by objectives is not going to be realized. This does not mean that MBO should be assigned to the circular file of administrative reform efforts that have failed. What passes for MBO in government might still fulfill meaningful planning and control functions, but principally for centralized decision-makers.

21. Joel Havemann, "Is MBO Becoming SOP at OSHA?" *National Journal Reports* 7 (July 26, 1975): 1075. Also see Jerry McCaffery, "MBO and the Federal Budgetary Process," *Public Administration Review* 36, no. 1 (January–February 1976): 37.

Even in governmental agencies where objectives are force-fed to the subordinates, there is often participation in developing the action plan for achieving those objectives. Of course, it is difficult to say whether the MBO process contributes something new in this action-planning phase or whether such planning went on before MBO. Surely, there is nothing in the action-planning phase that would disrupt smooth management unless the action plans are subject to such extensive, time-consuming review that the original planning becomes a paper-pushing exercise.

The reporting, or tracking, and adjusting phases provide the institutionalized feedback that is essential to management by objectives. Just as PPBS foundered on the rocks of the impossibility of cleanly dividing work by function, so MBO has run into difficulties where one organization is dependent upon another for either setting or meeting its objectives. The functions of governmental agencies sometimes overlap. Agencies sometimes must depend on other agencies to meet their objectives. Furthermore, as Frank Sherwood and William Page have pointed out:

> The expression, pursuit, and achievement of objectives of a governmental unit are frequently and significantly conditioned by external phenomena. . . . External phenomena include legislators, clientele groups, decisions of other governmental units, mass communication media, economic conditions, courts, special interest, and other private organizations.[22]

Public managers, especially those involved in intergovernmental relations, have far less control over the resources needed to achieve their objectives than their private sector counterparts do.

Evaluation and Measurement in MBO

Even if one is willing to cast aside the participation elements of management by objectives, one is left with a solid core of program evaluation. Evaluation, especially while a program is developing, is necessary if management is to recognize that changes must be made to enable the program to reach its goals. The elements of good program evaluation share the same analytical base whether the evaluation takes place through PPBS, MBO, or ZBB.

Program evaluation through any of these budgeting systems depends on two factors: (1) program goals must be clearly stated, and (2) appropriate measures must be devised that will really show whether those goals are being achieved. While it may be true that the goals of govern-

---

22. Frank P. Sherwood and William J. Page, Jr., "MBO and Public Management," *Public Administration Review* 36, no. 1 (January–February, 1976): 10.

mental programs may be harder to define than those of some private sector organizations, there is a certain sting to George Odiorne's admonition, "If you cannot count it, measure it or describe it, you probably don't know what you want and you can often forget it as a goal."[23] Generally it is possible to formulate precise goal statements in most government agencies, even though it may not be politically wise to do so. Perhaps the Occupational Safety and Health Administration (OSHA) has the goal that by the end of the fiscal year, 90 percent of all employed Americans will be working in firms that have met or exceeded all safety standards, provided OSHA is given a certain level of resources. Such a statement may imply that OSHA is going to harass American businesses until they comply or go out of business. People might prefer to work in safe places, all things being equal; but given a choice between working in a place that fails to meet safety standards and being out of work, people might prefer to continue working. Precisely stating a goal might stimulate antiagency political forces—in this case, labor and business— to trim the agency's sails.

Developing reliable and valid measures to assess how close an agency is coming to its goals, however, is not always easy. In areas where the process itself, rather than any specific goal, is valued, it is virtually impossible to establish meaningful, measurable goals. How can we measure the extent to which the Department of Justice protects freedom of speech? By the number of arrests of speakers? By the number of arrests of those trying to stop free speech? Although there are some areas of government where measures of objectives are not useful at all, in most agencies some goal-related measures can be developed.[24]

Some measures may not really show how close an agency is getting to its goal. A program's goal might be to improve health in the inner city areas. The number of nurses that the particular program might train would be a measure of output of the program, but it does not necessarily measure how close the program comes to achieving its goal. The number of nurses trained would give an executive some notion of the cost of training each nurse but relatively little knowledge of whether the pro-

---

23. George S. Odiorne, *Personnel Management By Objectives* (Homewood, Ill.: Dorsey Press, 1971), p. 119. Odiorne is a successful MBO consultant who plays down the participative role in MBO.
24. A government study of productivity measures in 1971 reported that half the work done in government was susceptible to meaningful measurement. *See* Thomas D. Morris, William H. Corbett, and Brian L. Usilaner, "Productivity Measures in the Federal Government," *Public Administration Review* 32, no. 6 (November–December, 1972): 755. *Also see* Peter F. Drucker, "The Deadly Sins in Public Administration," *Public Administration Review* 40, no. 2 (March–April 1980): 103–106.

gram was contributing to its real goal. *Impact* or *accomplishment* or *effectiveness measures* attempt to assess program performance in relation to goals. Such measures are much more difficult to develop than output measures such as the number of nurses graduated or applications processed. Most of the measures used in MBO are output rather than impact measures.

There is a danger that the choice of a measure, especially of output measures, might contribute to an agency's failure to achieve its goal. Harry Hatry has raised the problem of *perverse measurement.* Dealing with the closely allied field of productivity measurement, Hatry noted that some measures encourage some employees to take actions that look good on the measures but might not be in the public interest.[25] If garbage collection efforts are to be assessed on the basis of tons collected, some employees might be inclined to water the garbage down before taking their truck to the weighing station. Wet garbage weighs a lot more than normal garbage. The garbage-truck crew could pick up a half-truckload of legitimate trash and turn on the hose to raise the weight to that of a full load while they relax over coffee and donuts. Similarly, if the measure adopted is number of full truckloads of garbage per crew, a way to beat the system would be to take a full truckload into the dump but drop only half of it. The crew would only have to pick up the equivalent of a half-load to have another full truck. They could still enjoy the coffee and donuts while the trash did not get picked up.

Measures with a high potential for becoming perverse occur regularly in public agencies. At least one community action program takes the number of meetings held as an indicator. If you are being evaluated on the basis of the number of meetings held, how do you act? If professors at a university are evaluated by the number of students currently writing dissertations under their direction, does it make sense for the professors to push those students to complete their work? Of course, any measurement system can be perverted to serve individual rather than agency goals. Management by objectives generally assumes that professional pride and trust engendered by the participative process will confine such efforts to beat the system to a few. Since meaningful participation in the selection of objectives seems to be lacking in federal MBO, there is a potential danger of measurement manipulation by disgruntled federal employees.

Although there can be abuses of measures, there are valid indicators for a wide variety of programs. The Urban Institute has developed and

---

25. Harry P. Hatry, "Issues in Productivity Measurement for Local Government," *Public Administration Review* 32, no. 6 (November–December, 1972): 777–778.

tested such indicators for many of the functions of local governments.[26] Among the kinds of measures developed was a scale for assessing street cleanliness. The scale values were related to photographic and written descriptions, and trained observers assigned a scale rating based on the degree of cleanliness of the assigned area. For example, "condition 1" would be used to describe a clean area. Condition 2 would be moderately clean; condition 3 would be moderately littered; and condition 4 would be heavily littered. The trained observer would have a set of photographs that corresponded to each of these conditions, so he or she could keep a standard idea of what a "moderately littered" area would be, for example. This technique was successfully used in New York City under the name Project Scorecard. Similar photographic rating scales have been used by Washington, D.C., Savannah, Nashville, and St. Petersburg.

The use of such an indicator enables managers and workers to set some objectives regarding the level of cleanliness of the streets. For example, if management found that the streets in a certain area averaged a 2.5 value and that the streets in another area of town averaged 2.3, it might want to channel resources to the more littered area to make those streets cleaner. Or management might use the information to justify an increased budget and mobilize the support of the people who live in the dirtier area. Or management might devise some reward scheme based on competition among those working in various areas of the city to see which groups could show the most improvement on the street cleanliness rating. With the more precise information regarding street cleanliness, management could attempt to make changes. It would have some targets, and greater accountability could be enforced.

The Urban Institute has developed measures for social services programs such as recreation and libraries, too, but it is not alone in the effort to improve public management through indicators. Working independently, other scholars and practitioners have contributed to this effort. For example, John Aplin and Peter Schoderbek note that the criteria for assessing any service program should include these factors:

1. *Definition of the type of service to be provided (i.e., delivery of meals to elderly people in their homes).*
2. *Specification of quality of service delivered (i.e., meeting 100 percent of minimum daily caloric and vitamin requirements of elderly individual).*

---

26. *See* Harry P. Hatry, Louis H. Blair, Donald M. Fisk, John M. Greiner, John R. Hall, Jr., and Philip S. Schaenman, *How Effective Are Your Community Services?* (Washington, D.C.: The Urban Institute, 1977).

3. *Estimation of all* major *consequences or outputs of the organization's activities related to service delivery.*
4. *Definition of the target group—area of coverage/responsibility (in essence, determination of total clientele possible for service).*
5. *Establishment of desired clientele penetration levels (i.e., reach 35 percent of eligible recipients).*
6. *Economic constraints (i.e., within parameters dictated by funding and administrative support).*
7. *Time dimensions—a future point in time when evaluation and replanning is to occur.*[27]

With this kind of information, management can redirect resources if the indicators suggest that targets are not being met. The ability to use information to make adjustments so that the organization can achieve its objectives is the essence of good management.

Assessing MBO

Management by objectives has received mixed reviews in federal government. An article praising MBO in the Department of Health, Education and Welfare (HEW), written by Rodney Brady, has been influential in spreading the gospel of MBO.[28] Within HEW, now the Department of Health and Social Services (HSS), others criticized the program for (1) creating paperwork, (2) failing to provide resources consistent with the objectives, (3) creating objectives out of time phase with the budget, and (4) depending on state and local governments for delivery of services while objectives were unilaterally set by the federal government.[29]

Although the participative elements of MBO seem to have been dropped in the federal case, management by objectives has retained its effectiveness as a control device. Executives generally believe having some hard, measurable data is better than having none. Even if the data do not directly measure program impacts, they do provide some notion of what the public is getting for tax dollars spent. By specifying goals and measures, upper-echelon executives believe they increase their control over subordinate agencies. This belief may give them the confidence to provide leadership to bureaucratic units that seem highly susceptible to falling into the cozy, symbiotic patterns with agency, clientele, and legislative committee relations.

27. John C. Aplin, Jr. and Peter P. Schoderbek, "How to Measure MBO," *Public Personnel Management* 5, no. 2 (March–April 1976): 93.
28. Rodney H. Brady, "MBO Forces to Work in the Public Sector," *Harvard Business Review* 51, no. 2 (March–April, 1973): 65–74.
29. Sherwood and Page, "MBO and Public Management," p. 7.

As Sherwood and Page have suggested:

> It is likely that MBO will find its greatest expression as a tactic in a hierarchical strategy of leaderhip. Despite pressures for a more humanistic value orientation in society, the fact is that hierarchical patterns of leadership still dominate our organizations. MBO is an advantageous strategy in its goal clarity, in eliciting achievement motivations as objectives become clear, in its tracking wherein high achievers can see results of work, in improved capability to exercise data-based control, and in increased capability to provide rewards . . . in terms of demonstrated performance.[30]

Excessive reliance on quantitative measures has its dangers. If public agencies are evaluated on the number of cases they successfully handle, they may be reluctant to take difficult cases. Instead they may engage in "skimming" or "creaming." Skimming involves handling the easier cases first. For example, it is easy and relatively cheap to run a methadone clinic if many heroin addicts want treatment and voluntarily come to the clinic. Costs per participant soar once the easy cases have been dealt with, because the agency has to set up an outreach program to attract hard-core, often criminal, heroin addicts who might have been the main target group for the program. The great increase in costs needed to meet the agency's real target group may seem outrageous compared to the costs of dealing only with the easy cases.

MBO's emphasis on measures makes it a quantitative management system. Budget officers who have a fiscal orientation are inclined to support programs that appear to be relatively efficient. Since harder cases involve more resources and result in fewer "successes," MBO-oriented budget systems might discourage an agency from handling hard assignments. MBO, like any quantitative management system, must be carefully monitored to balance programmatic and fiscal concerns.[31]

Zero-Base Budgeting

WHILE the Office of Management and Budget was force-feeding management by objectives to agencies of the federal government, a "new" budgeting technique was being developed and implemented in the pri-

---

30. Ibid., p. 11.
31. For a discussion of programmatic versus fiscal orientations, *see* John Wanat, *Introduction to Budgeting* (North Scituate, Mass.: Duxbury Press, 1978), chapter 4.

FIGURE 10.3
Steps to Zero-Base Budgeting

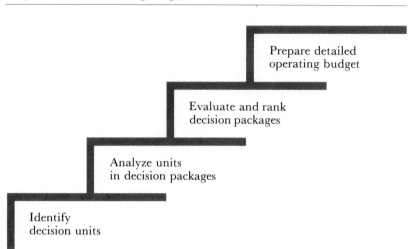

Prepare detailed
operating budget

Evaluate and rank
decision packages

Analyze units
in decision packages

Identify
decision units

vate sector and in a few governmental jurisdictions. That technique, zero-base budgeting (ZBB), became President Jimmy Carter's symbol of good management, and many elected officials at all levels of government looked to ZBB as the way to control government expenditure through better management technique. As with other systems and techniques that we have discussed, ZBB was supposed to centralize budgetary decision-making by routinely giving superiors in the hierarchy better information concerning tentative decisions made at lower levels.

Zero-base budgeting, as developed by Peter Pyhrr for the Texas Instruments Company, the State of Georgia, and the federal government, seeks to allow virtually all programs—both old and new—to be reviewed through the budgetary process.[32] ZBB involves several steps, which are presented in Figure 10.3. The first step is the identification of *decision units.* Decision units are the lowest level at which meaningful management decisions are made. An organization implementing ZBB has considerable flexibility in determining what "meaningful" means. Therefore, decision units are not completely synonymous with the program elements of program budgeting. Implicitly, in zero-base budgeting, all

---

32. Peter A. Phyrr, *Zero-Base Budgeting: A Practical Management Tool for Evaluating Expenses* (New York: John Wiley, 1973), chapters 3, 4, and 5. *Also see* his "Zero-Base Approach to Governmental Budgeting," *Public Administration Review* 37, no. 1 (January–February 1977): 1–8.

the decision units of government constitute a program structure when logically grouped for review at higher levels.

Each decision unit should have an identifiable manager who has the authority to establish priorities and budget for all the activities within the decision unit. There is a great deal of flexibility built into the notion of a decision unit if the only requisite is for a responsible manager to speak for the unit. Graeme Taylor presents an example of how an organization could set up alternative decision units:

> Consider an organization that operates neighborhood health centers, each of which offers a variety of health services such as tuberculosis control, venereal disease control, lead poisoning control, maternal and child health clinics, and so forth. The decision units may variously be (a) each center, encompassing all health services provided within the center, (b) each separate health service provided in each center, or (c) each health service aggregated across all centers.
>
> If each center has a manager who is responsible for resource allocation within the center, then the individual centers may be logically selected as decision units. If each health service within a center has an identifiable manager responsible for resource allocation within that service, each service within a center could be viewed as a separate decision unit. On the other hand, if resource allocation decisions within health services are made system-wide by identifiable managers at the organization's headquarters, then the individual health services aggregated across all centers would be logical decision units. The key criterion is how responsibility for resource allocation decisions is distributed.[33]

Another element to consider when setting up decision units is the total number of units that will eventually be developing *decision packages* which will have to be ranked, then reviewed. Many decision units may develop too many decision packages, making the system unwieldy. The second step in the zero-base budgeting process demands that each decision unit develop several decision packages for aspects of its programs. Each decision package spells out the detailed description of program objectives, ties the objectives to the amount of resources needed to carry out the program, and presents a cost-benefit analysis to justify each aspect of the program. There are two roles for decision-package development. The first is to suggest alternative ways of performing existing functions, and the second is to analyze the impact of performing existing functions in the same ways but at different levels of activity. For example, if a "meals on wheels" program is part of the responsibility of a par-

33. Graeme M. Taylor, "Introduction to Zero-Base Budgeting," *The Bureaucrat* 6, no. 1 (1977), reprinted in Fred A. Kramer, ed., *Contemporary Approaches to Public Budgeting* (Cambridge, Mass.: Winthrop, 1979), pp. 152–153.

ticular decision unit, one decision package might consider using a centralized kitchen and delivering the food to the elderly in small vans. An alternative package might analyze the costs and benefits of having the food cooked on the road in converted recreational vehicles that could also be used for the delivery. A package dealing with the level of activity might analyze the costs and benefits of providing meals to 35 percent of the target population. Another decision package might consider the costs and benefits of expanding the service to include an additional 5 percent of the target group.

The third step in ZBB involves ranking each decision package. The manager of each decision unit ranks his or her decision packages. All the packages ranked by first-level managers are sent up the hierarchy to be reviewed and ranked against decision packages from other decision units. In the course of this review, superiors can change the rankings of decision packages sent up by any decision-unit manager. If all the decision packages were reviewed and ranked against all others as they went through the review process, ZBB would be caught in a deluge of paper. Although Jimmy Carter stated that all programs would have to be justified from a zero base,[34] the practical problems of implementing the technique have forced the agencies to concentrate their review on decision packages whose incremental costs exceed some arbitrarily set percentage of last year's appropriation. In effect, this means that zero-base budgeting is not operating from a base of zero dollars, but rather from a base that is some percentage—usually 75 or 85 percent—of last year's appropriation. Just as the base in traditional budgeting virtually eliminated review of established programs, decision packages that fall within 75 to 85 percent of the previous year's appropriations are immune from review at higher levels. The higher levels concentrate their review and ranking efforts on the decision packages whose costs exceed the arbitrary cumulative cost level.

The arbitrary figure based on last year's appropriation is called the *minimum funding level.* The minimum funding level assumes that the entire program should be discarded if higher authorities choose not to allocate funds to support the agency at its minimum funding level. In his study of ZBB in Georgia, Thomas Lauth discovered how budget officers treated the minimum funding level provisions of ZBB. In Georgia at the time of his study, the minimum was 85 percent of the previous year's appropriations. Lauth quoted several budget officers:

---

34. Jimmy Carter, "Jimmy Carter Tells Why He Will Use Zero-Based Budgeting," *Nation's Business* 65, no. 1 (January 1977): 24.

The minimum level is not of much use . . . we work backward to get it.

The minimum is a waste of time . . . no one looks at that. We determine where we want to be and work back to 85%.

No one pays any attention to it. In 1975 when we had to rework our budgets because of the revenue shortage, we made cuts without any reference to the minimum. You certainly could not expect anyone to come up with say 10% in each program. Some programs are untouchable. We would get 10% department-wide by taking most of it out of a couple of less important programs.

The minimum level is worthless. We (Legislative Budget Office) don't look at it . . . the departments merely take their 'current' and lop off 10 or 15% to satisfy the requirement of submitting a minimum funding level.

See that machine over there? (A desk calculator) I prepare my current level which to my way of thinking is not the same dollars as this year, but what it will take to provide the same level of services . . . then I hit those keys and multiply by .85 of the current to get the minimum.[35]

Zero-base budgeting, therefore, is not as thorough as its name implies. In practice, it does not mean justifying programs from a zero base. A budgeting system that used a real zero base was tried in the United States Department of Agriculture (USDA) in the early 1960s, but was discarded after a year. The system proved to be a paper exercise which took many extra person-hours and mounds of paper but did not produce a budget that differed substantially from the typical incremental budgeting process. In general, the attempt at zero-based budgeting in the USDA concentrated on new programs and large increases in old programs, which is exactly the way incrementalism would have handled the budget-making process.[36] It is possible, and may be desirable, to have some agencies at some times engage in real zero-based budgeting. To predicate an entire budgeting system on such an activity, however, may be more trouble than it is worth.

Assessing Zero-Base Budgeting

The variants of zero-base budgeting used in government today do not budget from a clean slate with a zero base. Instead, as we have seen, decision packages are usually developed by using the costs to produce the current level of services or a limited cutback in services. To a degree, we

35. Thomas P. Lauth, "Zero-Base Budgeting in Georgia State Government: Myth and Reality," *Public Administration Review* 38, no. 5 (September–October 1978): 423.
36. Aaron Wildavsky and Arthur Hammann, "Comprehensive Versus Incremental Budgeting in the Department of Agriculture," in Fremont J. Lyden and Ernest G. Miller, eds., *Planning-Programming-Budgeting: A Systems Approach to Management* (Chicago: Markham, 1968), pp. 142–161.

would expect any budget system to yield budgets that change in small increments from year to year, because so many expenditures are relatively uncontrollable in the short run. Therefore, it is not surprising that ZBB usually produces budgets that are incrementally different from the previous year's budget. Allen Schick's comment concerning Jimmy Carter's first budget could characterize most ZBB-produced budgets in government: "The first president to promise a zero-base budget has delivered the most incremental financial statement since Wildavsky canonized that form of budget-making more than a dozen years ago."[37]

Although the outcomes of ZBB seem similar to what one would have expected under traditional incremental budgeting, there may be some advantages to the system. One advantage of ZBB over PPBS and MBO is that it is easier to implement than the other systems. In the federal government, agencies quickly conformed to the ZBB process. The Office of Management and Budget had learned from earlier mistakes in trying to implement PPBS and MBO. This time, ZBB became *the* way to submit the budget, not an ancillary submission justifying the standard budget documents. This time, separate staffs were not established to carry out the budget innovation. Instead, the regular budget offices worked on ZBB.

To some observers, however, the speed at which ZBB forms were accepted indicated their nonthreatening character.[38] In the federal government, ZBB initially did not call for additional information. It did not require reorganization. The aim of this flexible approach was to make the process by which programs are reviewed more systematic. Indeed, much effort has been spent on developing intricate ranking techniques that would paint a pseudoscientific gloss on decision packages that had been approved.[39] Most people with governmental experience would expect such ranking systems to be revamped if they produced politically unacceptable recommendations. They were.

Zero-base budgeting as practiced in governments is a systematic, incremental budgeting system. Each decision package above the mini-

---

37. Allen Schick, "The Road from ZBB," *Public Administration Review* 38, no. 2 (March–April 1978): 177.
38. Certainly Schick feels this way about the federal experience. Lauth tends toward this view because of the Georgia experience. James D. Suver and Ray L. Brown, "Where Does Zero-base Budgeting Work?," *Harvard Business Review* 55, no. 7 (November–December 1977): 76–84, see the budgeting aspects of lesser importance than other changes that were made in Georgia and Wilmington, Delaware.
39. *See* Mark J. Versel, "Zero-Base Budgeting: Setting Priorities through the Ranking Process," *Public Administration Review* 38, no. 6 (November–December 1978): 524–527.

mum level required to keep an agency operating represents a marginal increment. The most important marginal increments are added first, then progressively less important decision packages are added until a *budget constraint* is reached. A budget constraint is an arbitrary amount of money that higher executives or central budget officials have suggested as the expenditure target for the agency. The real action in ZBB, as in traditional incremental budgeting, is the analysis of decision packages or programs that bring the agency to expenditure totals near the budget constraint. But generally, ZBB forms and procedures are applied across the board, even in programs and areas where there is no need to deliver the detail required by ZBB.

Daniel Ogden has suggested that zero-base budgeting be conducted under certain conditions.

> In practice, zero basing is expensive and time-consuming. A good manager uses it when he expects the gains will outweigh the costs. Few managers would deny that analyzing and defending the entire budget is a useful tool in selected circumstances. For example, when an agency has encountered a significant change in program demands and must shift its resources to cope more effectively with the change, a good manager will call for a zero based budget to reestablish a defensible base. Even very stable, continuing programs can be usefully zero based occasionally, perhaps once in five or seven years.[40]

Using ZBB more selectively might improve the performance of the technique and enable it to meet some of the expectations of the users. Currently in the federal and state governments using ZBB, there is a discrepancy between the expectations of the budget participants and what they really get from zero-base budgeting (see Table 10.3).

Although there are considerable negative features of ZBB, there have been some positive effects. ZBB was designed to get program managers more involved in the budget process. This has been accomplished, along with greater knowledge and respect for other programs. More information has been channeled to the top managers. This has increased their control over subordinate units. ZBB has also presented some funding-level choices to the central budget officials. But improvements in ZBB—especially the kind needed to show the cost savings and increased productivity demanded by anxious taxpayers—have not been forthcoming.

Most of the attempts to implement ZBB in governments may not be

---

40. Daniel M. Ogden, Jr., "Beyond Zero Based Budgeting," *Public Administration Review* 38, no. 6 (November–December 1978): 528. Perhaps Ogden confused true zero-base budgeting with ZBB, but his points are still valid.

TABLE 10.3
Expectations and Results of ZBB in the Federal Government

ZBB Participants

	What They Often Get	
What They Want	*Negative*	*Positive*
Legislative representatives: (To serve the voters' desires) An effective information source	An executive branch tool	Two State Legislatures receive valuable information and use it
OMB staff: (To serve the President's desires) Program cuts Alternative program approaches Several choices of funding levels Knowledge of agency priorities	Program growth justifications Old warmed-over ideas Submissions that double and quadruple Information that many programs do not lend themselves to ZBB	Several funding level choices Agencies' managers' program priorities
Top managers: Greater control More complete information An influence over the organization's priorities	Justification for additional expenditures Volumes and volumes of paper Endless forms with little substance Staff morale problems	Increased control More information about the organization Solutions to certain problems
Program manager/corporate managers: More money for their programs More influence in establishing priorities	Forms that make no sense Forms calling for information that is not available Caught up in the details of budgeting	Knowledge and influence over other programs Justifications which support program growth
Budget officers: Help to form the budget Adequate justifications	Left out of the decision-making process No time for budget analysis Become trackers of forms and numbers	More effective budget Funding alternatives for programs Established priorities

Source: *Streamlining Zero-Base Budgeting Will Benefit Decisionmaking,* Report PAD-79-45 (Washington, D.C.: U.S. General Accounting Office, September 25, 1979), p. 12.

worth the effort. Usually these attempts are system-wide efforts that typically generate more paper than changes. But there are numerous applications of simplified zero-base budgeting that ties program evaluation to the budget process for *some* programs. Simplified systems such as those advocated by Joseph Wholey show considerable promise as a means to give "policymakers more control over government programs and staff activities, and [give] program managers and their staffs the chance to participate in informed priority setting."[41] These simplified ZBB systems call for decision packages for a limited number of programs and do not require explicit priority rankings of all programs. Furthermore, these systems use available program evaluation techniques. As Wholey notes, "With the close involvement of policymakers who want and will use specific information on program performance, these evaluation processes produce information needed to improve government efficiency and effectiveness."[42]

Summary

THE budget process is one of the strongest managerial controls to enforce accountability. Ever since V. O. Key bemoaned the lack of budgetary theory in the 1940s, public managers and public policy scholars have sought to develop ways to answer his question: "On what basis shall it be decided to allocate X dollars to Activity A instead of Activity B?"[43] The managers and scholars have suggested a number of answers, many of them touted as panaceas.

Performance budgeting—tying work-load measures to various governmental activities—was supposed to be the answer in the 1950s. Planning-programming-budgeting systems devised by economists were to be the way of the 1960s. Management by objectives was to pick up the pieces of earlier budget reform failures in the early 1970s. Zero-base budgeting is today's answer, and variants of all these reforms are probably just over the horizon. All these answers to the Key question have failed to deliver what their most zealous supporters promised.

The public budgeting techniques have failed to live up to the expan-

---

41. Joseph S. Wholey, *Zero-Base Budgeting and Program Evaluation* (Lexington, Mass.: Lexington Books, 1978), p. 14.
42. Ibid., p. 15.
43. V. O. Key, Jr., "The Lack of a Budgetary Theory," *American Political Science Review* 34, no. 4 (December 1940): 1137.

sive expectations of their advocates because, as Aaron Wildavsky has pointed out, they failed to recognize that politics is a legitimate way to answer Key's question.[44] Some decision-makers, borrowing from business experience and welfare economics theory, have tried to substitute rationality in the form of dollars-and-cents analysis for political judgments. Although only a handful of the most ardent supporters of these techniques would argue that economic standards must be substituted for political ones, the forms and processes of governmental budgeting in many jurisdictions have been affected by these new techniques. Public budgeting is still political, but the techniques of political accommodation in the budgetary process in the United States have been changing in the past two decades.

No single reform has revolutionized public budgeting. Instead, the effect of these reform efforts has been evolutionary. There is a bit of truth in Richard Rose's tongue-in-cheek assertion regarding one of these reforms. Rose concluded "that MBO has evaporated, becoming a part of the climate of management, albeit a part whose specific influence is limited and incapable of precise measurement."[45] The essence of these reforms has raised managerial attention toward better information and better analysis. The appendix to this chapter presents one analytic technique that is easy to use in a variety of situations.

Modern management techniques using better information and better analysis can be applied to budget-making without recourse to labels such as PPBS, MBO, or ZBB. Good public managers can exert better control over subordinate units if they choose control systems that fit their management styles.[46] For some managers, PPBS might be worth the time and effort needed to develop the system to the limits of its theoretical capacity. For most other managers, the elements of MBO might be more useful. Still others may find that the institutionalized incrementalism of ZBB with an analytic overlay fits their styles.

From a management perspective, the goal of all these budget reform efforts is to make better policy decisions supported by better information and analysis. Joseph Wholey has reported on several successful variants of ZBB implementation. These applications of ZBB did not follow the Peter Pyhrr prescription to the letter but did enhance the chances of

44. Wildavsky, *Politics of the Budgetary Process,* chapter 4.
45. Richard Rose, "Implementation and Evaporation: The Record of MBO," *Public Administration Review* 37, no. 1 (January–February 1977): 70.
46. Cortlandt Cammann and David A. Nadler, "Fit Control Systems to Your Management Style," *Harvard Business Review* 54, no. 1 (January–February 1976): 65–72.

FIGURE 10.4
Government Policy and Management Environment

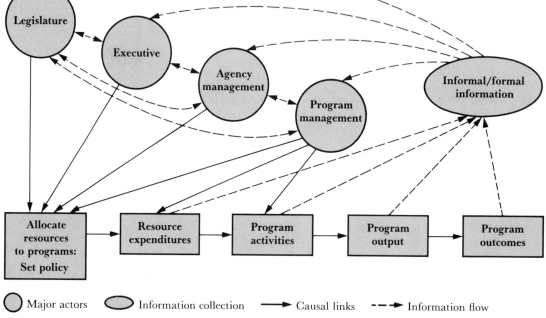

SOURCE: Reprinted by permission of the publisher, from *Zero-Base Budgeting and Program Evaluation* by Joseph S. Wholey (Lexington, Mass.: Lexington Books, D. C. Heath and Company, Copyright 1978, D. C. Heath and Company).

making better policy decisions. Wholey recognizes the need for formal information systems to supplement the informal political channels.[47] Figure 10.4 shows the relationships between information and actors in the policy process.

Better formal information routinely channeled up the hierarchy by the kinds of modern budget systems presented in this chapter is a tool for centralization. A degree of centralization is necessary if citizens are to hold elected executives accountable for the actions of public bureaucracies. Wholey's diagram suggests that such information could be used to break up the policy subsystems that seem to develop around agencies and bureaus. But the diagram also suggests that there is a legislative role

---

47. Wholey, *Zero-Base Budgeting and Program Evaluation.*

in accountability. Because of the nature of the legislative committee systems, this role tends to have a decentralizing effect, which supports the existence of policy subsystems. In the next chapter we turn our attention to legislative controls on public bureaucracies.

Suggestions for Further Reading

Hatry, Harry P., Louis H. Blair, Donald M. Fisk, John M. Greiner, John R. Hall, Jr., and Philip S. Schaenman. *How Effective Are Your Community Services? Procedures for Monitoring the Effectiveness of Municipal Services.* Washington D.C.: The Urban Institute, 1977.

Jun, Jong S., ed. "Symposium on Management by Objectives in the Public Sector." *Public Administration Review* 36, no. 1 (January–February 1976).

Kramer, Fred A., ed. *Contemporary Approaches to Public Budgeting.* Cambridge, Mass.: Winthrop, 1979.

Lee, Robert D., Jr., and Ronald W. Johnson. *Public Budgeting Systems,* 2d ed. Baltimore: University Park, 1977.

Levine, Charles H., ed. *Managing Fiscal Stress.* Chatham, N.J.: Chatham House, 1980.

McCaffery, Jerry, ed. "Symposium on Budgeting in an Era of Resource Scarcity." *Public Administration Review* 38, no. 6 (November–December 1978).

Merewitz, Leonard, and Stephen H. Sosnick. *The Budget's New Clothes.* Chicago: Markham, 1971.

Morrisey, George L. *Management by Objectives and Results in the Public Sector.* Reading, Mass.: Addison-Wesley, 1976.

Pyhrr, Peter A. *Zero-Base Budgeting: A Practical Management Tool for Evaluating Expenses.* New York: John Wiley, 1973.

Schick, Allen, ed. *Perspectives on Public Budgeting.* Washington, D.C.: American Society for Public Administration, 1980.

Wholey, Joseph S. *Zero-Base Budgeting and Program Evaluation.* Lexington, Mass.: Lexington, 1978.

Wildavsky, Aaron. *The Politics of the Budgetary Process,* 3rd ed. Boston: Little, Brown, 1979.

The Discounting to Present Value Technique as a Decision Tool

The technique of discounting to present value is widely used as a routine part of investment analysis in the private sector. The technique has wide possible use in the public sector, too, but many who might be able to use it to clarify aspects of decisions, especially in the smaller jurisdictions, act as though discounting techniques do not exist. In what situations do you think discounting would be useful in your community? Can you develop a hypothetical case where the analysis would be sensitive to the discount rate? In what ways can general administrators arm themselves to be able to cope with doctored analysis?

THERE ARE SEVERAL DISADVANTAGES to some formal program budgeting systems. They are expensive to develop and operate, and they strike many people as simply another management fad that simply will not be able to compete in an arena where the needs of political decision-makers are paramount. Yet practically all observers of public administration at all levels of American government are appalled by the lack of systematic planning and analysis in governmental decision-making. This lack of systematic planning and analysis is acute in the smaller jurisdictions where community leaders are unable or unwilling to commit the level of resources needed to implement a system similar to that established in Pennsylvania[1] or Washington State.[2] Still, it is possible to use some relatively simple economic analytic techniques to explore more adequately the implications of certain kinds of decisions.

---

1. Robert J. Mowitz, "Pennsylvania's Planning, Programming, Budgeting System," in David Novick, ed., *Current Practice in Program Budgeting (PPBS)* (New York: Crane, Russak, 1973), pp. 169–80.
2. Tory N. Tjersland, "PDS Is a Better Way," *Governmental Finance* 4, no. 1 (February 1975): 10–18.

The discounted cash-flow method for capital budgeting can be used in a wide variety of small jurisdiction activities. Just about any local government service that could be contracted to private suppliers or to another governmental unit represents a potential use for the discounted cash-flow method. Should a town invest in new refuse disposal equipment? Or would it be more economical to contract to private carters? Should a jurisdiction invest in its own computer facility? Or should it contract out for specific computer services? Which decision would be a better use of scarce resources?

Generally, in most jurisdictions questions such as these are not often raised, let alone analyzed. If a town has provided garbage collection services in the past and a few new trucks are needed, the sanitation agency requests funds in its budget to purchase new trucks. Since the town wants to have its trash picked up, it will generally set aside the needed funds to support this legitimate, accepted, and expected governmental service. On the other hand, if a jurisdiction has been contracting out for a computerized payroll system, sooner or later, if there is a chance of getting money out of the capital budget, someone is going to suggest that the jurisdiction develop its own computer capability. After all, if the city had its own computer facility, it could perform many more useful functions. The decisions that are made in these cases are generally based on the political acceptability of the service being performed or the availability of capital funds. Rarely, in smaller jurisdictions especially, are such decisions based on meaningful economic analysis.

Governmental finance officers in the smaller jurisdictions are used to dealing with alternative costs of performing various functions. But often they are tied to the concepts of simple accounting methods that treat dollars as constants over time. According to this view, a dollar spent or received today is the same as a dollar spent or received next year. Intuitively, we know that a dollar spent or received in the future has less value than today's dollar. We know that inflation alone erodes the buying power of money. Also, we know that we can never be sure of what our dollar will buy in the future. We have to deal with uncertainty. We often have data that purport to show the future cost of contracting out for a service for a period of years versus the cost of providing that service in-house. If we treat this data as simply accounting for dollars, "future dollars are unrealistically and erroneously treated as bearing the same weight as present dollars."[3] In addition, any investment decision repre-

---

3. Charles T. Horngren, *Cost Accounting: A Managerial Emphasis*, 2d ed. (Englewood Cliffs, N.J.: Prentice-Hall, 1967), p. 416.

sents some opportunity costs, which should be considered in an analysis.

The discounted cash-flow method recognizes that a dollar received or spent, say, five years in the future is not the equivalent of a dollar received or spent today. Therefore, more meaningful comparisons of alternatives requiring different amounts of expenditure at different times can be made.

The Discounted Cash-Flow Method

THE discounted cash-flow method or discounting to present value is a cost-accounting technique that does not require a large staff or an enormous computerized data-processing center for many problems facing governmental jurisdictions. It is a simple technique based on compound interest. We are all familiar with compound interest as it relates to our deposits in a savings bank. If we deposit $1000 in the bank today and we know the rate of interest, we can use a table of compound interest to show us how much we will have after a specified number of years.

Discounting to present value, as shown in Table A, is like a compound interest problem in reverse. In discounting to present value, we know how much future savings are expected from the choice of one alternative over the other. If we know the interest rate, we can use a table to find the present value of the anticipated savings.

TABLE A
Discounting to Present Value Is Like a Compound Interest Problem in Reverse

Compound Interest		Present Value
Known	Dollar value today	Unknown
Known	Interest rate	Known
Unknown	Future dollar value	Known

The choice of the interest or discount rate for public sector investment is subject to wide controversy among economists. Low discount rates make high initial investment projects that have relatively lower operating and maintenance costs appear more economically viable. High discount rates favor projects with a smaller ratio of initial investment costs to operating and maintenance costs. Although a case can be made that a fair discount rate for public sector projects should be 10 percent,[4] for our purposes, we will assume that the effective discount rate will be the current cost of borrowing money for that jurisdiction.

Example: To Invest or to Contract Out for Garbage Collection

FLAGTOWN has been collecting garbage from homeowners in town trucks with town employees. The trucks are in poor shape and must be replaced. The town manager realizes that she has a choice. The town can invest in new trucks or can contract with a private carting company. The manager gathers data concerning the possible savings that could be made if the town chooses one or the other of these alternatives. She finds that the private company will charge $65,000 per year to handle the town's garbage collection operation. She also finds that the cost of three new trucks—the town's initial investment cost if it is to remain in the garbage collection business—would be $40,000. In addition to the initial costs, the town manager estimates annual operating costs. Including such items as wages and salary, benefits, gasoline and oil, maintenance and repair, as well as miscellaneous expenses, the town manager comes up with an annual operating estimate of $55,000. Furthermore, the expected life of the trucks is five years each. It is assumed that they will have no salvage value.

Discounting to present value can help the town manager determine which choice is more economical to the town in this case. First, she computes the annual savings from town operation versus contracting. The town can expect annual operating and maintenance savings of $10,000 ($65,000 − $55,000 = $10,000). Assuming these annual savings occur for five years, the town reaps a savings of $50,000 (5 years × $10,000 = $50,000), minus the initial costs of the trucks, which was $40,000. Without

---

4. Jacob A. Stockfisch, "The Interest Rate Applicable to Government Investment Projects," in Harley H. Hinrichs and Graeme M. Taylor, eds., *Program Budgeting and Benefit-Cost Analysis: Cases, Text and Readings* (Pacific Palisades, Calif.: Goodyear, 1969), pp. 187–201. In an era of double-digit inflation, the rates will be higher. Stockfish based his figures on data developed during a period of 5 percent inflation.

discounting, the town apparently saves $10,000 ($50,000 − $40,000 = $10,000) over five years by handling the garbage with town trucks and workers. The decision appears to be clear-cut.

But we cannot be certain what is going to happen up to five years in the future, and we do have to put up the money for those trucks right now. Can we really expect that degree of savings? What about the pressure of the town employees for a union? Will there be state-mandated cost-of-living increases? Since we don't really know what is going to happen in the future, we should give the information about the more distant future less weight than information concerning the near future. In short, we should discount that information in a systematic way.

Assuming an 8 percent discount rate, because that is the current cost to the jurisdiction of borrowing money, we can proceed to discount the future year savings according to the present value of $1.00 table, a portion of which is presented in Table B. The discounting procedure is relatively simple. Multiply the annual estimated savings for the first year times the present value of $1.00 at 8 percent for that year. This figure is $0.926. In a like manner, multiply the annual savings for the second year times the present value of $1.00 at 8 percent two years hence. This figure is $0.857. Treat the other years in a similar manner, as in Table C. By adding up the discounted values for each of the five years and subtracting the intitial investment amount, $40,000 for the trucks, we find that our proposed $10,000 savings has evaporated. In fact, by using the present value method, we find that we probably will not realize a savings from having the town handle the garbage collection if the cost of money is assumed to be 8 percent.

If we assume a 6 percent interest rate, as was done in Table D, however, we find that there is some savings if the town handles garbage collection by itself. When the outcome of a problem can be changed from

TABLE B
Present Value of $1.00

Year	6%	8%
1	.943	.926
2	.890	.857
3	.840	.794
4	.792	.735
5	.747	.681

TABLE C
Computing the Present Value of the Estimated Savings at 8 Percent

Year	Savings in that Year		8% Discount Factor		Value Present
1	$10,000	×	.926	=	$ 9260
2	10,000	×	.857	=	8570
3	10,000	×	.794	=	7940
4	10,000	×	.735	=	7350
5	10,000	×	.681	=	6810
		Total present value of annual savings			$39,930

If total present value of savings exceeds amount required for initial investment, that investment should be recommended.

$$\$39,930 - 40,000 = -\$70$$

TABLE D
Computing the Present Value of the Estimated Savings at 6 Percent

Year	Savings in that Year		6% Discount Factor		Present Value
1	$10,000	×	.943	=	$ 9430
2	10,000	×	.890	=	8900
3	10,000	×	.840	=	8400
4	10,000	×	.792	=	7920
5	10,000	×	.747	=	7470
		Total present value of annual savings			$42,120

If total present value of savings exceeds amount required for initial investment, that investment should be recommended.

$$\$42,120 - 40,000 = \$2,120$$

favoring one solution to favoring another solution with just a minor change in the discount rate, that analysis is said to be sensitive to the discount rate. In this analysis, a relatively minor change in the discount rate changes the recommendation from contracting out for the service at 8 percent, to a recommendation that the town invest in its own garbage collection capability at 6 percent.

In this particular problem, since the estimated savings is exactly the same for each year of the proposed life of the investment, there is a short-cut table that could have been used. By using Table E, the present value of $1.00 received annually for n years, we could find our answer

TABLE E
Present Value of $1 Received Annually for *n* Years

Years	6%	8%
1	.943	.926
2	1.833	1.783
3	2.673	2.577
4	3.465	3.312
5	4.212	3.993

Copyright by The President and Fellows of Harvard College.

TABLE F
The More Direct Method Used Only When Annual Savings Are Constant

	6%	8%
5 year factor	4.212	3.993
	×	×
× Annual savings	$10,000	$10,000
	$42,120	$39,930
− Initial investment	− 40,000	− 40,000
	$2,120	− $70

If total present value of savings exceeds amount required for initial investment, that investment should be recommended.

more directly. Using Table E, we find the appropriate discount rate and the number of years that we expect to get our annual benefits. The table gives us the coefficients for five years—4.212 for 6 percent and 3.993 for 8 percent. In Table F, we multiply each coefficient by the annual estimated savings and come up with exactly the same answers that we found in Tables B and C. This more direct method, however, can only be used when the estimated savings or benefits are constant for each year for the life of the project.

Potential Uses and Abuses

ALTHOUGH only one hypothetical example has been presented here, the technique is applicable to virtually every government program for which alternative ways of accomplishing the program's goals are available. This opens an astonishing array of potential programs that may benefit from this type of analysis. There are alternative ways of handling computer services, street paving, even police services. Some of these services may be more economically provided by contracting out. Other services may be more economically provided by having the jurisdiction develop its own capability.

The technique of discounting to present values can also be useful in determining the relative economic value of various major capital investment projects that might face a jurisdiction. Discounting to present value might shed light on the relative costs of an industrial park, downtown urban renewal, and housing for the elderly. The technique might give us some insight into the possible cost consequences of delay in carrying out plans in some of these projects. For example, if it takes several years more than planned to attract a developer for a downtown urban renewal scheme, the present value of the benefits of renewal will be sharply reduced, since the method more highly values benefits that accrue earlier in a project and downgrades benefits that will not be realized until far into the future.

Of course, we must recognize that discounting is only an economic technique. It can add to our knowledge about various alternatives, but in a political world it would not be the sole criterion upon which a decision would be made. Analysis might show that resources could be spent more economically on an industrial park than on housing for the elderly, but the city may feel the need for better housing for the elderly. The technique can merely show decision-makers what the true economic cost of their decision is. It cannot dictate that all governmental decisions should be made on economic grounds.

Since analysis is often used to justify decisions that political leaders want to make,[5] it is instructive to see how an analyst using the discounting to present value technique might be able to develop analytic work guaranteed to please his or her superiors. Several methods by which the analyst using the present value technique would be able to alter the outcome of the analysis by marginally changing a few assumptions are presented below:

1. *increase annual returns or savings*
2. *prolong life of the asset*

---

5. Fred A. Kramer. "Policy Analysis as Ideology," *Public Administration Review* 35, no. 5 (September–October 1975): 509–517.

3. *reduce amount of the investment*
4. *lower the discount rate*
5. *increase annual returns in the earlier years.*

This may be an overly cynical view of analysis, but as long as some analysts approach their work in the manner of hired guns, a skeptical attitude might well be in order.

Despite the above warning, discounting to present value is a simple technique that could have wide applicability in government decision-making in the smaller jurisdictions. Discounting to present value can bring a more correct picture of costs into the decision calculus involving choices among alternatives by recognizing future uncertainty. Although such analysis can improve the level of information available to a decision-maker, legitimate political factors will continue to be recognized in governmental decision-making.

CHAPTER ELEVEN

Controlling Administration through the Legislative Branch

THE STUDY OF PUBLIC management focuses on executive action. Management innovations such as management information systems (MIS) and the centralizing budget systems such as program and zero-base budgeting are attempts to enforce administrative accountability through the hierarchy. In the American tripartite checks-and-balances governmental system, legislatures and courts are also important factors affecting agencies and their programs. In this chapter we will explore some of the legislative techniques for enforcing administrative accountability—or at least the legislature's view of that accountability. Because political executives and individual legislators have different political roots, the executive's view of accountability and the legislators' views do not necessarily coincide.

Legislative Supremacy

FOR most of the first 125 years of the United States, legislatures at all levels were the dominant force in government. This dominance was reflected not only in legislative law-making initiatives, but also in control of administration. Woodrow Wilson, one of the intellectual fathers of public administration, attributed congressional dominance to the committee system, which permitted Congress to enjoy the fruits of division of labor. Through the specialization of committees, Congress "entered more and more into the details of administration until it [had] virtually taken into its own all the substantial powers of government. . . . [Congress] was getting into the habit of investigating and managing everything."[1] During the nineteenth and early twentieth centuries, legislatures, controlled and organized by strong political parties, ran America at all governmental levels.

The growth of governmental functions, along with excesses of corrupt political bosses, created a climate in which executive-oriented public administration flourished. Except for the commission form of government at the local level, in which local legislators also served as executives in charge of specific departments, public administration reformers from Wilson's academic days until the present have advocated restraints on legislative meddling and greater freedom for administrators. From roughly the end of World War II until the Vietnam War, legislatures at

---

1. Woodrow Wilson, *Congressional Government* (New York: Meridian Books, 1956), pp. 49–50. *Also see* Allen Schick, "Congress and the 'Details' of Administration," *Public Administration Review* 36, no. 5 (September–October 1976): 516–528.

all levels in the United States allowed much of their control over administration to erode.

This erosion is the result of two kinds of legislative action: (1) construction of loose substantive legislation, and (2) acquiescence to executive-oriented initiatives, including management innovations designed to centralize executive decision-making. In 1958 Kenneth Culp Davis, an administrative law expert, concluded that typically laws were written so loosely that in effect they were telling the responsible agency, "Here is the problem; deal with it." Or even worse, Davis suggested: "Sometimes [the statute] has not even said 'Here is the problem.' It does less than that. It says instead: 'We . . . don't know what the problems are; find them and deal with them.' "[2]

Aside from delegating broad substantive powers to administrative agencies, Congress has supported many management innovations that have strengthened the independence of the executive branch. The merit system gave career bureaucrats a more independent base than the spoils system had. The Budget and Accounting Act of 1921 established a central Bureau of the Budget (BOB) to channel agency requests to the appropriations committees of Congress. Before that, congressional committees had handled requests directly from the agencies. The Budget and Accounting Act, however, did establish the General Accounting Office (GAO) as an arm of Congress. More recently, the executive branch has befuddled Congress with a succession of new budgeting systems.

Complexity is the reason for erosion of congressional power over administration. Congress is generally unwilling and unable to deal with the complexities of trade policy, nuclear energy, cancer research, drug testing, and most of the other highly technical areas in which modern governments are concerned. The complexities of the budget are such that the appropriations subcommittees cannot scrutinize expenditures for agencies the way they could fifty years ago. The executive budget process aggregates data so that examination of certain details is impossible unless Congress demands that the data be presented in some other way. State and local legislatures have lost some of their powers to deal with administration for these reasons, too.

This complexity has been supported by two ideological factors, according to Allen Schick. These factors are *nonpartisanship* in international affairs and what Theodore Lowi called *interest group liberalism* in domestic

2. Kenneth Culp Davis, *Administrative Law Treatise* (St. Paul, Minn.: West, 1958), and *Supplement* (1965), quoted in Theodore J. Lowi, *The End of Liberalism* (New York: W. W. Norton, 1969), pp. 302–303.

politics.[3] Nonpartisanship is an expression of faith in the executive to handle crises in a benevolent manner. Congress learned to trust the executive in foreign policy matters, and this sense of trust affected other areas as well. It was not until the Vietnam War that the spirit of nonpartisan trust was broken. Interest group liberalism legitimizes the use of governmental power to grant benefits to organized, powerful interests. If interest group liberalism is the dominant public philosophy and the bureaucratic agencies dispense the benefits, a strong congressional presence hindering the flow of these benefits would be self-defeating. Instead of checking the administrative role in dispensing the benefits, Congress (through its committees) joined in the symbiotic relationships that we have called policy subsystems. Nonpartisan acceptance of the executive branch and congressional complicity in interest group liberalism discourage Congress from taking a powerful role in holding agencies accountable.

Greater Congressional Concern

EVEN though legislatures in general have allowed much of their power to hold administrators accountable to slacken since the nineteeth century, some have not abandoned the administrative ship. Schick points out that Congress can selectively exert strong powers on administrators.

> When it wanted, Congress (or its members or committees) continued to meddle in administrative particulars, intervening in behalf of interests, writing restrictions into legislation, using its investigatory powers to spotlight an administrative problem, holding on to old administrative prerogatives. At will, Congress could penetrate to the smallest administrative detail, but these usually were pinpricks, mere nuisances compared to the countless matters which escaped legislative control.[4]

Among the more well-known pinpricks of congressional intrusion into the heart of bureaucracy have been the Golden Fleece awards. The Golden Fleece is given monthly by Senator William Proxmire, a Wisconsin Democrat, for the "biggest, most ridiculous or most ironic example of wasting federal tax funds." Among projects that have received the awards since April 1975 are a study on why people fall in love, the ex-

---

3. Schick, "Congress and the 'Details,' " *Also see* Lowi, *The End of Liberalism,* chapter 3.
4. Schick, p. 517.

periment on how long it takes to cook breakfast, a study of why people are rude on tennis courts, and a grant to measure anger in monkeys and humans based on jaw-clenching. Since many Golden Fleece awards involve academic studies, Proxmire has offended university-based scientists. The existence of these awards has tightened the procedures for judging research grants, according to a deputy director of the National Science Foundation, but these newer procedures, designed to screen out potential Golden Fleece winners, have created more paperwork.[5]

There is some evidence, however, that Congress would like to exert more control over administrators. To a large degree, congressional efforts stem from a lack of faith in the executive branch, which grew during the Vietnam years. The breakdown in nonpartisanship in foreign affairs was a wedge that allowed Congress to express its concerns in a variety of administrative areas. The Watergate scandal sufficiently weakened the president's political position to allow Congress to reexert itself. During the 1970s, congressional attempts to regain control over the details of administration were strongest in the budget process.

We have already talked a bit about the Congressional Budget and Impoundment Control Act of 1974. That act established procedures for the Congress to discuss national priorities and deal with the budget as a unified statement of such priorities rather than piecemeal, through the fragmented appropriations process. It also made Congress more independent of the executive branch because it created the Congressional Budget Office (CBO) which serves three functions that meaningful control requires: "(1) monitoring the economy and estimating its impact on the budget, (2) improving the flow and quality of budgetary information, and (3) analyzing the costs and effects of alternative budgetary choices."[6] Although Congress has had difficulties in meeting its budget deadlines and reconciling the various budget resolutions in recent years, it has strengthened its capacity to scrutinize executive budgets.

The impoundment control provisions of the act have also strengthened congressional capacity to deal with the executive branch and to have more control over administration. Impoundment is an executive branch decision not to spend appropriated funds. At the federal level, some impoundment has occurred in virtually every administration since President Thomas Jefferson's refusal to spend appropriations for new gunboats after the Louisiana Purchase. Many people recognize that

5. See Arlen J. Large, "Unlike Jason, People in the Capital Don't Want Golden Fleece," *Wall Street Journal,* May 16, 1978, p. 1.
6. Aaron Wildavsky, *The Politics of the Budgetary Process,* 3rd ed. (Boston: Little, Brown, 1979), p. 228.

some limited power to withhold funds in the interest of good management and economy is a legitimate executive power. The Congressional Budget and Impoundment Act, however, was a response to President Nixon's efforts to change congressional priorities by refusing to spend money that Congress had appropriated for certain purposes, especially in the areas of education, criminal justice, manpower, and community development.

The act created two categories of impoundment: *rescissions* and *deferrals*. A rescission occurs if the president refuses to spend all or part of an appropriation to carry out congressionally approved purposes. If a president wants to substitute his judgment for congressional will, as shown through the appropriations process, and to cancel a program by refusing to spend money on it, he must file a rescission proposal with Congress. The rescission cannot take place unless Congress approves the proposal within forty-five days. A deferral is a proposal to delay obligations and expenditure until later in the fiscal year, not to cancel expenditures. Deferral proposals must also be submitted to Congress, but they become effective unless either house of Congress passes a resolution disapproving them. For a rescission to take effect, Congress must take action to approve it; for a deferral to take effect, Congress must not take any action.

Since different congressional action is required for rescissions and deferrals, it is important who determines when a proposed impoundment is really a rescission, even though it has been called a deferral. The act gives this power to the comptroller general, the chief officer of the General Accounting Office. The GAO has an important role in monitoring impoundments and determining what congressional action is required in particular cases. The GAO has taken the executive branch to court on several occasions over the definition of rescission and deferral.

The impoundment provisions have given Congress more information on administrative activities of the executive. Since all rescissions and deferrals, even ones that do not deal with policy changes, must be submitted to Congress, the impoundment control process is somewhat unwieldy. It is also subject to executive-legislative game-playing. For example, during the Ford administration, many appropriations that were in excess of the President's budget requests were sent back to Congress as deferrals or rescissions. Louis Fisher has noted that the "sheer volume of the requests . . . undermined the prospect for careful congressional review."[7]

---

7. Louis Fisher, *Presidential Spending Power* (Princeton, N.J.: Princeton University Press, 1975), p. 201.

Sunset Laws and Oversight

CONGRESSIONAL efforts to regain control over administration through the budgetary process have required great increases in staff and resources. Most governmental jurisdictions have not given legislators the staff support they need to confront the executive branch through the budget process. But there are two key legislative processes that enable legislatures to exert controls on administration. The one that we have discussed most is the appropriations process, through which agencies get the funds they need to operate. The other key legislative process is the authorization process, through which legislatures decide whether agencies should exist and what programs they should pursue. In the past decade, several state legislatures have tried to improve their oversight capacity through the authorization process.

Governmental programs often seem to be immortal. Herbert Kaufman found that agencies, once authorized, seldom die.[8] Instead they continue to make successful claims on public resources, simply because nobody spends the energy to end their authorization. *Sunset laws* periodically and automatically end programs unless the legislature takes action to renew the program authorization. Sunset legislation shifts the burden of proof from those wanting to end or terminate a program to those wanting to renew a program. The popularity of this idea, which has been advocated by the public interest lobbying group Common Cause, has been sunset laws passed in almost twenty states. A sunset bill has been introduced in each Congress since 1977.

There are two categories of sunset laws, those that require automatic termination of virtually all programs and those that concentrate review on regulatory programs. The first sunset law was passed in Colorado in 1976 with the support of the Colorado chapter of Common Cause. The Colorado law called for periodic review and automatic termination of all the forty-one regulatory and licensing boards. The termination dates for these boards were scattered over a period of several years so that the sunset review could deal with a manageable number of agencies—thirteen or fifteen—each year. New regulatory legislation included sunset provisions, too. Extensive performance audits were conducted by the state auditor's office, and additional program evaluation help was provided by graduate students from the University of Colorado. The agencies under review also developed detailed program evaluations sup-

---

8. Herbert Kaufman, *Are Government Agencies Immortal?* (Washington, D.C.: The Brookings Institution, 1979).

ported by federal grants. The results of the review were mixed. Some agencies were abolished; some were given expanded duties; but most were found to be functioning in an acceptable manner.[9]

Alabama's experience with sunset legislation indicates some problems that are to be expected if the sunset concept is expanded to cover most governmental agencies. In 1977 the Alabama legislature, through its eleven-member joint "super-sunset" committee, held hearings on 207 state agencies and units of government. The recommendations of the committee for all 207 agencies had to be voted up or down in the Alabama House of Representatives within a three-hour period. It stretches the imagination to believe that a committee could effectively consider program evaluations on 207 agencies during the year. Furthermore, the final legislative approval of the committee's actions hardly fits the view of a legislature as the deliberative voice of the people. Common Cause official Bruce Adams claimed, "The Alabama legislators acted like the citizens of ancient Rome, who decided the fate of defeated gladiators with a simple gesture of thumbs up or down."[10]

Instead of the early Alabama experience, "sunset laws are designed to ensure meaningful program evaluation, to introduce the possibility of termination, to merge duplicative programs and rationalize program structure, and to eliminate conflicts and competition between programs."[11] In short, the purpose of sunset legislation is to provide meaningful legislative oversight of administration. Legislatures, however, have been in the oversight business for many years and have had access to some institutional support that could help them handle the oversight function. At the federal level, Congress can call on the General Accounting Office, the Congressional Research Service of the Library of Congress, and independent research organizations such as Brookings Institution or universities. The Congressional Budget Office might develop the capacity to provide individual members with programmatic and evaluative data, too. Generally, state and local legislators lack the resources available to Congress, but they could tap state and local universities to help them with program evaluations.

Of the institutions designed to help Congress, the General Accounting Office has performed investigatory functions for members of Congress in recent years. Until the 1960s, the main job of the GAO was to conduct

---

9. Neal R. Pierce and Jerry Hagstrom, "Is It Time for the Sun to Set on Some State Sunset Proposals?" *National Journal* 9, no. 23 (June 18, 1977): 937–939.
10. Ibid., p. 939.
11. Robert D. Behn, "The False Dawn of the Sunset Laws," *The Public Interest* no. 49 (Fall 1977): 105.

Why Sunset Laws Will Not Lead
to Major Changes

Advocates of sunset laws reason that if Congress only had to undertake a real evaluation and make a real decision, a significant barrier to termination would be overcome. But the lack of evaluation and decision is only a small obstacle to termination. There are other more important factors that contribute to the durability of public programs and that a sunset law would do little to overcome.

Any government program has its own constituency: those who benefit directly from it and those who take a personal, if less selfish interest in it. The agency administering the program recruits and cultivates this constituency to ensure continued political support, for it can be relied upon to complain loudly, forcefully, and personally at any suggestion that the program be terminated.

Public-opinion polls reveal a pervasive unhappiness with inefficient and ineffective government, and the advocates of sunset laws suggest that this public mood can be transformed into political support for terminating inefficient and ineffective programs. But the only characteristic common to those who share this mood is a general unhappiness with government; if you ask precisely which programs are inefficient and ineffective there is little agreement. Moreover, people do not believe it inconsistent to declare: "Too many programs don't work and should be terminated. But not my program. It's a good one."

SOURCE: Robert D. Behn, "The False Dawn of the Sunset Laws," *The Public Interest* no. 49 (Fall 1977): 113.

audits of government expenditures. The image of the agency was that of an army of bookkeepers wearing green eyeshades, perched on high stools, laboring over their ledger books. Since the 1960s, however, the GAO has developed a capacity for management analysis and program evaluation in addition to its accounting and auditing roles.

Today, the GAO initiates its own studies of a wide range of government operations and investigates allegations raised by individual members of Congress. The full-scale studies can range from use of simulations as an aid to decision-making in the Department of Defense to problems implementing revenue-sharing in diverse communities. Sometimes these studies generate enough interest to have their recommendations reflected in legislation. A negative report on the proposed Cheyenne helicopter encouraged the House Appropriations Committee to terminate the project in 1974.

Generally, legislatures have not used the resources they already have to carry out their oversight responsibilities. There is little reason to believe that the mechanics of sunset legislation will drastically improve legislative ability to oversee administration.

Most observers of American politics believe legislatures should be more involved with oversight. Studies of their behavior have established that legislators have two basic goals: to survive in office and to have an impact on policy. The impact on policy can be future-oriented—developing new legislation—or reactive—reviewing bureaucratic activities. Pressures of time force legislators to decide how best to achieve their survival and policy goals. Often the administrative oversight function is given lowest priority.[12]

Barriers to Oversight

Seymour Scher has suggested some barriers to effective legislative oversight of administrative activity:

1. *Congressmen see greater rewards in legislative policy-making and constituent service than in oversight.*
2. *They view the bureaucracy as an "impenetrable maze."*
3. *They are reluctant to endanger mutually rewarding relationships with bureaucrats.*
4. *They see personal contacts as more beneficial for constituent service than committee investigations.*
5. *They fear provoking reprisals from powerful interests by disturbing the policy subsystem.*
6. *If they seek gains from the president, they will avoid embarrassing him.*
7. *Committee staff routines tend not to provide for real oversight.*[13]

To Scher, meaningful oversight of administrative agencies could only occur if individual members mobilize the committee structure of Congress aggressively to check the agencies. But if one of the prime goals of a legislator is political survival, aggressive oversight of agency actions might do the legislator more harm than good. To make an agency appear less of an "impenetrable maze," the legislator would have to develop his or her own expertise in the specific area of interest. This would

---

12. *See* Morris S. Ogul, *Congress Oversees the Bureaucracy* (Pittsburgh, Pa.: Unversity of Pittsburgh Press, 1976); R. Douglas Arnold, *Congress and the Bureaucracy: A Theory of Influence* (New Haven, Conn.: Yale University Press, 1979); David R. Mayhew, *Congress: The Electoral Connection* (New Haven, Conn.: Yale University Press, 1974); and Randall B. Ripley and Grace A. Franklin, *Congress, the Bureaucracy and Public Policy*, 2d ed. (Homewood, Ill.: Dorsey, 1980).
13. Seymour Scher, "Conditions for Legislative Control," *Journal of Politics* 25, no. 3 (August 1963): 526–551.

take a considerable amount of time and effort and might not aid the legislator's chances of political survival.

Even if a legislator were able to develop considerable expertise through long service on a particular committee or by prior experience, he or she might be reluctant to upset the symbiotic, mutually rewarding relationships implied in the triangular model. Personal contacts and smooth relationships with the agency are seen as being more productive for individual constituent problems—"casework"—than aggressively ferreting out more generalized abuse. Furthermore, attempts to uncover generalized abuses might provoke powerful clientele interests that were the beneficiaries of questionable agency actions. These interests might be in a position to affect adversely the conscientious legislator's electoral prospects. By not attempting to highlight administrative abuses that systematically favor certain interests, legislators keep the level of conflict low. They are able to solidify their ability to serve their own constituents by not investigating the patterns of interest group liberalism. As the late speaker of the House of Representatives, Sam Rayburn, a Democrat from Texas, used to say: "The best way to get along is to go along."[14]

Often the agencies can provide the best reasons for "going along." Agencies are not powerless when it comes to dealing with legislators who are supposed to control them. Perhaps the most striking example of agency power was shown by the Federal Bureau of Investigation (FBI) from 1950 through 1971. For over two decades the FBI got 102 percent of its recommended amount in the president's budget.[15] Most political scientists attributed the FBI's rare ability to deal successfully with Congress to the standing in public opinion of its former director, J. Edgar Hoover, to favorable views of the agency in general, to strong support by Congressmen John J. Rooney of Brooklyn, who chaired the appropriations subcommittee with jurisdiction over the FBI, and to Hoover's practice of lending FBI personnel to understaffed committees on Capitol Hill. The domestic intelligence investigations conducted by Senator Frank Church in 1975 and 1976 turned up the real story of the agency's power. Hoover's investigators had extensive files on the private behavior of many members of Congress.[16] Knowledge of the sexual and drinking

---

14. Quoted in Tom Wicker, *JFK and LBJ: The Influence of Personality upon Politics* (New York: William Morrow, 1968), p. 44.
15. *Current American Government* (Washington, D.C.: Congressional Quarterly, Spring 1974), p. 64.
16. "Intelligence Activities and the Rights of Americans," final report of the Senate Select Committee on Intelligence Activities (the Church Committee), Washington, D.C., April 1976.

habits of members of Congress enabled the FBI to blackmail legislators to maintain support for the agency.

Of course, not all agencies are in a position to blackmail legislative committees or individual legislators, but agencies have ways of helping legislators who might be in a position to help them. A concise list of areas of legitimate agency discretion where specific agency decisions can help the political career of individual legislators follows:

1. *regulations determining how a program will be implemented*
2. *geographic and programmatic patterns of spending*
3. *timing of spending and other programmatic decisions*
4. *decision about location of facilities*
5. *disposition of individual "cases" of persons seeking a specific agency ruling.*[17]

A simple correlation between the exalted position of southern Democrats in the committee structure of Congress during the 1960s and early 1970s and the disproportionate share of Washington's investment in the South suggests that agencies are not blind to who can butter their bread. As our model of symbiotic behavior would suggest, they are appreciative.

Aside from using formal powers to help those in positions to help them, the agencies show deference to their congressional controllers in informal ways. Although members of Congress are not legally granted the right to announce beneficial administrative actions affecting their districts, agencies routinely allow representatives and senators to make such announcements and to claim credit for getting the benefits for their districts. Agencies generally realize that by serving their clientele and well-placed legislators, they can maintain a low profile while still generating the political support necessary to keep them in business. As we have seen, the resolution of conflict at the administrative level involving interested parties of legislators and clientele tends to reinforce policy subsystems that may not be accountable to the more generalized interest of the public as a whole.

Conditions Favoring Oversight

In cases where the legislature is helping an agency distribute benefits to a happy clientele, there is little reason for legislators to cause trouble in paradise by exercising excessive oversight. Unless a scandal receives wide exposure in the media, distributive programs run by such agencies as the

---

17. Ripley and Franklin, *Congress, The Bureaucracy and Public Policy,* pp. 80–86.

Departments of Agriculture, Transportation, Labor, Commerce, Housing and Urban Development, Education, and a number of other federal agencies will be immune from congressional investigation. In regulatory arenas, however, aggressive regulation by an agency can upset the regulated interests, who will complain to Congress. Regulation that is in the interest of the regulated will not spark such complaints. Neither will mild, almost symbolic regulatory actions. Aggressive regulation of powerful interests, however, is sure to turn on the spotlight of legislative oversight.

During the 1970s the Federal Trade Commission (FTC) changed its image from that of the "little old lady of Pennsylvania Avenue" to that of a tiger in support of consumer protection. The FTC was created in 1914 with a broad mandate to prevent "unfair methods of competition" and "unfair and deceptive" trade practices. Until the mid-1970s the FTC was considered ineffective. A report by Ralph Nader charged that it was caught up in trivial details and should be abolished or changed drastically.[18]

It changed. Congress gave the FTC power to issue industrywide trade rules in 1975, and new commissioners emphasized consumer protection. Under the leadership of Republicans Lewis Engman and Miles Kirkpatrick, the FTC undertook major antitrust actions against the large oil companies and the ready-to-eat cereal companies. It also began to draft the industrywide rules that eventually led to considerable opposition. Under the Democratic chairman, Michael Pertschuk, the FTC continued its consumer protection focus by attacking the used car, funeral, and home insulation industries, among others. Under Pertschuk, the FTC proposed the highly controversial rule dealing with children's television advertising.

Although any attempts at meaningful regulation are bound to upset specific companies and industries, the FTC's attempt to develop a truth-in-advertising rule for children's television programs mobilized a coalition of politically powerful forces. Pertschuk was outspoken in his desire to protect young consumers from the alleged benefits of sugar cereals and plastic toys. He and the FTC incurred the wrath of the Kellogg Company, the Toy Manufacturers of America, and a coalition of groups representing the advertising industry. These groups undertook sophisticated lobbying campaigns designed to curb FTC power in 1979 and 1980. Robert Katzmann observed at the time that during the 1970s,

---

18. Edward F. Cox, Robert C. Fellmeth, and John E. Schultz, *The Nader Report on the Federal Trade Commission* (New York: R. W. Bacon, 1969).

"congressmen were apt to praise the lofty ideals of the FTC; now that those ideals have moved from symbolism to concrete actions, the legislators have had to deal with well-financed groups affected by agency efforts."[19]

The lobbying efforts bore fruit. Several investigative committees looked hard at FTC decision-making processes. They advocated legislative vetoes of the commission's proposed industrywide rules and put the FTC on a reduced month-to-month budget. The FTC responded by backing away from strong consumer protection positions, in other areas as well as in matters affecting children's television. New rules for product warrantees issued in May 1980 showed a new flexibility. Obviously, the people at the Federal Trade Commission had learned that to get along, they had to go along.

Whereas the conditions that present barriers to legislative control of administrative activity generally hold, there are times when other conditions prevail. Some situations actually encourage meaningful investigations by legislative bodies. Such conditions prevailed during 1975 and 1976 with regard to the Central Intelligence Agency (CIA) and more generalized domestic intelligence operations. Allegations of abuse by the CIA and FBI had surfaced during the Watergate investigations. With a Republican president, who was interested in standing for election, and a Democratically controlled Congress, which included several potential presidential candidates, the time was ripe for an investigation that might bring additional unfavorable light on the excesses of the Nixon years. The Ford administration sought to preempt a congressional investigation by conducting its own study of CIA and FBI activities under Democratic presidents as well as under the Republican Nixon. It was fairly obivous that such an investigation would be a whitewash to protect the White House by emphasizing that Democratic presidents engaged the CIA and FBI for illegal political purposes, too.

The conditions that prevailed in the mid-1970s, therefore, were the direct opposite of the conditions that generally prevail. The revelations that had sent a president into virtual exile at San Clemente provided a climate whereby the public was interested in knowing more about agency activities that had gone on under a blanket of secrecy. Since the Republican president had pardoned former President Nixon and had instituted an investigation designed to embarrass Democrats who controlled Congress, Democratic congressional leadership was willing to

---

19. Robert A. Katzmann, "Capitol Hill's Current Attack Against the FTC," *Wall Street Journal,* May 7, 1980, p. 26.

fight for its good name. There were individuals, notably Senator Frank Church, who saw their own political interest furthered by undertaking such an investigation. A further condition that favored a meaningful investigation of the CIA and FBI was the increased level of confidence that congressional members had in their institution as a result of its role in the impeachment proceedings against President Nixon.

Summary

IN Congress and a handful of the state legislatures that have well-developed staff systems, there is the potential for legislators to control administration at a more general level than specific casework for constituents. In addition to improving staff resources, Congress has passed legislation to make the agency policy-making process more open. Congress has passed the Freedom of Information Act (1974) and the Federal Advisory Committee Act (1972).[20] Legislatures at other levels of government have passed "sunshine laws" declaring various administrative meetings open. Some jurisdictions have appropriated money for program evaluations, especially for new programs. Congress already has the tools to pursue greater oversight. So do several other jurisdictions.

Generally, these tools are not used to their capacity, because there are political costs to using them. Most legislators, therefore, see their oversight role as principally relating to casework—helping constituents in their dealings with administrators. Casework does provide a check on administration. It keeps bureaucrats on their toes, and it does correct some injustices, but as Kenneth Culp Davis pointed out, there are dangers to legislative meddling in administrative areas. Legislative casework tends to harm the cause of fair and just administration because "some legislators put pressure on administrators for favorable action irrespective of the merits."[21]

Casework by legislators tends to support the closed system of conflict resolution at a low level of conflict. Powerful interests that lose decisions at the administrative level can decide unilaterally to raise the level of conflict by taking the issue to the courts or to the legislative arena. They have the resources to do this. Smaller interests often do not. The smaller interest who seeks help from the legislator must rely on that legislator's relationship with the agency. Success for the smaller interest will be de-

20. PL 85–619, 72 Stat. 547, and PL 92–463, 86 Stat. 770.
21. Kenneth Culp Davis, *Discretionary Justice: A Preliminary Inquiry* (Baton Rouge: Louisiana State University Press, 1969), p. 149.

termined, to a large degree, by the informal actions of the legislator. Under the casework focus, the established decision-making policy subsystems will not be altered. The "who gets what," which is the heart of politics, will only be changed for that particular case. The "private expropriation of public authority," which Theodore Lowi decried in *The End of Liberalism,* will continue.[22]

When we look at the legislative role in controlling administrative action, we can readily agree with Davis:

> Legislative supervision of administration appears on the surface to be a mass of confusion—appropriations committees pulling administrative policies in one direction and substantive committees in some other direction, individual members of both kinds of committees helping constituents to pull agencies in still another direction in particular cases, lobbying directed to key legislators in order to influence policies made by bureaucrats, legislative enactments designed to reverse or to modify administrative positions, legislative investigations for the purpose of [affecting] business pending before agencies . . . , committee chairmen pressuring agency chairmen and committee staffs pressuring agency staffs, administrative action notably in defiance of the will of legislative committees.[23]

This "mass of confusion" supports the status quo. Political factors encourage legislators not to make trouble by exercising systematic and intensive oversight. This lack of enthusiasm for oversight fosters decentralized policy subsystems in distributive policy areas. We have seen that executives can sometimes use management innovations such as improved budgeting systems to affect these policy subsystems to a limited degree. In the next chapter, we turn our attention to the influence of the courts on administrative actions.

Suggestions for Further Reading

Arnold, R. Douglas. *Congress and the Bureaucracy: A Theory of Influence.* New Haven, Conn.: Yale University Press, 1979.

Heaphey, James J., ed. "Symposium on Public Administration and Legislatures." *Public Administration Review* 35, no. 5 (September–October 1975).

Harris, Joseph P. *Congressional Control over Administration.* Washington, D.C.: The Brookings Institution, 1964.

---

22. Lowi, *The End of Liberalism,* p. 102.
23. Davis, *Discretionary Justice,* p. 146.

Mayhew, David R. *Congress: The Electoral Connection.* New Haven, Conn.: Yale University Press, 1974.

Ogul, Morris S. *Congress Oversees the Bureaucracy.* Pittsburgh, Pa.: University of Pittsburgh Press, 1976.

Ripley, Randall B., and Grace A. Franklin. *Congress, the Bureaucracy, and Public Policy,* 2d ed. Homewood, Ill.: Dorsey, 1980.

Wayne, Stephen J. *The Legislative Presidency.* New York: Harper & Row, 1978.

Wilson, Woodrow. *Congressional Government.* New York: Meridian Books, 1956.

CHAPTER TWELVE

Administrative Law
and Judicial Control

Public administration is grounded in public law. Agencies cannot exist unless enabling acts are passed through the legislative authorization process. Agencies cannot do anything unless they have funds, which must be approved through the legislative appropriations process. Laws that establish programs are not self-executing. They must be administered, and administration implies discretion. When laws apparently conflict and when affected interests claim that administrators have violated procedures or acted beyond the limits of their discretion, the courts directly affect administrators.

In this chapter we will see how courts deal with administrative problems in three broad categories: (1) administrative law, (2) judicial review of administrative decisions, and (3) direct judicial intervention in administration. Administrative law traditionally deals with the power of agencies and the discretionary authority of administrators. We will discuss the legal views of delegation of power from the legislature to specialized administrative agencies, the processes by which agencies regulate economic behavior, and judicial review of administrative action. Direct judicial intervention in administration is a relatively new phenomenon. Federal district court judges in school desegregation, prison reform, housing, and mental health class action cases have dictated the specific means needed to achieve the ends of the court decisions. This type of judicial intervention has far-reaching consequences for public management and all the actors involved in the environment of public administration.

Delegation of Power

Administrative law is principally concerned with the quasi-legislative and quasi-judicial roles of the "independent" administrative agencies. These independent regulatory agencies—those listed in Table 12.1—are independent in the sense that the president cannot remove agency heads at will. Instead, the president appoints commissioners when their terms, which overlap that of the president, expire. Although administrative law is heavily involved with the regulatory problems of these agencies, the principles and problems of administrative law are also applicable to agencies that have regulatory powers within the standard executive departments. Administrative law deals with the Food and Drug Administration (FDA), which is in the Department of Health and Human Services, and the Bureau of Public Roads in the Department of

---

TABLE 12.1
Major Independent Regulatory Agencies

Interstate Commerce Commission (1887)
Federal Trade Commission (1914)
Federal Power Commission (1930)
Federal Communications Commission (1934)
Securities and Exchange Commission (1934)
Civil Aeronautics Board (1938)
Atomic Energy Commission (1953), now Nuclear Regulatory Commission (since 1975)

Transportation, as well as with the Interstate Commerce Commission (ICC), the original independent regulatory agency.

Any law that is passed by a legislative body will grant some discretionary power to those administrators who are supposed to implement the law. In the case of most regulatory agencies, which deal in highly specialized matters that are often affected by rapid changes in technology, legislative bodies have tended to delegate a great deal of discretionary power to them because they expect the specialized agency to develop the expertise necessary to maintain meaningful regulations in times of change. Implicit in the broad grants of discretionary power to regulatory bureaucracies is that specialized agencies can deal with the types of problems likely to arise in specific areas better than the generalist-oriented legislatures or courts can. These specialized administrative bodies have been delegated the "full ambit of authority necessary . . . to plan, to promote and to police, [which covers all the] rights normally exercisable by government as a whole."[1]

On a few occasions, however, Congress has drastically limited agency discretion in highly technical matters. The *Delaney clause* of the 1958 amendments to the U.S. Food, Drug and Cosmetic Act is such an example. The Delaney clause, which is named after its sponsor, Congressman James J. Delaney of New York, automatically bans food additives from the marketplace if they are found to induce cancer in animals or humans. When the Delaney clause was adopted, much less was known about the prevalence of carcinogens than is known today. Research has found that some carcinogens—nitrites, for example—are ingested through the air as well as through hot dogs. A reporter noted: "People even generate nitrites in the saliva of their mouths, so a zero risk from

---

1. James M. Landis, *The Administrative Process* (New Haven, Conn.: Yale University Press, 1938), p. 15.

nitrites is impossible."[2] The strict Delaney clause limited the flexibility of the Food and Drug Administration in dealing with saccharin and nitrites—both substances shown to produce animal cancers—but the political furor caused by the application of the clause forced changes in its interpretation.

The broad delegation of rule-making and enforcement power to the agencies presents a constitutional problem. For much of American constitutional history, the Supreme Court has followed the judicial doctrine of " nondelegation."[3] In 1892 the Supreme Court unequivocably stated, "That Congress cannot delegate legislative power . . . is a principle universally recognized as vital to the integrity and maintenance of the system of government ordained by the Constitution."[4] If the Court were to rely only on the separation of powers mentioned in the Constitution, very limited delegation would be permitted. Quite the opposite has happened, although the nondelegation doctrine has never been retracted by the Supreme Court.

As Ernest Gellhorn has noted: "The practical necessities of modern government demanded delegation of law-making authority. The doctrine of separations of power could not become the altar upon which governmental operations meeting the country's felt needs could be sacrificed."[5] The Court has recognized that the Constitution provides that Congress "can make all laws which shall be necessary and proper. . . ."[6] Therefore, Congress can make laws delegating its legislative powers to agencies for the sake of expediency. The nondelegation doctrine does not apply here, according to the judicial reasoning, if Congress provides the agency with standards or limits. The standards are supposed to provide guidelines for the use of the discretionary power. If the standards are specific, the courts can use those standards to see whether agencies violate them. With specific, standards, the courts would be in a good position to control administration.

But the standards that Congress has used in delegating power to agencies are often vague. The concept of "public interest, convenience,

---

2. P. J. Wingate, "Reason to Applaud: FDA Handling of Nitrite Problem," *Wall Street Journal*, September 8, 1978, p. 16. *Also see* Linda E. Demkovich, "Saccharin's Dead, Dieters Are Blue, What Is Congress Going to Do?" *National Journal* 9, no. 21 (June 4, 1977): 856–859.
3. This is more generally called the "delegation doctrine," but since it maintains that legislative power cannot be delegated, the author prefers the more descriptive term "nondelegation." *See* Ernest Gellhorn, *Administrative Law and Process in a Nutshell* (St. Paul, Minn.: West, 1972), pp. 12–17.
4. *Field* v. *Clark*, 143 U.S. 649, 692, quoted by Gellhorn, p. 12.
5. Gellhorn, p. 15.
6. Article I, section 1.

or necessity" does not give much guidance to the Federal Communications Commission. Neither does "just and reasonable rates" provide meaningful guidance for the Interstate Commerce Commission; but as Theodore Lowi has suggested, other aspects of the ICC Act of 1887 clearly marked jurisdictional limitations and specified railroad abuses.[7] But a striking example of ambiguous standards was the Federal Trade Commission Act of 1914, which "so poorly defined the key term, 'unfair method of competition,' that the Supreme Court invalidated order after order issued by the FTC through most of the first 20 years of its life."[8] Since the mid-1930s, the courts have accepted standards that are so flexible as to be virtually useless as control devices that would permit them to tell clearly whether an agency had exceeded its delegated authority.

The last time the Supreme Court challenged the vagueness of standards was during the Great Depression, when a majority of the "nine old men" on the Court blasted the National Industrial Recovery Act in *Panama Refining Company* v. *Ryan* and unanimously shot it out of the water in *Schechter Poultry Corporation* v. *The United States*.[9] The *Panama Refining* case was the first time that the Court had declared a delegation void. Although some scholars have maintained that the Court went out of its way to seek an excessively narrow interpretation of what constituted a standard, there were some very real problems with the petroleum code that had been developed by the National Recovery Administration (NRA). As Louis Jaffe has noted, "There had not been devised, prior to NRA, any required, authorized, or even standard method of publishing administrative rules or decisions."[10] The codes were supposed to be filed with the secretary of state and published each year with the statutes at large. In the case of the petroleum code, copies had not been published, nor were they available to the affected parties. Evidently, copies of the petroleum code were only in the desk drawers of some NRA officials. To make matters even weaker from the point of view of the government's position in the case, when the original copy of the code was found, government brief writers found to their shock that the code had inadvertently been amended out of existence. The immediate effect of the *Panama Refining* case was to encourage Congress to provide for a system for

---

7. Theodore J. Lowi, *The End of Liberalism: Ideology, Policy, and the Crisis of Public Authority* (New York: W. W. Norton, 1969), pp. 129–132.
8. Attributed to Louis L. Jaffe, *Administrative Law* (Englewood Cliffs, N.J.: Prentice-Hall, 1959), pp. 60–61, by Lowi, p. 132.
9. 293 U.S. 388 (1935) and 295 U.S. 495 (1935), respectively.
10. Louis L. Jaffe, *Judicial Control of Administrative Action* (Boston: Little, Brown, 1965), p. 61.

publishing administrative rules and regulations through the *Federal Register* and the *Code of Federal Regulations.*

By bringing the delegation question into the opinion, the *Panama Refining* case showed that the justices of the Supreme Court could go out of their way to find grounds for disposing of administrative action that they did not favor. In the *Schechter* case, however, the Court unanimously agreed that the power to formulate codes of "fair competition" for all industries to promote industrial recovery was simply too broad a delegation of legislative authority, and as such the court declared it unconstitutional. The Court also noted the lack of procedural protections available to those affected by the codes. This concern for procedural protections and due process is a recurring theme in judicial control over administration. We will return to it later.

Since *Schechter,* however, the Court has consistently upheld delegation. As Ernest Gellhorn has noted, "The authority to determine 'excessive profits,' to 'liquidate' savings and loan associations, to fix 'maximum prices and wages,' and to 'allocate' vast quantities of water among water-short states are among the many delegations which have been upheld."[11] When Congress agrees to pass laws with such vague standards, it is really recognizing that there is little agreement on what constitutes standards necessary for regulation. Congress deals with the issue on a symbolic level. It passes regulations establishing a specialized arena in which specialized conflicts can be resolved. These specialized arenas become inaccessible to the public at large and become the province of interested groups seeking tangible rewards from government. These groups seek to settle their disputes at a low level of conflict deep within the bowels of bureaucracy. If they do not get their way, however, they will seek to pursue their interests through judicial review.

Informal Administrative Regulatory Procedures

IN most regulatory activity, the vague, ill-defined mandates from Congress leave many political questions and conflicts unresolved. Perhaps the key political question facing regulatory agencies is whom to prosecute. Congress can authorize agency action, but it generally does not

---

11. Gellhorn, *Administrative Law,* p. 19.

compel an agency to act in all cases. Assuming the Federal Trade Commission (FTC) develops a recognized definition of an "unfair and deceptive trade practice," it is not required to prosecute every such alleged practice. No regulatory agency has the resources to check out every allegation, let alone prosecute each potential case. Whether an agency makes an example of a large, powerful violator or goes after many small, less powerful violators is a matter of politics as well as managerial strategy.

Even in the cases a regulatory agency such as the FTC or the FDA looks into, the agencies are not required to proceed by issuing formal complaints, which would activate formal enforcement mechanisms. In all the arenas of American politics, there are formal and informal means of resolving conflicts. The ongoing regulatory process relies heavily on informal means to gain compliance, although formal procedures are in the background giving teeth to informal agency efforts. The main reason that agencies seek to use informal procedures is cost. Formal procedures put heavy demands on an agency's manpower and time. An agency has the choice between gaining compliance by tying up resources in a few formal complaint actions that can serve as examples and using less costly informal means. Again, these are management strategies that have political consequences.

There are several informal means that agencies use to gain voluntary compliance. Agencies use the *Federal Register* and professional journals to make policy announcements, and they circulate press releases. These straightforward efforts at communication serve to apprise the agency clientele of proposed policy changes or the effect of court rulings on existing policy. In an effort to avoid the chaos that surrounded the petroleum code, most regulatory agencies today realize that compliance is difficult unless one knows the rules with which he or she is supposed to comply.

The regulatory agencies encourage informal communications between agency staff and agency clientele. Much informal advice is given to people who request information over the telephone or through written inquiries. The informal advice is sometimes referred to as an *advisory opinion*.[12] Technically, an advisory opinion is an opinion of a tribunal that is dealing with an abstract or hypothetical situation. In an advisory opinion, the rights of the parties that requested the opinion are not at stake. American judicial practice does not allow for advisory opinions in

---

12. Kenneth Culp Davis, *Administrative Law and Government*, 2d ed. (St. Paul: West, 1975), pp. 288–290.

the general courts, but regulatory agencies are permitted to speculate on hypothetical problems brought to them by their clientele.

It seems reasonable that agency clientele would want to find out the agency's reaction to some proposed activity before it gets involved with that activity only to find out that it has violated some regulation. However, advisory opinions are not legally binding on the agency that issues them. For example, a toy company might ask an agency for an advisory opinion as to whether the agency would allow it to manufacture and market plastic thumbscrews without some warning label. The agency person who responds to the inquiry might feel that since there were no prohibitions specifically against plastic thumbscrews, such a product could be manufactured and sold to children. On the basis of this informal advice, the toy company might invest heavily in the equipment and staff needed to assure the thumbscrews would hit the market in time for the Christmas rush. The agency would still have the authority to prosecute the toy manufacturer if other agency personnel, higher in the hierarchy or more knowledgeable about the pernicious use of thumbscrews, convinced the agency staff that marketing of thumbscrews without a warning label was indeed against agency rulings. Even though the toy company based its decision on the advice of a member of the regulatory agency, it could be prosecuted because advisory opinions are not legally binding on the agency.

Informal advice might be dangerous to clientele on another level. As Gellhorn has suggested, "Requesting an [advisory] opinion . . . draws the agency's attention to a matter which otherwise might go unnoticed."[13] For example, if a political science professor thought he or she could write off a vacation to Jamaica as a research expense, it might be better not to contact the local office of the Internal Revenue Service (IRS) in advance. Even though the professor might have a real research interest in Jamaica, a hard-pressed IRS examiner might not readily see the relation of a January trip to the Caribbean and the professional growth of the professor. Furthermore, the IRS employee might note that the professor seems like a tax cheater whose returns should be audited.

Although there is no way to avoid calling agency attention to a possible problem if one seeks an advisory opinion, many regulatory agencies have established ways to increase the reliability of information that is given in response to specific questions. One way is that many agencies voluntarily consider themselves bound by advisory opinions. Another way is by issuing *declaratory orders*. A declaratory order has the same effect

---

13. Gellhorn, *Administrative Law*, p. 116.

as any other kind of legal order or judgment issued by a tribunal except that the agency issuing it merely declares what its decision is. But that declaration does not imply coercion and does not command that some punishment be enforced. When the ICC holds hearings to determine what commodities are "agricultural" in terms of laws regulating truckers, it issues declaratory orders at the end of the proceedings declaring that certain commodities are or are not to be considered agricultural.[14] Declaratory orders are based on more formal procedures than we have been dealing with heretofore. They are reviewable by courts, whereas advisory opinions are not, and they clearly state what an agency position is on a given issue.

Formal Regulatory Procedures

THE bulk of regulatory enforcement is accomplished by voluntary compliance encouraged through informal agency-clientele relationships. These informal relationships can influence when and against whom formal charges, which might carry criminal and civil penalties, should be brought. They may influence the conditions under which an agency and an offending party might agree to a *consent order.* Informal relationships might influence whether the agency will regulate aspects of whole industries by far-reaching, quasi-legislative *rule-making procedures* or whether it will develop a body of interpretations of its own enabling legislation through slower *adjudicatory procedures,* which resemble judicial law-making.

Consent orders are one of the more interesting political aspects of administrative law. The Administrative Procedures Act of 1946 (APA), which sought to limit the chaotic maze of procedures that each regulatory agency developed independently, requires that agencies give respondents in complaint cases an opportunity for settlement "when time, the nature of the proceeding, and the public interest permit."[15] If an agency has investigated an alleged violation by a regulated company and feels that it has a case against the company, the agency often seeks to comply with the APA by allowing the company to request consideration of a settlement before the complaint actually goes through adjudication procedures. The outcome of this negotiation is often a consent

14. Davis, *Administrative Law,* p. 291.
15. Administrative Procedures Act 60 Stat. 237, reprinted in appendix to Gellhorn, p. 290.

order whereby the alleged offending company agrees to stop whatever it was doing, but the offending company and the agency agree not to call whatever it was doing a violation of the law. As Gellhorn pointed out: "A consent order usually does not include an admission of material facts or of a law violation. The agency exchanges this avoidance of almost certain civil liability for the added cost savings and greater coverage of its orders."[16]

For example if the Federal Communications Commission finds that a radio station has not devoted the minimum time required by the "fairness doctrine," which mandates that opposing political candidates be given equal air time, the agency can negotiate with that station rather than automatically start formal procedures to revoke its license. The agency might avoid costly, time-consuming adjudicatory procedures by agreeing with the station that the station will not violate the fairness doctrine in the future. Such an agreement or consent order would not stipulate that the station violated the fairness doctrine in the past. By not admitting guilt, the station would not be liable to possible civil charges brought by the candidate who was the victim of the station's failure to follow the fairness doctrine in the first place.

Agencies have a great deal of latitude in negotiating whether to issue consent orders. Generally this kind of discretionary decision, which could have enormous impact on who gets what, is not reviewable by the courts.

It is the suspicion here that agencies tend to give offending companies a break by entering into consent orders. It is assumed that the agencies generally have the goods on the offending companies, but the agencies decide to let the companies off through the consent order mechanism in the name of expediency. Perhaps the public interest is served by agencies' regulating by consent order rather than through formal adjudication. Certainly, the consent decree is widely used. By one knowledgeable estimate, up to nine-tenths of the cases in some agencies are resolved by consent orders or similar exercises of the negotiating power.[17]

There is, however, another side to consent orders. Consent negotiations could be used to harass innocent regulated parties. Davis stressed this aspect of consent negotiations:

Much administrative action rests upon the kind of consent which bars the regulated party from effective remedy. Yet that consent is often

---

16. Gellhorn, p. 109.
17. Kenneth Culp Davis, *Administrative Law and Government* (St. Paul, Minn.: West, 1960), p. 99.

coerced. The radio station unwillingly discontinues a profitable program, the bank terminates a practice it wants to continue, the issuer of securities reluctantly agrees to a highly objectionable action, because the alternative of fighting out the question in an expensive or publicized formal proceeding involves greater loss or risk of loss than peacefully yielding.[18]

Sometimes, however, alleged offenders do not accept consent orders from regulatory agencies. Instead, they fight. In 1973, the Securities and Exchange Commission charged Arthur Young and Company, one of the "Big Eight" national accounting firms, with failing to uncover a $30 million fraud in an oil-drilling company that they had audited. Rather than settle, the firm challenged the SEC. Six years later, after spending $3.5 million in legal fees, the accounting firm was vindicated. Most companies do not have that kind of money to protect their reputations. They settle, says one corporate lawyer, because "litigating the federal government can be nothing but a disaster." David Ferber, the SEC's solicitor, thinks the real reason is that "usually we got the goods on them."[19]

Clearly, the decision to prosecute and to take a regulated company through the adjudicatory jungle is a great power to force compliance. The Administrative Procedures Act specifies that each agency must publish its adjudicatory procedures and these must conform to the provisions of the act. The first step of adjudication involves the filing of a formal complaint. This is followed by an administrative hearing using procedures that are very similar to those of a federal court. The proceedings are open to the public and are conducted in an orderly, dignified manner by a hearing examiner or administrative law judge. Generally, the atmosphere at the hearing is a bit less formal than in a courtroom. Since there are no juries, the rules of evidence are a bit looser. Witnesses may be presented and cross-examined, and the parties may be represented by legal counsel.

But the administrative hearing is only the beginning of a long, slow process involving agency appeals up through the commissioners of the independent agency, then further appeals through the federal courts. The resources needed to mount a major legal defense and to fight an administrative decision all the way to the Supreme Court are enormous, but many cases—those involving multi-million-dollar potential gains or losses—do go all the way up. In recent years, about one-third of the cases

---

18. Ibid., p. 104.
19. Stan Crock, "More of SEC's Targets Are Going into Court Rather than Settling," *Wall Street Journal,* July 16, 1979, p. 1.

the Supreme Court has decided to hear in any given session involved administrative law questions.

Given the legal aphorism "Justice delayed is justice denied," there is a question as to whether the lengthy, drawn-out process, which is in effect reserved for the rich because of the expense, really produces justice. Similarly, there is a question whether the adjudicatory process is an effective way to regulate. Surely, as we have seen, the ability to take offenders through this adjudicatory mill enhances the potential power of the regulators. If adjudication were not available, regulation would have no teeth whatsoever. But developing regulations through adjudication is needlessly limiting, when one considers the alternative—rule-making.

An agency's rule-making power—especially its ability to make substantive rules in addition to procedural rules—is the heart of modern regulatory action in the United States, and one of the reasons for the delegation controversy, which we discussed earlier. Rule-making is legislative power that has been delegated to administrative agencies. Substantive rules state administrative judgments about future events and activities of the regulated parties.

So that new rules cannot be slipped by an unsuspecting clientele, the APA commands that the agency publish advanced notice or proposed rule changes in the *Federal Register,* give interested parties the opportunity to participate through formal hearings or submissions of written material, and publish the adopted rule thirty days before it is to go into effect. But conflicting commands from other sections of the APA and other legislation have created a situation whereby much rule-making does not go through this process. Instead, the notification of rule changes may not be circulated widely but may be limited to people or interests selected by the agency or to an advisory committee. Furthermore, the agencies are not bound by the evidence presented at the hearings should they actually be held; they may consider data from other sources.[20]

In recent years, Congress and the courts have required elaborate procedures of administrative rule-making by the independent regulatory agencies. Commissioners are now expected to behave as impartial judges even when they engage in rule-making. Jeremy Rabkin has suggested some of the reasons for this:

> Having delegated an extremely broad regulatory authority to the commission, Congress naturally prefers to think—or at least prefers the public to think—that decisions will be guided by expert determination rather than political judgment. The courts, apparently despairing of adequate

---

20. Gellhorn, *Administrative Law,* pp. 127–129.

congressional oversight, seem to have concluded that more formal rule-making procedures will ensure better administrative decisions. Strenuous efforts to maintain the *appearance* of expert impartiality on the part of the commissioners follow, then from the doubts about their political accountability. . . . Indeed, the more the commissioners keep up the appearance of sober impartiality the easier it is for Congress to avoid calling them to account.[21]

Part of the reason that the Federal Trade Commission failed in its efforts to enforce advertising standards for children's television was the strong position taken by its chairman, Michael Pertschuk. This brought down the wrath of Congress and the courts on the FTC.

Powerful interests that fail to get their positions supported in the final rules adopted by the agency may seek to raise the level of conflict to the legislature. Legislative enactments supersede administrative rules on the same subject. Alternatively, if a powerful interest is prosecuted on the basis of an unfavorable rule made by the agency, that interest might want to fight the agency through the adjudicatory procedures and the courts, in hopes of a reversal.

Judicial Review of Administrative Action

IF an interest loses a battle at the administrative level, that party may wish to escalate the conflict, hoping for a different decision in another arena. Judicial review is an alternative to seeking legislative changes that would have the effect of changing the administrative decision. Judicial review of administrative decisions is supposed to be limited to questions of law rather than questions of fact. The administrative agencies, with their specialized knowledge, are assumed to be better able to ascertain facts in complicated, specialized situations than regular judges are. But in practice, this distinction between questions of law and questions of fact is not all that clear.[22] In effect, in complicated cases, interested parties that have the financial resources necessary to mount a legal battle can find grounds for bringing administrative decisions before the regular courts for review.

In a candid article discussing the issues in judicial review of adminis-

---

21. Jeremy Rabkin, "Rulemaking, Bias, and the Dues of Due Process at the FTC," *Regulation* 3, no. 1 (January–February 1979): 45. Emphasis added.
22. Jaffe, *Judicial Control*, pp. 546–550.

trative action, a former judge, Irving Kaufman, admitted that "appellate judges cannot possibly be as familiar as the administrative agency with the factual controversies or the specialized knowledge involved in many agency decisions."[23] Even though judges might have difficulty dealing with the factual material in the case, Kaufman held that "it is both impossible and improper for a judge reviewing administrative decisions to decide a case in a vacuum without at least partially immersing himself in the complex of facts."[24] Since the facts would tend to be more the province of the administrative agency, Kaufman suggested that the judge's role was to carve out issues that do not require administrative expertise. Among the kinds of issues that are the proper concerns of judges are the fundamental concepts of fairness, due process, and common sense.

In applying judicial expertise to administrative decisions, judges must consider several questions that provide the basis for judicial review. Perhaps the first question is whether the administrator's action was authorized by statute law. Here the issue involves delegated authority. Assuming that the administrator has the authority to act, the question arises whether the administrator properly interpreted the applicable law. A second question involves abuse of discretion. Was the choice supported by the evidence? And a third question—one of the favorites of lawyers—was the process fair? Was the constitutional mandate of due process of law followed by the administrator in coming to a decision? These questions provide judges with wide latitude potentially to set aside administrative decisions.

Sometimes judges have an intuitive sense, according to Kaufman, that justice is not being done.

> At that point [judges] may search for a peg upon which to hang a decision. With the voluminous records which burden the arms of the law clerks and the minds of the judges in agency cases, . . . enterprising lawyers (for once their minds are made up, judges become advocates and write their decisions accordingly) *can usually find error upon which to base a reversal.*[25]

It would be too strong to hold that judges can easily reverse any administrative decision, but they can generally find technical grounds in complex cases if they are so disposed. That is why regulated companies that

---

23. Irving R. Kaufman, "Judicial Review of Agency Action: A Judge's Unburdening," *New York University Law Review* 45, no. 2 (April 1970): 201.
24. Ibid., p. 203.
25. Ibid., p. 209. Emphasis added.

have the resources to appeal administrative decisions hire top legal talent and pay them huge fees.

For example, judges might not have the expertise to determine how chemical plants must end the dumping of medically harmful effluents into rivers by 1983 as provided for in an Environmental Protection Agency (EPA) rule, but they can find grounds to reverse the rule. While upholding the agency's authority to make such a regulation, a court felt that the EPA's record, although substantial, "failed to disclose a reasonable basis for a belief that a new technology will be available and economically achievable" to cut pollution to prescribed levels.[26] The effect of the decision in the case, which was brought by several large chemical companies, was to allow the companies to continue discharging pollutants into the nation's rivers. The court did note, however, that the EPA could redraft its rules. Furthermore, the court virtually dismissed the industry contention that rules controlling the level of pollution would force the chemical plants to close. Still, the effect of the decision was to support the interests of the major pollutors over those of the public. Perhaps the regulations drafted by the EPA were too vague, but in an area of technological change maybe regulations have to be vague to deal with, and even encourage, new developments.

Whereas a powerful interest, like the chemical industry, is able to allocate the resources necessary to force a contrary administrative ruling into another arena of conflict, smaller interests are in effect prisoners of administrative decisions. As Davis has said, "Litigation expense makes much administrative action unreviewable from a practical standpoint."[27] There is a degree of irony in the situation because the due process clause was designed to protect relatively powerless individuals from unreasonable, illegal governmental action. Now, because of the high costs of a legal defense, powerful interests can seek due process protection while less powerful interests and individuals cannot.

At the federal level, however, help for the less powerful may be on the way. In 1980 Congress passed the Equal Access to Justice Act, which says federal agencies must pay the legal expenses of those who successfully fight agency actions that are not proper. The burden is on the agency to show that its actions were "substantially justified."[28] To be eligible for reimbursement for legal expenses, an individual cannot have a

---

26. Reported in Victor K. McElheny, "Court Asks Clearer Rules for Phosphate Pollutants," *New York Times,* April 30, 1976.
27. Kenneth Culp Davis, *Discretionary Justice: A Preliminary Inquiry* (Baton Rouge: Louisiana State University Press, 1969), p. 155.
28. P.L. 96–481, October 1980.

net worth of more than $1 million; and a business's net worth cannot exceed $5 million. Nonprofit organizations and labor unions qualify regardless of organizational wealth or size.

Direct Judicial Intervention

WHEN constitutional rights are involved, however, the courts have gone out of their ways to protect classes of affected individuals. Generally, court decisions involving rights establishes the right—for example, the right of accused persons to have lawyers—and assumes that without direct supervision, others will see that the right is granted. In the right-to-counsel example, police, prosecutors, and lower court judges are all supposed to see that persons accused of crimes have access to legal help. But in an increasing number of areas (some not even involving constitutional rights), judges have developed elaborate plans for assuring that the established right is protected. Direct judicial intervention has put the courts (often the federal district courts) in the business of managing school systems, mental hospitals, prisons, and other institutions.

One of the more outspoken critics of this new, detailed judicial activism is Nathan Glazer. He notes that the school desegregation orders are the models for direct judicial intervention in the other areas. Usually a school desegregation order

> includes a detailed and elaborate plan for school assignment, and may also require the closing of some schools, the construction and repair of others, the employment of additional personnel, the purchase or rental of buses and other equipment, specifically defined consultation with various elements in the community, elections to advisory boards, regular reporting, and the employment of specified agents of the courts and their reimbursement at defined rates, fixed procedures for the suspension and expulsion of students and so on.[29]

The rationale for this extensive judicial intervention in administration is that school officials resisted implementing simple court orders establishing the right to attend integrated schools.

In dealing with numbers of white, black, and other minority students, it is possible to develop a plan that will achieve the judicial goal of de-

---

29. Nathan Glazer, "Should Judges Administer Social Services?" *The Public Interest* no. 50 (Winter 1978): 65. *Also see* Glazer, "Toward an Imperial Judiciary?" *The Public Interest* no. 41 (Fall 1975): 104–123.

segregation. School boards probably could have come up with such plans themselves, but the political environment of the agencies might have prevented them from doing so. If they had responded to certain powerful forces in their environment, they might have resisted the court's will and therefore been subjected to additional court efforts.

The notion of resistance of state officials to integrating public schools has apparently served as an analogy to failures in other areas. Glazer contends that judges act as though state officials in prisons, mental institutions, and so on have failed because they are resisting court efforts to establish certain rights. Glazer claims that state inaction in certain areas is based not on resistance but on incapacity. "[That] the state did not know how to rehabilitate prisoners, or cure the mentally ill, or run a good housing project, or ensure that parents receiving money for the care of children raised them properly becomes associated, in the minds of judges, with resistance."[30]

Whether it is a matter of willful resistance or of state incapacity, once judges begin operating in the insulated world of legal reasoning, they can greatly upset the environment of public management. As Justice Benjamin Cardoza suggested, there is "the tendency of a principle to expand itself to the limit of its logic."[31] In legal theory, it is not a great leap from establishing a right to establishing the administrative requirements necessary to see that right implemented. When a judge is dealing with a right, that right is to be protected. Cost does not enter into the legal equation. The source of funds needed to protect a right is not of judicial concern. Neither are programs, or even other rights in other areas that might suffer if the judicial order is carried out. The judge is only required to deal with the substance of the case at hand.

As long as this direct judicial involvement was limited to one policy area—schools—the immediate effect on the overall public policy–public management environment was not large. Now that judges have established the precedent that conditions in jails and mental health institutions violate individual rights, they may be on a path that leads to greater judicial involvement in other social services. Indeed, District Court Judge Arthur Garrity, who issued detailed orders to desegregate Boston schools, issued similarly detailed orders to improve conditions in the apartments managed by the Boston Housing Authority. Another judge from the same district court issued an order requiring the Com-

30. Ibid., p. 69.
31. Quoted in Justice Robert Jackson's dissent in *Korematsu* v. *United States,* 323 U.S. 214 (1944).

monwealth of Massachusetts to hire 200 additional social workers. Clearly, direct judicial intervention is spreading.

Abram Chayes sees this movement of public litigation resulting in specific judicial orders to be a positive and irreversible trend. He argues that the judiciary, although it should act cautiously in directly managing institutions as part of the relief sought by the plaintiffs, has some advantages in ordering highly specific remedies. Among the advantages are these:

1. *The judge's profession insulates him from narrow political pressures. . . . He is governed by a professional ideal of reflective and dispassionate analysis of the problem before him. . . .*
2. *The solutions can be tailored to the needs of the particular situation and flexibly administered or modified as experience develops. . . .*
3. *The procedure permits a relatively high degree of participation by representatives of those who will be directly affected by the decision. . . .*
4. *The court, although traditionally thought less competent than legislatures or administrative agencies in gathering and assessing information, may have unsuspected advantages in this regard. Even the diffused adversarial structure of public law litigation furnishes strong incentives for the parties to produce information. If the party structure is sufficiently representative of the interests at stake, a considerable range of relevant information will be forthcoming. . . . The judge can engage his own experts to assist in evaluating the evidence. Moreover, the information that is produced will not be filtered through the rigid structures and preconceptions of bureaucracies.*
5. *The judicial process is an effective mechanism for registering and responding to grievances generated by the operation of public programs in a regulatory state.*[32]

Chayes admits his list presents an optimistic view of judicial capabilities.

There is much to recommend decisions by philosopher-kings capable of hearing all the arguments, then giving reasoned responses covering almost all details. Whether district court judges fit this mold is something experience will determine. Glazer is not convinced. He notes that judges are limited to the evidence presented before the court and that in public law litigation, the plaintiffs often do a better job. The plaintiffs are often represented by bright young lawyers and professors galvanized with a cause and a chance to make legal history. He points out that "sometimes the civil servants who are formally testifying on behalf of the defendant will in effect join with the plaintiffs to present testimony to the judge justifying greater appropriations for staff and facilities from the legislature, thus hoping to get by judicial order what they could not get through budgetary presentations to executive and legislature."[33] In-

---

32. Abram Chayes, *Harvard Law Review* 89, no. 7 (May 1976): 1307–1308.
33. Glazer, "Should Judges Administer Social Services?," p. 70.

deed, the experts a judge would get to help him or her would be professionals who would probably have stronger programmatic than fiscal concerns. As such they would support professional claims on resources and not be concerned about the effects on other policy areas.[34] The judge may thus be faced with a budget strategy rather than an adversary proceeding.

The budgetary implications of direct judicial intervention in administration are serious. Harry Miller, a critic of public law litigation, expresses this concern.

> Given [states' or municipalities'] limited resources, their compliance with federal court decrees must require budget-juggling that shifts funds from other needs that must also be met. The court examines only one area of need at a time; advocates who come before it demanding increased resources for state hospitals are not accompanied by advocates for increased expenditures on police, or health, or education, or any of the other needs met by the states. The state budget-making process must deal politically with this welter of competing demands, doing the best it can to trade off and compromise. . . . Judicial intervention in the process, through setting fiscal priorities on the basis of whatever demand happens to come to a court's attention, is difficult to justify in a representative democracy.[35]

Summary

OUR vision of fair administration assumes that judges do not have a monopoly on protecting individual rights. Administrators should be, and generally are, concerned that their efforts to plan do not violate the legitimate rights of interested individuals and groups. In part this concern for the rights of clientele encourages the informal contact that results in agencies bending over backward to be "reasonable"—and not aggressively enforce certain rulings that might upset the symbiotic balance that has been developed among the agency, the clientele, and the legislature.

The courts, legislatures, and public bureaucracies have various degrees of overlapping authority. As Martin Shapiro has pointed out, they all are involved with law-making—the courts and bureaucracies serving

---

34. See John Wanat, *Introduction to Budgeting* (North Scituate, Mass.: Duxbury Press, 1978), pp. 55–56 for the programmatic versus fiscal orientation.
35. Harry L. Miller, "The 'Right to Treatment': Can the Courts Rehabilitate and Cure?" *The Public Interest* no. 46 (Winter 1977): 107–108.

as supplemental law-makers.[36] Even though the great bulk of administrative decisions are neither reviewed by courts nor the immediate concern of legislators, there has been continuing interest in assuring that bureaucrats appear to be controlled. The citizenry is symbolically reassured if it thinks that administrative action is protected from the arbitrary use of authority by vigilant legislators or courts.

We have seen here, however, that checks on administration by these other institutions are often illusionary. There are political reasons that mitigate against meaningful oversight of the bureaucracy by the legislature. There are financial reasons that administrative action cannot be appealed through the courts except by more wealthy, powerful interests. Allowing the courts to impose their will on the other political and administrative actors through judicial decrees can have repercussions in other policy areas. There are limitations to legislative and legal controls over public managers. This does not mean that we should ignore all legislative and judicial means for controlling administrative action. But perhaps it means we must look elsewhere to understand the nature of just administration in the United States. The final chapter will discuss administrative responsibility and the future of public management.

Suggestions for Further Reading

Berger, Raoul. *Government by Judiciary.* Cambridge, Mass.: Harvard University Press, 1977.

Davis, Kenneth Culp. *Administrative Law and Government,* 2d ed. St. Paul, Minn.: West, 1975.

———. *Discretionary Justice: A Preliminary Inquiry.* Baton Rough, La.: Louisiana State University Press, 1969.

Fritschler, A. Lee. *Smoking and Politics: Policy Making and the Federal Bureaucracy,* 2d ed. Englewood Cliffs, N.J.: Prentice-Hall, 1975.

Horowitz, Donald L. *The Courts and Social Policy.* Washington, D.C.: The Brookings Institution, 1977.

Jaffe, Louis L. *Judicial Control of Administrative Action.* Boston: Little, Brown, 1965.

Relyea, Harold C., ed. "Symposium on the Freedom of Information Act." *Public Administration Review* 39, no. 4 (July–August 1979).

Shapiro, Martin. *The Supreme Court and Administrative Agencies.* New York: Free Press, 1968.

---

36. Martin Shapiro, *The Supreme Court and Administrative Agencies* (New York: Free Press, 1968), especially pp. 12–29.

CHAPTER THIRTEEN

Administrative Responsibility and Public Management

In CHAPTERS 10, 11, AND 12, we discussed ways to control bureaucrats in a democracy. We want to control bureaucrats to make sure they carry out their functions in accordance with goals determined through the processes of representative government. We want to control bureaucrats so they do not violate the general wishes of the citizenry. We want to control them so they do not make arbitrary decisions that violate individual rights. In our presentation we have seen that there are many ways to control bureaucrats through the three branches of government. Although political difficulties often impinge on the effectiveness of any of these measures, there is a clear capacity within the governmental system of the United States to control bureaucrats.

But in a rapidly changing society, perhaps the emphasis on control is misplaced. Of course we want to hold bureaucrats accountable for their negative actions, and we would like to ensure against their potential abuse of power, but perhaps, as Kenneth Culp Davis has suggested, "fear of bureaucracy may have overemphasized excessive zeal and underemphasized administrative arteriosclerosis."[1] Perhaps administrative responsibility is more than just being held accountable for malfeasance and misfeasance. Perhaps we expect something more from our public managers and employees.

In this chapter we will look more closely at the roles of public administrators and our expectations for their actions in a democratic society. We will discuss the complexities of administrative responsibility and the management problems that will emerge in the future.

Responsible Administrators and the Public Interest

MODERN public administration recognizes that public policy-making involves both political and administrative components. As Carl Friedrich has stated:

> The concrete patterns of public policy formation and execution reveal that politics and administration are not two mutually exclusive boxes, or absolute distinctions, but that they are two closely linked aspects of the same process. Public policy, to put it flatly, is a continuous process, the formation of which is inseparable from its execution. . . . Politics and administration play a continuous role in both formation and execution,

---

1. Kenneth Culp Davis, *Administrative Law and Government* (St. Paul, Minn.: West, 1960), p.109.

FIGURE 13.1
The Relationship of Politics to Administration in Public Policy

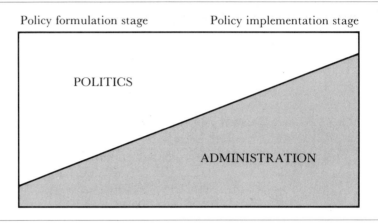

Policy formulation stage   Policy implementation stage

POLITICS

ADMINISTRATION

though there is probably more politics in the formation of policy, and more administration in the execution of it. [See Figure 13.1.] Insofar as particular individuals or groups are gaining or losing power or control in a given area, there is politics; insofar as officials act or propose action in the name of public interest, there is administration.[2]

As long as an element of discretion is available to administrators, they are in a position to determine "who gets what" in a given situation. Since virtually all laws and rules leave some discretion to those who administer them, public administrators are political actors.

Just and responsible administration implies that the administrators are not simply powerless pawns in a political game whose outcome is completely determined by considerations of power. Just and responsible administration implies that administrators are expected to play an active role in improving public policies. As political actors, they are expected to use their power resources—principally their expertise—to bring about outcomes that are in the public interest." Indeed, many laws give administrators the mandate, if not the wisdom, to act "in the public interest."

2. Carl J. Friedrich, "Public Policy and the Nature of Administrative Responsibility," in Carl J. Friedrich and E. S. Mason, ed., *Public Policy* (Cambridge, Mass.: Harvard University Press, 1940). This essay has been widely reprinted. Page references here are to its appearance in Francis E. Rourke, ed., *Bureaucratic Power in National Politics,* 3rd ed. (Boston: Little, Brown, 1978), p.401.

So the notion of just and responsible administration in a democracy demands that bureaucrats act in the public interest. But does a public interest really exist? For all issues? And if so, how are administrators to know what the public interest is?

Just what the public interest means, let alone how it can be achieved, has been strongly debated in political science. One critic of the concept, Glendon Schubert, has suggested that the public interest has been used in different ways by three broad types of political theorists whom he called rationalists, idealists, and realists.[3] To Schubert, the rationalists assume that, at any particular time, there is a common good that is a reflection of the common interests and goals of a given society. It is the duty of public officials to carry out the popular will, which is the expression of the common good. Even though the rationalists are agreed that there is a common good—a public interest—out there in a society, they disagree on how this common good is made known to public officials.

Some rationalists maintain that the common good is expressed through the electoral process and through the positions of the political parties. Others maintain that public opinion as measured by polls is the proper way for representatives to determine the popular will. There is therefore a clash between the party rationalists, who tend to worship the ideal of a British-like disciplined party system, and the popular rationalists, who feel individual legislators should carry out the wishes of their constituents. All those whom Schubert called rationalists, however, agree that there is a public interest, and it can be determined by elected officials. To these people, administration is merely the implementation of policy, which has been determined by the elected officials' ability to state the public interest. Few public administrators hold this view.

Idealists, on the other hand, support a view of the public interest that is developed independently of what the public itself may view as its interest. According to Schubert, idealists "believe that the public interest reposes not in the positive law made by men, but in the higher law, in natural law."[4] In this view, each public official, in communion with his or her own conscience, decides what is in the public interest. The indi-

3. The most concise statement of Schubert's views are to be found in his essay "Is There a Public Interest Theory?" in Carl J. Friedrich, ed., *The Public Interest, Nomos V* (New York: Atherton, 1966), pp. 162–176. The following discussion is drawn from pp. 164–171.
4. Ibid., p. 166.

vidual interpretation that goes on in such a process is antithetical to democracy.

Schubert feared that the idealist position governs much of public administrative theory. To Schubert, "Administrative engineers advise administators to be creative manipulators and to resist the seductions of interest groups. Guild idealists warn ... of the danger of party politics, and demand that administrators be given elbow room for the exercise of craft and conscience." Tied to the idealist view of the public interest are, according to Schubert, "elitist notions of superior intelligence and wisdom."[5] Elitism in this sense has nothing to do with a power elite posited by C. Wright Mills and others.[6] Rather, it is a kind of moral elite of academics and social planners who have normative notions of what a just society should be. Because of the antidemocratic bias in such a view of the public interest, Schubert could not support it.

Public Interest Realists

WHEREAS the rationalist and idealist views of the public interest presuppose different political systems from what we have in the United States, the realist position glorifies the apparent political reality of pluralism. Pluralism, according to a leading critic, William Connolly,

> portrays the system as a balance of power among overlapping economic, religious, ethnic, and geographical groupings. Each "group" has some voice in shaping socially binding decisions; each constrains and is constrained through the processes of mutual group adjustment; and all major groups share a broad system of beliefs and values which encourages conflict to proceed within established channels and allows initial disagreements to dissolve into compromise solutions.[7]

Schubert saw three varieties of the realist position, all of what are rooted in pluralist theories of American democracy: (1) strict countervailing pressure of interacting groups; (2) "psychological realists," who focus on

---

5. Ibid., p. 167.
6. C. Wright Mills, *The Power Elite* (New York: Oxford University Press, 1957). Elite rule is often contrasted with pluralism, *See* Peter Bachrach, *The Therory of Democratic Elitism* (Boston: Little, Brown, 1968), and William E. Connolly, ed., *The Bias of Pluralism* (New York: Atherton, 1969).
7. William E. Connolly, "The Challenge to Pluralist Theory," in Connolly, *The Bias of Pluralism,* p. 3.

the conflict of interests in the minds of decision-makers; and (3) "due process–equilibrium realists," who deal with the legal and economic environment in which decision-makers operate. It is fairly clear that the crass pull and tug of groups based on positions of raw power is an oversimplification of the way policy decisions are made. But the psychological and due process–equilibrium realists present a more sophisticated view of pluralism in action.

To the psychological realists, decision-making by government policymakers is an active process of mediation among conflicting group interests. This mediation includes the decision-maker's knowledge and understanding of broad values in society. Among these values are the components of the democratic ethic—freedom, equality, and opportunity—that can lead the decision-maker to consider interests other than those that are explicitly favored by contending interest groups. It is difficult to assess the value-balancing process within a decision-maker's head—even though that balancing act goes on within rough limits prescribed by the society's value system. Therefore Schubert felt bound to reject the psychological realists' position, too, because he saw himself as a positivist social scientist.

The thinkers Schubert called due process–equilibrium realists deal with the world outside the decision-maker's head and thus with supposedly observable phenomena. According to this theory of the public interest, Schubert claimed, "people accept democratic decision-making processes because these provide the maximum opportunity for diverse interests to seek to influence governmental decisions at all levels."[8] The job of the official decision-makers becomes one of encouraging the access of these interests to the policy-makers. Their aim is to maintain continuity and stability in the policy-making process. Of course, this continuity and stability will only be maintained if the more powerful interests in society generally get what they want from the policy process. But the public interest is supposedly obtained as long as all relevant interests have had the ability to state their cases. Schubert's view of the due process–equilibrium camp recalls Murray Edelman's notion of symbolic versus tangible rewards in a policy system. The mass of players get symbolic rewards inherent in having played the policy game. The winners, usually the more powerful, gain tangible rewards.[9]

Schubert concluded that the concept of the public interest is too fuzzy

---

8. Schubert, "Is There a Public Interesr Theory?," p. 170.
9. Murray J. Edelman, "Symbols and Political Quiescence," *American Political Science Review* 54, no. 3 (September 1960): 695–704.

to be of analytical relevance. He claimed it makes no operational sense and should be discarded. Others have challenged this view. Brian Barry, a political philosopher, has suggested that people who are "able to *use* a concept may nevertheless talk rubbish *about* it." Barry conceded that all too often the "public interest" has been used as a smokescreen to cover the decisions of politicians and bureaucrats that tend to support the most effectively deployed interests. Despite this, Barry argued that the notion of the public interest points to a "fairly clearly definable range of considerations in support of a policy, and if it is a very popular concept at the moment, all this shows is that (for better or worse) these considerations are highly valued by many people at the moment." Barry saw the public interest as a viable concept that explains the legitimate interests of people on a particular issue. He pointed to ordinary speech patterns whereby people often explain their actions as being in their interests as members of some class or category—"as a parent," "as a businessman," "as a student." To Barry, there are some issues that people find themselves favorably disposed toward as members of the public at large.[10] Barry looked to officials to protect this interest:

> Interests shared by few can be promoted by them whereas interests shared by many have to be furthered by the state if they are to be furthered at all. Only the state has the universality and the coercive power necessary to prevent people from doing what they want to do when it harms the public and to raise money to provide benefits for the public which cannot, or cannot conveniently, be sold on the market.[11]

Barry's position, therefore, is very close to Schubert's description of the psychological realists. Although it may be difficult to measure the kind of value-balancing that goes on in a decision-maker's head, it does not follow that such an activity does not occur.

Several longtime observers of the American administrative scene have come to similar conclusions. Robert Presthus has called the public interest "a normative myth that sometimes helps officials to achieve a working compromise between claims of various publics without sacrificing the interest of the inarticulate, unorganized majority."[12] This notion that the public interest—the general interest of the unorganized—can be a guiding spirit in policy-making is shown in Paul Appleby's classic description of what goes on in the closed hearings at the final stages of

10. Brian Barry, "The Public Interest," in Connolly, *The Bias of Pluralism*, pp. 160, 173.
11. Ibid., p. 175.
12. Robert Presthus, *Public Administration*, 6th ed. (New York: Ronald, 1975), p 420.

"There's getting to be a lot of dangerous talk about the public interest." [*From* The Herblock Gallery (*Simon & Schuster, 1968*)]

the preparation of the president's budget: "It is not made in a public arena, but the public is somehow well represented. This is one of the most mystifying of governmental phenomena."[13]

Friedrich's View of Administrative Responsibility

WE can see that administrative responsibility in political bureaucracy is bound up with the notion of a public interest that is to be protected by administrators as a kind of trust for the unorganized citizens. If we want to demystify "the most mystifying of governmental phenomena," we

13. David B. Truman, *The Governmental Process*, 2nd ed. (New York: Alfrd A. Knopf, 1971), p. 449.

need to develop a set of criteria with which the administrator would be able to gauge his or her own actions against the yardstick of the public interest. Carl Friedrich has presented a widely accepted view of administrative responsibility in a modern democratic state. That view suggests two criteria.[14]

Friedrich took the position that in any complex society, there would always be a great deal of discretion left to public administrators. He felt that controls on bureaucrats merely to prevent them from doing wrong were not enough to make them act responsibly. Acting responsibly entails acting innovatively to solve problems that perhaps were only vaguely outlined in the laws authorizing agency action. Friedrich proposed a two-factor test of administrative responsibility, which he thought would encourage the bureaucrat to act with intelligence and flexibility in changing situations. These two factors, the criteria upon which he sought to judge administrative responsibility, are (1) technical knowledge and (2) popular sentiment.

Clearly, certain complex problems demand that the administrator have technical competence to deal with them properly. Depending on the situation, technical knowledge of accounting or finance may be needed if the official is to be able to choose some alternatives over others. If a local administrator were not able to understand the financial aspects of a grant proposal, the entire application might be rejected, making it much more costly to provide certain services to local residents. Under other conditions, perhaps, expertise in civil engineering would be necessary to evaluate cost projections for alternative highway bridge sites across a river. A purely technical solution would involve cost and engineering studies that would be able to show which site best conformed to technical criteria.

But, Friedrich held, responsible administrative action must conform to a dual standard—technical knowledge *and* popular sentiment. Purely technical solutions do not automatically guarantee political responsibility. A decision based completely on financial data might ignore human needs in such areas as health, welfare, and education—needs that might not have been accounted for through traditional financial analysis. Similarly, the "better" site for the highway bridge might entail the dislocation of many people and perhaps the destruction of a firmly rooted ethnic community. In cases like these, popular sentiment determines the political—and administrative—responsibility of the action.

Popular sentiment, like the public interest, is not easily measured. On

---

14. Friedrich in Rourke, *Bureaucratic Power*, pp. 403–409.

some issues, there is no popular sentiment as such. Not many people have taken a stand on the liquid fast-breeder nuclear reactor, for example. Is popular sentiment to be defined by legislative bodies? Should it be defined by public opinion polls? Should it be defined by various interested parties? And what happens if there is conflict, as surely there will be, among these expressions of popular sentiment? How is the administrator supposed to judge political responsibility? Friedrich's answers to all these questions are something like the story of the learned professor who heard an argument from a brilliant student. "You're right," said the professor. Then another student made an equally brilliant counterargument. "You're right," said the professor. Then another student from the back noted that both of these students could not be right. "You know," said the professor, "you're right, too!"

Friedrich believed that responsible administrators would try to use any means of communication available to them to assess popular sentiment. Legislative communications, public opinion polls, and responses of affected groups would all contribute to the administrator's notion of popular sentiment. But are the sentiments of the affected groups more important than generalized opinion of the public at large? Friedrich did not give firm guidance on how such communications should be weighted.

Instead, Friedrich maintained, the administrator "has the task of anticipating clashes between the administrative efforts at effectuating a policy and the set habits of thought and behavior of the public which constitute its 'environment.' "[15] This "law" of anticipated reactions applies directly to clientele and legislators. By implication, it would apply to what bosses might think of a subordinate's actions, and it might even apply to what the general public might think of a particular policy if they knew of it. On its surface, the law of anticipated reactions gives great flexibility to administrators because *they* anticipate how people will react and are free to act accordingly. The only real check on an administrator's action, to Friedrich, is his or her own moral position. This is the antithesis of external control.

Criticism of Friedrich

FRIEDRICH'S original position on administrative responsibility appeared in 1940 and sparked a heated debate with a fellow political scientist,

15. Ibid., p. 408.

Herman Finer.[16] To Finer, the very heart of democratic government was the ability of elected institutions to check government officials who exercised power. Finer thought Friedrich was rationalizing the administrator's use of discretionary power at the expense of external controls. Without meaningful controls on administrators, democracy itself would be in danger.

Finer agreed that much legislation creates the situations for administrative discretion. He clearly saw that legislative bodies are too bogged down in antiquated procedures to review legislation sufficiently and provide meaningful oversight. He also saw that most legislatures lack the technical capacity to deal with complex issues. Whereas Friedrich said that is the way things are, let us develop an administrative democracy, Finer argued that the electoral institutions should be strengthened to enable them to overcome their own institutional shortcomings. As Finer said, "The legitimate conclusion from the analysis of the relationship between [legislatures] and administration is not that administration should be given its head, but on the contrary that legislative bodies should be improved."[17]

Theodore Lowi echoed Finer's argument in the late 1960s with his call for "juridical democracy." While noting that legislation had often been poorly constructed in the past, Lowi did not see that political conflicts should be settled informally at the administrative level through bargaining among agency, clientele, and legislative committee. Instead he advocated tighter law, which could then be more adequately reviewed by the courts, and tighter legislative control.[18]

It would be unfair, however, to paint Friedrich as some kind of moral elitist who did not see the external control aspects of the administrative responsibility question. In a later work, Friedrich recognized that an individual administrator's discretion would be affected by disciplinary measures and promotion controls exercised through the hierarchy, financial measures such as budgetary control through the legislature, and civil and criminal penalties pronounced by the court. Still, he maintained that professionalism—adherence to professional and technical norms—tempered by the individual's view of popular sentiment is the most important control.[19]

16. Herman Finer, "Administrative Responsibility in Democratic Government," *Public Administration Review* 1 (Summer 1941): 335–350. T)his article has been widely reprinted and appears in Rourke, *Bureaucratic Power,* pp. 410–421.
17. Rourke, *Bureaucratic Power,* p.417.
18. Theodore J. Lowi, *The End of Liberalism* (New York: W. W. Norton, 1969), chapter 10.
19. Carl J. Friedrich, *Constitutional Government and Democracy,* 4th ed. (Waltham, Mass.: Blaisdell, 1968), pp. 418–428.

Finer was principally concerned with the possibility of what he called *"over*feasance, where a duty is undertaken beyond what law and custom oblige or empower" an administrator to do. His warning that we "must beware of the too good man as well as the too bad; each in his own way may give the public what it doesn't want," rings true when one considers the careers of Robert Moses and J. Edgar Hoover.[20] But for people racked with frustration in trying to get government to act, the problem often seems to be administrative overcautiousness rather than administrative overfeasance. From our perspectives of classical and neoclassical organization theories and the view of political bureaucracy as a triangle of symbiotic relationships defining policy subsystems of agency-clientele-legislative committee mutual benefits, we get a different view on Friedrich's idea of control through anticipating reactions.

Organization theory and political reality suggest that conservatism and immobilism, rather than overfeasance, are the most likely results of anticipating reactions of others. Unless the demand for change becomes a salient political issue, public bureaucracies tend to maximize the security of the individual bureaucrats and minimize the dislocation of affected interests, even if such activity involves altering agency goals. Certainly, this has been the case in the past, and there are no indications that the situation will change in the future unless organizational changes that alter the political positions of participants in the policy process can be incorporated. Friedrich's reliance on anticipated reactions of the other participants as a major control factor, without structural realignments, provides the rationale for inaction.

Theory of Nonmarket Failures

IN a mixed economy, private sector managers do not have to wonder about concepts of administrative responsibility that have concerned us. There is no need for balancing professional values against democratic values, for example. In the private sector, market values—money, the "bottom line"—are presumed to be the favored values. Private managers must pay attention to the laws, rules, and regulations. They can run

---

20. The Finer quotes are in Rourke, *Bureaucratic Power,* pp. 413–414. For a biography of Robert Moses, *see* Robert A. Caro, *The Power: Robert Moses and the Fall of New York* (New York: Random House, 1974).

afoul of the courts, but the standard by which private sector managers are judged is determined by the market forces and the managers' responses to those forces.

Capitalism assumes that the market is an efficient and equitable allocator of resources in a society. Under some conditions, however, the market does not produce efficient or equitable outcomes. Under those conditions of *market failure,* government may intervene in the market through regulation, the purchase of public goods, or administration of transfer payments. Government involvement seeks to produce more socially preferable outcomes than the market itself can produce. Markets are judged on their abilities to allocate resources efficiently and equitably. Market failure means it has failed to do so.

Markets fail to live up to the ideal type because of imperfections. Markets assume levels of price and product information that might not be widely available to consumers and producers. In extreme cases, they can be manipulated by interests controlling market share, distribution facilities, or production technology. Therefore, market imperfections are one cause of market failure and a reason for government to step in to achieve the goals of a properly functioning market—efficient and equitable distribution.

Markets fail when the price paid for a good does not reflect the true cost of producing that good. For example, usually the consumer of chemicals does not pay for all the costs, including air and water pollution, that went into producing the product. Instead, there are *externalities* or spillovers. The community may "pay" for increased water and air pollution with increased cancer rates, although individuals living around the chemical plant were not involved in any market transaction with the chemical company. Again, the market has not operated in an efficient or equitable manner; therefore government or nonmarket mechanisms may be brought to bear on the problem.

Markets cannot put a price on pure public goods such as national defense. Nor do markets encourage projects with very high initial investments and the possibility of increasing returns and declining marginal costs, such as supersonic transport planes. In these cases, like the other forms of market failure, nonmarket mechanisms (usually government authority) may make the allocation decisions.

Implied in the concept of governmental intervention to correct market failure is the notion that the nonmarket mechanism results in a more efficient or more equitable distribution of resources than the market would have allowed. Intuitively, however, we know that the nonmarket mechanism has some problems. Holding up the criteria usually used to judge markets—efficient and equitable distribution of outcomes—Charles Wolf has suggested a theory of *nonmarket failures*.[21]

Wolf identifies four types of nonmarket failures: (1) *internalities,* (2) unreachable goals and rising costs, (3) derived externalities, and (4) distributional inequity of power. Because nonmarket agencies lack well-defined impact measures, the main criteria for guiding, regulating, and evaluating an agency and its personnel are internal. These *internalities* encourage behavior that works against efficient allocation or equitable distribution of resources. Budget growth is an example of an internality. "Lacking profit as a measure of performance, a non-market agency may view its budget as the proxy goal to be maximized."[22] As an example, Wolf cites postmasters who used to be paid according to the number of employees, the number of branch offices, and the number of trucks they had. Under those conditions, there was not much incentive to deliver the mail efficiently.

Similarly, other forms of internalities can work against the efficient achievement of agency goals. Wolf suggests that professional values, operating in an environment where budget expansion is also valued, may favor the latest professional advances without considering their costs and benefits. He cites military and health care professionals as examples. Another internality is the control of information, which can be used as an internal power source. Sometimes people protect their own data from others in the organization who could use it to help the organization reach its goal. Internalities favor the private interests of people within organizations at the expense of the organization as a whole.

Wolf claims there is a tendency for nonmarket organizations to exhibit rising costs to meet unrealistic goals of poorly conceived programs. He claims that political actors are more interested in short-term action than in long-term consequences. They may respond to political demands by proposing solutions that are not feasible. Can all Americans have dignified jobs? If that is the agency goal, a lot of money will be spent in vain trying to reach it. Meanwhile, internal pressures will force the budget to rise while the agency seeks to accomplish an impossible task.[23]

Another kind of nonmarket failure occurs when governmental intervention creates unanticipated side-effects. Often these occur in areas far

---

21. Charles Wolf, Jr., "A Theory of Non-Market Failures," *The Public Interest* no. 55 (Spring 1979): 114–133.
22. Ibid., p. 122.
23. Ibid., p. 126. Wolf calls this category "redundant and rising costs," but we will avoid confusion over the term *redundant* by not using it now.

from the policy area in which the governmental action originally took place. For example, trade restrictions and a "Buy American" sales campaign aimed at helping domestic manufacturers may inhibit weapons standardization for the North Atlantic Treaty Organization (NATO). A home mortgage policy that favors the suburbs might lead to the decline of urban amenities.

The final type of nonmarket failure that Wolf discusses relates to power. In any policy area there is the tendency for policy subsystems to develop. The participants in these policy subsystems, namely the agency officials, the clientele, and the members of legislative committees, have considerable power in the particular policy area. As Wolf suggests:

> The power may be exercised with scruple, compassion, and competence. It may be subject to checks and balances, depending on the law, on administrative procedures, on the information media, and on other political and social institutions. Nevertheless, such redistribution of power provides opportunities for inequity and abuse.[24]

Power differentials among competing groups can skew the distribution of government benefits to the more powerful groups, regardless of notions of equity.

Nonmarket Failures and Responsibility

MARKET failures exist, but only a devout Marxist would advocate throwing out the market altogether. Similarly, the existence of nonmarket failures should not call for the end to government involvement in many areas. The theory of nonmarket failure points to several tendencies of public agencies that produce ill-defined products or products whose worth is not readily assessed. Furthermore, these features of much government work are aggravated by the lack of competition in the public sector. The theory of nonmarket failure raises some rough standards that should be considered in our discussion of responsibility.

Agencies overly concerned with internalities, such as budget growth as the indicator for organizational success and information control as an internal power tool, will not produce socially preferable results. Socially

24. Ibid., p. 129.

preferable results are defined in the theory of nonmarket failure to be those that are efficient or equitable. A growing budget is not necessarily an indication that the manager is buying off internal critics or ignoring program results in favor of the prestige conferred by a rising budget, but it may be. Tight information control systems do not necessarily indicate that information is being used to serve individuals rather than the organization, but they might.

The theory of nonmarket failure suggests that some programs may be poorly thought-out responses to political demands. They may have impossible goals. Continuing to throw money at such programs will not help them achieve these goals and will be neither an efficient nor an equitable use of resources. That a program has impossible stated goals, however, might not mean that its unstated, or latent, goals are impossible to attain. An educational program with wide community participation may not raise reading levels by the desired amount, but it might improve the sense of community in the area. This latent goal may be more important than the stated goal. Achieving a higher degree of community solidarity in an area might provide the basis for community development. A responsible administrator should recognize the worth of latent goals as well as the stated ones. But the responsible administrator must also recognize that some programs are born to fail. Under some circumstances, programs should be terminated.

The theory of nonmarket failure urges us to look for unexpected consequences of governmental action. Although we cannot hold administrators responsible for some kinds of unanticipated consequences which spring up far afield from their agencies' missions, we can assess their behavior once the problems have been brought to their attention. If environmental programs have spillovers affecting international relations, as in the case of the supersonic transport plane, the Concorde, some responses might be more "responsible" than others. The degree to which responses are more or less responsible would depend on the circumstances. Obviously, if the environmental program led to the brink of war, the responsible response would be different from what it would be if only minor trade relations were involved.

Nonmarket failure theory notes that governmental programs often redistribute power in a policy area. This distribution of power can be inequitable. Generally, as we have seen, policy subsystems develop around agencies that are acting in a policy area. The interest group liberalism that often characterizes these policy subsystems locks some interest into and others out of power. Responsible administrators should work to

413

open these systems to democratic values, as expressed through the elected officials and the individual citizens. Responsible administrators should act to protect the powerless.

A Suggestion for Change

THE discussion of administrative responsibility raises many interesting questions. An understanding of administrative responsibility provides some rough measures by which to assess public management. Unfortunately, these rough measures do not give firm guidance for all cases. We cannot trust government administration solely to the judgment of good persons, and there are limitations on the oversight capacities of the legislatures, courts, and political executives. Perhaps there is a structural change that might encourage a flexible, intelligent, responsible public bureaucracy by harnessing forces that appear to have worked in the private sector—competition and competence.

Since the Brownlow Committee in 1937, it has been an article of faith of American public administration that government should be organized to prevent duplication and overlapping of services. The Hoover Commissions, President Nixon's Ash Council, and innumerable efforts to reorganize the governments of the various states have all sought to wipe out areas of duplication in the name of administrative efficiency and cost saving. As Martin Landau has pointed out:

> The logic of this position . . . calls for each role to be perfected, each bureau to be exactly delimited, each linkage to articulate unfailingly, and each line of communication to be noiseless—all to produce one interlocking system, one means-end chain which possesses the absolutely minimum number of links, and which culminates at a central control point.[25]

Yet all these reorganizations have laid the groundwork for more studies and commissions, because even with the reorganization, government bureaucracies still were not deemed to be effective.

Perhaps reorganizations on these lines are doomed to failure because the individual links in the means-end chain cannot maintain a commitment to the overall public welfare. Organization plans designed to wipe out duplication establish agency monopolies over particular policy

---

25. Martin Landau, "Redundancy, Rationality, and the Problem of Duplication and Overlap," *Public Administration Review* 29, no. 4 (July–August 1969): 354.

areas. Policy subsystems come together around these areas, and the symbiotic relationships that define such subsystems tend to limit the consideration of policy alternatives. Limiting the consideration of alternatives at any place in the chain is bound to affect some aspects of public welfare and governmental effectiveness adversely. Reorganizations on these lines create the conditions for nonmarket failures.

It may be possible, however, to break these self-rewarding policy subsystems by encouraging agency competition over jurisidictions. Different agencies dealing with slightly different aspects of the same problem might be responsive to slightly different clientele. Friction that might develop between the agencies might more readily be raised to a higher—more open—level of conflict, because with more agencies involved, there would be more legitimate policy arenas available. There would be less likelihood that the same interests could control all such arenas. The agencies and the bureaucrats who staff them might find that they would be forced to develop more creative responses to problems or to abandon areas that had been within their jurisdictions. The threat of loss of jurisdiction, as Matthew Holden has suggested, provides a powerful bureaucratic incentive.[26]

Using the concept of redundancy from information theory, Landau has provided a theoretical rationale for encouraging competition and overlap among agencies:

[The concept of redundancy] sets aside the doctrine that ties the reliability of a system to the perfectability of parts and thereby approaches the pragmatics of systems in action much more realistically. That is, it accepts the inherent limitations of any organization by treating any and all parts, regardless of their degree of perfection, as risky actors. . . .
   [In information theory] the probability of failure in a system decreases exponentially as redundancy factors are increased.[27]

Redundancy in public organizations might do the same, thus making government more effective.

Dan Felsenthal has developed a method for evaluating the desired amount of redundancy needed to make an administrative system avoid failure. His system is based on three factors:

1. *by how much is the system's probability of failure reduced by introducing . . . redundant components;*

---

26. Matthew Holden, " 'Imperialism' in Bureaucracy," *American Political Science Review* 60, no. 4 (December 1966): 943–951.
27. Landau, "Redundancy," p. 350.

2. *what is the cost associated with the installation and maintenance of this component; and*

3. *what is the cost associated with the system's failure.*[28]

If these probabilities and costs can be estimated, a public manager would advocate a redundant component if its "expected cost (i.e., its cost multiplied by the probability of the system's adequate operation) is smaller than the system's expected failure (i.e., the cost of failure multiplied by its probability."[29]

But despite formal rationalization through pseudoscientific techniques, advocating competition and overlap within public bureaucracy is heresy in American public administration. For years the notion that duplication automatically means waste has been accepted by politicians, taxpayers, and even the bureaucrats themselves. The major thrust of program budgeting and a variety of more traditional feedback techniques—"reports, inspections, the 'grapevine,' investigations, and centralized administrative services"[30]—has been predicated on a single agency's being responsible for a single policy area or single bureaucratic units being responsible for single aspects of policy. Changing the existing pattern of organization and the acceptance of the logic behind that pattern will not be easy.

Certainly it would not be politically viable to duplicate all the administrative units that make up American public administration. That is not being advocated here. But it is possible to use some of the slack that is available in bureaucracy now. Few observers of bureaucratic behavior would question that the majority of bureaucrats are working and working hard. But many have questioned whether some of this work is directed toward worthwhile goals. Often bureaucrats are forced to spend much of their time satisfying the information needs of their organization itself rather than dealing with the actual problems that the agency is supposed to solve. This is another aspect of internalization, one of the causes of nonmarket failures.

Such a situation presents an opportunity for change. The efforts to satisfy internal informational needs of an agency are really one method of trying to gain effective government. Relaxing some of these internal demands would free many bureaucratic work hours. This time could be put to use to serve the same purpose—administrative control for effec-

28. Dan S. Felsenthal, "Applying the Redundancy Concept to Administrative Organizations," *Public Administration Review* 40, no. 3 (May–June 1980): 250.
29. Ibid., p. 250.
30. Herbert Kaufman, *Administrative Feedback* (Washington, D.C.: The Brookings Institution, 1973), pp. 24–25.

tive government—by creating alternative work groups that would be in competition with each other to provide services for the people. Such competition might encourage the natural political feedback mechanisms to work more effectively.

Furthermore, competition might inspire individual creativity among the bureaucrats themselves. The establishment of competing work groups—competing to provide more effective service—might provide more avenues for bureaucratic advancement based on performance. If bureaucrats perceive mechanisms for encouraging competition within and among agencies as helpful to their careers, they might be strong supporters of such competition.

Perhaps competition among work groups would encourage increased cooperation within each work group. If work is set up to accomplish meaningful, understandable goals, people might find that they are more open to sharing the organizational humanistic values such as full and free communication, which seem to have been useful in solving problems.

If competition provides more meaningful outlets for individual bureaucrats, they may experience greater job satisfaction. This potential job satisfaction might create a healthier atmosphere in which the bureaucrats may be more open to the environmental changes and legitimate political demands of the expanded feedback network. Perhaps increased job satisfaction will obviate the need of some individuals to engage in the "bureaupathic" behavior described by Victor Thompson.[31] A service orientation may even supplant the self-protective orientation characteristic of some unbending and unresponsive bureaucracies.

Perhaps encouraging competition within and among agencies would even save the public's money. In an atmosphere of greater competition and more meaningful work, public bureaucrats may be able to perform much of the work that is presently contracted out to high-priced private firms. Private consulting firms have sprung up around most major government centers to facilitate what Taylor Branch has called the exchange of white paper for green.[32] When governments contract out most of the interesting work to highly paid professionals who often duplicate the skills of professional civil servants, they send the challenging jobs outside the agency, leaving skilled bureaucrats with little meaningful

31. Victor Thompson, *Modern Organization* (New York: Knopf, 1961), pp. 152–153.
32. Taylor Branch, "We're All Working for the Penn Central," in Charles Peters and James Fallows, eds., *Inside the System,* 3rd ed. (New York: Praeger, 1976), p. 161.

work. With the exciting professional work being sent outside the agency, highly motivated and competent professionals often leave government to work for the private consulting firms. By encouraging challenging work within the bureaucratic structure, governments may be better able to hold professional talent.

If all these things occurred as a result of encouraging competition within bureaucratic structure, administrators could be powerful agents for change in American society.

Public Management and the Future

SPECULATION about the possible effects of increased competition within bureaucracy may open up a door to a new future for public bureaucracy. But the political and organizational realities with which we have dealt through this book suggest that public bureaucracies will continue to operate in the next twenty-five years along much the same lines as they have operated in the last twenty-five years.

There will be some obvious changes, especially in the larger jurisdictions—the national government and the larger states and cities. These governments will continue to be innovators in more refined budgeting and personnel systems. Furthermore, they will be innovators in applying technology to public management problems. This does not mean that they will necessarily be the most effective governments, but they will soon operate in a technological environment that the smaller jurisdictions can expect to see by the turn of the century.

One of the major changes that will occur is the widespread acceptance of the electronic office in public management. Electronic typewriters and word processors are already commonplace in the larger jurisdictions, and the technology exists to alter the style of communication based on staff meetings and memoranda stacked on desks. Computer terminals on each bureaucrat's desk might change the pejorative image of "paper-pusher." There may not be paper to push. What managers now keep in file cabinets and on their desks can be stored in a computer and viewed on a desk-top screen with the push of a few buttons. Messages and memos can never be "lost." Managers will have access to mounds of data and the technical capacity to send that data to others instantly. Portable terminals will enable managers and their subordinates to take their desks with them wherever they go. A telephone coupling is all that is required to tie the public bureaucrat to the computer net.

The public administrator of the future might expect to get calls at all hours of the day or night from legislators looking after the interests of their constituents. The legislator will expect the efficient civil servant to get the needed information at the touch of a few buttons on his or her terminal. No longer will the excuse be, "I'll have to check into that and get back to you in a couple of days." Administrators will have the capacity to get the requested information directly and send it to the legislator's terminal almost immediately. Legislators may have the technical capacity to enhance their political clout. If a bureaucrat attempts to give a legislator the runaround, the legislator could file charges against the offending bureaucrat right from his or her terminal, and the message could go both to the bureaucrat's boss and to the personnel file. The "Third Wave" will inundate public management.[33]

Despite the changes in hardware and the stresses that change might bring, the problems and opportunities of public management will remain very similar to those that exist today. Strong political and administrative leadership, when combined with exciting new ideas for solving problems, will probably ignite sparks in some agencies at some times. Those who expect some magic formula that will energize all public bureaucracies and inspire them to new heights of service to the public will be disappointed.

A new generation of public managers armed with technological and managerial skills and aware of the environment of public management may be able to make public bureaucracies more effective. We may not be able to develop an optimum solution to James Wilson's "bureaucracy problem,"[34] but we may create a climate in which more is expected and demanded of public bureaucracies. More effective government may be the result.

Suggestions for Further Reading

Friedrich, Carl J., ed. *The Public Interest, Nomos V.* New York: Atherton, 1966.
Lowi, Theodore J. *The End of Liberalism: The Second Republic of the United States,* 2d ed. New York: W. W. Norton, 1979.

33. Alvin Toffler, *The Third Wave* (New York: William Morrow, 1980). The third wave is the information revolution. The first and second waves were the agricultural and industrial revolutions.
34. James Q. Wilson, "The Bureaucracy Problem," *The Public Interest* no. 6 (Winter 1967): 4. *See also* chapter 1 above.

Martin, Roscoe C., ed. *Public Administration and Democracy.* Syracuse, N.Y.: Syracuse University Press, 1965.

Mainzer, Louis C. *Political Bureaucracy.* Glenview, Ill.: Scott, Foresman, 1973.

Ostrom, Vincent. *The Intellectual Crisis in American Public Administration,* rev. ed. University, Ala.: University of Alabama Press, 1974.

Redford, Emmette S. *Democracy in the Administrative State.* New York: Oxford University Press, 1969.

Waldo, Dwight. *The Administrative State.* New York: Ronald, 1947.

A Personal Note to Students Doing Term Papers

THIS BOOK HAS BEEN an introduction to public administration. It has not covered in depth all the problems facing public administration. Nor has it dealt with many of the policy issues that are the real concern of public administration. I hope that you study some policy issue in depth as part of your introductory course in public administration. You can become an expert in some policy area through solid term-paper research. You can find out how rewarding a feeling it is to be really familiar with a particular policy area.

The term paper should be a learning experience. It should enable you to dig deeply into the substance of a particular topic and, more important, develop your research, logical thinking, and writing skills. Although the facts and ideas that you deal with in your paper will probably be forgotten, the tools developed while working on the paper will remain, it is hoped, throughout your life.

Many of the issues raised in the text should provide you with some ideas for paper topics. I have included suggestions for further reading to help lead you to additional materials. Based upon the papers that I have received in several years of teaching, I have several specific suggestions that will make your papers appear more professional. Some of these ideas have been borrowed from one of my former professors, the late Roscoe C. Martin. I have found them useful and I hope you will too.

1. Break up the material into manageable units. Paragraphs should not be so short as to leave the reader breathless. I have raced through papers with five or six short paragraphs on each page. Neither should paragraphs go on for more than a page. This tends to cloud the issues with which the writer is trying to deal. Topical

headings every three or four pages help the reader follow the line of thought.

2. Try to limit the use of colloquialisms and "bureaucratese." Sometimes the writer's natural style is so loose as to make serious consideration of the topic impossible. Bureaucratic reports are notorious for having words like "finalize" and "prioritorize." There is a place for technical bureaucratic terms like "interface," but generally plain English will suffice.

3. Abbreviations certainly are acceptable, but spell them out the first time, indicating the abbreviation to be used subsequently. For example, "The General Accounting Office (GAO) performs the audit function during the budgetary cycle. Recently the GAO has come under fire."

4. Brief quotations of three typewritten lines or less should be incorporated in the text and enclosed in quotation marks. Longer quotations should be set off from the text by indenting and single-spacing the passage. Quotation marks are not needed when long quotations are treated in this manner.

5. Since plagiarism is frowned upon, always give credit to other persons' ideas and data when you use them in your paper. Extensive footnoting and accurate quotation will avoid problems.

In any good paper, I expect to see some explicit theoretical component. Some theoretical component is absolutely essential if you are to analyze rather than merely describe. Even a description implies some theoretical perspective. You will probably have more success in dealing with your topic if you make that perspective explicit in your paper.

Good luck.

Index

431